Total War and 'Modernization'

Total War and 'Modernization'

Edited by
Yasushi Yamanouchi,
J. Victor Koschmann,
and Ryūichi Narita

East Asia Program
Cornell University
Ithaca, New York 14853

The Cornell East Asia Series is published by the Cornell University East Asia Program and has no formal affiliation with Cornell University Press. We are a small, non-profit press, publishing reasonably-priced books on a wide variety of scholarly topics relating to East Asia as a service to the academic community and the general public. We accept standing orders which provide for automatic billing and shipping of each title in the series upon publication.

If after review by internal and external readers a manuscript is accepted for publication, it is published on the basis of camera-ready copy provided by the volume author. Each author is thus responsible for any necessary copy-editing and for manuscript formatting. Submission inquiries should be addressed to Editorial Board, East Asia Program, Cornell University, Ithaca, New York 14853-7601.

Number 100 in the Cornell East Asia Series.
© 1998 J. Victor Koschmann. All rights reserved
ISSN 1050-2955
ISBN 1-885445-60-1 hc
ISBN 1-885445-00-8 pb
Printed in the United States of America
13 12 11 10 09 08 07 06 05 04 03 02 01 00   10 9 8 7 6 5 4 3 2 1

⊗The paper in this book meets the requirements for permanence of ISO 9706:1994.

Contents

III. Total War and Social Integration

Preface

This volume is the product of a binational research effort among scholars centered at Cornell University in the U.S. and the Tokyo University of Foreign Studies in Japan. For a period of three years beginning in 1992, we engaged in collaborative research aimed at a reassessment of Japanese society in the period around World War II. The results of that project include not only the essays presented here, but another group as well, soon to be published in a second volume entitled *The Deconstruction of Nationality*. Both volumes have already been published in Japanese.[1]

The collapse of the Berlin Wall symbolically marked the end of the Cold War, which had determined the world's power structure ever since the end of World War II. However, relief from the burden of the Cold War did not necessarily mean the beginning of an era of peace and emancipation. Indeed, the dissolution of whatever stability had been preserved through confrontation between the two superpowers inevitably uncovered new problems. Most of these emerging problems are related to global capitalism's nascent destabilization of the nation-state, linchpin of the world power structure since the dawn of the modern era. And despite the waning of the nation-state, no alternative basis for world order is on the horizon.

Although the globalization of capital has indeed eroded the power structure of the nation-state, it has not fundamentally transformed our political and economic institutions, which owe their basic character to the system-integration and homogenization carried out during the era of World War II. Nation-states' programs of system integration have long-since disciplined our bodies and molded our life attitudes, to the point even of prescribing the content of linguistic communication. How might this legacy be overcome? Clearly we cannot rely on high-level negotiations among government bureaucrats or elite managers of multinational corporations. Indeed, more hope would seem to lie at furthest remove from those dealings, in the critical scrutiny of habitual patterns of daily life (what Pierre Bourdieu calls 'habitus') that might give rise to a new set of attitudes. Needless to say, if this critical scrutiny occurs only at the abstract level of individual self-reflection it will not achieve significant results. To have an impact it must be carried out in the social context of cultural friction and clashes of identity, that is, through participation in what Mary Louise Pratt has referred to as 'contact zones'.[2]

In orienting our research project toward this set of issues, we began with our common suspicion that general mobilization during World War II brought nation-states to the stage of system integration, and with that as the starting point we attempted to come to grips with some of the problems of modernity in the second half of the twentieth century. Surely neither democracy, as the typical political system of postwar societies, nor the welfare state, as their characteristic economic structure, are unrelated to the systematic social unification and consolidation initiated during the era of world war. Democracy had to be severely constrained by political loyalty to the nation-state under that new consolidation, and the welfare state that emerged out of it was unimaginable without systematic social integration. In order to achieve that degree of integration, the nation-state has had to differentiate clearly between those who belong to it and those who do not, and the inevitable result is a structure of exclusion and discrimination. The recent prevalence of protest movements based on ethnic identity is closely related to those state structures of exclusion and discrimination.

We have pursued our research from a standpoint opposed to that which assumes from the beginning that Japan, Germany and the United States are qualitatively different societies as the inescapable result of their divergent cultural traditions. We begin rather from the perception that all three have been subjected to the waves of change that have swept over the globe in the past half-century and to that extent have undergone similar historical experiences. Of course, that does not mean that we find among them no differences that are likely to lead to conflict. We recognize that they have in many ways been differently formed through local processes of social institutionalization, but we have not focused systematically on those processes in this project.

Research from the perspective outlined above is impossible to contain within the usual boundaries of academic specialization. From the beginning, therefore, we chose not to define our project in terms of any particular approach, whether social scientific, historical, philosophical or literary, but welcomed opportunities for interchange across these boundaries. This early decision to disregard specialization in research, as itself one of the many barriers that have been erected in the late-modern era, contributed greatly to deepening our mutual understanding. The project's success depended from the outset on interaction among participants from the different social contexts of Japan, Germany, and the United States as well as from different academic discipines, but we experienced nothing like the "clash of civilizations" or "collisions among specialties." Indeed, we found ourselves engaged in the radical experiment of pursuing mutual interaction among diverse intellectual orientations in order to promote the formation of a new intellectual identity, and it has given us great pleasure to find that this experiment has succeeded, at least in a small way, as these volumes testify.

In conclusion, we are pleased to acknowledge that our research project was supported by a scientific research grant from the Japanese Ministry of Education; we also received research support from the Rōdō Mondai Risāchi Sentā of Tokyo. Without this generous support we could not have carried out the project in the first place, let alone meet the costs of translating the essays. The mountain of vexing administrative business that accompanied the project was dealt with by our editorial administrator, Itō Shōko, and project administrators Kishimoto Yukiko and Saeki Satoko. We deeply appreciate their devoted service.

For the English version, we are indebted to the translators, who are credited at the end of each essay; to Laura Hein, who read the translated essays in manuscript form and contributed many helpful comments and criticisms; to Coraleen Rooney, who expertly transformed the manuscript into camera-ready copy; and to Karen Smith, who supervised production of the book.

The Editors
Tokyo, August 21, 1995

Notes

[1] Yamanouchi Yasushi, Victor Koschmann, and Narita Ryūichi, eds., *Sōryokusen to gendaika* (Tokyo: Kashiwa Shobō, 1995); and Sakai Naoki, Brett DeBary and Iyotani Toshio, eds., *Nashonaritei no datsukōchiku* (Tokyo: Kashiwa Shobō, 1996).

[2] Mary Louise Pratt, *Imperial Eyes: Travel Writing and Transculturation* (London & New York: Routledge, 1992).

Introduction to the English Edition

J. Victor Koschmann

The essays included here first appeared in Japanese in December 1995, in a book that has attracted substantial attention among Japanese readers. It has attracted attention because its contents are revisionist in the best sense. By "revisionist," I mean that they are critically disposed, in various degrees, toward the mainstream, "progressive" historiography that predominated in Japan in the early years after World War II—a historiography that itself reacted critically against the academic and nationalistic histories of wartime. By revisionist "in the best sense," I mean to distinguish clearly the revisionism represented here from another, reactionary variety that in the early-1960s and after sought to rehabilitate major aspects of the wartime order while also implicitly vindicating the postwar establishment as the culmination of a modern Japanese success story. It is in direct opposition to this other form of "revisionism" that the authors represented here seek to criticize "postwar democracy" by illuminating from various angles the threads of continuity that continue to link postwar ideology and institutions to their wartime predecessors. Yet the iconoclastic effect of this strategy can fully be understood only in contrast to the historiography that became dominant in the period following Japan's defeat in 1945.

The approach to Japan's modern history that predominated from the early-postwar period down to the early 1960s, and retained considerable influence even in the 1980s and beyond, was the result of a partial convergence between the official view of the war imposed by the Occupation Army and that espoused by leftwing forces, including the resurgent Communist party, that had been influenced by the prewar faction of Marxist scholars called the Kōza-ha (lectures faction). This approach was premised on the assumption that the authoritarianism and expansionism that characterized Japan's history between 1931 and 1945 could be attributed primarily to pathological factors peculiar to Japan, usually interpreted via a theory of premodern particularism versus modern universalism. In short, "premodern residue" became the key to interpreting Japan's entire modern history, including especially the wartime period. Accordingly, inasmuch as the reforms that followed Japan's defeat were explicitly designed to eliminate premodern irrationality and to complete Japan's democratic revolution, the postwar era tended to be sharply distinguished from wartime in this historical approach. It was as if history had begun anew in the autumn of 1945. The final corollary was the assumption that further "modernization" was the panacea for whatever irrational, exploitative, or undemocratic elements might still exist in postwar society.

For at least the first two decades of the postwar era, this historical paradigm formed a fundamental component of the world view that undergirded "progressive," or "renovationist" (*kakushin*), political forces in Japan, including the opposition parties, major elements of the labor movement, and a variety of mass movements that united beneath the banners of "peace and democracy" and finally culminated in the struggle against the Japan-U.S. Security Treaty in 1960. Therefore, to challenge the historical paradigm was implicitly to betray the progressive postwar ideology of "peace and democracy" that defended the "no war"-clause (Article Nine) in the Constitution and held the line against conservative revanchism in education, law enforcement, women's rights, and other areas.

Nevertheless, since the 1980s the above paradigm has slowly begun to give way to a new perspective that interprets "wartime" as intimately connected to—and, indeed, the fundamental condition for—'postwar', and thus dispels the illusion that the "postwar" must be treated as an historical era sui generis. In one way or another, all of the essays included in this volume spring from this post-1980s historical strategy. Inasmuch as they all depart in one way or another from the historical consciousness that has informed progressive politics in postwar Japan, some of them will doubtless be interpreted as taking a conservative or rightwing line. For example, some readers might still feel that any retreat from the dichotomy between wartime "dark valley" and postwar Enlightenment is tantamount to exculpating the wartime regime and facilitating postwar trends toward re-militarization and authoritarianism. Therefore, it is important to realize that the predominant intent of these essays is quite different. That is, most of the contributors believe that a penetrating understanding and, ultimately, critique of the system called "postwar democracy" is possible only when one recognizes not only its deep continuity with wartime but its thorough modernity. At the end of his essay on education, for example, Ōuchi suggests that the institutional innovations of wartime as well as postwar are pervaded by "none other than the problem of modernity itself." That is, for the most part the contributors feel that the ills of the postwar era are, first of all, predominantly modern rather than residually premodern; and second, that they result not primarily from Japanese peculiarities but rather from tendencies that are in greater or lesser degree common to all "advanced" capitalist nations. Of course, this does not preclude them from recognizing also the ways in which aspects of Japanese society differentiate it from others, as both Amemiya and Saguchi suggest.

Because the post-1980s historical perspective involves the sense that in some ways we are *still in* the total-war system, it destroys the self-evident nature of the postwar/wartime split, thereby not only making it possible to envision more continuity between wartime and postwar, but also rendering accessible a wide range of possible forms of complicity between the two eras. Among the implications of this awareness of continuity between wartime and postwar is a parallel sensitivity to two other junctures that are marked by relative discontinuity: first, between what might be called the "wartime/postwar era" (1930s to 1970s?) and the "prewar" era that immediately preceded it, and second, between the "wartime/postwar era" and a more recent period, extending roughly from the late-1970s or 1980s down to the present. The former disjuncture is explicitly posited in essays by Yamanouchi, Okazaki and Ōuchi, but is implicit in several others; the latter is implied in Yamanouchi's reference to the new social movements, and is referred to in other ways by Amemiya and Iwasaki.

The essays construe the complicity between wartime and postwar in a variety of contending ways. For Yamanouchi, the transition from the prewar to the wartime/postwar era—not only in Japan but in Western Europe and the U.S.—is to be understood broadly as the shift from a class society, theorized most compellingly by G. W. F. Hegel and Karl Marx, to a system society, whose preeminent theorist was the American sociologist Talcott Parsons but which has also been compellingly analyzed in its various dimensions by thinkers as diverse as Herbert Marcuse, Michel Foucault, and Milan Kundera. Most of the other essays, and especially those by Iwasaki, Amemiya, Ōuchi, Satō, and Koschmann, also adhere broadly to this general conception of wartime-postwar continuity.

Yet within, or paralleling, that general, systemic form of consistency are a number of more specific links between wartime and postwar. Hooks and Jussaume connect wartime and postwar by identifying a process of "paradoxical transformation" in the role of the state in relation to civil society. In their view, the originally weak American state was able to mobilize great infrastructural power during the war and then, after the war, to remain relatively strong and militarized; Japan, on the other hand, found itself unable during the war to exercise strong control over the private economy—despite its despotic police powers—and then after the war reverted to a less intrusive, civilized state. As they point out, their analysis calls into question the common image of the postwar American state as the guarantor of free enterprise in contrast to the Japanese state's "strong and intrusive" exercise of industrial policy.

In his study of the women's movement leader Oku Mumeo, Narita focuses on the systematic mobilization of women as active subjects of the nation that was carried out during wartime and resumed in the context of postwar democracy. That is, Narita illustrates an aspect of the process of Gleichschaltung, which Yamanouchi glosses as "enforced homogeneity," and suggests how the social integration and mobilization of women and of the private sphere continue autonomously after the war through women's organizations like Shufuren. Similarly, Koschmann focuses on conceptions of subjectivity, suggesting via the thought of the economic historian Ōtsuka Hisao that influential postwar conceptions of democratic subjectivity were virtually identical with those that during wartime had supported mobilization and the expansion of national productivity.

Sugiyama explicates the theories and analyses of modern Japan's political economy that were set forth, both during and after the war, by leading members of the so-called "civil-society school," which also includes Ōtsuka Hisao and the social policy expert Ōkōchi Kazuo. Focusing on the economists Hirata Kiyoaki and Uchida Yoshihiko, Sugiyama shows how the claim to have "resisted" fascism allowed members of the civil-society school to retain their influence after the war and to contribute profoundly to the influential debates on civil society that emerged in the 1960s.

Iwasaki's analysis reveals profound irony in the intellectual connection between wartime and postwar, suggesting that the "debate on subjectivity," which has been portrayed as quintessentially "postwar" in its concern with freedom and historical agency, was "merely a poor and emaciated repetition" of more penetrating discussions carried on during wartime. Irony is also evident in Satō's account of the mass media. As he points out, the literary critic and conservative publicist Etō Jun has blamed the Occupation for initiating an information control system that suppressed Japanese feelings and historical consciousness in postwar Japan; Etō thereby negates, in effect, the postwar historical orthodoxy that equated wartime with thought control and postwar with freedom and democracy. Yet, Satō proceeds to turn Etō's argument around, suggesting that the postwar Occupation's modern surveillance system, based on the elicitation of self-control, was already anticipated in Japanese wartime planning. Thus, for Satō, continuity consists in the postwar execution of plans that had been first articulated at the height of total war. This form of continuity is also posited by Ōuchi, who shows that wartime plans for, and limited reforms in the direction of, a more universal, equal, and scientific system of education were, in effect, carried out in radical fashion by the Occupation authorities. In Ōuchi's view these ideas and reforms were part of a single modernization process that continued virtually uninterrupted from the 1930s into the postwar period.

By way of contrast, Amemiya conceives of wartime-postwar continuity in an interrupted mode, in that for him the pattern of "forced homogenization" (Gleichschaltung) is first generated largely from the bottom up during mobilization for total war, and then is imposed from on high in the era of high growth from the mid-1950s through the 1960s. Intervening between these homogenizing moments was a period in the early 1950s when Japan was characterized by "multiple, autonomous spaces and communities beyond the state and big capital."

An etiological approach to continuity, in which postwar effects are produced by wartime causes, is most clearly represented in the model of "path dependence" employed by Okazaki. In his institutionalist perspective, sunk costs and the complementarity among institutions that were created de novo during the total war emergency made it much more likely that the same or similar institutions would be appealed to in the early-postwar years, and again in the midst of the coordination failure among various industries that followed the Dodge Line. In Okazaki's view, the legacy of wartime institutionalization lives on in Japan's less than "pure" market system. Saguchi suggests that in Japan, as in the U.S. and Europe, wartime patterns of labor relations "powerfully constrained" their postwar counterparts. These patterns included tendencies to work toward a need-based wage and to conceive of equality and legitimacy as flowing from the workers' contribution to the national economy.

Our sense of the generic nature of the various forms of war-postwar continuity that are evident in the various essays is heightened by the elements they hold in common with the German patterns identified by Prinz. His model of "Janus-faced modernization," highlighting negative as well as positive implications of modernization, resonates with points made by virtually all the contributors, but especially Yamanouchi, Sugiyama, Narita, Ōuchi, Satō and Koschmann. Similarly, what Prinz characterizes as an openness to the "relative modernity" of society under fascism is highlighted by Yamanouchi, Sugiyama, Iwasaki, Ōuchi and Satō. "Mobilization and the question of participation" is the main theme of analyses by Koschmann, Narita, Saguchi and Satō, and the "modernizing function" of fascist mobilization for total war, which typically takes the form of Gleichschaltung, is specifically thematized by Yamanouchi, Ōuchi, and Amemiya. Clearly, the problematic of wartime-postwar continuity can play a creative role in both the German and Japanese cases, and more comparative work should be done.

We hope that despite—or perhaps in part because of—their differences as well as similarities in approach, periodization, scope, and relationship to existing historiography, these essays will stimulate a reassessment of dominant historical assumptions, and encourage students as well as established practitioners to explore new approaches in the field of modern Japanese historical studies.

Japanese names are rendered in accord with Japanese practice, surname first. Thus, in the case of Abe Shigetaka, Abe is the surname, Shigetaka the given name.

Notes

[1] Examples of this reactionary brand of revisionism are: Hayashi Fusao, *Daitōa sensō kōteiron* (Tokyo: Banchō Shobō, 1964); and Hayashi Fusao, *Zoku-Daitōa sensō kōteiron* (Tokyo: Banchō Shobō, 1965).

[2] Influential histories of the war that employ the early-postwar approach include GHQ, *Taiheiyō sensōshi: Hōten jiken yori mujōken kōfuku made* (Tokyo: Takayama Shoin, 1946); Rekishigaku Kenkyūkai, ed., *Taiheiyō sensōshi*, 5 vols. (Tokyo: Tōyō Keizai Shinpōsha, 1953-54; and Tōyama Shigeki, Imai Seiichi, Fujiwara Akira, *Shōwa-shi* (Tokyo: Iwanami Shoten, 1955).

Contributors

AMEMIYA Shōichi

Professor, Ibaraki University; Japanese politics

Gregory HOOKS

Associate Professor, Washington State University; politics, comparative sociology

IWASAKI Minoru

Associate Professor, Tokyo University of Foreign Studies; philosophy, political thought

Raymond A. JUSSAUME

Associate Professor, Washington State University; comparative sociology, development

J. Victor KOSCHMANN

Professor, Cornell University; modern Japanese history

NARITA Ryūichi

Professor, Japan Women's University; modern Japanese social history

OKAZAKI Tetsuji

Associate Professor, University of Tokyo; Japanese economic history

ŌUCHI Hirokazu

Lecturer, Matsuyama University; sociology of education

Michael PRINZ

Lecturer, Bielefeldt University; 19th and 20th century German social history

SAGUCHI Kazurō

Associate Professor, University of Tokyo; labor relations

SATŌ Takumi

Associate Professor, Dōshisha University; modern German history

SUGIYAMA Mitsunobu

Professor, University of Tokyo; history of Japanese social science

YAMANOUCHI Yasushi

Professor, Ferris University; history of social theory; historical sociology

Total-War and System Integration: A Methodological Introduction

Yamanouchi Yasushi

TOTAL-WAR AND SOCIAL REORGANIZATION

A summary of the prevailing conception of Japan's modern history would probably go something like this: During the fascist period, Japan veered off the normal course of maturation that has been followed by modern societies and took an aberrant path. The trend toward democracy that had developed in the Taishō period (1912-1926) came to a standstill during this period and in its stead an authoritarian system supported by an irrational, ultranationalistic ideology forced the people of the nation down the deviant path of mobilization for war. Defeat in 1945 brought the postwar reforms, which returned Japanese history to the track of democracy as it had begun to develop in the Taishō period. The postwar reforms were then the starting point and foundation for all subsequent Japanese history, from 1945 to the present.[1]

When this interpretation of modern Japanese history is projected on to world history, World War II becomes a confrontation between an irrational, absolutist form of fascist system (including Germany, Italy and Japan) and a rational, democratic New Deal-type of system (including the United States, England and France).[2]

It is still possible to find a certain plausibility in the above conception. Yet it also leaves a number of problems unsolved. Can it truly be said that the New Deal-type democratic system has guaranteed us a desirable society?

1

Certainly, in contrast to the overtly totalitarian regimes it can be called democratic, but it has brought about domination by mammoth national bureaucracies and in all organizations, whether commercial, academic, or medical, it has created centralized hierarchies presided over by specialists. In these respects, this type of society must be considered fraught with problems in regard to the conduct of democracy. Even the labor movement, which was once expected to serve as a critical force in opposition to increasing bureaucratic ossification, has been institutionalized as one more component of the system. In the New Deal form of democracy, all sectors of society have been converted into colossal organizations, and opposition movements no longer threaten the survival of the system. Indeed, these tendencies are symptomatic of what might be called a variety of totalitarianism.[3]

Although I call them New Deal-type societies, we must not forget that they went through irreversible changes in the course of the two world wars.[4] By virtue of the characteristics noted above, the New Deal-type societies were highly efficient in mobilizing personnel and economic resources and thus highly suited to the conduct of war. Yet, an even better explanation might be that the New Deal-type societies, as well as the fascist-type societies, were fundamentally reorganized as a result of the general mobilization required in the course of two world wars. If such is the case, before we hastily portray modern history as a confrontation between fascism and the New Deal, we must reinvestigate that history in light of the social reorganization demanded by a total-war regime. The differences between the two types—fascist and New Deal—ought to be considered as an internal and subordinate issue to be addressed after completing an analysis of the social reorganization brought about under the total-war systems.

How should we define the reorganization that was precipitated by the total-war systems? We can begin by noting the reality that modern societies have, since their inception, been stratified so as to distinguish between elite citizens and the others. As powerful nation-states, modern societies cannot exist without political integration, but such nation-states also presume an image of the ideal citizen, authorized by religious values. In Japan, for example, the Imperial Rescript on Education, promulgated in 1890, provided the criteria for such a citizen. In the United States, the values of the WASP (White Anglo-Saxon Protestant) probably fill this role. Only those who conform to this image are recognized as genuine citizens, while the other members of society are consigned to second or third-class status. Among the inferiors by this measure are, first, the working class. In terms of formal legality, there are no grounds for considering blue-collar workers to be second-class citizens, but when it comes to negotiations with their capitalist employers in a market economy, they are at an overwhelming disadvantage. This is the origin of workers' struggles. In the case of Japan one notes that, after experiencing a period of unprecedented prosperity following the First World War, the labor movement was stirred by the influence of the Russian revolution and in tandem with the rural tenant movements brought about a period of social crisis.

Others who had to be content with the status of second-class citizen included women and ethnic groups such as Koreans in Japan and African-Americans in the U.S. These groups were deprived of their legitimate rights as national citizens, sometimes via legal restrictions openly stipulated, at other times through ineradicable social prejudice.[5]

Under the total-war system, human as well as natural resources had to be completely mobilized in order to make war. Therefore, citizens of inferior status inevitably constituted a serious obstacle to the conduct of total war. In so far as the inferior-status groups have not been accorded full legitimacy as citizens, and are not put in positions of responsibility, they will lack the internal motivation to become active agents of the total-war effort. As regards the "synchronization," or enforced homogeneity (*Gleichschaltung*) that was carried out by Nazi Germany, Schoenbaum asserts that it contained what may rightly be called "Hitler's social revolution." On the one hand, the Nazi ideology taught that the German people were destined to rule the world and pursued policies of discrimination against non-German peoples and the elimination of the Jewish people, in particular. On the other hand, in a time of total war the Nazis struggled under the rallying cry of "a common destiny" to abolish social-status discrimination within the very group that was to bear the burden of ruling the world. If we understand the policy of "enforced homogeneity" not in the first sense but in Schoenbaum's second sense, then we should recognize that this was not a policy adopted exclusively by the Nazis. Rather, it is the policy adopted by all the nations that played a leading role in World War II (including the New Deal-type nations.)

The total-war system attempted to unite all the people under the slogan of a common destiny as citizens of a single national community and to intervene against the momentum toward social exclusion and conflict that had been inherent in modern societies since their inception. The policy of "enforced homogeneity" was pursued under the extraordinary and irrational circumstance of war, but its implementation was not confined to such circumstances. The policy promoted rationalization in that it supported the inevitable social revolution required in a time of all-out mobilization of human resources for war. It was expected that through "enforced homogeneity" all members of society would share the burden of the social functions required to prosecute the war. The total-war system would eradicate the impetus toward social exclusion (born of the modern status order) and social conflict, rationalizing the entire society toward the single end of conducting war in the most efficient, functional manner. The prerequisites of the total-war system are a keen awareness of the potential for intrasocietal conflict and turmoil, the active incorporation of these impulses within the system, and their redirection through reform to enable them to contribute to social integration. Thus conceived, the total-war system undoubtedly played an important transitional role on the way to the establishment of a system society that is organized on the basis of functionalist principles. Although each nation returned to a peaceful and routine social order at the close of the Second World War, such a return did not signify a restoration of prewar conditions. Even after the Second World War, nations continued to opt for the type of social reorganization based on functionalist principles that had been accelerated by the total-war system; and they restored their way of life in that manner.

On the basis of the above perspective, I argue in this introduction that the reorganization achieved through the total-war system comprised a "shift from a class to a system society."[6] Whether my hypothesis is valid can only be determined on the basis of future historical research; for the time being, I will examine the interpretations advanced by Talcott Parsons, the originator of the modern system-theory of society, in order to determine the extent to which his conception of a system society corresponds to the reorganization actually carried out under the total-war system. If it becomes clear that the birth of social-system theory is intimately related to the historical reality of the total-war period, it would show the appropriateness of framing the problem in terms of a "shift from a class to a system society." First, we must refer back to Hegel, who in the early-nineteenth century had already demonstrated an approach to "social consciousness" that can reasonably be associated with system theory. Conceived during the period of the old imperialism, after the Thirty Years War between France and Great Britain when the "crisis of the *anciens régimes* of Europe" that had been brought about by the French Revolution had become clearly apparent,[7] Hegel's system displays a problem-orientation and method very similar to those embraced by Parsons in an age when the "general crisis of capitalism,"[8] had been intensified by the First World War, the Russia Revolution, and the panic of 1929. In both cases, system theory appeared just as one historic period came to a close and a new one was being born. Hegel's approach was eventually inherited by Marx, but from Hegel's system theory which encompassed the triad of family, civil society and state, Marx drew exclusively on the dimension of civil society (capitalism) in order to delineate the organization of class-society as distinct from traditional and status-based societies. In contrast, Parsons documented the shift from a class- to a system-society that occurred against the backdrop of the age of total warfare.

When this reality is recognized, it becomes apparent that the following additional problem must be addressed. Although the system theories of Hegel and Parsons are similar, obvious differences must be accounted for. Hegel's system theory appeared just as "class society" was emerging, while Parsons's appeared in the period of the "shift from class to system society." Thus, by comparing them, we should be able to gain valuable insights into the true character of the metamorphosis that was undergone in that transition. The following study will attempt, first, to apprehend the formation of system theory as a product of the period of "the general crisis of capitalism," or total war, and second to investigate the character of the transformation that occurred between nineteenth-century and present-day society in light of the differences in theoretical framework between the system theories of Hegel and Parsons.

FROM HEGEL TO PARSONS
The Possibility of Social Order

According to Niklas Luhman, the distinctive character of social-systems theory is fully evident in the question, "how is social order possible?" According to Luhman, before the appearance of system theory the social sciences had presupposed, uncritically, the actual existence of societies as fixed and stable orders. The aim of the social sciences was thus to investigate these social orders so as to clarify their objective structure. In effect, the fundamental task of the social scientist prior to the advent of system theory was to ascertain a social structure that he presupposed with certainty to exist and to make clear the well-regulated nature of the laws that governed the interior of that structure. For this variety of social science, whose style was perfected during the nineteenth century, certainty itself became the goal of scholarship; uncertainty was nothing less than the principal negative factor detracting from the truth of the social sciences. For the nineteenth-century variety of social science, each advance in the investigation of an uncertain world transformed that world into the realm of the certain, which could then be ruled by reason and knowledge. Such was the primary goal of the social sciences.

Yet, according to Luhman, the social sciences are today no longer capable of fully retaining objective science as their distinctive characteristic. This is because the complex specialization of social functions has developed to such extremes that society has further fragmented into multiple subordinate systems. Each of these subordinate systems possesses its own self-referential autonomy, and reduces or simplifies the unpredictable complexity that arises out of its relationship with other subordinate systems and transforms that complexity into something more manageable. This simplification or reduction is in itself the process of transforming complexity so that it can be processed by the human intellect. However, this process does not imply total knowledge of the object of study. Simplification or reduction are ultimately expedients employed to transform complexity into an object that is provisionally manageable and orderly. The complexity of the object itself remains unknowable, locked within a mysterious shroud of darkness. In Kantian terms, the complexity, as the "thing in itself," remains outside the realm of human knowledge. But, that is not the end of the matter. The social act of interpretation itself produces a chain reaction that leads to a new realm of unpredictable complexity.

For the earlier brand of social science, uncertainty was intolerable, an object to be overcome. However, from the standpoint of system theory, uncertainty is not immediately deemed abnormal; on the contrary, that the functional processes of society are everywhere confronted with uncertainty is taken to be the normal state of affairs. Because the social sciences cannot exclude uncertainty, they require a new method that encompasses and accommodates it. In Luhman's conception, uncertainty and normality are no longer mutually exclusive, binary opposites. The task of system theory, therefore, is to discover "how to theoretically integrate uncertainty and normality." The question of "how is social order possible?" did indeed announce the methodological transition from nineteenth-century to modern social science.[9]

The proposition that the objective existence of social phenomena cannot be taken for granted and that therefore the social system must take upon itself the task of continually reconstructing the social order, says a lot about the current state of the social sciences in the wake of the "general crisis of capitalism." The social order is no longer a given; nor is there inherent within the process of unstable change an order (the dialectic), as Hegel and Marx would have it, governed by logical or historical laws. Rather, social order is possible only by virtue of the ability of the system continually to manage the uncertainty that confronts it. This proposition reveals how the social system has been able to transcend the "general crisis of capitalism." This proposition incorporates methodologically the disturbances of the social system that had been revealed by the crisis. The social system is not stabilized by the actual existence of an immovable social order. After the "general crisis of capitalism" there emerged a system society that had successfully internalized the shifts and strains in the social order. Although society was still enveloped in uncertainty, it was now able to manage that uncertainty without being brought to the point of crisis. "System society," therefore designates a society that, although still faced with constant crises, has reached a stage where it is able to manage those crises by reducing their concrete manifestations to moderate levels which may then be neutralized.

Modern Society in Light of System Theory: Hegel

For Hegel, the advent of modern society signified precisely the emergence of a state of crisis that called forth unrelenting instability. The young Hegel was a student of theology when he encountered the French revolution, and it signified the start of an age of new possibilities. However, the bloody power struggles that surfaced in the course of the revolution, along with the panics and economic recessions that regularly struck England, which had previously experienced the industrial revolution, gradually made Hegel skeptical of modern society. In his *Philosophy of Right*, which is based on lectures he delivered in the decade of the 1820s, Hegel has already advanced his concern to a point far removed from his early enthusiasm for the French revolution. He had now come to be fascinated by the question of "how is social order possible?" For Hegel, elucidation of the objective structural relations of modern society would never make clear the true state or secret of the social order as a thing in itself. His *Philosophy of Right* grasped the objective, structural relations of capitalism, which were then emerging in full form at the level of "civil society." But this "civil society" was none other than a state of ethical and spiritual division that would never be stabilized unless complemented by systemic links to the other social realms—that of the family, which was a natural ethical body, and the state, which was the ethical body on a rationally reflective level. As is well known, Hegel explained the systemic relations of modern society according to the logic of transition from base to apex, moving from the family to civil society and on to the state; in other words, he explains the system by ascending from bottom to top. As we shall see, Parsons explains such systemic linkages in terms of a horizontal process of exchange along the boundaries of various subsystems that all exist on the same plane.

Hegel's *Phenomenology of Spirit*[10] of 1807, poised between his days as a student of theology and the period of the *Philosophy of Right*, is best seen as retaining a heavy dose of the youthful Hegel's fervor for the French revolution. This text brings to the fore the prospect of a new order ripe with possibilities in the wake of the crisis of the *anciens regimes*. This becomes clear through an examination of the logic of "mutual recognition," which serves as the methodological axis of the *Phenomenology of Spirit*, and the structure of the "master-slave dialectic" which was derived from that logic.

As regards the point that the *Phenomenology*'s methodology represents a period of crisis, the most acute reading of the work has been provided by Alexandre Kojève. In Paris during the tension-racked period between the two world wars, Kojève conceived an epoch-making reading of the *Phenomenology*, which overturned the traditional understanding of the work. The keys to

Kojève's discovery were Heidegger's *Being and Time* and the newly discovered *Economic and Philosophic Manuscripts* of Marx, which attracted much attention at the time.[11]

It must not be forgotten that Heidegger's *Being and Time* was conceived during the First World War, an age rife with blood and gunpowder, and that it responded to the memory of the unprecedented carnage that had relegated to the seemingly distant past the almost bucolic nature of war as people had known it. Marx's *Economic and Philosophic Manuscripts* were written in 1848, in anticipation of the upheavals that would rock all of Europe. In any case, Hegel's theory of "mutual recognition" was greatly influenced by Hobbes' grim vision of the tumultuous English revolution of the seventeenth-century. In essence, as a philosopher of the age in which the old European order was in crisis, Hegel constructed a system using as raw material his experience of that crisis. In such an age, people are hardly guaranteed a life of tranquillity. Accordingly, philosophy in such an age must confront the threat of death and adopt a style that treats of life by investing meaning in that threat.

Hegel viewed the development of human history as the unfolding of "consciousness of freedom," but this "consciousness" could only be realized through the experience of a "struggle for mutual recognition" in which one's own existence was put at risk. In this struggle, the person who is able to assert himself without fear of death commands recognition from the others and assumes the seat of the master. In contrast, one who, fearing death, retreats from the scene of battle, recognizes the dignity of the master and submits to him as a slave. The master plays the active role in the development of the "consciousness of freedom," and the slave is confined to a passive role. Nevertheless, once established, the master-slave relationship must eventually be reversed in the following stage. This is because the master's victory in the struggle for recognition establishes his humanity, but in the process liberates him from the necessity to work. Liberation from labor involves, at the same time, alienation from labor. The master's existence is thus devoted entirely to the unilateral enjoyment of the wealth produced out of the slave's labor and, in this sense, becomes a passive existence. In contrast, the slave goes out into and transforms the natural world through his own labor. By transforming the natural world, the slave brings it into the humanly constructed, historical world; moreover, through his act of creation the slave also transforms himself. Indeed, the slave transforms himself to the point of excluding the master, ultimately driving him to his death. That is roughly Kojève's account of the argument in *Phenomenology of Spirit*. It is evident that in interpreting the "struggle for mutual recognition" Kojève applied Heidegger's point of view, and in his interpretation of the "dialectic of master and slave" he adopted the approach of Marx.[12]

As finite beings who must die, humans participate in the struggle for recognition within the limits of the inevitability of death, and it is precisely this struggle for recognition that makes possible the development of the "consciousness of freedom." Moreover, the *Phenomenology of Spirit* represents Hegel's perception of new possibilities emerging out of the crisis of the old European order. Although members of the old aristocratic class, who had been the masters in the society governed by status, had lost the right to rule, and a civil society based on the victory of former slaves' labor had appeared, this civil society betrayed the hopes that Hegel had vested in it. That is, for Hegel, by this time the crisis of the *anciens régimes* of Europe was no longer uppermost. He realized that the appearance of civil society itself was bringing about a new crisis. Thus, in *Philosophy of Right*, Hegel has nothing more to say about the "master-slave dialectic."[13] Rather, once he situated civil society as merely one structural element in the total social system, the dialectic became a way of thinking about the relationship between civil society and the other two realms, the family and the state. In this process of reorientation, Hegel's target was the social philosophy of utilitarianism, which viewed civil society as an autonomous domain. As he hardened his stance against the social philosophy of utilitarianism, Hegel clearly intended that the dialectic, that is, the system theory of the *Philosophy of Right*, should serve as a "critique of political economy." As will be evident below, Talcott Parsons also developed a unique "critique of political economy" on the basis of his own thoroughgoing, consistent critique of utilitarian social theory. Thus, such a "critique" is by no means a monopoly of Marx or Marxists. For both Hegel and Parsons, the development of a system theory itself could not help but be a "critique of political economy."

It is by no means easy to grasp the overall logic of the *Philosophy of Right*, as within it a number of apparently contradictory threads coexist. I will begin by summarizing what appears, on a first reading, to be the clearest line of argument.

"Ethical Life," the third section of the *Philosophy of Right*, is constructed according to the logic of transition, which begins at the level of the family, shifts to civil society, and finally arrives at the state. The family is an "immediate or natural ethical body." In it the various conflicting moments of subjectivity (*Subjektivität*) and objectivity (*Objektivität*), or particularity (*Besonderheit*) and universality (*Allgemeinheit*), remain dormant, sealed in by an ethics based on the natural ties of blood. In the transition to civil society, these various forces split apart, become separate, and begin to act. Each particular individual now becomes independent, separated from the ties of family, and transformed into the purest particularity, seeking only to attain individual goals. Of course, since the particularity of the individual is incomplete and one-sided it requires connections to others. Here, the mutual ties that bind particular individuals have already transcended the stage of individual particularity and have attained the state of universality; and, yet, because it lacks an ethic, it is devoid of content and nothing but a formal universality. The universality that exists at the level of the civil society is merely a formal relationship among individuals and can attain a higher stage only through rational reflection. That is, the substantial whole (*substantielles Ganz*) is fully attained only by shifting to the level of the state. Individuals can recover their ethical existence when they reach the stage of self-consciousness as citizens of the state (*Philosophy of Right*, paragraphs 157 and 255).

The universality of civil society that Hegel discovers in the *Philosophy of Right* is not a true universality endowed with substance, but merely an unstable universality superimposed over a situation of ethical division. This is because, from the standpoint of one who has been transformed into the purest particularity, others exist only as the necessary means to the realization of one's own ends. The narrow confines of communities based on blood or territorial ties had certainly been transcended with the establishment of civil society. However, the transformation of people into means at the hands of others—*Versachlichung* is the term used later by Marx and adopted by Max Weber to designate the commodification of social relations—had become a universal practice (*Philosophy of Right*, paragraph 182).

Hegel could not help but be strongly conscious of the problematical nature of formal universality, or commodification, as it emerged in civil society. As is well known, that was the basis for his argument against utilitarian social theory, especially the utilitarian theory of the state. The utilitarian social theory based the state on social contract theory. But, for Hegel, this did not constitute a theory of the state but was merely a discourse that took the logic of contract, appropriate only at the level of civil-society, and applied it to the state. That is, the social-contract theory's rationale for the existence of the state was confined to securing the wealth of the citizenry and guaranteeing their personal freedom (*Philosophy of Right*, paragraphs 182 and 258). In contrast, Hegel countered with the organic theory of the state. In his view, true meaning resided only in the state as a substantial, public entity. The state did not consist in a series of contracts made with disparate individuals, but was a social organism whose existence preceded that of the citizen (*Philosophy of Right*, paragraph 145).

As we trace his argument, we become fully aware of the extent of Hegel's conservatism. The conservative Hegel did not fail to devote careful consideration to the composition of a national legislature. His theory of the legislature was built upon the premise of preserving medieval status relationships. One legislative house was to be selected from those whose "status was based on substantial relations," in other words, the agricultural class and landed gentry, while the other house was to be selected from among those whose "status was based on individual desire or the labor that mediated it," in other words, the traders and artisans who made up civil society. The foundation of the lives of those who constituted civil society was set in the ever-fluctuating world of market relations. Hegel felt great apprehension at the thought that members of civil society might penetrate to the center of national power and seek to dominate the realm of politics. The agricultural classes and landed gentry are referred to in terms of the "status of natural ethics," but the political significance of the existence of those who possessed such status resided in the fact that many of them had hereditary rights to property (*Erbgut*), based on primogeniture (*Majorat*). It was not simply a matter that this form of property was isolated from civil society in the sense of being cut off from commercial market relations and held semi-permanently as a unitary parcel of hereditary property. It was rather that, by virtue of a stability which preceded that of the modern state, it could endure without "the protection of the state," and had actually done so (*Philosophy of Right*, paragraphs 303, 305, and 306). It was on the basis of the family's independence from the relations of civil society and its stable assets that, for Hegel, "the family is the primary ethical root of the state." But we must also take into account the occupational group (*Korporation*), which was seen as the "second ethical root of the state." In contrast to the family, which existed outside civil society, the occupational group originated in the guild systems of the medieval era and existed within civil society. Its appointed role was to restrain the commodification of civil society from within (*Philosophy of Right*, paragraphs 201 and 255).

When compared to the Hegel of the period of *Phenomenology*, the Hegel of the *Philosophy of Right* is much more skeptical toward civil society. It would be simple to criticize Hegel's retreat into skepticism as a matter of his growing conservatism. However, we must also consider that Hegel now recognized that the advent of civil society implied not only the possibility of dynamic economic development but also a profound clash of interests and inevitable moral degeneration. When the commodification of human relationships becomes pervasive, that is, as human beings increasingly employ one another as means and, in effect, treat one another as things, social order is likely to become extremely unstable and uncertain. Thus, in a manner befitting the first system theorist, Hegel wrestled in his own fashion with the task of "how to theoretically integrate uncertainty and normality."[14]

But our consideration of Hegel must go on a bit further. In addition to the above-mentioned main thread of the *Philosophy of Right*, there is also in Hegel another divergent, somewhat contradictory strain of thought. This other strand brings Hegel in close proximity to utilitarian social thought and, finally, unravels his system theory from within.

Let us first examine his theory of the family. According to Hegel, the family must ultimately be based on an "agreement freely entered by both personalities," that of the man and the woman. It must be noted that Hegel's statement implies a critique of status society in which marriage did not then constitute an agreement between free personalities but was rather a union of one house with another (*Stamme oder Hauser*). Hegel was consistent on this point. In his view, property belonged to the couple, whose union was based on free will, never to the "household." He also based his arguments regarding the inheritance of family property on the premise of an independent, free personality. According to Hegel, the exclusion of daughters from family inheritance or disinheriting other children for the sake of the eldest son had to be declared violations of the principle of freedom of property (*Philosophy of Right*, paragraphs 162, 172, and 180). Regarding the education of children in the home, Hegel specified that the goal is that "of raising children out of the instinctive, physical level on which they are originally, to self-subsistence and freedom of personality and so to the level on which they have power to leave the natural unity of the family" (*Philosophy of Right*, paragraph 175). This reflects an essentially modern theory of family. An inquiry into the concrete evolution of Hegel's theory shows that, rather than natural and direct ties of blood, he emphasizes the modern principle of a free, independent personality. In terms of this thread of logic, Hegel's theory of the family already belongs on the level of civil society. If this is the case, it would seem directly to contradict his theory of the legislative system, which is based on social status. That is, as noted above, in his theory of the national legislature, Hegel introduced premodern relations in the form of *Erbgut* based on *Majorat*, and also proposed to control the instability of civil society through recourse to the natural stability of the family system. It is not at all unreasonable that in regard to this point the young Marx called Hegel's argument in *Philosophy of Right* incoherent, and severely criticized it as the "worst sort of mosaic" that tried to reconcile the modern and the medieval.[15]

What of the theory of civil society? Here too, the specific contents of Hegel's conception are strikingly at odds with how they might seem at first glance. Ethical rules have been abandoned in civil society, giving rise to relations in which "the particular becomes the primary determinant of the private self." Yet, the impression this conveys of civil society in a state of ethical division is actually incorrect, according to Hegel. Such an impression is actually the illusion typical of those who are trapped in the position of the individual, private self. Human beings who live in civil society operate to the last as individuals on the level of formal universality and are subjectively conscious of themselves as individuals with self-interest. Nevertheless, the subjectively self-interested individual unconsciously and objectively serves the development of the universal spirit (*Philosophy of Right*, paragraph 181). The conception of the "cunning of reason" (*List der Vernunft*) that appears in the *Philosophy of History*, is in this sense already anticipated in the argument of the *Philosophy of Right*. This thread of argument draws Hegel close to the economics of Adam Smith et al., and makes him heir to the English utilitarian social thought that spread in Smith's wake. Expressly mentioning Adam Smith, J.B. Say, and David Ricardo by name, Hegel began to speak of the possibility that civil society could be studied scientifically. It appeared to be disorderly, unregulated, and lawless. However, in civil society "this medley of arbitrariness generates universal characteristics by its own working; and this apparently scattered and thoughtless sphere is upheld by a necessity which automatically enters it. To discover the necessary element here is the object of political economy." Hegel compares economics to astronomy: Just as astronomy had discovered the orderly laws governing the movement of the solar system "which displays to the eye only irregular movements," economics discovers the universal laws operating in the sphere of civil society that is animated by particularistic activity (*Philosophy of Right*, paragraph 189).[16]

Civil society, which appears to be in a disorderly state of ethical division, is in reality equipped with an internal self-regulating mechanism. Once this is realized, one begins to see that the logic of the state and that of organic theory are constructed differently. Already concealed within Hegel's theory of the state was an idea that would bring about the dissolution of the organic theory of the state which is his original standpoint. It appears that Hegel was intrigued by and followed closely the argument between Malthus and Ricardo over the nature of financial panic. Inherent within civil society is an impulse for disintegration due to its ethically-divided state. As an economic phenomenon, this appears as a collision between the interests of consumers and producers. Hegel accurately grasped the condition that would later be explained by J. M. Keynes as insufficiency of effective demand, and thus provided the following solution to the problem. "This interest invokes freedom of trade and commerce against control from above; but the more blindly it sinks into self-seeking aims, the more it requires such control to bring it back to the universal. Control is also necessary to diminish the danger of upheavals arising from clashing interests and to abbreviate the period in which their tension should be eased." As was appropriate for a theorist arguing from the standpoint of the organic state, Hegel sought regulation by the state against economic fluctuations and therefore seems to have recognized the superiority of the state over civil society. However, that is actually not the case. This is because the role of the state here is theorized from the viewpoint of abbreviating "the period in which their tension should be eased," which is based on the premise that the civil society already contains a self-regulating capability. That is, even in the absence of control from above, tension would be "eased through the working of a necessity of which they themselves know nothing" (*Philosophy of Right*, paragraph 236). The role of the state, here, is analogous to that of a kind of nursemaid who is reluctant to augment artificially the natural, self-healing capability of civil society.

Despite his professed advocacy of the organic theory of the state, Hegel's thinking as manifested in *Philosophy of Right* had been exposed to the seductive power of the logic of utilitarian social theory. If civil society were equipped with an internal self-regulating capacity, and if it were possible to create a field of study, i.e., economics, that would illuminate this self-regulating capacity within civil society—just as astronomy illuminated the movement of heavenly bodies—then Hegel's system theory, in which the recovery of ethical substantiality was predicated on the triad of the family, civil society, and the state, would probably be deprived of its foundation. Hegel's *Philosophy of Right* already contained the logical moment that would undo his system theory from within. In fact, nineteenth-century social science did proceed toward the dissolution of the Hegelian synthesis, dividing into sociology, anthropology, political science, economics, and so forth. That each of the various fields of study monopolizes a discreet sphere, and that the scientific character of each is guaranteed by the self-contained completeness of its own sphere, has provided the rationale for that dissolution. Economics, in particular, is armed with a persuasiveness that finally brought even Hegel to his knees. Nevertheless, the experience of World War I brought an era in which one had to admit to the "crisis of European sciences" (Edmund Husserl).[17] The "general crisis of capitalism" had made absolutely clear what was to blame for the dissolution of the Hegelian synthesis. A return to Hegel was inevitably discussed at this point. Yet, any return to Hegel would have to be one that took fully into account the dissolution of the Hegelian system. Talcott Parsons responded to this problematic state of affairs in *The Structure of Social Action* (1937).

Functionalist Reorganization of Contemporary Society: Parsons

The social sciences had reached an apparent dead-end, and were at a standstill. Underlying their desperate situation were the limitations of the utilitarian philosophy on which the social sciences had previously relied. In his maiden work, *The Structure of Social Action* (1937), Talcott Parsons attempted to provide a new direction for social theory based on the perception that there was no possibility of breaking through the contemporary impasse—the condition we have been calling "the general crisis of capitalism"—so long as utilitarian social theory remained the premise. The task undertaken in *The Structure of Social Action* was truly impressive in scope. On the one hand, the work probed the German tradition of idealist philosophy, so different in character from utilitarianism, and arrived at Max Weber's conceptual framework for social action. On the other hand, it sought out the French tradition of thought, extracting the idea of normative integration from Durkheim.[18] Parsons had now arrived at a position critical of the premises of the utilitarian view of social action, and proposed instead the concept of voluntarism. Since it is impossible to recapitulate his argument in its entirety, we will focus on Parsons' discussion of Hobbes and Locke in the first part of *Structure*, and the critical understanding of utilitarian social theory to which it leads him.

According to Parsons, the character of utilitarian social theory is summarized in the following four points. First, its emphasis on individual autonomy means that it lacks the opportunity for community and social reciprocity, and portrays the world atomistically. Second, as a result of its assumption that individuals are motivated in terms of rational means-ends relationships, it is unable sociologically to evaluate motivation that arises in realms such as religion or ritual that transcend instrumental rationality. Third, and conversely, it vigorously promotes the kind of scientific thinking that determines cause and effect relations on the basis of positivistic, empirical observation. Fourth, it treats as random and outside the purview of scientific investigation any motivations for individual action that are not determined by the rational selection of means to reach a given end (*Structure*, pp. 51-60).

The economic activity that unfolds within civil society appears at first glance to be completely arbitrary and dominated by individual instrumentalism, or the rational selection of means. Absent is any normative adjustment of behavior in accord with social communality. One thinker in the tradition of utilitarian social theory made the difficulties surrounding this point his central theme from the beginning. It was Thomas Hobbes, of course, who portrayed civil society as a "war of all against all" and argued on that basis for the necessity of constructing the state "Leviathan" through the social contract.

Parsons discovered the wellspring of his own thought in Hobbes, who, although a founder of utilitarian social theory, is apt to be regarded as heterodox. In the reified, instrumentalist world where the "war of all against all" must constitute the normal condition, social order could only be maintained by establishing an external regulator with powerful authority. Although Hobbes had participated in the incipient stage of utilitarian social theory, because he had most thoroughly argued the "problem of order" Hobbes was, according to Parsons, the one thinker deserving of attention in the attempt to establish a new social science in an age of general crisis. And yet, Parsons did not become an uncritical Hobbesian. In place of Hobbes' powerful external regulator Parsons established a regulating function that operated within the system of civil society itself. For Parsons, even power (as will be discussed below) ceased to be something impinging on civil society from outside and was now resituated within the system as an integrating mechanism that sustained the systemic relations of civil society. On this point, Parsons' conception differs from those of both Hobbes and Hegel. However, a discussion here of his differences with Hegel would be premature. First, we must confirm that Parsons and Hegel were both thinkers born of social crisis.

The "randomness of ends" and, consequently, a serious "Hobbesian problem of order"—these are the problems of modern society that are inevitably brought into the open by utilitarian social theory. In the sense that he took Hobbes' conceptions as his starting point, Parsons' orientation was very similar to that of Hegel, who saw civil society as being in a state of ethical fracture. Parsons, like Hegel, was a thinker who lived in an age of crisis and sought to overcome that crisis.

Parsons' approach depreciated the value of Locke, who had previously been deemed the most orthodox theorist of the initial period of utilitarian social theory. Locke prepared the way for Adam Smith by introducing, in the fifth chapter ("Of Property") of his *Two Treatises of Government* (1690), the archetype of the labor theory of value, premised on the logic of "ownership based on labor." However, in that Locke's argument was oblivious to the "Hobbesian problem of order," it lacked scientific rigor when compared to that of Hobbes. In his "wishful postulation" (*Structure*, pp. 97f), Locke assumed unlimited tillable land and supposed that all people would be linked equally through their own labor to the bounty of nature. Because he never doubted this wishful thinking, Locke failed to realize the colossal gap between "established fact" and his "implicit normative assumptions." Locke overlooked the important point that the stability of the social order (an established fact) is sustained as a result of a preexisting social agreement made by people on the basis of certain fixed norms. Parsons therefore criticized the utilitarian viewpoint on social activity, positing against it the position of voluntarism. Contradicting Locke, Parsons argued that divergent social interests would never experience a "natural identity of interest" (*Structure*, p. 101). This was also stressed by Hobbes. Absent the intervention of some regulator, there would be no reconciliation. Whereas Hobbes sought this regulator in the Leviathan state, Parsons found it in normative agreement among the constituent members of society. Utilitarian social thought after Locke had ignored the unique importance of normative agreement for the social order. That is, such thought had allowed "implicit assumption" to take the place of "established fact." As a heterodoxical thinker, Hobbes was an exception in the history of utilitarian social thought.[19]

The above account shows Parsons' appraisal of Locke to be strikingly low. Nevertheless, one also detects a tone at variance with this critique. It results from Parsons' effort to interpret as a valuable scientific legacy the tradition of classical economics, from Locke to Adam Smith. According to Parsons, Locke's exclusion of the problem of the "stability of order" may be dubbed a "fortunate error." This is because "[u]tterly dependent logically on this 'erroneous' premise there grew up what is perhaps the most highly developed theoretical system in the social sciences [that is to say economics] with correct results—within certain limits" (*Structure*, p. 101). Parsons went back to the philosophical antecedents of economics to develop his own critique. However, his critique of economics differed from Marx's in that it was not intended to overturn the foundations of utilitarian social philosophy, which had begun with Locke. In conceiving of the development of a voluntaristic theory of action derived from utilitarianism, Parsons intended to reposition the utilitarian viewpoint within the limited, partial system (expressed in the terms of later system-theory as a subordinate system) of the goal-oriented rationalism of market activity. Parsons' critique did not constitute a revolution against economics. It made clear the existence of a higher theoretical plane where consideration was devoted to the relationship of normative agreement to economic activity,[20] and thereby resituated economics in an appropriately limited, functional sense. It was an unambiguous critique of economics in the sense that it made clear that economics could never be a self-contained science; alone it was insufficient to analyze the character of the impending crisis. But this was not to say that it was utterly sterile; it was endowed with a paradoxical significance, for despite having been established on an "erroneous premise," it developed into the "most highly developed theoretical system."

The readjustment in theoretical position that was carried out in relation to economics was also applied to other fields such as political science, commercial economics, and the sociology of the family and of organization. In this way, Parsons resituated the separate domains of the social sciences, which had developed since the nineteenth century, within the more comprehensive framework of a system theory centering on the voluntarist theory of action. If we were to organize Parsons' conception in terms of a basic framework, the following two points would be most important.

First, value systems, which generally originate in religion and which motivate human action, are confined to a role as normative propositions at a high level of abstraction. In order for these abstract, normative propositions to operate in concrete social situations, each of the following three processes must be accounted for: A) the value system must be the common property of the members who constitute society and it must be internalized in the personality of each member; B) the value system is institutionalized on differentiated levels of society; C) the value system fulfills the function of integrating members of society on the level of various collective bodies. (For discussion of the internalization, institutionalization, and integration of collective bodies, see Parsons, "Authority, Legitimation, and Political Action," in *Nomos*, 1958.)[21]

Second, it is necessary to consider what sort of relationships exist among the main subordinate systems of society—for the present, the following four: politics, economics, family, and organization. Parsons explained the interrelationship among these subordinate systems using a diagram of boundary exchanges; through these boundary exchanges, not only the various subsystems but also each member who belongs to a collective body within a subsystem contribute to the efficient and functional operation of society. (On the functional operation of system-society, see Parsons, *Economy and Society*, 1956.)[22]

We will make no further effort here to explore the contents of the system theory to which Parsons devoted himself during his middle period except simply to confirm that, having concentrated his energy on clarifying the issue of the possibility of establishing social order despite the "general crisis of capitalism," Parsons was able to see that all social elements and processes were arranged to "contribute" to the functional operation of the entire system. Parsons' emphasis on harmony appears most prominently in his reinterpretation of two categories that had previously been considered sources of social conflict and/or class confrontation, in other words, profit in economics and power in political science.

According to Parsons, profit is not the reward for success won by the survivor in a life-and-death struggle, nor is it the excess value wrung from labor by the capitalist. It is rather a compensation for services rendered—here, the service of organizational integration—that differs little from the stipend that is received by the conductor of an orchestra. For Parsons, the capitalist is in charge of the social function of system integration, and thus "contributes" to the operation of the social system. A consequence of this type of thinking is the emergence of a definition of profit in which it is ultimately indistinguishable from the wage received by the laborer (*Economy and Society*, p. 269).[23]

Similarly, power is no longer seen as an expression of the minority's exercise of control over the majority, but now defined "as the generalized capacity of the social system to cause something to be done for the benefit of collective goals" ("Authority, Legitimation and Political Action," p. 186). For Parsons, power was not exercised unilaterally by a certain group of people against the weaker ones, but was an indispensable function possessed collectively by all members who constitute society. Ultimately, all members of society, with the exception of a few social deviates, receive the blessings of power's integrative function rather than being injured by it. Power is diffused throughout all realms of society, mutually maintained by all members of society, and mutually exercised. Thus, power merges with authority in a one-dimensional, systemic function that benefits the collectivity. Authority as defined by Parsons—"just collective action performed effectively"—forms the basis of "the institutionalization of the right of 'leaders,' who anticipate the support of the members of the collective body" ("Authority, Legitimation and Political Action," p. 186) and is essentially equivalent in content to power. According to Parsons, authority and power are merely systemic functions that contribute to sustaining the stable operation of society.[24]

SYSTEM SOCIETY AND THE TRANSFER OF PRIVATE LIFE
INTO THE PUBLIC SPHERE

Power, according to Parsons, is not a small elite's capacity for rule over the majority of the members of society, but a function of the system that contributes to society's stable operation. The power that Max Weber had once interpreted as linked to the special capacity of charisma, was now for Parsons a general operation whose functional significance was supported by all members of society. Power was represented as functioning throughout all of society as something that all citizens were potentially qualified to exercise. According to this definition, a power holder is merely the leader of a collectivity analogous to the captain of a college baseball team. He fulfills the role of leader simply because he happens to meet the requirements for office, and when his term is up, he returns to being an ordinary team member.[25] Therefore, power pervades society as a system-maintenance function exercised reciprocally. It is no more than the normative mechanism through which the collectivity maintains itself under elected leaders. Parsons' representation of power here is strangely similar to the concept of power expressed by Michel Foucault through the metaphor of the Panopticon.[26] If there is a major difference between the two conceptions, it would be that while Foucault firmly adhered to a critical stance in his investigation of power in modern society, Parsons saw in it the key to overcoming crisis, and assigned it positive significance. Neither saw power as an external mechanism of oppression, and both treated it as a form of self-discipline internalized into the everyday-consciousness of the citizen. The same phenomenon that Foucault took as internalized surveillance Parsons had previously understood as the internalization of values. Foucault's internalization of surveillance and Parsons' internalization of values are key processes in the self-sustaining function of the social system.

Foucault found the advent of modern society in the conversion to self-discipline through the internalization of surveillance, while Parsons considered it in the context of the "general crisis of capitalism." Despite these differences, the distance between the two is not very great. What Foucault located in the discursive transformation that accompanied the formation of modern society, Parsons found in the Reformation, based on his reading of Max Weber's sociology of religion. While Foucault focused his attention on the period of modern society's formation, Parsons believed that only in the new world of the United States of America could the values and norms formed during the Reformation become fully operative functionally throughout the entire social system.[27] In contrast to European societies which were still constrained by class, Parsons believed that the shift to a system society had occurred early in the United States. More concretely, in the U.S. the managerial revolution had occurred early along with the rapid spread of the joint-stock company.

In contrast to class societies where capitalists are both owners and managers and thus power is linked directly to a particular personality, contemporary societies are dominated by joint-stock companies in which the ownership of capital is institutionally differentiated from the managerial function. Moreover, as a result of the successive subdivision and thus proliferation of shares in such societies, capital ownership has moved out of the hands of individuals to become collectivized in investment organizations such as insurance companies, pension funds, and investment trusts. In contemporary society, where the joint-stock company is pervasive, the classical figure of the capitalist has now disappeared, and, with the development of corporate bureaucracy the power and authority that were once concentrated in the person of the capitalist have been institutionalized within the objective duties of the functionary.[28] Under the objective institutionalization of power characteristic of contemporary society, even those who subjectively see themselves as members of the working class have already become indirect owners of capital through participation in legally established insurance and pension arrangements. The liberation of power from any direct association with specific personalities, and its institutionalization in accord with the subdivision of roles within society, have brought about a fundamental change in the structure of classical capitalist society. In the course of two world wars, this transformation merged with the processes of social mobilization demanded by the nation-state.

Spurred on by the wartime sense of common destiny throughout a national community, the total-war system initiated a variety of social-policy measures. These wartime social-policy measures vastly expanded the social institutionalization of power across the entire society as the result of the need to replace class conflict with institutionalized negotiations between labor and capital, to dilute ethnic discrimination by means of the principle of equal rights for all citizens, or to compensate citizens for the deaths or injuries sustained by those who fulfilled their military duties. Social policy in the age of total war intensified the social institutionalization of power that had begun on the level of the joint-stock enterprises, converting it into a public principle to which society as a whole had to conform.[29] Parsons' sociology emerged in response to such an era of change.

Perhaps this is the appropriate place to reformulate and summarize the differences between Parsons' and Hegel's system theories. In Hegel's case, the possibility of social order is explained in terms of vertical development, shifting in turn from the family, the site of natural ethics, to civil society, in which ethics are in a state of disintegration, and finally to the state as the locus of rational ethics. The self-development of the ethical spirit is central and the progression of that spirit from natural synthesis through disintegration, and on to reintegration at the rational level, constitute the core of Hegel's dialectically-formed system theory.

In Parsons' system theory, on the other hand, the ascending development from nature to reason has been erased. Vertical relationships certainly provide one theoretical component in Parsons as well, but this time they are situated in a top-down process, in which the value system produced out of the Reformation is: a) internalized as the motivation for action by members of society, and b) institutionalized in structures charged with the various, specialized functions of society. In contrast to the central axis of the internalization and institutionalization of the value system, the four major subordinate systems of family, business, politics, and organizational integration are arranged and intersect across a horizontal plane. The interrelationship of these four major subsystems can be clarified if one diagrams a square in which each corner is occupied by one of the four, and diagonal lines connect opposite corners, resulting in six lines which link family and business, business and government, government and organizational integration, organizational integration and family, organizational integration and business, family and government. Parsons used the term boundary exchange to describe the relationships designated by these six lines that connect subordinate systems. For example, the family provides a worker to a business enterprise, and in exchange the business pays the family a money wage. With the wage the family, in turn, purchases a business-produced commodity. And so on.

The special characteristics of Parsons' diagram are, first, that it does not adopt the Hegelian view that the state occupies a particularly high level of rationality; second, it erases the Hegelian view that civil society is in a state of ethical fracture; third, it eliminates the conception of the family as a locus of natural ethics and as therefore different in character from the state or civil society. In Parsons' diagram of boundary exchange, the state occupies no special place and appears only in the form of the government. In relation to the other subsystems of family, business, and organizational integration the government simply provides those services that only a government can carry out. For Parsons, the state is not distinguished from civil society by virtue of some supposedly special character, but has been dragged down to the level of civil society. This fate is shared by the family, which is no longer the locus of natural ethics, external to society; it merely provides specific services to the other social subsystems.

Despite his consistent criticism of utilitarianism, Parsons' system theory (in contrast to Hegel's) is, in a sense, the culmination of utilitarian social theory in that it eliminates the theory of the state as an organic body. The state ceases to exist as an all-encompassing community whose existence precedes that of the citizen. However, from another point of view, it can be said that Parsons reconstructed Hegel's structure in a form appropriate to the contemporary system society. This is because in Parsons' conception, built around the central axis of the dual process of institutionalization and internalization of the value system, the citizens appear less as human individuals than as cells comprising the social organism. Despite whatever autonomy they might possess, the individual cells of living bodies "contribute" to the organic operation of the whole body. In the same manner, in Parsons' formulation the citizen is situated within a complex network spanning the interior of the social system, and exists in order to fulfill an allotted function. The organic totality, conceived by Hegel while focusing on the level of the state, was transferred by Parsons to the more comprehensive scale of the system society. Parsons' system theory is in a sense the latest edition of the Hegelian organismic theory. As indicated by the central concepts of self-organization and self-reference, the social system—whether Parsons' or the new, refined edition fashioned by Luhman—is conceived in terms of the autopoeisis characteristic of organic life.[30]

Parsons' system theory lost its authority once its status-quo oriented conservatism was pointed out in the late 1960s. Parsons believed that the style of American democracy that reached its zenith with the New Deal was the best model for the world, and was confident that other societies would converge on the American model in any case. It must be considered only natural that this kind of optimistic modernism was destroyed when it came face to face with the social unrest of the 1970s.[31] Since then, the New Deal has been stripped of its former glory and has now begun to be the object of criticism. Nevertheless, if one removes the status-quo ideology from Parsons' thought, it is possible to reconstruct his vision of contemporary society from a critical perspective. Indeed, as noted above, in several of its aspects, Parsons' image of contemporary society resembles that of Michel Foucault.

When we adopt such a perspective, Marcuse's earlier vision of contemporary society (as manifested in the United States) as a kind of totalitarianism can no longer be said to completely miss the mark. The warning that contemporary society could be seen as a refined and polished totalitarian world can be found in the statements of Milan Kundera as well. According to Kundera, no matter how much it might seem to differ from the West, the totalitarianism that enveloped Eastern Europe after 1945 is not of an entirely different character from that of modern society in Western Europe. That is, the latter might be categorized as an extremely refined variety of totalitarianism. Nor is modern Japanese society exempt; one often hears it characterized as a cleverly crafted totalitarian order. Recent comments by the historian of economic theory, Uchida Yoshihiko, and the political scientist, Fujita Shōzō, come to mind in this connection.[32]

When Kundera stated that the Eastern-European society of the recent past was scarcely unique and that contemporary Western-European society is also a variety of totalitarianism, he correctly focused on the problem that in such a society the private lives of individuals are caught up in the realm of the collectivity so that "public life and private life become one." It might, of course, legitimately be said that "private life and public life are, in essence, two different worlds." However, in contemporary society sensationalist exposés often destroy the tranquillity of individuals' private lives. The one thing that Kundera considers indispensable is the modicum of individualism that would prevent others from arbitrarily entering the precincts of the self. This sort of individualism, as can be understood from Kundera's reference to it as a sense of shame (*la pudeur*), is not the active individualism expressed in the social activism of contemporary civil society but a passive individualism wrapped in silence and isolated from the sites of social activity.[33] In individual life, which involves physical experience, it is necessary to preserve the secret times and free spaces that allow an individual to step back from society's demands for conformity or participation and quietly to reconsider his or her responsibility. This private time and free space, even if passive and inactive in their initial stages, are the indispensable conditions enabling one to take an active stance, in that they give rise to considered judgments.

WARTIME JAPANESE THINKING ON SOCIAL POLICY

The total-mobilization system of the Second World War provided the occasion for a massive reduction in this passive individualism. The Japanese economist Ōkōchi Kazuo, active in this period, pointed to the flaw in the social sciences that resulted from their tendency to ignore the realm of individual consumption. Economics had seen production as the central economic issue, while devoting little active discussion to consumption at the level of the family. Ōkōchi argued for the importance of consumption as well as production in the general analysis of economic phenomena, but in fact consumption had previously been seen as a purely materialistic process, too vulgar to warrant discussion, and thus seldom analyzed in a scientific fashion. Yet, general economic livelihood, including consumption, is not simply an individual matter, but belongs in the sphere of the "total national economy." In his justification of consumer activity, Ōkōchi argued that it was key to maintaining and preserving productive activity. From his point of view, "for the economic whole, consumption is positive social activity." Therefore, he contended that consumption, which had been regarded as "merely" the domestic economy of the housewife, must be relocated as a central economic issue. In wartime, the economics of consumption as well as production was "a life or death matter."[34]

Under the circumstances of the time, it is no doubt true that underlying Ōkōchi's emphasis on the importance of consumption was the rational judgment that a stop had to be put to the military dictatorship's tendency to conduct irrational confiscations without second thought for the citizens' livelihood. After the war, therefore, Ōkōchi was able to repeat with pride such statements that he had made in opposition to the military dictatorship. However, it cannot be denied that Ōkōchi's logic was never directed against the war as such, but was rather aimed at rationalizing the wartime economy from the perspective of mediating the relationship between production and consumption. Suggesting that it was necessary to "convert the traditional modes of consumption that have been our age-old custom into cooperative communal ones," Ōkōchi indicated the way to mobilize economic livelihood in the interest of more rational operation of the wartime economy. He resisted the military dictatorship, yet actively contributed to the wartime mobilization system. The leadership role played by Ōkōchi in postwar Japanese social science is not unrelated to the stance he took toward the wartime system. Therefore, the trajectory on which postwar Japanese social science was established should not be sought in resistance to total war, but rather in the process of contributing to the rationalization of the wartime system, as represented in the case of Ōkōchi. In this regard, it should not be overlooked that at the time of the postwar dismantling of the zaibatsu, Ōkōchi argued against disturbing the rationalization standards established for Japanese industry during the war, and was supported in this by an influential group of economists.[35] The wartime economy possessed a certain degree of economic rationality in its own right, and Ōkōchi felt that the reforms achieved as a result of that rationality should not be reversed or allowed to lapse. Moreover, Ōkōchi contended that rather than the postwar reforms, it was the wartime mobilization system that was responsible for creating the configuration of labor power that was the main pillar of accelerated postwar growth.[36]

By granting public significance to the consumption carried out in the private sphere, Ōkōchi's theory of consumption published during the war made an unprecedentedly positive contribution. This point is crucial for the argument we want to make. In the sense that it helped liberate family life from the traditional sphere of domesticity and brought it into the realm of civil society, Ōkōchi's theory of consumption stands as indisputably consistent with the logic of modernization. At the same time, we cannot overlook that in attaching public significance to the site of consumption, he dragged it out of private, hidden locations into the glare of public space. That is, the rationality inherent in Ōkōchi's argument contributed to the wholesale restriction of the space available for Kundera's passive individualism and sense of shame.

As is evident from Ōkōchi's thought, the wartime mobilization system played a major role in the historical composition of everyday life in contemporary society. Family life, which for Hegel had been the locus of natural ethics, had now lost the autonomy that was latent in its detachment from the state and civil society. In Ōkōchi, it was given communal significance as a sphere of activity that was indispensable to maintaining and preserving the productive activities of business enterprises, and was incorporated into the general circulatory system of society. His thought lacked a system theory. However, Ōkōchi clearly realized that the subsystems of family and business enterprise were incomplete spheres that could not function by themselves. He also realized that the state had to contribute to the rational operation of business enterprise by maintaining and preserving labor power and providing for its social allocation. Here, the state and the family contribute as subsystems, on the same horizontal plane as civil society, to the systematic operation of the total social process. Thus, Ōkōchi's thought actually corresponds in large measure to that of Talcott Parsons.

In contemporary society, where "public life and private life are one" (Kundera), the realm of civil society, which Hegel distinguished from the family and the state, has lost its autonomy and been transformed into a subsystem on the same horizontal plane as others. The family has been "civil-societized" and surrounded by the publicity that pervades civil society. Similarly, the state has lost its uniquely Hegelian significance as the locus of rational reflection and has been "civil-societized" via metamorphosis into the welfare state. It is now an agency for supplying and maintaining services of the sort appropriate to the civil-society level. Indeed, civil society itself has lost the special features that distinguished it from the family and the state. It now takes partial charge of the services once shouldered by the family and plays the role of subcontractor in carrying out policies mandated by the state. In this way, contemporary society, as the Italian sociologist Alberto Melucci would have it, presents the aspect of "a seamless fabric of organizations linking public character and private character in an inseparable form."[37]

Finally, regarding the possibility of resisting the totalitarian character of contemporary society, let's refer to the strategy of Habermas. Habermas contends that one must critically relativize the functional rationality that characterizes system-society, and argues that what makes that possible is communicative rationality.[38] However, if Melucci and Kundera are correct in their view that public and private have merged to the point of inseparability, it is difficult to see how Habermas's strategy can be effective. At this stage, it must be said that Habermas's attempt to distinguish between the realms of system integration and social integration, and to make the latter into a base from which to defend one's life-world against colonization by the former, has ceased to be a meaningful option.[39] It has already become impossible to distinguish the life-world from the publicity of the political system.

THE POSSIBILITY OF TRANSCENDING THE NATION-STATE

The rationalization precipitated by the age of total war subsequently brought about a system that subsumed all spheres of life, private and public, into the cyclical rotation of the system. The postwar Japanese Constitution's unambiguous proclamation of democracy suggests that it has now reached its apex. Nevertheless, the content of this democracy has been largely constrained by the system society, the course for which was set by wartime mobilization. The welfare-state that has now become a reality is linked inextricably to the warfare-state.[40] Under these circumstances, the democratic reforms institutionalizing social equality will not diminish the domination and integration of the nation-state. Democratic reforms under these conditions cannot be free from the nation state's tendency to further tighten social integration.

What sort of remedy can be prescribed to deal with the dilemma plaguing contemporary society? Here, we should probably take note of the dissident groups known as the "new social movements."[41] Past social movements have been carried out and supported, in the main, by social strata that did not receive sufficient political or social benefits from the nation-state. By appealing to the state for a fair appraisal of their social value, these social elements campaigned to win their rights as citizens. Once they secured these democratic rights, the earlier social movements tended to opt for social integration as citizens. As this earlier variety of social movement was characterized by its members' orientation toward integration as citizens of the nation-state, the realization of their demands led to their institutional incorporation within the system. As this occurred, however, it inevitably gave rise to other social groupings within and outside the nation-state, which were again left out of the process of integration. Democratic rights that had been won through integration into the system inevitably led to the structural institutionalization of exclusion and discrimination.

In contrast, the leaders and supporters of the new social movements are not restricted to a particular social class or stratum. In these movements, people who sympathize with the symbolic aims espoused by the movement assemble without regard to social origins. These movements emphasize the expression of new aesthetic or cultural values related to their members' own lifestyles and do not seek the institutionalization of their own rights as citizens at the nation-state level. Classic examples are probably the citizens' movements that have appeared in response to problems of environmental pollution and abuse of natural resources. A recent form of such movements is represented in the enhanced concern for death with dignity, which respects the individual's capacity to choose and opposes modern medical practice, which blindly seeks only the extension of human life. The death-with-dignity movement bespeaks the formation of new attitudes toward a medical technology that has been pushed to its limits. It forces us to realize that the development of high technology results, on occasion, in severe injury to personal dignity. A portion of the feminist movement, and parts of the movement pressing for the reappraisal of ethnic values, as well as some parts of the movements to develop or preserve the traditional lifestyles of a particular region probably belong in the category of new social movements.

To summarize, the new social movements express a self-conscious determination to abstain from integration into the system and thereby to resist the brand of capitalism that was begun in early-modern times and that has now reached the stage of system society as a result of the total-war regime; they also oppose the ceaseless tide of rationalization unleashed by system society capitalism. One of the most important characteristics of these movements is that their members do not aim to establish their own rights as citizens within the nation-state. Instead, part of the essential character of such movements is their wariness of being submerged within the system as the result of a facile institutionalization of easily-won rights. This allows many new social movements to be especially open to the possibility of international solidarity.

Marx once thought that the high-level productivity brought about by capitalism would transcend national boundaries, regions, classes, and status barriers, making universal solidarity a possibility. Marx contended that the working class, in contrast to the capitalist class for whom the state was an indispensable mechanism of oppression for class rule, partook of a world-historical destiny to realize the universal solidarity that had been made possible by capitalism (*The Communist Manifesto*). However, the working class has betrayed Marx's expectations by integrating itself into the nation-state system. The new social movements, in contrast, have taken as their starting point the very place where Marx failed. They hold no rosy expectations of the high-level productivity brought about by capitalism; instead, they problematize the inhumanity and irrationality that have necessarily accompanied the rationalization brought about by capitalism's productivity. These movements are, in fact, social products of capitalist development, oppositional movements brought about by capitalism's supra-national activities. Indeed, just like earlier forms of social movement, these new phenomena are internal to the capitalist system itself. Nevertheless, they do not attach a positive significance to capitalism's accelerated expansion of the productive forces, but focus rather on the negative concomitants of that expansion. In this respect, they are groping for a standpoint outside the capitalist system.

Marx's vision of human liberation as the final outcome of capitalist development is indelibly marked by the Christian theology he inherited via Hegel. The vision of a "realm of freedom" lying just beyond the development of the productive forces (*Das Kapital*, Vol. 3, "The Trinity Formula") is a classic example of the religious desire for salvation. In contrast, the thought of the new social movements can be said to be related to the tradition of Ludwig Feuerbach, who influenced the young Marx in the period of Marx's *Economic and Philosophic Manuscripts*. Through his critique of Christianity, Feuerbach exposed the desire for salvation inherent in Hegel's philosophy. In contrast to Hegel, who sought a unity of philosophy and theology, Feuerbach affirmed human life in the face of the inescapable reality of death. Feuerbach urged us to accept bravely the grim reality that the world of perfect salvation is never going to come. Humans can understand one another and experience solidarity precisely because they live in a world of suffering. It was on the basis of the solidarity of suffering (*Leidendeswesen*) rather than high hopes for further expansion of the productive forces, that Feuerbach defined himself as a socialist.[42] Indeed, what is necessary even now is not the socialism of the later Marx, but rather the Feuerbachian socialism that influenced the young Marx.

Even in contemporary society there remain many problems that cannot be overcome except through the agency of the traditional type of social movement. For this very reason, such movements must not precipitately be replaced by the "new social movements." However, the relative importance of the new movements is undoubtedly increasing. Further technological development is irrepressible, as is the generation of further irrationality out of the rationalization that dominates the modern world. Development of the new social movements will be increasingly important, but at the same time the character of that locus of power known as the nation-state, whose origins paralleled those of the modern world itself, will also continue to be transformed.

Translated by Michael Jamentz

Notes

[1] Two works can be mentioned as representative of the established view, Mitani Taichirô's *Shinpan Taishō demokurashi-ron* first published in 1974 and revised in 1995 (Tokyo: Tokyo University Press), and Matsuo Takayoshi's *Taishō demokurashi* first published in 1974 and revised in 1994 (Tokyo: Iwanami Shoten). According to Mitani, Taishō democracy "built a foundation for liberalism by advocating the independence of non-statist values in opposition to statist values." This liberalism "formed the political tradition that is linked to postwar democracy." (See the postscript to *Shinpan Taishō demokurashi-ron*.) Matsuo, likewise, understood Taishō democracy as essentially a "movement supported by the consciousness of a broad spectrum of working people," and says that "It was possible for postwar democracy to take root in Japanese society only to the extent that it was preceded by Taishō democracy." (See Matsuo's introduction.)

It is noteworthy that both works refer to historical realities that threaten the very basis of their arguments. According to Mitani, "democratic elements that legitimized citizen participation in the exercise of power were not necessarily weak in modern Japan's political tradition." That is, by virtue of citizen participation in the exercise of power, democracy was practiced without liberalism, and this, for Mitani, is the origin of the problems of the Shôwa era. Thus, it follows from Mitani's argument that democracy absent liberalism might easily be transformed into totalitarianism. According to Matsuo, movements of the working masses were vulnerable to intellectual "contamination" by "imperialism" and "great-power consciousness." But, if such is the case, does it make sense to sever Taishō democracy from the succeeding period of the wartime-mobilization system? And is it justifiable to separate the war-mobilization system from postwar democracy? Would it not be better to regard Taishō democracy as having from the beginning contained the social and political seeds of its destruction and recognize that these seeds of destruction also prepared the way for the wartime system? Moreover, did the wartime system not contain abundant elements that prepared the way for the political and social structures of postwar democracy? This essay is my attempt to respond to the point of view represented by Mitani and Matsuo.

In contrast to the "discontinuity theory" of Mitani and Matsuo, Ōuchi Tsutomu argued for continuity across the wartime and postwar eras based on the Marxist methodological conception of state-monopoly capitalism. Ōuchi, *Kokka dokusen shihonshugi* (Tokyo: University of Tokyo Press, 1970.) However, since the 1980s, there have been studies that extend the argument for continuity beyond the economic sphere to illuminate a wide-ranging transition during and after the war that affected all social processes. According to Ōishi Kaichirō's formulation, such studies "seek to discover the distinguishing characteristics of the postwar Japanese economy within that of wartime by focusing attention on the 'social revolution' that occurred during the course of the war, and reevaluating it as the 'legacy' for the postwar period." (Ōishi, *Joshō: Dainiji sekaitaisen to Nihon shihonshugi, Nihon teikokushugi shi* 3 (Tokyo: University of Tokyo Press, 1994.) He characterizes the following works as representative of this new trend: Yamanouchi Yasushi, "Senji dōin taisei no hikakushiteki kōsatsu," *Sekai* (April 1988); Yamanouchi, "Senji dōin taisei," *Shakai keizai shigaku no kadai to tenbō*, ed., Shakai Keizai Gakkai (Tokyo: Yūhikaku, 1992); Amemiya Shōichi, "Taisei ikō to shakai: Doitsu, Itaria, Nippon no senzen to sengo," *Ibaragi Daigaku kyōyō gakubu kiyō*, 21 (1984); Amemiya, "Sōryokusen taisei to kokumin saisoshiki," *Shiriizu Nihon kin-gendai shi: kōzō to hendō* 3 [Gendai shakai e no tenkei] eds., Banno Junji et al. (Tokyo: Iwanami Shoten, 1993); Okazaki Tetsuji, "Senji keikaku keizai to kigyō," *Gendai Nihon Shakai* 4 [Rekishiteki zentei], ed., Tokyo Daigaku Shakai Kagaku Kenkyūjo (Tokyo: Tokyo University Press, 1991). Although its standpoint differs from that of the present volume, see Hara Akira, ed. *Nihon no senji keizai* (Tokyo: Tokyo University Press, 1995) as representative of the most recent trends in the study of the wartime economy of Japan.

[2] Studies that portray the Second World War as a confrontation between democratic, New Deal-type systems and autocratic fascism are well represented by Sekiguchi Yoshiyuki and Umezu Junichi's *Ōbei keizaishi* (Tokyo: Hōsō Daigaku Kyōkai, 1987) republished in 1991. Endō Teruaki ed., *Kokka to keizai: Furansu dirijizumu no kenkyū* (Tokyo: Tokyo University Press, 1982) takes the same stance.

The standpoint of Sekiguchi et al., who formed an influential current in postwar social science, is extremely close to that of the German Gesellschafts-geschichte group represented by H. U. Wehler and J. Kocka. (See Heinreich A. Winckler Herausgegebe von, *Organisierter Kapitalismus*, 1974, translated by Hozumi Toshihiko et al., *Soshiki sareta shihonshugi*, Nagoya University Press, 1989.) Wehler and Kocka's argument on organized capitalism—which emphasizes the distinction between the organized capitalism of "authoritarian, fascist systems" and that of "mass democratic social states"—was introduced in detail by Ono Eiji, who also shared the point of view of Sekiguchi et al. throughout his study of German social history (Ono, *Gendai Doitsu shakaishi kenkyū josetsu* (Tokyo: Iwanami Shoten, 1982).

[3] Marcuse issued the clearest warning that the New Deal form of society was approaching some form of totalitarianism. (Herbert Marcuse, *Reason and Revolution*, Epilogue, 1954, translated by Masuda Keisaburō et al., *Risei to kakumei* [1954 nenpan epirōgu] (Tokyo: Iwanami Shoten, 1961). The shift from capitalism

to organized-capitalism was positively appraised by Wehler and Kocka who felt it contained the potential for a "mass democratic social state," but Marcuse saw it as indicating a decline into totalitarianism. Marcuse expanded and developed the point of view expressed in *Reason and Revolution* throughout his later work, *One Dimensional Man: Studies in the Ideology of Advanced Industrial Society*, 1964, translated by Ikimatsu Keizō and Misawa Ken'ichi as *Ichijigenteki ningen* (Tokyo: Kawade Shobō Shinsha, 1974). For a more recent pronouncement, see Milan Kundera, *Les testament trahis*, 1993, translated by Nishinaga Yoshinari, *Uragirareta isho* (Tokyo: Shūeisha, 1994). Kundera recounts just how cruel the totalitarianism of Eastern Europe was before the fall of the Berlin Wall; but such an account does not show that Western societies are free or liberated. Kundera indicates that modern Western society is also sinking into a variety of totalitarianism, albeit of a different character from that prevalent in the former Eastern Europe. See in particular the ninth section, "La, vous n'etes pas chez vous, mon cher" (You are not in your own home, there, my dear).

Likewise, one frequently encounters pronouncements that post-New Deal American society has ceased to function effectively as a democratic society. Best known in Japan is Theodore J. Lowi, *The End of Liberalism: The Second Republic of the United States* (second edition, 1979, translated by Muramatsu Michio, *Jiyūshugi no shūen* (Tokyo: Bokutakusha, 1981). In investigating the actual condition of the TVA, Selznick was forced to come to the conclusion that the original will of the Congress and federal government had been broadly distorted by the co-optation of local interests. Philip Selznick, *TVA and the Grassroots*, 1953. Mancur Olson's *The Logic of Collective Action*, 1965, (*Shūgōkōi-ron*, translated by Yoda Hiroshi and Morita Toshio, Minerva Shobō, 1983) dealt with the issue of the appearance of the Freedom Riders in the midst of the organized society. These works are of the same genre and are also well known in Japan. In the field of socioeconomic history, to which I have devoted long years of study, see Douglas North's critique of the neoclassical economic model and argument for the new institutionalist approach. In Japan, this work was seen as an innovative response to the stagnation of the New Deal-type society. (Douglas C. North, *Structure and Change in Economic History*, 1989, translated by Nakajima Masato, *Bunmeishi no keizaigaku*, Shunjūsha, 1989.)

It is also necessary to mention Scott Lash and John Urry's *The End of Organized Capitalism*, 1987, as representative of the most recent trends in the field. Despite their mutual opposition, Wheler and Kocka and Marcuse all adopted the concepts of Rudolf Hilferding and share the idea that modern society belongs to the stage of organized capitalism. However, according to Lash and Urry, the label organized capitalism is no longer appropriate to describe the character of contemporary society, which has entered what the philosophers call the Post-Modern era. The view of Lash and Urry is surely correct. It can be imagined that in passing through two world wars, advanced industrial society moved from the stage of class society to that of system society, but that system society, having consummated its first stage in the advent of "post-industrial society" (Daniel Bell), should probably be seen as now entering a second stage. Lash and Urry's thesis in *The End of Organized Capitalism* expresses this reality.

Superb in analyzing Japanese society at the stage of organized capitalism, Ronald Dore's *British Factory-Japanese Factory: The Origins of National Diversity in Industrial Relations*, 1973 (translated by Yamanouchi Yasushi and Nagayasu Kōichi, *Igirisu no kōjō-Nihon no kōjō*, first published in 1987 and reissued in an enhanced edition by Chikuma Shobō, 1993), depicts an industrial society that no longer conforms to the realities of present-day Japanese society, which has entered the post-industrial stage. This may also be explained as a shift from the first stage of the system society (industrial society) to the second (post-industrial society.)

[4] It should be noted that a textbook of American economic history states the following. "In World War I we encountered the first in the nearly continuous sequence of crises that have engaged the American economy in the twentieth century. The actions then taken and the lessons learned provided a rough blueprint of things to come. It is a curiosity of American economic history that so much of the war's institutional apparatus has been used to cope with crisis after crisis since 1918." "... [I]n the New Deal emergency of the 1930s the techniques of war mobilization reappeared in various guises and have remained the main options for meeting emergencies by federal action ever since. The importance of World War I for institutional evolution has been neglected in most U.S. economic history textbooks, although it's well known among specialists." (Jonathan Hughes, *American Economic History*, 2nd edition 1987, p. 413.) As for Japanese-language literature on the topic, the following work, which pioneered a new path in the field, focuses on the wartime mobilization system during the Second World War. (Kawamura Tetsuji, *Pakkusu Amerikāna no keisei: Amerika 'Senji keizai shisutemu' no bunseki*, Tōyō Keizai Shinbunsha, 1995). For a study linking the formation of modern English society to the system of wartime mobilization, see A. Marwick, *Britain in the Century of Total War*, 1968, and B. Waites, *A Class Society at War, England 1914-18*, 1987.

As regards the German case, one should note the existence of a tradition of scholarship that recognizes the Nazis' contribution to the promotion of modernization notwithstanding their irrational violence. Of course, this tradition is heretical in relation to orthodox historical studies. It includes Ralf Dahrendorf, *Society and Democracy in Germany*, German edition 1965 and English edition 1967, and David Schoenbaum, *Hitler's Social Revolution: Class and Status in Nazi Germany 1933-1939*, 1966 (translated by Ōshima Michiyoshi and Ōshima Kaori, *Hittorā no shakai kakumei*, Shōritsushobō, 1978. Recently, this scholarly tradition, linked to critical doubts regarding modernization, has led to new developments in the field. Examples are Detlev J.K. Peukert, *Die Weimarer Republik: Krisenjahre der Klassischen Moderne*, 1987 (translated by Ono Kiyomi et al.,

Waimāru kyōwakoku—kotenteki kindaika no kiki, Nagoya University Press, 1993) and Peukert, *Max Weber's Diagnose der Moderne*, 1989 (translated by Sasabe Yukitaka and Ono Kiyomi, *Makkusu Vēbā: kindai no shindan*, Nagoya University Press, 1994) and Michael Prinz and Rainer Zitelman, *Herausgegeben von, National Sozialismus und Modernisierung*, 1991.

The following two works, which appear destined to have a major influence on the field, are not based on individual case studies of the U.S., England, Germany or Japan, but focus attention on the importance of wartime mobilization systems in terms of reforming sociological theory: Anthony Giddens, *The Nation-State and Violence*, 1985; and Christopher Dandecker, *Surveillance, Power and Modernity: Bureaucracy and Discipline from 1700 to the Present Day*, 1990. Giddens shows that modern societies have consistently been formed by nation states in the course of their preparation and mobilization for war. According to Giddens, neither Marxist nor liberal sociology deal adequately with this point. Giddens identifies Otto Hintze and Max Weber as forerunners of his own argument. Dandecker, as is suggested by his subtitle, links Max Weber's theory of bureaucracy with Michael Foucault's notions of power and discipline, and contends that war plays a central role in the formation of identity and surveillance by the modern nation-state. According to Dandecker, the expansion of democratic citizen's rights was not contradicted by the expansion of the nation-state's power in the conduct of war, but rather the two were mutually complementary. Giddens and Dandecker's works make a critical, direct attack on the orthodox current of thought represented by T. H. Marshal, *Class, Citizenship and Social Development*, 1964.

[5] As regards the important issue of trends in the participation of women, who were second-class citizens, in the wartime mobilization system, see Narita Ryūichi's analysis of the Japanese case in this volume. Regarding the typical perspective of Japanese social scientists on the problem of colonization, Kan San Jun argues that insofar as it sees colonization in terms of the spread of modern civilization and is unconsciousness of the second-class-citizen status of colonized peoples, it lacks consciousness of the problems of political subordination and ethnic identity. See Kan San Jun, in *Shakaikagaku no hōhō*, vol. 3 (Tokyo: Iwanami Shoten, 1993).

As for the case of the Japanese-Americans, whose second-class status was reinforced by their forced placement in concentration camps, one work among many is Takezawa Yasuko, *Nikkei Amerikajin no esunishiti*, Tokyo University Press, 1994.

This author has little knowledge of the significance of mobilization during the Second World War for African-American citizens of the U.S., but the following account indicates that the starting point of the civil-rights movement of the late 1960s was in the period of the Second World War. Alan M. Osur, *Blacks in the Army Air Forces during World War Two*, 1980. For a bibliography related to Japanese-American and African-American citizens during the war see Richard Polenburg, *War and Society: The United States, 1941-1942*, 1972.

[6] This point of view is entirely my own, and is not necessarily subscribed to by other contributors. Indeed, while I attempt to distinguish clearly between *kindaika* (modernization in the classical sense), on the one hand, and *gendaika* ("modernization" as employed in the title to the present volume), signifying the advent of the contemporary system society, on the other, a number of the other authors do not distinguish between the two.

In distinguishing between these terms in this manner, I have in mind the actual shift from a type of capitalist society that was deeply imbued with the characteristics of a class society of the classically modern (*kindaiteki*) sort, to a variant of capitalist society that is heavily integrated and systematized. Moreover, in regarding the age of total war as the focal point of a "shift from a class to a system society," I have in mind the following facts. First, in the formative process of system society, class conflict was institutionalized in the form of labor negotiations, which were mediated by the nation-state. Likewise, through the intervention of the state, a route to social advancement (in which the expansion of educational opportunities played an important role) was established, thereby institutionalizing a form of social mobility that transcended class barriers. Second, Hegel assigned each of the elements of modern society—family, civil society, and state— a special place that was irreducible to either of the other two. However, as a result of total war, the boundaries between nation-state and civil society, and civil society and the family, became blurred and subject to interpenetration. Interpenetration between the nation-state and civil society brought about what has became known as the welfare state, and that between family and civil society forced private life into the public sphere and also caused the privatization of public space. Third, as a result of the above processes, "modern society" (*gendai shakai*) has reached a stage unlike that of the classically modern (*kindai*). In this new stage, class conflict and other social struggles have ceased to serve as major agents of historical change, but are rather continually subjected to rules and eventually institutionalized. However, a new set of problems then arises. Other systems that are not easily absorbed by the social system, for example the bodily system and ecological system (the system of the natural environment) seriously conflict with the social system.

Of course, these new problems will also either be solved or evaded in accordance with the response of the social system. Yet, the social system cannot manage this new series of problems solely within its own sphere as was the case with class conflict and other social struggles. Indeed, they can be dealt with only if fundamental changes are made in the social system itself. The historical changes that are occurring in contemporary society are all related in one way or another to the axis of fundamental transformation in the social system in response to this new series of problems.

In coming around to the above viewpoint, I was influenced by the writings of Karl Löwith, especially his "Vico Grundsatz: verum un factum convertuntur. Seine theologische Pramisse und deren sakulare Konsequenzen," 1968, *Samtliche*

Schriften, 9, 1986 (translated by Uemura Tadao and Yamanouchi Yasushi, *Gakumon to wareware no jidai no unmei*, Miraisha, 1989). See also Yamanouchi Yasushi, "Vico to Sumisu, soshite Marukusu—Kimae Toshiaki 'Topika to rōdō no rinri' ni yosete," *Tokyo Gaikokugo Daigaku Kaigai Jijō Kenkyūjo kenkyū hōkoku* 49 (1989), and "Shisutemu shakai to rekishi no shūen," *Shakaikagaku no hōhō* (The Methodology of the Social Sciences), Vol. 1, 1993, Iwanami Shoten.

[7] Uchida Yoshihiko made a lasting impression on the Japanese study of economics. In his famous *Keizaigaku no tanjō*, Uchida struggled toward a new interpretation of Adam Smith's *The Wealth of Nations* (in his *Chosakushū*, Vol. 1, Iwanami Shoten, 1988). Uchida explained the formation of *The Wealth of Nations* in relation to the age of "mercantilist imperialism" that centered on the confrontation between England and France. In Uchida's interpretation, *The Wealth of Nations* sought to provide an answer to the "crisis of civilized Europe" that was brought about by confrontation among the great powers in the age of mercantilist imperialism. The foundation of Smith's solution, according to Uchida, was an international alliance between physiocratic economists and the thought of Jean-Jacques Rousseau. Needless to say, Uchida's conception was to some degree a projection of his own experience during the "crisis of modern civilization" that had been precipitated by World War II. In the body of this essay, I attempt to extend Uchida's contentions to the period of the 1990s and to develop them further. For a retrospective look at the development of his own thought, see the collection of Uchida's essays, which may be considered his testament, titled *Kangaete kita koto, kangaeru koto*, 1983, in *Uchida Yoshihiko chosakushū*, Vol. 1. As regards the place occupied by Uchida's thought in wartime and postwar Japan, see my "Shimin shakaiha no keifu to regyurashion riron," in *Regyurashion paradaimu: shakai riron no henkaku to tenbō*, edited by Ebizuka Akira and Ogura Toshimaru, Tokyo: Seikyūsha, 1991) and the chapter by Sugiyama Mitsunobu in this volume.

[8] The notion of a "general crisis of capitalism" was propagated by Marxists in the Comintern when faced with the rise of fascism. I was brought back to this rather musty old term in the course of my attempt to characterize the historical moment at which Talcott Parsons formulated his social theory. The all-too-facile rejection of Parsonian theory in contemporary social thought is the result in part of a failure to realize that it was formulated as an attempt to respond to an era of crisis.

[9] Niklas Luhmann, "Wie ist soziale Ordnung moglich?," *Gesellschafts Struktur und Semantik*, 1981 (translated by Satō Tsutomu, *Shakai shisutemu riron no shiza*, Bokutakusha, 1985.

[10] *Hegel's Phenomenology of Spirit*, translated by A. V. Miller, 1977. Translated in two volumes by Kaneko Takezō, *Seishin genshōgaku*, the first volume in 1971 and the second in 1979 (Tokyo: Iwanami Shoten).

[11] Alexandre Kojève, *Introduction to the Reading of Hegel: Lectures on the Phenomenology of Spirit*, edited by Allan Bloom, 1980. On Kojève's interpretation of Hegel's *Phenomenology* see Michael S. Roth, *Knowing and History:*

Appropriation of Hegel in Twentieth-Century France, 1988, and Yamanouchi Yasushi, "Shisutemu shakai to rekishi no shūen, op. cit.

[12] Regarding the strong influence of Heidegger on Kojève's interpretation of *Phenomenology of Spirit*, see Roth, op. cit.

[13] *Hegel's Philosophy of Right*, translated by T. M. Knox, 1967. Japanese translation by Fujino Wataru and Akazawa Masatoshi, *Hō no tetsugaku* (Tokyo: Chūō kōronsha, 1967).

[14] See Luhman in note 9 above.

[15] "Contribution to the Critique of Hegel's Philosophy of Law," 1843, *Marx-Engels: Collected Works*, Vol. 3, 1975, "Hēgeru kokuhōron no hihan," *Marukusu-Engerusu zenshû I* (Tokyo: Ōtsuki Shoten, 1995).

[16] For the youthful Hegel's reception of economics, see Georg Lukacs, *Der junge Hegel: Uber die Beziehungen von Dialektik und Ökonomie*, 1967, translated in two volumes by Ikimatsu Keizō and Motohama Kiyomi, *Wakaki Hēgeru* (Tokyo: Hakusuisha, 1969); and Manfred Riedel, *Studien zu Hegels Rechtsphilosophie*, 1969 (translated by Shimizu Masanori and Yamamoto Michio, *Hēgeru hōtetsugaku: sono seiritsu to kōzō*, Fukumura Shuppan, 1976).

[17] Edmund Husserl, *Der Krisis der europaischen Wissenchaften und die tranzendentale Phanomenologie*, 1936. Translated by Hosoya Tsuneo, *Yōroppa shogaku no kiki to senkenteki genshōgaku* (Tokyo: Chūō kōronsha, 1970).

[18] Talcott Parsons, *The Structure of Social Action*, 2 vols., 1968. Translated by Inagami Takeshi and Kōtō Yōsuke, *Shakaiteki kōi no kōzō*, in five installments, 1976-1989, Bokutakusha. There have been countless studies of *The Structure of Social Action* undertaken by Japanese sociologists. Among them, see Takagi Kazuyoshi, *Pāsonzu to Amerika chishikishakai* (Tokyo: Iwanami Shoten, 1992).

[19] For a work that argues for the impact on the early Parsons of the "Hobbesian problem of order," see John O'Neil, "The Hobbesian Problem in Marx and Parsons," *Explorations in General Theory in Social Science: Essays in Honor of Talcott Parsons*, edited by Jan J. Loubser et al., Vol. 1, 1976. There has been a debate in Japan regarding how to compare the early Parsons to the Parsons of his middle period when he began to develop his system theory. For a synopsis see my *Gendai shakai no rekishiteki isō* (Tokyo: Nihon Hyōronsha, 1982), note 2 of the second section ("'Hobbesian social order' and the critique of Utilitarianism") of Chapter Six, "The Problem of Marx and Weber in Parsons," pages 201-2.

[20] From the standpoint of Parsons, who stressed the significance of norms and values in the integration of the social system, the neglect of those factors in the Marxist method had to be criticized. As regards Parsons' criticisms of Marx, in addition to the pertinent portions of *The Structure of Social Action*, see also "Social Classes and Class Conflict in the Light of Recent Sociological Theory," *American Economic Review*, No. 39 (1949), found in *Essays in Sociological Theory*, revised edition, 1954; "Some Comments on the Sociology of Karl Marx," *Sociological Theory and Modern Society*, 1967. For the arguments in Japan regarding

these issues, see the third section of Chapter Six, "The Elevation of Analytical Abstraction and Overcoming Marx," in Yamanouchi, 1982.

[21] Talcott Parsons, "Authority, Legitimation, and Political Action," *Structure and Process in Modern Societies*, 1960.

[22] Talcott Parsons and Neil J. Smelser, *Economy and Society: A Study in the Integration of Economic and Social Theory*, 1956. The Japanese translation, in two volumes, by Tominaga Ken'ichi, *Keizai to shakai* (Tokyo: Iwanami Shoten, 1958 and 1959).

[23] Parsons, 1956, p. 269. Japanese language version, Vol. 2, pp. 127-8. As regards Parsons' theory of profit, see the summary in Yamanouchi, 1982, pp. 246-9. I have borrowed the metaphor of the "orchestra conductor" here from Karl Marx, who, in the third volume of *Das Capital*, argued that even socialist societies would require the business executive but that his role, equivalent to that of the conductor, would differ from the kind of domination exercised by the owners of capital.

[24] Parsons, 1960, pp. 181, 186. As regards Parsons' theory of power, see the summary in Yamanouchi, 1982, pp. 272-285. Parsons distinguished his own theory of power, formulated from the viewpoint of system integration, from what he called the "zero-sum conception." In the latter conception, as represented in the theories of Max Weber and Harold Lasswell, power was defined as "the capacity of one unit in the system to reach a goal by overcoming the opposition of another unit." In contrast to this, Parsons concluded that power was nothing other than the function of system integration. Indeed, according to Parsons, the concept of power in C. Wright Mills' *The Power Elite*, 1956, was based on the same "zero-sum conception." "The Distribution of Power in American Society," *Politics and Social Structure*, 1969 (translated under the supervision of Shinmei Masamichi, *Seiji to shakai kōzō* (Tokyo: Seishin Shobō, 1973).

[25] Talcott Parsons, "Introduction to: Max Weber," *The Theory of Social and Economic Organization*, translated by A.M. Henderson and Talcott Parsons, 1974. For a summary, see Yamanouchi, 1982, pp. 263-71.

[26] Michel Foucault, *Surveilier et Punir; Naissance de la prison*, Editions Gallimard, 1975.

[27] For a work that takes the social order of the United States to be an extension of the Reformation, see Talcott Parsons, *The System of Modern Societies*, 1971. Translated by Ikado Toshio, *Kindai shakai no taikei* (Tokyo: Shiseidō, 1977).

[28] Parsons took up the problem of the general spread of the business corporation in Chapter Five, "Institutional Fluctuation and Growth in Economy," *Economy and Society*, discussing the systematic fluctuation of contemporary society.

[29] As regards the system integration of society precipitated by the age of total war, see the works mentioned in note 4 above, especially those of Giddens and Dandecker.

[30] Many commentators have remarked on the autopoiesis of Luhman's system theory, but the following will suffice for the present. Wolfgang Lipp,

38

"Autopoiesis Biologisch: Autopoiesis Soziologisch: Wohin fuhrt Luhman Paradigmawechsel?" in *Kolner Zeitschrift fur Soziologie und Sozialpsychologie*, Heft 3, Jg. 39 (1987).

[31] For a work representative of the wave of criticism aimed at Parsons, the following is well known in Japan. Jere Cohen, Lawrence E. Hazelrigg and Whitney Pope, "De-Parsonizing Weber: A Critique of Parson's Sociology," *American Sociological Review*, Vol. 40, No. 2 (1975). Shinmei Masamichi's *Tarukotto Pāsonzu* (Tokyo: Kōseisha Kōseikaku, 1982) introduced the critique of Parsons by Cohen et al.

[32] See Uchida's *Kangaete kita koto, kangaeru koto*, op. cit., and Fujita Shōzō, *Zentaishugi no jidai keiken* (Tokyo: Misuzu Shobō, 1995).

[33] Kundera, op. cit. p. 302; p. 298 in the Japanese translation.

[34] Ōkōchi's "Seikatsu riron to shōhiriron," in *Sumisu to Risuto*, found in the third volume of *Ōkōchi Kazuo chosakushū*, Seirin Shoin Shinsha, 1969. Additionally, see "Kokumin seikatsu no riron," 1943, "Shōhiron to shakai seikatsu," 1943, both collected in *Ōkōchi Kazuo shū* 6 (Tokyo: Rōdō Junpōsha, 1981).

[35] Ōkōchi's "Rōdō seisaku ni okeru senji to heishi—senji rōdō rippō ni okeru iwayuru 'isan' ni tsuite," 1949, collected in *Ōkōchi Kazuo shū*, Vol. 2 (Tokyo: Rōdō Junpōsha, 1981). Usami Seijirō, Inoue Harumaru and Uchida Yoshihiko expressed views corresponding to Ōkōchi's in their article "Sensō keizai no isan," *Chōryū*, January 1948. However, these three withdrew their support of Ōkōchi shortly thereafter.

[36] Ōkōchi's "'Sangyōhōkokukai' no mae to ato to," *Kindai Nihon keizai shisōshi* 2, edited by Chō Yukio and Sumiya Kazuhiko (Tokyo: Yūhikaku, 1971). For Ōkōchi's significance, see my "Sanka to dōin—senjiki chishikijin no purofiiru—," *Chiiki funsō to sōgo izon* 3.17 (1993), and also "Senjiki no isan to sono ryōgisei," *Shakai kagaku no hōhō* 3 (Tokyo: Iwanami Shoten, 1993) which is a condensed version of the above "Participation and Mobilization." Regarding The Industrial Patriotic Association see Saguchi Kazurō, *Nihon ni okeru sangyō minshushugi no zentei* (Tokyo: Tokyo University Press, 1991) or his article included in this volume.

[37] Alberto Melucci, *Nomads of the Present: Social Movements and Individual Needs in Contemporary Society*, edited by John Kean and Paul Mier, 1989, p. 171. For a work that incorporates Melucci's point on the significance of critical social movements in contemporary society, see my "Shisutemu shakai no gendai teki isō—aidentiti no fukakuteisei o chūshin ni," in *Shisō*, June/July, 1991.

[38] Jürgen Habermas, *Theorie des kommunikativen Handelns*, 2 vols., 1981, translated by Kawakami Rin'itsu, et al., *Komyunikeishonteki kōi no riron*, published in three consecutive volumes (Tokyo: Miraisha, 1985, 1986, and 1987). See also Axel Honneth et al., "The Dialectics of Rationalization: An Interview with Jürgen Habermas," *Telos*, No. 49 (Fall 1981).

[39] For a critical statement regarding this problem in Habermas, see Johannes Berger, "Die Versprachlichung des Sakralen und die Entsprachlichung der

Ökonomie," in *Zeitschrift fur Soziologie*, Jg. 11, Heft 4 (October 1982). For the author's criticism of Habermas' point, see Yamanouchi, 1991.

[40] Regarding the suggestion that the "welfare state" is a "warfare state" as well, see Dandecker, op. cit., p. 222f.

[41] The following remarks on "the new social movements" owe much to Melucci, op. cit. See also Yamanouchi Yasushi and Yazawa Shūjirō, "A. Melucci e no intāvyū/ 'Atarashii shakai undō to kojin no henyō'," *Shisō*, March 1995.

[42] L. Feuerbach, *Das Wesen des Christentums*, 1841, translated by Funayama Shin'ichi, *Kirisutokyō no honshitsu*, in two volumes (Tokyo: Iwanami Bunko, 1965), *Vorlaufige Thesen zur Reformation der Philosophie*, 1842, translated by Matsumura Kazuto and Wada Raku, "Tetsugaku kaikaku no tame no zanteiteki meidai" in *Shōrai no tetsugaku no konpon mondai* (Tokyo: Iwanami Bunko, 1967). On Feuerbach's critique of religion and the theoretical foundation of "a life of suffering," see my "Shoki Marukusu no shimin shakaizō," in *Gendai shisō*, March 1977 and May 1977.

I. Total War and Structural Change

National Socialism and Modernization: Recent Debates in the Federal Republic of Germany

Michael Prinz

This essay deals with recent interpretations in the German press and historiography of National Socialism in relation to "modernization." It provides a summary of different strands of discussion related to the question of National Socialist "modernity" and its modernizing effects, while trying, at the same time, to illustrate and concretize the several approaches.

The varying use of theoretical tools in historical analysis often reflects not only the shifting tides of scientific interest but also current social developments and public debates. The question of modernization and National Socialism presents no exception to this rule. The debate on National Socialism in Germany since the end of World War II has taken a peculiar and somewhat strange course. It did not reach its greatest intensity when the war ended and the consequences of Nazi rule affected German society most directly. It did not even peak, as one might otherwise expect, in the 1960s when two preconditions came together: immediate interest on the part of a younger generation and a distance in time that psychologically could facilitate turning around and looking back to an awful past. Instead, the most intensive phase of research and publication on National Socialism has emerged in the 1980s and the early 1990s. Never has the interest among the general public been as great and diversified as in this decade. Whether this willingness to deal intensively with the years between 1933 and 1945 will continue, or if it represents something like a climax before a final downturn, remains to be seen. Thus the claim, often repeated by various authors, that Germany's National Socialist past is about to be forgotten (!) has no real basis.

The explanation that is usually given for this development is a psychological one. It was necessary for a whole new generation with a certain degree of "neutrality" and inner distance to emerge before German society was able to confront the crimes of its past.

Another explanation points to deficiencies in traditional historiography and its methods. The kind of scholarly, sober and abstract presentation that has been characteristic of the German historiographical tradition since the late 19th century has been held responsible for the resistance of the general public to reflecting upon and accepting emotionally the historical legacy of the Nazi regime. This argument was developed especially to account for the effects on public opinion of the American film, "Holocaust."[1]

Nevertheless, there are good reasons to believe that a mainly psychological explanation for the current boom in research and publication on the National Socialist past in Germany is much too superficial. This becomes obvious when one delves into the discussion itself. Debate centers especially on the question of National Socialist *modernity*, that is, the *modernizing effects* that it supposedly had.

Generally speaking, current debates on modernization are not at all limited to the profession of history.[2] Concepts of modernity and post-modernity are popular in the other social sciences as well, pointing to real change in contemporary society. Throughout the Western World one encounters the notion that we are living on the edge of a new epoch that has departed from the kind of evolution we have witnessed since the last third of the 18th century. This has been reinforced by new technologies like the computer and the microchip, the proliferation and effects of atomic energy and genetic engineering, and the rise of material wealth throughout much of Western Europe and Japan, to the point where these societies are thoroughly dominated by a saturated middle class.

On the other hand, these developments are accompanied by a widespread feeling of crisis for which the German term "angst" has become a symbolic marker. Some such feelings are attributable to the fact that the most advanced industrialized countries have solved many of the classical problems of modernization and are now confronting a future for which there is no historical design or current model. Then, there are the specific risks inherent in some of the new technologies,[3] illustrated dramatically in transnational disasters such as Tchernobyl.

The shift in public mood has led in societies such as Germany to profound changes in the traditional party structure, which had guaranteed stability for nearly half a century after World War II. These changes, in turn, are reflected in the spread of social theories that paint a bleak picture of further evolution along the well-known paths of modern civilization. These theories no longer interpret modernization as a process of emancipation and integration, promoting welfare and equality, but as a process of disintegration accompanied by suppression, tightened discipline, and even totalitarian tendencies.[4] The sense of crisis among many intellectuals in Western Europe during the 1970s and 1980s explains, too, why the triumph after the downfall of socialism in Eastern Europe has, in general, been astonishingly subdued.

What has all this to do with renewed interest in the history of National Socialism on the part of historians and social scientists? In combination with a critical, pessimistic, sometimes even catastrophic view of the future, National Socialism is often used as the clearest illustration of the potential dangers of further evolution.[5] National Socialism functions as the lighthouse at the edge of civilization in a situation where, to some, other points of moral orientation no longer seem valid. It is not by chance that the most important impulses to treat National Socialism as a "possibility of modernization," or, as is often said, as an expression of the "janus-faced character of modernity,"[6] did not come from faculties of history but from historians attached to other departments like medicine, psychiatry, psychology, pedagogy, architecture, planning and sociology. This desire to project a certain phase of German history as a warning on the wall of western civilization is not limited to Germany. To use history in such a way requires a theory capable of universalizing a specific historic experience so that its "lessons" might be applied in what often are very different contexts. With the demise of Marxism the concept of modernization remains the only theoretical framework left for such a task. That these developments carry a potential threat—moral, political and scientific—should not be overlooked but rather seriously addressed in a program of research guided by this framework.[7]

It is questionable whether dissatisfaction with modernization provides a suitable starting point for studying the practice and consequences of National Socialism. If one looks at the history of West Germany after World War II— one may cite the example of Japan as well—then the most pervasive impression is of a highly unlikely and therefore still impressive resurrection of a nation that underwent dictatorship, military defeat and devastating destruction, and has been divided for most of its postwar history. The swift rise of Germany and Japan from the ashes of disgrace to remarkable economic, social and political stability has lost none of its fascination. On the contrary, the most recent experiences of travel from dictatorship to democracy illustrate how bumpy the road can be. Accordingly, the historic examples of the German and Japanese postwar histories still merit our attention.

* * * * *

The basic ambivalence of postwar history, susceptible to interpretation either as the path to global ecological crisis and a computerized Orwellian state produced by science running out of control or, in contrast, as a success story ending in social and democratic stability, is also reflected in the discussion of modernity in relation to National Socialism.[8]

One can distinguish four different ways of framing that discussion: 1) National Socialism as an example of *"Janus-faced" modernization*; 2) the *"relative" modernity* of German society in the Nazi era; 3) National Socialism as a *mobilizing force* and the question of *active participation*; 4) "Hitler's social revolution" and the *modernizing function* of National Socialism.

The first approach deals with some central elements of National socialist rule: the exclusion and extermination of minorities—the mentally impaired, homosexuals, gypsies, Jews—and the active role of technocratic elites in this process. The argument linking these events to modernization runs as follows.[9] A central element of modernization is the continuous extension of the "system"—composed of market, state and science[10]—at the expense of the individual and collective "life world" (Habermas). A typical indicator of its progression is the emergence within social policy of the idea and practice of "prevention." "Prevention" marks a new phase of thinking in place of the traditional strategy represented by the idea and institution of social insurance. Instead of compensating for social problems retroactively, the new current within social reform tries systematically to change society, its members, and their behavior in order to prevent accidents and disorder. Prevention may be viewed as an authorization for technocrats to "rationalize" society as a whole with extremely illiberal implications.[11]

The extension of control is only one aspect of this development. The other is *exclusion*. Several factors contribute to it. In order to control society as a whole one must have a definite, clearly shaped idea of what is "normal" and what is not. By creating an definite picture of normality, social reformers develop the capacity to distinguish between individuals who merit support when in need and others who should be excluded. Support and encouragement, on the one hand, and disregard, exclusion, even extermination, on the other, are considered to be two interrelated aspects of modernization in the realm of social policy.

A second factor leading to exclusion of the "unfit" is the desire for reputation and success on the part of certain professionals, such as doctors, welfare workers and others responsible for assisting and caring for the ill and insane. People who resist such therapy, either willingly or unwillingly, tend to represent failure on the part of those professions in the public eye. In a modern society, where only success counts and where different groups tend to compete for income and prestige in the social hierarchy, the temptation to get rid of the unfit seems irresistible, either by fobbing them off on another profession with a more "caring" image or, if that is not possible, getting rid of them more literally and definitively. Under certain conditions, such tendencies can lead to the idea of a biological "final solution of the social question."[12]

In this argument, only roughly sketched here, typical elements of modernization such as professionalization, orientation towards success and competition, the idea of prevention in place of insurance, centralization of control within the social state, and concepts like total social rationalization and planning are put together in a theoretical frame that is supposed to explain National Socialist practice systematically. Such elements no longer appear as crimes committed by insane individuals but as the culmination of general tendencies characteristic of the process of modernization.[13]

Efforts have been made to apply a similar approach to the Holocaust. It has been argued in several highly controversial studies that the mass killing of the European Jews was part of an overall, utilitarian program of "rationalization" to "solve" the problem of "overpopulation" in Eastern Europe and create enough space for partial decentralization and a more sound social and population structure. The point of departure for these studies is the discovery that among the "brain trusts" of the SS it was clear that Eastern Europe was not at all sparsely populated—as Hitler had supposed in "Mein Kampf"—and therefore had to be "cleared" of an "abundant" native population in order to gain "living-space" for the Aryan race.[14]

This is not the first effort to link the Holocaust to "economic rationality." Previous efforts were undertaken especially by orthodox-Marxist authors. Neither those nor the current arguments are convincing. The genocide of the European Jews ran counter not only to all humane standards but to even a rudimentary utilitarian approach. What principle of rationality can explain why, while Nazi commissioners were desperately hunting throughout the occupied territories for qualified armament workers, 40,000 Jewish metalworkers were send to the gas chambers. In addition, that kind of argument gives no idea at all why a capitalist profit motive should have led to such consequences only in Germany.

The same criticism can be made of studies which attribute sterilization and euthanasia to modernization, although these studies seem generally more convincing because they can point to similar discussions of eugenics and selective reproduction in other western countries, such as Great Britain and the United States.[15] At least in their early stages these discussions are surprisingly similar to those in Germany during the 1920s. Generally speaking, the interpretation of Nazi crimes as the expression of a "janus-faced" process of modernization tends to underestimate gravely the importance of politics. The contribution of such an interpretation lies in helping us to understand better why so many modern professionals have cooperated voluntarily with the regime.

The second way of framing the issue listed above, that of National Socialist "modernity," is frequently raised in studies on the economy, society and culture of the 1930s without any attempt to be systematic. In many cases, the motive is historiographical. National Socialism has been portrayed in the media as well as by the general public and historians as a hermetically closed system. It has been viewed as the result of an absolute rupture that may have had certain preconditions in Germany's pre-1933 society but that was otherwise completely separated from the rest of German history. The idea of a closed system has also been applied to the Third Reich's relations with the outside world.

The contrast between the political systems before and after 1945 is so overwhelmingly sharp that, understandably, the historical interest has focussed mainly on outstanding aspects of that difference, such as the Nazi regime's terrorism, violence, lawlessness, forced emigration policies, mass killings, megalomaniacal ideas of world domination and archaic notions of racist superiority. The perception of a politically and ideologically induced prewar regime is strengthened by the central interest on the part of historians of the Third Reich in the decision-making process and the power structure. To balance this one-sided emphasis, social and economic historians have tended to stress continuities in many fields. They have tried to demonstrate what had nearly been forgotten: that for the great majority of contemporaries the years between 1933 and 1938 did not represent a phase of preparation for another war but an era of fast economic recovery and of "normality" after the turmoil of the final Weimar years.

In a most impressive study, Hans Dieter Schäfer, of Regensburg University, has pieced together evidence showing that many trends of cultural and economic modernization continued in the years preceding World War II.[16] Even in 1940 and 1941, American films were shown in German cinemas. Thus, film stars like Marlene Dietrich, who had emigrated in 1933, reappeared on the screens. Hollywood stars like Greta Garbo, Katherine Hepburn, and Joan Crawford were definite role models for Berlin secretaries. During the war the foreign minister, Joachim von Ribbentrop, went to considerable lengths to get copies of Mickey Mouse films. Moreover, the Coca Cola company which had been founded in Germany in 1929 expanded rapidly under Nazi Rule. Bottling plants rose from 5 in 1934 to 50 in 1939.[17] At the same time, gains in productivity permitted the lowering of prices for cars and made them available to a larger cross-section of the general public, even though Hitler's Germany still lagged far behind the United States in this respect. Contrary to the notion of a hermetically closed society, the number of foreign visitors rose, using several weekly transport services from Hamburg to New York. Camping became popular as a form of tourism. More students from Germany studied at English Universities in 1937 than from all other European nations combined.[18] And none of these developments were suppressed, but rather were liberally documented in the general press.

Facts such as the above constantly elicit surprise from today's audiences. Their image of the Third Reich has been formed by the historical writing in postwar Germany, and therefore it is difficult for them to believe that such icons of modernity as Walt Disney, Coca Cola, and IBM coexisted with Nazi-rule and the praising of an archaic Germanic past. Other "discoveries" of modern elements attached to National Socialist rule have been made. They might not seem as spectacular as those mentioned, but their significance for specialists is often even greater. The plans that the Nazi brain trust for social policy—the "Arbeitswissenschaftliches Institut" (Scientific Institute for Labor Studies)—drew up for a postwar National Socialist Germany contained for the first time in the debate on social reform the idea of a "dynamic pension" for the elderly, i.e. a pension whose level would be determined not by former payments but by the rising living standards of the younger generation.[19] This idea of a "contract between generations" was put into practice in 1957 by the West-German chancellor Konrad Adenauer and has long been regarded not only as a keystone of social and democratic stability in West-Germany but as an ingenious invention of postwar politicians.[20]

In 1972, when psychiatrists in West Germany discussed the reform of facilities for the mentally impaired, they discovered to their surprise that their ideas regarding more humane treatment for mental illness had already been developed in Weimar by the same people who later advocated and actively participated in the National Socialist program of euthanasia during the 1930s. A closer look suggested the explanation already mentioned above: This seemingly inconceivable development resulted from the social Darwinist idea of securing all available means to help the curable while getting rid of the incurable.

Other studies have shown that the 1930s brought a leader and other principals in the regime who not only were fond of motor races and sports cars but who reflected on how to integrate pedestrians and automobile traffic. The solutions—pedestrian subways and an inner city district without cars—became common in West Germany only in the late 1960s and early 1970s. Even the idea of integrating the famous motorways, the "Autobahnen," into the landscape by taking the construction material for the bridges and roadside vegetation from the different regions through which the motorways passed, originated in Germany under National Socialist rule.[21]

The observation that German Society under National Socialism contained more modern elements and developments than one might have expected provides an important correction to the notion that the Third Reich was only a bizarre interlude in German history. It indicates that the system was not so much out of step with the ongoing process of modernization in other countries, and in Germany itself, as one might expect. Finally, it indicates the limits of political and ideological manipulation. Thus, a one-sided picture is diffused, but no clear alternative emerges. Before drawing far-reaching conclusions from these facts one should also bear in mind that many of the modern elements cited above represented only ideas and plans that were not carried out until 1945.

This leads to the third important approach to National Socialist modernity, that of mobilization. Contrary to the thesis of "relative modernity," which has a rather diffuse meaning, this approach deals with a clear-cut question. The late director of the Institute of Contemporary History in Munich, Martin Broszat, presented it clearly: "What helped National Socialism gain its extraordinary ability to attract and mobilize followers?"[22] Where lay the social and psychological roots of the regime's ability to stretch and overstretch the potential of a historic society for building up as well as in tearing down, often in close relationship to each other? These questions direct research to the problem of "social motivation" among the key supporters of the regime.[23] The groups Broszat had in mind could be found in strategic positions in the armament plants of the Third Reich, in the highly effective propaganda machinery, controlling and exercising the sterilization and euthanasia program, preparing and starting the Holocaust, planning the exploitation and extinction of the Slavic people, directing the war economy especially during the so-called "Speer era" and finally drawing the contours of a postwar Nazi "social state."[24] They were often younger than the average of the population and came from the ranks of the self-employed or dependent new middle class. They thought of themselves as victims of traditional, petrified social structures that hindered highly motivated groups from gaining the high income and prestige that they claimed a right to. This self-perception made them responsive to the new opportunities and careers that German society after 1933 seemed to offer.

Again, one should note that desire for a career and upward mobility was only one element in the motivation of these groups. The Nazi technocrats were not so unpolitical as they pretended to have been when, after 1945, they sought to defend their involvement in the Nazi system. There is a certain danger in taking an ideology of defense and justification for granted. When studying the behavior of certain groups—for instance, the doctors involved in medical experiments in the concentration camps—one is powerfully confronted with the question of how it was possible for these individuals to leave even a modicum of civilized norms so far behind. Explaining this phenomenon certainly requires additional arguments. It can be argued convincingly that political and ideological indoctrination played only a minor role in the social motivation of these strategic groups.

Similarly, the finding that opportunities for upward social mobility increased during the Third Reich does not mean that the structures which generated such expectations and permitted more mobility than in the Weimar Republic were the result of progress in modernization. Some of these chances for mobility resulted indirectly from the effects of charismatic rule: those who, often accidentally, had sufficient access to the "Führer" to present him with an ambitious project[25] sometimes made a career that might have been unthinkable in normal structures determined by election, achievement or seniority.[26] Other cases were the result of the reign of terror that gave groups within the party an edge over their adversaries. The constant necessity for improvisation due to the systematic overstretching of resources by the regime promoted the career of outsiders, with the most prominent example being Albert Speer, architect and manager of the war economy from 1942 onwards. One should bear in mind that improvisation is usually not the most efficient way to run a modern enterprise and that the ability to attract Hitler's attention may not necessarily lead to effective and durable results in the way of economic modernization.[27]

Bearing in mind the danger of reproducing the verbal strategies used by Nazi technocrats to defend their involvement in a totalitarian regime, it would also be wrong and unrealistic to assume that the motivation of these groups consisted only in mere fantasy or, in other words, that Nazi propaganda was so effective as to create a world of sheer make believe. Although a thorough investigation is still lacking, it is highly probable that the opportunities for social and political careers increased through the expansion of the military, the state and the party administration, as well as their multiple branches. With this development, traditional patterns of selective social recruitment should have been weakened and levelled out, thus promoting the process of social modernization. Some of these modernizing effects were planned and brought about "intentionally," while others resulted from unplanned structural peculiarities of the regime.

Whoever looks for identification, engagement and consent under the Third Reich can no longer omit the role of the blue collar workers. Studies into the social policies of some of the main German enterprises in the 1930s, such as Krupp, Siemens, and United Steelworks, have shown that although the position of management was strengthened by the new factory laws, the managers tended to adopt a new management style. This was partly because a relatively high percentage of workers on the shop floor occupied posts within the hierarchy of the Nazi labor organization, the German Work Front (DAF). Although the rights of this organization had been severely reduced in comparison with the trade unions, it represented a huge bureaucratic machine within the company and thus contributed to the further weakening of patriarchal traditions within many firms.[28]

Another important trait of National Socialist policy at the workplace was the attempt to level differences between the blue and the white-collar workers.[29] These differences existed in many respects: in the way the management addressed each group in formal declarations, the way punctuality and attendance were controlled, the duration of holidays, the availability of recreation facilities, in profit-sharing schemes, and in the outfitting of houses and apartments owned by the firms. The process of levelling was extended to the collective wage agreements and the institutions of state social policy. It was also accompanied by propaganda to raise and correct systematically the social image of the working class within German society. Many, often cleverly executed, symbolic measures were used to integrate the workers, such as sending philharmonic orchestras to the factory floor. The resultant rise in the spirit and prestige of blue collar workers vis-à-vis the bourgeoisie was in some respects paralleled in the individual careers of many members of the professional classes in these years. Together with slowly rising incomes and job security it clearly contributed much to the willingness of the workers to lend their support to the regime.[30]

The fourth approach, which includes the thesis of "Hitler's social revolution" and the modernizing function of National Socialist rule, is addressed primarily by two authors: the American historian David Schoenbaum and the Anglo-German sociologist Ralf Dahrendorf.[31] Both begin with the notion that German society before 1933 differed from other Western countries with respect to the number and strength of traditional and illiberal elements, which contributed significantly to the rise of National Socialism. Such elements included, for instance, an influential, antidemocratic agrarian elite (the Prussian Junkers), a strong tradition of militarism and an army that acted as a state on its own, a tendency to formalize social roles and block social mobility thereby turning the lower ranks of society into outcasts, the role of the "estate" as a model for social policy, the containment of women within the spheres of church, childcare and kitchen, the retreat of important groups such as the blue-collar workers and the Catholics into separate, densely organized "societies" of their own; the lack of "public values," i.e. of a democratic political culture, uneasiness with conflict as a necessary element of modernization, etc. Whoever is acquainted with recent discussions in German historiography will recognize the well-known theory of the "peculiarities of modern German history" that lies behind these assumptions.[32]

Contrary to Schoenbaum, who merely describes some of these elements, Dahrendorf has tried to find a commonly applicable formula for the features that made up Germany's "deficit of modernization" and its "divergence from the West." This formula is to say that the "social role of citizenship" hadn't been established in Germany's pre-Nazi society. Via the "cunning of history"

(Hegel), this argument contends, the very regime that rose out of illiberal traditions and blockades of modernization became their liquidator and pushed modernization in Germany decisively forward. How did the heir turn into a liquidator?

In Dahrendorf's perspective it was the process that the Nazis themselves called "synchronization" (Gleichschaltung), i.e. the rapid dissolution and trans-formation of the entire intermediate power structure in order to establish to-talitarian rule, that changed the face of German society forever. For the first time in modern history all members of German society were brought into direct contact with each other and the state without the shelter of traditional roles. This did not refer, for instance, only to the workers or the youth but to the employers, the middle classes and even the military, which lost its special status and was placed under direct political control—something the Weimar Republic had never achieved.[33] While old institutions were abolished, such new mass organizations as the state youth and party, the compulsory labor service, the labor front and many other centralized professional leagues took their place. The role of the "people's comrade," which was to become the model for social organization in the Third Reich, resembled in its structure and lack of traditional elements the social role of "democratic citizen" on which the second German democracy could successfully be built.

Dahrendorf's thesis about the involuntary "push of German society into modernity" caused by National Socialism was formulated for the first time back in 1965. It took quite some time before historians started to use it as a framework for analyzing National Socialism and its consequences. It's not possible here to give a detailed account of the research which is still continu-ing in many fields.[34] Instead, I will try to outline some general results and observations by concentrating on two social groups that have been examined rather well: the white collar employees[35] and the catholic milieu.[36]

The existence of a clearly defined white-collar stratum which distanced itself vigorously from the blue-collar workers, as well as the formation of a peculiar catholic society within Germany's national, mainly protestant soci-ety may both be seen as expressions of the deep divisions within pre-Nazi Germany.

In both cases 1933, the year of the National Socialist rise to power, repre-sents a clear rupture. Many of the catholic mundane organizations—the Chris-tian trade unions, the consumer cooperatives, the youth organizations, the choral societies, etc.—were dissolved and disappeared completely. The same happened with the special associations of white-collar employees. They all ceased to exist within a few months after the National Socialist seizure of power and were melted into the anonymous mass organizations of the totali-tarian state.

The modernization perspective suggests that the measures taken by National Socialism had a durable effect on the structure of Germany's society. This seems to be true in both cases. Neither the Christian trade unions nor the special associations of white-collar employees were reconstructed after World War II in a way that may be compared with the 1920s. Does this prove the thesis of a "social revolution" and a "decisive push" towards social and political modernization by National Socialism?

For instance, if one examines the long term evolution of organized Catholicism in the cities and compares it with developments in the countryside one finds that there is a strong correlation between urbanization and the organizational attachment of Catholics to their church. This makes it probable that certain developments we now tend to attribute to National Socialist rule may have been the result of gradual modernization. More or less the same holds true for the "collar-line" between blue- and white-collar workers. There were clear signs of erosion already during the twenties.

From within Germany, scholars often tend to concentrate on what seem to be significant changes since the war rather than on what has remained and still constitutes part of their actual environment. The influential role played by the catholic church throughout German history is an example.[37] It should not be overlooked that the catholic hierarchy as such remained untouched during the twelve years of National Socialist rule. It was protected effectively by a concordat between the Nazi government and the Vatican. What was abolished were just the mundane organizations. Projects of "oral history" have shown that Catholics often fiercely resisted atheist tendencies within the Nazi Party, clung to their religious symbols and continued to participate in worship.[38] The same conclusion may be drawn from National Socialist social policy. It clearly tried to level some of the differences between white- and blue-collar workers but it stopped short of a radical abolition leaving, for instance, the most important factor of pension insurance untouched. In other cases such as artisans, small shopkeepers, judges, advocates, doctors, and pharmacists, National Socialism went even further and endowed these groups with traditional, illiberal instruments with which to regulate their labor market and fight outsiders.[39]

Taken together, these observations throw new light on the question of the modernizing effects of National Socialism in general. The regime apparently combined different strategies. In contrast to the radical challenges that it looked for and the needs of permanent mobilization, it chose to mix conservative and modern elements in order not to risk social unrest and instability. Moreover, it seems that Dahrendorf underestimated the influence that certain social groups retained and exercised in the process of decision making in the Third Reich, thus counteracting the more dynamic elements. Nevertheless, the notion stills holds that—among other factors such as the consequences of military defeat, allied rule, the economic boom of the 1950s, and the peoples' own ability to learn from bad experiences—National Socialism itself was an important factor in the modernization of Germany's social structure, without which it might not have come about in such a short span of time.

* * * * *

This paper has outlined four approaches related to the modernity of National Socialism and the question of its modernizing effects. It has stressed mainly the differences among these related approaches. The thesis of National Socialism as the expression of a janus-faced modernization process tries to explain especially the barbaric elements of the regime while most of the others concentrate on more favorable aspects—the reasons for widespread consent, or the question of how the regime contributed involuntarily to the founding of a stable democratic order after its own defeat. But there are important common traits as well. All approaches refer to aspects of the much neglected social history of National Socialism. They all, in one way or another, include, or at least imply, systematic comparison. Finally, they stress the need for putting the Nazi years back into the continuum of national and international history.

If this overview has seemed complicated and abstract, that can hardly be denied. Applying the concept of modernization as a framework to interpret National Socialism requires intensive methodological reflections in order to avoid relativizing a totalitarian dictatorship and its barbaric aspects. The least desirable result of research within this framework would be a modernization of National Socialism itself.

Notes

[1] The film not only introduced into the everyday language the word "Holocaust," that had not been known and used up to that point. It provoked a series of televised debates on German war crimes. In the discussions that accompanied the film, the directors of the three official German Television corporations pointed helplessly to a steady stream of documentaries on the Third Reich that preceded the "Holocaust" film. But none seemed to have an effect comparable to that of an individualized presentation of the Holocaust by presenting the fate of a single Jewish family. Some historians went so far as to call the effect of the film the "Cannae of German contemporary history," citing the example of the disastrous and historic defeat of the Romans at the hands of Hannibal. Within German historiography the "Holocaust" film contributed much to legitimizing and

popularizing "oral history" and the "history of everyday life." See Martin Broszat, "'Holocaust' und die Geschichtswissenschaft" (1979) in: Martin Broszat, *Nach Hitler. Der schwierige Umgang mit unserer Geschichte.* Beiträge von Martin Broszat, München 1986, S. 271-286.

² A useful recent introduction is Hans van der Loo, Willem van Reijen, *Modernisierung. Projekt und Paradox*, München 1992; from an historical perspective, Hans-Ulrich Wehler, *Modernisierungstheorie und Geschichte*, Göttingen 1975; an example of discussions within West German sociology is *Die Modernisierung moderner Gesellschaften. Verhandlungen des 25. Deutschen Soziologentages in Frankfurt am Main 1990*, hg. i.A. der Deutschen Gesellschaft für Soziologie von Wolfgang Zapf, Frankfurt 1991.

³ A much discussed study is Ulrich Beck, *Risikogesellschaft. Auf dem Weg in eine andere Moderne.* Frankfurt/M, 1986.

⁴ Influential is Norbert Elias, *Über den Prozeß der Zivilisation*, 2 vols., Frankfurt 1977.

⁵ One can best illustrate the relationship between these developments by citing a concrete example. In 1984 a major population census was due to be carried out in West Germany. It should have included an additional questionnaire for sociological purposes, but public protest and a campaign of civil disorder erupted in opposition to the census. At the height of the campaign two historians, Götz Aly from Berlin and Karl Heinz Roth from Hamburg, published a study under the title "Complete Registration: Population Census, Identification, and Selection under National Socialism." Ostensibly, it dealt with a survey in 1939 that the Nazis had carried out to prepare for euthanasia and the extinction of the Jewish population. In fact, it drew direct parallels between the two events, arguing that in both cases irresponsible scientists had prepared the way for totalitarian tendencies in the state machine and its bureaucracy. See Götz Aly, Karl Heinz Roth, *Die restlose Erfassung. Volkszählen, Identifizieren, Aussondern im Nationalsozialismus*, Berlin, 1984.

⁶ D. Peukert, *Grenzen der Sozialdisziplinierung. Aufstieg und Krise der deutschen Jugendfürsorge 1878 bis 1932*, Köln, 1986.

⁷ Norbert Frei, "Wie modern war der Nationalsozialismus?," in: *Geschichte und Gesellschaft* 19, 3 (1993), S.367-387; for the discussion in general see from a Marxist point of view—Joachim Petzold, "War Hitler ein Revolutionär? Zum Thema Modernismus und Antimodernismus in der Faschismus-Diskussion," in: *Blätter für deutsche und internationale Politik* 23 (1978), S. 186-205; Werner Abelshauser und Anselm Faust, "Wirtschafts und Sozialpolitik. Eine nationalsozialistische Sozialrevolution?" in *Nationalsozialismus im Unterricht, Studieneinheit* 4, Deutsches Institut für Fernstudien an der Universität Tübingen, Tübingen 1983. H. Matzerath/H. Volkmann, "Modernisierungstheorie und Nationalsozialismus," in: J. Kocka (Hrsg.): *Theorien in der Praxis des Historikers*, Göttingen 1977, S. 86-116. From a sociological perspective, Jens Alber, "Nationalsozialismus und Modernisierung," in: *Kölner Zeitschrift für Soziologie*

und Sozialpsychologie 41. Jg. 1989, S. 346-365; for criticism of the approach, see Hans Mommsen, "Nationalsozialismus als vorgetäuschte Modernisierung," in: *Der historische Ort des Nationalsozialismus. Annäherungen.* Walter H. Pehle (Hg.), Frankfurt/M. 1990, S. 31-46.

[8] For recent studies, see the reader, Michael Prinz, Rainer Zitelmann, *Nationalsozialismus und Modernisierung*, Darmstadt 1991. It contains 12 examples.

[9] For a summary, see Detlev Peukert, *Volksgenossen und Gemeinschaftsfremde. Anpassung, Ausmerze und Aufbegehren unter dem Nationalsozialismus*, Köln 1982; an informative reader is: Frank Bajohr u.a. (Hg.), *Zivilisation und Barbarei. Die widersprüchlichen Potentiale der Moderne*, Hamburg 1991.

[10] See Jürgen Habermas, *Theorie des kommunikativen Handelns*, Bd. 1, Frankfurt 1981, S. 255ff.

[11] See Peukert, *Volksgenossen*, S. 278.

[12] On the use of the term "final solution of the social question" see Hans-Ludwig Siemen, *Das Grauen ist vorprogrammiert. Psychiatrie zwischen Faschismus und Atomkrieg*, Gießen 1982, S. 132; "Beiträge zur nationalsozialistischen Gesundheits- und Sozialpolitik 1: Aussonderung und Tod." *Die klinische Hinrichtung der Unbrauchbaren*, Berlin 1989, S. 7; a good summary of the debate is Franz-Werner Kersting, Karl Teppe and Bernd Walter, "Gesellschaft—Psychiatrie—Nationalsozialismus. Historisches Interesse und gesellschaftliches Bewußtsein," in: Nach Hadamar, *Zum Verhältnis von Psychiatrie und Gesellschaft im 20. Jahrhundert*, hg. von Franz-Werner Kersting, Karl Teppe and Bernd Walter, Paderborn 1993, S. 9-62.

[13] Hans-Walter Schmuhl, "Reformpsychiatrie und Massenmord," in: *Nationalsozialismus und Modernisierung*, S. 239-266.

[14] Götz Aly and Susanne Heim, *Vordenker der Vernichtung. Auschwitz und die deutschen Pläne für eine neue europäische Ordnung*, Frankfurt 1993; Karl Heinz Roth, *I. G. Auschwitz. Normalität oder Anomalie eines kapitalistischen Entwicklungssprunges*: 1999 4 (1989), S. 11-28. For description of National Socialist economic planning and war aims see Albrecht Ritschl, "Die NS-Wirtschaftsideologie—Modernisierungsprogramm oder reaktionäre Utopie?," in: *Nationalsozialismus und Modernisierung*, S. 48-70.

[15] For the history of the eugenics movement in England, see Mark Haller, *Eugenics. Hereditarian Attitudes in American Thought*, New Brunswick, New Jersey, 1963; John Macnicol, *The Movement for Family Allowances 1918- 1945: A Study in Social Policy Development*, London, 1980; Matthew Thomson, Paul Weindling, "Sterilisationspolitik in Großbritannien und Deutschland," in: Nach Hadamar, *Zum Verhältnis von Psychiatrie und Gesellschaft im 20. Jahrhundert*, hg. von Franz-Werner Kersting, Karl Teppe and Bernd Walter, Paderborn 1993, S. 137-149. For the support of Hitler's plans on eugenics by English groups see the article in: *Eugenics Review* 25 (Juli 1933), S. 77f. A study of the relationship between the socialist movement and eugenics in England is Michael Freeden,

"Eugenics and Progressive Thought. A Study in Ideological Affinity," in: *Historical Journal* 22 (1979), S. 645-671; Diane Paul, "Eugenics and the Left," in: *Journal of the History of Ideas* 45 (1984), S. 567-590; for the same aspect in Germany, see Michael Schwartz, "Sozialismus und Eugenik. Zur fälligen Revision eines Geschichtsbildes," in: *Internationale wissenschaftliche Korrespondenz zur Geschichte der Arbeiterbewegung* 4 (1989), S. 465-489. A conclusive study on the whole subject is Peter Weingart, Jürgen Kroll and Kurt Bayertz, *Rasse, Blut und Gene. Geschichte der Eugenik und Rassenhygiene in Deutschland*, Frankfurt 1988.

[16] See Hans Dieter Schäfer, "Das gespaltene Bewußtsein. Über die Lebenswirklichkeit in Deutschland 1933-1945," in: Schäfer, *Das gespaltene Bewußtsein. Über deutsche Kultur und Lebenswirklichkeit 1933-1945*, München 1984, 2. edition, S. 146-208.

[17] Ibid., S. 151.

[18] Ibid., S. 161.

[19] See M. L. Recker, *Nationalsozialistische Sozialpolitik im Zweiten Weltkrieg*, München 1985; Michael Prinz, *Vom neuen Mittelstand zum Volksgenossen. Die Entwicklung des sozialen Status der Angestellten von der Weimarer Republik bis zum Ende der NS-Zeit*, München 1986, S. 299f.

[20] The point should be stressed that there seem to be no direct links betweens these plans and the introduction of this reform in 1957.

[21] Hitler's social and economic ideas are documented in Rainer Zitelmann, *Selbstverständnis eines Revolutionärs*, Stuttgart 1989 3. ed.

[22] Martin Broszat, "Plädoyer für eine Historisierung des Nationalsozialismus," in: ders., *Nach Hitler. Der schwierige Umgang mit unserer Geschichte. Beiträge von Martin Broszat*, hg. v. Hermann Graml and Klaus-Dietmar Henke, München 1986, S. 159-173, Zit. S. 160.

[23] Vgl. Martin Broszat, "Soziale Motivation und Führer-Bindung des Nationalsozialismus," in: *Vierteljahrshefte für Zeitgeschichte* 18 (1970), S. 390-407.

[24] See Karl Heinz Roth, *Intelligenz und Sozialpolitik im "Dritten Reich." Eine methodisch-historische Studie am Beispiel des Arbeitswissenschaftlichen Instituts der Deutschen Arbeitsfront*, München 1993.

[25] Professor Ferdinand Porsche and the history of the "Volkswagen" is a famous example of such an encounter.

[26] See Ian Kershaw, *Hitlers Macht. Das Profil der NS-Herrschaft*, München 1992 (English 1991).

[27] See Volker *Berghahn, Unternehmer und Politik in der Bundesrepublik*, Frankfurt 1985, p. 188.

[28] See Wolfgang Zollitsch, *Arbeiter zwischen Weltwirtschaftskrise und Nationalsozialismus. Ein Beitrag zur Sozialgeschichte der Jahre 1928-1936.* Göttingen 1990; Matthias Frese, *Betriebspolitik im "Dritten Reich." Deutsche Arbeitsfront, Unternehmer und Staatsbürokratie in der westdeutschen*

Großindustrie 1933-1939, Paderborn 1991. A summary of recent publications is Matthias Frese, "Sozial- und Arbeitspolitik im "Dritten Reich." Ein Literaturbericht," in: *Neue Politische Literatur* 3 (1993), S. 403-446.

[29] See Prinz, *Mittelstand*; H. Trischler, *Steiger im deutschen Bergbau. Zur Sozialgeschichte der technischen Angestellten 1918-1945*, München 1988.

[30] See Ulrich Herbert, "Zur Entwicklung der Ruhrarbeiterschaft 1930 bis 1960 aus erfahrungsgeschichtlicher Perspektive," in: Lutz Niethammer and Alexander von Plato, *"Wir kriegen jetzt andere Zeiten." Auf der Suche nach der Erfahrung des Volkes in nachfaschistischen Ländern (Lebensgeschichte und Sozialkultur im Ruhrgebiet 1930 bis 1960*, Band 3), Berlin 1985.

[31] Ralf Dahrendorf, *Gesellschaft und Demokratie in Deutschland*, München 1963; by the same author, "Die neue Gesellschaft. Soziale Strukturwandlungen der Nachkriegszeit," in: Hans Werner Richter (Hrsg.), *Bestandsaufnahme. Eine deutsche Bilanz 1962*, München 1962; David Schoenbaum, *Die braune Revolution. Eine Sozialgeschichte des Dritten Reiches*, Köln 1968. English edition: *Hitler's Social Revolution*, New York, 1966.

[32] For the discussion, see D. Blackbourn and Geoff Eley, *Mythen deutscher Geschichtsschreibung*, Frankfurt 1980; *Deutscher Sonderweg—Mythos oder Realität?* München 1982.

[33] See Detlev Bald, "Von der Wehrmacht zur Bundeswehr. Kontinuität und Neubeginn," in: Werner Conze and M. Rainer Lepsius, *Sozialgeschichte der Bundesrepublik Deutschland. Beiträge zum Kontinuitätsproblem*, Stuttgart 1983.

[34] An important publication is Conze/Lepsius, *Sozialgeschichte*.

[35] Prinz, *Mittelstand*; Trischler, *Steiger*.

[36] See Wilfried Loth, "Integration und Erosion: Wandlungen des katholischen Milieus," in: Loth (ed.), *Deutscher Katholizismus im Umbruch zur Moderne* (= *Konfession und Gesellschaft*, Bd.3), Stuttgart 1991, pp. 266-281. Clemens Bauer, "Der deutsche Katholizismus und die bürgerliche Gesellschaft," in: Bauer, *Deutscher Katholizismus. Entwicklungslinien und Profile*. Frankfurt/M, 1964, pp. 28-53; Josef Henke, "Die Hochburgen der 'katholischen Parteien'. Materialien zum Wahlverhalten vom Kaiserreich bis zur Bundesrepublik Deutschland," in: *Deutschland in Europa: Kontinuität und Bruch. Gedenkschrift für Andreas Hillgruber*, ed. by Jost Dülffer and Bernd Martin, Frankfurt a. M. 1990, S. 348-373; Urs Altermatt, *Katholizismus und Moderne. Studien zur Sozialgeschichte der Schweizer Katholiken im 19. und 20. Jahrhundert*, Zürich 1989; Margaret Lavina Anderson, "Piety and Politics: Recent Work on German Catholicism," in: *Journal of Modern History* 63 (1991), 681-716; the best case-study is Werner Blessing, "'Deutschland in Not, wir im Glauben. . . .' Kirche und Kirchenvolk in einer katholischen Region 1933-1949," in: *Von Stalingrad zur Währungsreform. Zur Sozialgeschichte des Umbruchs in Deutschland*, ed. by Martin Broszat, Klaus-Dietmar Henke and Hans Woller, München 1988, pp. 3-112; for another region Wilhelm Damberg, "Katholizismus im Umbruch. Beobachtungen zur Geschichte des Bistums Münster in den 40er und 50er Jahren," in: Raimund Haas (Hrg.),

60

Ecclesia Monestariensis, Festschrift für Aloys Schröer zum 85. Geburtstag, Münster 1992, pp. 385-404; Klaus-Michael Mallmann, "Ultramontanismus und Arbeiterbewegung im Kaiserreich. Überlegungen am Beispiel des Saarreviers," in: Wilfried Loth (ed.), *Deutscher Katholizismus im Umbruch zur Moderne* (= *Konfession und Gesellschaft,* vol. 3), Stuttgart u.a. 1991, pp. 76-94.

[37] See the remark by the English historian, Alan Milward, in: *Vierteljahreshefte für Zeitgeschichte* 40 (1992), S. 457. A comparative study on developments in East Germany after 1945 is Christoph Kleßmann, "Relikte des Bildungsbürgertums in der DDR," in: *Sozialgeschichte der DDR,* edited by Hartmut Kaelble, Jürgen Kocka and Hartmut Zwahr, Stuttgart 1994, S. 254-270; Detlef Pollack, "Von der Volkskirche zur Minderheitskirche. Zur Entwicklung von Religiösität und Kirchlichkeit in der DDR," in: *Sozialgeschichte der DDR,* S. 271-294.

[38] See Blessing, *Deutschland.*

[39] Michael Prinz, "Der unerwünschte Stand. Lage und Status der Angestellten im 'Dritten Reich'," in: *Historische Zeitschrift* 242 (1986), pp. 327-359.

Warmaking and the Transformation of the State: Japan and the U.S. in World War II

Gregory Hooks and Raymond A. Jussaume, Jr.

INTRODUCTION

The increasing interconnectedness of the U.S. and Japanese political economies has been accompanied by a growing literature on the contrasting social, economic and political cultures that characterize these two nations. While many factors have been used to explain these differences, the important role of warmaking has largely been ignored. Specifically, few scholars have examined how the process of mobilization for, and the outcome of, the Second World War helped to alter the historical trajectories that had been evolving and create a new set of social conditions in those two nations upon which postwar social, economic and political developments were constructed.

The research presented in this paper is inspired by the recent calls for social scientists to take wars and their legacies seriously (Giddens 1985; Hooks and McLauchlan 1992; Mann 1984; Stein and Russett 1980; Tilly 1990). To gain insight into the distinctive characteristics of the contemporary Japanese and American political economies, our analysis emphasizes the transformation of the relationship between the state and leading businesses during World War II. This research on World War II economic mobilization concentrates on 1) developments in raw material industries, with a special emphasis on aluminum, and 2) the management of core defense industries that emphasizes a case study of the aircraft industry. Our research corroborates Giddens's (1985, p. 244) claim that wars have "produced transformations which have turned

The research reported on in this essay was supported in part by the U.S. Department of Agriculture under agreement number 88-33574-4054, and by the Faculty of Economics at Kanazawa University, Japan. Any opinions, findings, and conclusions or recommendations expressed herein are those of the authors and do not necessarily reflect the views of either of these institutions.

out to be of enduring significance." This provides evidence that the World War II economic mobilization played a pivotal role in molding the postwar Japanese and U.S. states and helps to reveal some of the paradoxical dimensions of Japan and the U.S. that are among the legacies of this war.

THEORETICAL BACKGROUND

It is tempting, but misguided, to impute homogeneity to the state. Rather, the state reflects patterns of uneven development (Hooks 1993). At any time, certain legislative committees and state agencies can be heavily influenced by business elites, and are obliged to be responsive to broad economic imperatives. Simultaneously, other state agencies pursue agendas that flow from the state's organizational goals, even though they may risk resistance from business elites and conflict with economic imperatives. Policy initiatives associated with military objectives often fit into the latter category. Unfortunately, because the social sciences have ignored wars, most theories of the state have examined economic and social policies without considering the degree to which warmaking has constrained and distorted state development (Caporaso 1989; Hooks and McLauchlan 1992). This tendency has resulted in an underestimation of the state building that has been instigated by U.S. military bureaucracies. Similarly, the tendency to treat prewar Japan as the militaristic antithesis of liberal society (Lasswell 1937) has impeded an understanding of the linkages between postwar Japanese civil society and prewar Japanese militarism.

The Paradoxical Dimensions of the U.S. and Japanese States

World War II, a war that would bind the fate of these two states, is central to unraveling the paradoxical features of the U.S. and Japanese states. The mobilization for this war propelled the shift from a Japanese garrison state to one that seeks to guide domestic industries and economic development through "administrative guidance" by empowering a managerial class that is inclined to work with government bureaucrats (Okazaki 1993). While the Japanese state thus became less intrusive, the U.S. state became more powerful at home and abroad. Specifically, World War II mobilization propelled the rise of the Pentagon and provided the material, administrative, and ideological foundation for the defense-oriented economic planning carried out by the U.S. state after the war (Hooks 1991).

Many observers assert that the contemporary Japanese state is strong and intrusive. The Japanese state is given credit for implementing an industrial policy that has guided the evolution of the Japanese economy (for example, see Dore 1986; Johnson 1982; Okimoto 1989). Proponents of free enterprise typically vilify the Japanese state for its active role in economic planning and technological development. Indeed, the success of the Asian economies has presented a major ideological challenge to the free market orthodoxies of the United States, its Western allies, and their agencies for foreign economic development like the World Bank and the IMF (Ozawa 1994). Interestingly, this view of the Japanese state builds upon the criticisms that were levelled at the highly militaristic prewar Japanese state. In Lasswell's view (1937), Japan was ruled by the prototypical "garrison state" in which the entire society was regimented to serve the militaristic state (see also Huntington 1957).

The very existence of an industrial policy suggests that the Japanese government plays a more deliberate role in directing the domestic economy than its American counterpart, although some scholars insist that the role of the Japanese government in sustaining economic development has been supportive rather than activist. They use examples of the successful formation of industrial districts (Friedman 1988), and the case of the automobile industry, where firms rejected government calls to rationalize that industry (Cusumano 1985), to argue that the Japanese government is not as influential in directing economic development as many observers want to believe. Our research lends support to those who paint a more nuanced picture of the Japanese state's role. It provides evidence that the wartime Japanese state, its despotism notwithstanding, was less capable of managing the domestic economy, and was in many respects more compromised in its dealings with private firms, than its American counterpart. These trends were reinforced by Japan's defeat to insure that the postwar Japanese state would be oriented towards economic, rather than military, objectives.

The U.S. state is no less paradoxical. On the one hand, the contemporary United States is routinely contrasted with the Japanese or West European states to provide a classic example of a "weak" and nonintrusive state (Krasner 1978; Weir and Skocpol 1985; Zysman 1983). But this classically "weak" state has been the world's leading military and political power for five decades. Moreover, maintaining this international hegemony has required the U.S. government to play a pivotal role in the design, development and production of armaments (Hooks 1990). This "paradox of external strength and internal weakness" (Krasner 1978) confounds those who try to pigeonhole the U.S. state.

The state can neither be reduced to the functions it performs or the interests of societal organizations, nor can the state's autonomy be asserted without historical inquiry (Hooks 1993; Quadagno 1992). Yet, the actual character and evolution of a state are molded by historically specific interactions with the economic, political, and cultural organizations in the society it rules and by that state's interaction in the interstate system (Block 1987; Mann 1986; Tilly 1990). Thus, to unravel the paradoxical transformation of the Japanese and U.S. states, we investigate the states' interactions with other organizations. Specifically, we stress "negotiated accommodation" (Tilly 1990), which refers to the bargaining between states and leading organizations over the manner in which mobilization proceeded. Negotiated accommodation involves calculating parties protecting their interests, which are often best protected by accommodating the demands of a potent negotiating partner (Mann 1986). The state brings a distinctive agenda to this negotiation because geopolitical dynamics external to the nation-state are central determinants of going to war and the strategies for waging war. The state negotiates to secure economic resources in return for protecting the economic and political clout of leading economic organizations.

Despotic and Infrastructural Powers

To analyze the relationship between the state and economic development, we "must distinguish between the two principal meanings of a strong regime: power over civil society, that is *despotism*; and the power to coordinate society, that is, *infrastructural* strength" (Mann 1988, p. 477, emphasis in original). Because it provides few constitutional guarantees, a despotic state can detain, torture, and kill its citizens. But a despotic state does not necessarily have the infrastructural power to manage and coordinate the economy. Economic governance refers to "the institutionalized economic processes that organize and coordinate activity among a variety of economic actors." When attempting to understand the state's infrastructural powers, the issue is the degree to which the state "as an actor and an institutional structure influences the organization . . . of economic activity" (Campbell and Lindberg 1990, p. 636).

Clearly the World War II Japanese state wielded far greater despotic powers than its U.S. counterpart. Purges of academics, socialists, Communists and union organizers began in 1932 and helped create a climate in which it became impossible to criticize the state (Reischauer and Craig 1978). For example, the Japanese state created "neighborhood associations" that usurped the traditional notion of neighborhood mutual aid associations to place every Japanese household in a *gonin-gumi*, or group of five families. These groups carried out state policies and maintained social order under the supervision of the government (Tsurumi 1986). In the United States, despite serious civil rights abuses, such as the incarceration of Japanese-Americans, democratic processes and institutions survived the war (Blum 1976; Polenberg 1972).

Too often, theories of the state and warmaking conflate the infrastructural and despotic powers of the state. In Spencer's "militant" societies and Lasswell's (1937; 1941) "garrison state," power is centralized in the military.

A militarized society is quick to go to war, thereby reinforcing the state's control over society. A hidden assumption is that a despotic state maintains the infrastructural power to directly control economic activity. However, this was clearly not the case with the World War II Japanese state. During this war, private sector firms, particularly those that belonged to the *zaibatsu*, took advantage of their infrastructural power to negotiate a great deal of autonomy for themselves. According to Okazaki (1993), the Japanese state increased its ability to create a planned economy towards the end of the war by eliminating the influence of stockholders in firms and transferring control to managers, staff and workers. Not only did this set the stage for the postwar trend for managers and employees to identify strongly with their firms, it also highlights the barriers that impeded the Japanese government's mobilization for war. If the focus is restricted to the state's sweeping despotic powers and deeply ingrained militarist ideology, it might be expected that the Japanese state would have responded to the severe shortages and stinging military defeats of 1943 and 1944 by restricting business autonomy and profits. Instead, even as evidence mounted that the war was being lost, the Japanese government guaranteed profits and enhanced the managers' freedom to manage their firms. "In sum, the Munitions Corporations Law introduced a corporate system whereby managers were guaranteed by the government a free hand in all dealings with stockholders, financial institutions, and workers and carried out a management style aimed at the pursuit of profits, shared with workers" (Okazaki, ibid., p. 199; see also Bisson 1945; Cohen 1949; Rice 1979; Roberts 1973).

It is often difficult to translate despotic and infrastructural power from one form to the other. The Japanese state experienced the difficulty of translating despotic power into infrastructural power in two respects. First, the government was prevented from taking direct control of industry because it needed the managerial expertise of those who supervised these firms and the cooperation of those who owned them. The second limit was a product of Japan's relatively small size and natural resource deficits. Wielding despotic power over its citizens did little to increase the Japanese state's access to the materials essential to waging a war of industrial attrition. The Japanese state did wield its despotic powers, particularly in its colonies, to gain access to raw materials for the private sector in hopes of assuring a level of economic production that could maintain it in power. However, this despotism could not match the infrastructural powers at the U.S. state's command.

The U.S. state commanded remarkable infrastructural power because it exercised dominion over a vast nation of continental proportions and the world's largest manufacturing economy. It is misleading to suggest that the U.S. state lacked despotic qualities. The United States gained control over the

North American continent through brutal wars that resulted in the dispossession and rapid decline in the population of the Native Americans. In fact, even as the United States fought World War II under the banner of democracy, citizens of non-European ethnic backgrounds were routinely treated despotically. These qualifications notwithstanding, the U.S. state was far less despotic than the Japanese state, while its infrastructural power was far more important to its success in war. During World War II, the U.S. state ascended to a position of economic and military hegemony, while leading U.S. firms grew larger and stronger. In Tilly's view (1990, p. 133), the U.S. state secured the resources required to maintain the world's most potent military organization in exchange for a generous accommodation with the leading financial and manufacturing corporations. By skimming from the world's largest economy, the U.S. accounted for a disproportionate share of the world's military spending during the war (Milward 1977) and continued to do so in the postwar era (Hooks and McLauchlan 1992). However, the U.S. state did not simply skim resources, it created the institutions to guide industrial production during the war and forged the "military-industrial complex" through which the state guided weapons production for decades to follow.

PREWAR CONTRASTS AND WARTIME MOBILIZATION

Gerschenkron (1962) placed great emphasis on the timing of industrialization to understand the prominence of the state's contribution to the modernization process. Among the nations that industrialized early, like the U.S., the state was not central to the process and impediments to subsequent statist interventions were built during the course of industrialization. By contrast, for late industrializers, such as Japan, the state played a direct and prominent role in amassing and allocating capital to infrastructural projects and industrial activity. Even after industrialization takes off, these states continue to play a pivotal role in economic development and governance. As the developmentalist state extends its role in managing society, the boundary between the state and society often becomes blurred. This can create the conditions for an erosion of the state's centrality at a later point in time (Rueschemeyer and Evans 1985, p. 56).

Japan

The modern Japanese state was born on January 3, 1868, when the Meiji Restoration was proclaimed. In the summer of 1853, Commodore Perry of the American Navy had arrived with demands that Japan open itself to trade with the U.S. and other Western nations. Unequal economic treaties were signed in

1858 between Japan and the United States, Holland, Russia, Britain and France (Halliday 1975), setting the stage for the political downfall of the feudal regime. Japan had been developing an indigenous form of capitalism before the arrival of Commodore Perry (Smith 1988). Cottage industries, particularly in textiles, had sprung up in peri-urban areas. Merchant trading houses, whose influence had grown as a result of their links to the aristocracy, managed the increasing volume of internal trade. The arrival of the European powers simply speeded up the process of change.

The Japanese state led the initial processes of industrialization and capital accumulation. It did so by extracting capital from agriculture, particularly the non-landlord classes (Tsunematsu 1966; Ohkawa 1969). The state extracted heavy taxes from peasants, suppressed consumption in rural areas, and promoted the investment of capital that landlords amassed through rents. Large scale industrial projects were created with government capital and imported technology. Many of these firms were owned initially by the national government. However, once they became economically viable, they were sold to private investors, often to politically well connected merchant houses (Bisson 1954). In this manner, the state played a direct role in creating large, private companies, and in particular the industrial combines known as the *zaibatsu* (Lockwood 1954).

By the early 20th century, the *zaibatsu* commanded the pinnacle of the Japanese industrial hierarchy (Hirschmeier and Yui 1981). As is common in present day Japan, parent firms subcontracted production to small, dependent firms.

> There was a considerable number of small workshops engaged in manufacturing parts and working to the orders of the factories; but most of the heavy engineering industry was concentrated in a few large firms, each with a wide range of output. The more important among these firms, moreover, were owned by the great business families with interests in many branches of large-scale enterprise (Allen 1946, p. 78).

The state did retain control of strategic infrastructural sectors, such as railroads and communications, as well as industries that failed to attract sufficient private capital. For example, the Yawata Iron Works was a government-owned firm created in 1901. While imports supplied two-thirds of Japan's steel as late as 1913, by the late 1920s Japan produced 70 percent of its own steel, with the Yawata Works being the dominant supplier (Allen ibid.).

Despite government ownership of several key industries, the *zaibatsu* gained greater influence and power. By 1930, the eight largest *zaibatsu* directly controlled 15 percent of joint stock capital in the country (Hirschmeier and Yui 1981). In 1945, the Mitsubishi *zaibatsu* had 1,000,000 employees, while the Mitsui *zaibatsu* employed approximately 1,800,000 individuals within Japan and possibly up to 1,000,000 additional employees outside of the country (Bisson 1945). Additionally, the *zaibatsu* indirectly controlled the capital and labor of subcontractors. It should therefore come as no surprise that

> In the 1920's and 1930's, representatives of the *Zaibatsu* interest entered in numbers into all the higher organs of government, normally occupying the leading posts in the Imperial Household Ministry, the Privy Council, and the House of Peers. Prime ministers in these two decades, even when they were military or naval men, were almost exclusively from conservative blocs that were linked closely to the combines. The Finance Ministry, along with Commerce and Industry, was often held by the *Zaibatsu* executives themselves, such as Ikeda Seihin, Ogura Masatsune (Sumitomo), Yuki Toyotaro (Yasuda), and Fujihara Ginjiro (Mitsui, Nissan), or by men who worked with them (Bisson 1954, p. 22).

Prominent military leaders and much of the officer corps were hostile to *zaibatsu* domination of economic policy and industrial development (Smethurst 1974). A number of "strategically placed senior army and navy officers felt uncomfortably restricted by disarmament conferences, the level of appropriations for the ministries, and with the balance of power between themselves and the leaders of the business community" (Hadley 1970, pp. 38-41). One group of army officers, originating out of the army accounting school, favored an economy controlled and planned by the military (Shiozaki 1979). One group of radical militarists went so far as to assassinate, in 1932, a finance minister, the chairman of the board of the Mitsui Holding Company and a prime minister.

One must be careful not to make too much of the ideological and other differences that divided the Japanese military and business elites.

> Admirals and generals, on retiring from active service, often sought and found high positions in the *Zaibatsu* combines. Trading branches of the big combines, such as Mitsui, operated comprehensive espionage and intelligence services for the Army and Navy ministries. In the 'thirties, expansion of heavy industry geared chiefly to munitions production brought lucrative contracts to the combines and accounted for a steadily increasing proportion of their activity (Bisson 1954, p. 22).

The military depended on large industrial conglomerates to produce war material. Conversely, the *zaibatsu* reaped economic benefits from the establishment of a centralized, colonialist government. Nonetheless, it is equally important to recognize that the Japanese state was not without divisions, both within the government and between different elements of the government and representatives of the leading business organizations. Political movements aimed at establishing political control over the military were established (Amemiya 1976), and big business was concerned about the power and independence of the military.

> The trend toward a controlled economy during the 1937-41 period, even under semiofficial auspices, was not wholly to the *Zaibatsu's* liking. They disliked the steady trenching of control on the private sector of the economy, even though the big monopoly concerns had not yet been materially affected by this process. . . . Above all, they feared that extremist elements in the military or the bureaucracy might seek to impose an extensive bureaucratic control system on a basis which would seriously challenge their vested prerogatives (Bisson 1945, pp. 19-20; see also Rice 1979, p. 689).

The desire of the military to force industry to serve the state and the desire of business interests to maintain huge profits throughout the war years continually undermined the authority of war planning bureaucracies. Japanese economic mobilization was marked by convulsive reorganizations and policy reversals. Thus, instead of being a unified and insulated militaristic state, the wartime Japanese state displayed a large measure of paralysis as it was forced to accommodate powerful business and military interests.

This struggle reached its climax when the government created the Munitions Ministry in 1943. By that time, it had become apparent that supplies of raw materials, including skilled labor and machine tools, were dwindling and that improved coordination of the economy was necessary (Rice 1979; Yamazaki 1991). Not surprisingly, this new ministry became the center of turf wars between the military services, the *zaibatsu,* and the civilian bureaucracy (Rice 1979). Over the objections of military leaders, in order to maintain the cooperation of the *zaibatsu* and other private sector interests, the government guaranteed their profits and left most munitions production in private hands (Okazaki 1993). In addition, the creation of the Munitions Ministry never eliminated conflicts between the Army and the Navy (Cohen 1949).

The ability of the Munitions Ministry to stimulate and coordinate war production was thus hampered by conflicts between the Army and the Navy, as well as between the armed forces and private corporations. However, the overriding constraint on Japanese mobilization was the acute lack of resources, including raw materials. Indeed, one of the reasons Japan had gone to war and expanded its empire into Northeast and Southeast Asia was to gain access to raw materials. The inability of the Japanese state to acquire essential materials reveals the limits of a despotic state. Even if the Japanese state had succeeded in brokering the interests of internal power factions, it would still have confronted an absolute deficit in resources and infrastructural power.

United States

Although many liberal and Marxist scholars assume that capitalist societies are not inherently warlike, nations such as the U.S. have been among the most prominent belligerents and big winners of the major wars of the 20th century. Further, the lethality of 20th century wars has far surpassed that of previous centuries (Mann 1984, p. 27; Tilly 1990, pp. 72-73). While no less warlike than its Japanese counterpart, the geopolitical setting, class structure and economic resources of the American state steered it down a different path. From the vantage point of Native Americans, Mexicans, and inhabitants of the various Caribbean and Latin American nations in which the U.S. intervened, the assertion that the pre-World War II U.S. lacked a militarist tradition is untenable. The editors of *Fortune* pointed out that between 1776 and 1935, the U.S. "filched more square miles of the earth by sheer military conquest than any army in the world, except only that of Great Britain. And as between Great Britain and the U.S. it has been a close race, Britain having conquered something over 3,500,000 square miles since that date, and the U.S. (if one includes wresting the Louisiana Purchase from the Indians) something over 3,100,000" (in Mills 1956, p. 177n).

Like many of its contemporaries, the pre-World War II U.S. state aggressively extended "the range of population and resources" under its control. When these states "encountered no one with comparable control of coercion, they conquered; when they met rivals, they made war" (Tilly 1990, p. 14). The American state's exceptionalism is first and foremost a consequence of its geopolitical setting. The U.S. destroyed a number of Native American civilizations, but much of this violence was decentralized and implemented by amateurs, not professional soldiers. The "technical and numerical superiority of the American frontiersman who confronted the American Indian made it unnecessary for a true warrior stratum and a large, disciplined administration of violence to emerge" (Mills 1956, p. 178). The wars among the great European powers and their competition to control a vast colonial empire in distant lands led these states to build large and professional military establishments. By contrast, the U.S. was buffered from European wars by the Atlantic and Pacific Oceans. It was able to steal, absorb, and develop a rich nation of continental proportions in the decades preceding World War II with a much smaller and far less professional military establishment.

By the early 20th century, the U.S. economy was the largest and most vibrant in the world, and the American state was in the enviable position of skimming the world's largest economy for its revenues. The United States maintained relatively low rates of taxation and devoted a small proportion of its revenues to national security. Nevertheless, the U.S. was one of the "great powers," and its military was among the largest and richest even before the World War II rearmament. The U.S. state's options were limited only by the structure of its domestic political economy. "Big business" emerged in the U.S. long before big government (Vogel 1978). As a consequence, the expansion of the American state in the 20th century occurred in the shadow of a powerful network of financial, manufacturing, and transportation corporations. The weak bureaucratic traditions and the strength of the dominant class did not prevent the growth of the state, but the resulting state structures were compromised (Skowronek 1982), the military bureaucracy included (Huntington 1957).

During the economic mobilization for World War I, the balance of power rested with economic elites. The Army and Navy maintained longstanding parochial institutions during this war, but in so doing, lost control of the larger mobilization. The inability of the military leadership or the White House to exercise control over the procurement activity of separate military bureaucracies contributed to the chaotic World War I mobilization. By the war's end, the War Industries Board, a quasi-state organization controlled by business leaders, exerted effective control (Cuff 1973; Skowronek 1982). But the World War I pattern would not be repeated during World War II. The U.S. ascent to hegemony followed a path in which the state secured the resources to pursue geopolitical goals in exchange for a generous accommodation with the dominant class at home (Tilly 1990). Despite its generosity toward and dependence upon leading firms, the U.S. state built and maintained the world's most potent military organization.

On the eve of World War II, monopoly sector firms were powerful enough to exercise a de facto veto over a number of state policies. Executives from these firms played a prominent role in the legislative and executive branches of the state. However, these firms did not exert control over economic governance comparable to the role played by Japan's *zaibatsu*. In the United States, antimonopoly laws played a decisive role in preventing the reemergence of large trusts that had dominated financial, industrial, and transportation sectors in the late 19th and early 20th Centuries (see Campbell and Lindberg 1990). The fragmentation of the capitalist class was complemented by the fragmentation of the U.S. state. Power was dispersed between the federal government and the many states, and the Constitution's checks and balances distributed specific powers among the executive, legislative, and judicial branches of the federal government.

The unevenness of economic and political power was manifest in the defense industries. Although the prewar U.S. produced few weapons, the state was far more influential, and monopoly sector firms less so, in the production of aircraft, ammunition, and other military goods. A positive sum mobilization for World War II was made possible by the fragmentation of political and economic power and the U.S.'s advantageous geopolitical situation. The raw materials needed for pursuing commercial profitability and military autarky were largely located in territory the U.S. had secured decades before. Delegating a measure of the state's power to leading firms to secure and process strategically important raw materials did not jeopardize national security goals. Conversely, the expansion of a national security state, including direct state management of a network of weapons production facilities, threatened neither the profitability nor the autonomy of civilian-oriented monopoly sector firms.

To fully appreciate the strength of the U.S. state, the emphasis must be placed upon its infrastructural power. A state's infrastructural power is bounded by the size of the economy it controls. As noted above, the World War II Japanese state was clearly more despotic than its American counterpart, but this despotism did not and could not compensate for its geopolitical and natural resource disadvantages. By contrast, the U.S. state wielded far greater infrastructural powers. During World War II, a technologically demanding war of industrial attrition, the infrastructural powers made possible by the U.S. state's earlier conquests and subsequent economic growth proved decisive in determining the outcome of the war and the subsequent transformation of the two states.

CASE STUDIES OF THE ALUMINUM INDUSTRY

Case studies of aluminum production in Japan and the United States shed light on the different dimensions of power and of the historically specific paths available to warring states. Tilly (1990) makes a compelling case that a state's choices are conditioned by the lack or availability of resources in its environment. Specifically, a state with limited economic resources under its control is tempted to compensate by mobilizing the means of coercion. The World War II Japanese state was very much constrained by the comparatively meager resources it could muster for a war of industrial attrition. As the following case study of aluminum reveals, the Japanese state could not overcome a deficit in infrastructural power by intensifying its despotism. In fact, the crisis in raw materials brought about a relative decline in the state's ability to control economic processes.

The United States, on the other hand, followed a very different trajectory. By virtue of early industrialization and its earlier conquests over Indian nations and Mexico, the United States was rich in raw materials and capital resources. While converting despotic power into economic resources proved to be impossible for Japan, the United States successfully converted its access to raw materials and capital into military power. As the contrasting case study of the U.S. reveals, the state was able to direct the activities of private producers to an unprecedented degree. The U.S. state never threatened to displace or permanently subordinate leading aluminum producers, nor did it claim the sweeping, despotic powers of the Japanese state. Nevertheless, due to its advantageous access to economic resources, the U.S. state exercised greater control over aluminum production than its Japanese counterpart. Thus, while the Japanese state became less intrusive and ultimately more civilianized, the U.S. became more interventionist and militarized.

Japanese Aluminum Production

The development of a Japanese empire was set in motion by the global political-economic environment of the late 19th Century and the modernization trajectory Japanese leaders selected. Japan was a resource poor country that needed raw materials to fuel its industrial and military expansion. Not only did Japan borrow military and industrial technologies from the West, it also mimicked the West's acquisition of colonies to gain access to raw materials. Aluminum, which is manufactured from bauxite ore, became an important material for military weapons production in the early 20th Century, especially in aircraft. Along with petroleum, bauxite became one of the indispensable raw materials for fighting the Second World War. No significant deposits of either of these raw materials have ever been found in the Japanese islands, and access to bauxite was especially limited. At the beginning of the war with the United States, stockpiles of petroleum products totalled two years of estimated consumption, but stockpiles of bauxite existed for only nine months production (USSBS 1946).

Nippon Keikin Seizou was the first private firm to successfully produce aluminum in Japan. However, due to global shortages of necessary inputs (i.e., cryolite and carbon) during World War I, no Japanese firms developed a full-scale production line at that time (Ishikawa 1975). In addition, domestic demand was not substantial and aluminum could always be imported, particularly from the United States. Table 1 reveals that aluminum imports grew during the late 1920s and the U.S. was, for a short time, Japan's primary source.

Table 1. Japanese Aluminum Imports: 1927-1933

Year	Total Imports	Imports from U.S.	Percentage of U.S. to Total
1927	99,659	25,459	25.55
1928	155,613	59,916	38.50
1929	205,022	108,500	52.92
1930	195,127	40,541	20.78
1931	89,907	2,387	2.65
1932	138,084	11,454	8.29
1933	120,646	1,143	9.47

Source: *Tōyō Keizai Shinpō*, 1936.

In 1929, Japan imported over 200,000 piculs (1 picul equals 132 to 133 pounds) of aluminum, with over half coming from the United States. Beginning with 1930, the year of the London Naval Conference and the passage of the Smoot-Hawley Tariff, both overall imports and those from the United States began to drop. By 1931, the year that Japan invaded Manchuria (Halliday 1975), Japanese aluminum imports had dropped significantly and imports from the U.S. had become negligible.

In 1934, following the precedent established by other economic development policies, the Japanese government began to push private industry to initiate full-scale aluminum production. In part, Japan had attacked Manchuria to gain access to aluminum shale and other raw materials. When other countries restricted Japanese access to basic materials in response to its aggression in Manchuria, the Japanese government declared the expansion of domestic aluminum production capacity to be imperative. Nichiman Aluminum first began producing aluminum in 1935, followed by Sumitomo Aluminum in 1936 (Ishikawa 1975). As was the case in most areas of industrial production, firms associated with the *zaibatsu* carved out a prominent role in aluminum and related metals production, particularly the Sumitomo, Mitsui and Mitsubishi *zaibatsu* (GHQ-SCAP 1951).

Although the state did play a direct role in producing aluminum in Manchuria, it did not do so within Japan. Instead, private firms were responsible for domestic aluminum fabrication. By 1937, Japanese firms were producing 31,000 tons of aluminum, an output level equal to 250 percent of aluminum imports (Table 2). Only the scarcity of bauxite ore constrained the further expansion of the aluminum industry. In 1937, Japan imported slightly over 100,000 tons of bauxite ore, of which nearly half came from Dutch controlled Indonesia and another quarter from British controlled Malaysia (Table 3).

Table 2. Sources of Japanese Aluminum Supply

Fiscal Year	Production of Alumina			Production of Aluminum Ingots	Imports[b]	Total Aluminum Supply
	From Bauxite	From other Bauxite[a]	Total Alumina			
1933	—	100	100	19	3,549	3,568
1934	—	2,424	2,424	1,002	5,227	6,229
1935	—	7,434	7,434	3,166	10,949	14,115
1936	—	13,167	13,167	5,707	10,241	15,948
1937	24,316	7,181	31,497	13,979	13,701	27,680
1939	53,956	11,240	65,196	29,559	36,701	66,260
1940	81,837	15,650	97,487	40,863	NA	NA
1941	136,837	15,046	151,883	71,740	NA	NA
1942	212,558	13,623	226,181	103,075	2,000	105,075
1943	304,734	13,757	318,491	141,084	3,000	144,603
1944	190,585	34,626	225,211	110,398	4,205	114,603
1945	1,621	14,598	16,219	6,647	1,070	7,717

Source: USSBS 1946; Appendix C.

"NA" indicates data not available.

[a] Includes production from aluminour shale, alum-clay, alunite, and scrap.

[b] 1942-45 imports obtained from Manchukuo only.

Table 3. Japanese Imports of Bauxite: 1936-1945

Year	Total	Indonesia	India	Indo-China	Greece	Malayan Union	Palau
1936	24,762	9,192	6,380	0	8,232	958	—
1937	101,149	46,663	10,510	0	15,992	27,984	—
1938	220,478	117,269	7,809	0	15,240	76,505	3,655
1939	352,458	202,081	0	0	31,693	104,692	13,887
1940	280,189	194,729	0	0	0	62,965	22,495
1941	146,711	58,059	0	3,215	0	26,140	59,297
1942	344,187	274,449	0	0	0	55,831	13,907
1943	818,084	594,589	0	0	0	138,555	34,940
1944	337,335	177,782	0	0	0	55,065	4,488
1945	1,800	1,800	0	0	0	0	0

Source: GHQ 1951.

This placed Japan in a very precarious position and helps explain why Southeast Asia became a prime target for Japanese expansion in 1941.

As noted in Table 2, production of aluminum and aluminum supplies increased steadily until 1943. Nevertheless, these production levels were never sufficient to meet the demands of aircraft producers, and ultimately the Army and the Navy. Japan's difficulties were compounded by its reliance on transoceanic shipping to import bauxite ore. Shipping was disrupted by the Allied sea-air blockade, and became especially unreliable after the Allies invaded the Philippines. In 1944, imports and production levels declined precipitously, forcing the government to reserve 100 percent of all aluminum supplies for aircraft production (USSBS 1947a and 1947b).

Between 1936 and 1945, as military imperatives mounted and Japan's strategic position declined, effective state "control" over aluminum production declined. Until the United States entered the war, planning for light metals production was performed by the Cabinet Planning Board and administered by the Light Metals Bureau of the Ministry of Commerce and Industry. The Light Metals Control Association, a *voluntary* industrial association until 1942, administered the government's plans (USSBS 1947a). In 1943, the Cabinet Planning Board and the Ministry of Commerce and Industry were replaced by the new Ministry of Munitions which centralized economic planning (Halliday 1975; Rice 1979). However, even as the state moved to centralize control over the planning process, it never threatened to acquire aluminum producing firms. Instead, the government provided subsidies to promote aluminum production through the Light Metals Control Co., a subsidiary of the Light Metals Control Association (USSBS 1947a).

Despite the Japanese state's uncontested despotic powers at home, it failed to consolidate its access to raw materials through international aggression, and did not use its powers to displace the owners and managers of leading firms. The civilian state apparatus, the military and big business continued to fight amongst themselves. The creation of the Munitions Industry was a desperate response to Japan's rapidly deteriorating raw material situation that failed to resolve conflicts between the civilian government, the military and business. Moreover, the creation of this agency did not shift power toward the state, nor did the state "achieve the tight economic control it sought because it remained ultimately dependent on the managerial talent and productive capacity of the private sector" (Rice 1979, p. 692).

Aluminum Production in the United States

In the U.S. experience, economic preeminence preceded and served as the foundation for military supremacy (Kennedy 1987). The United States became one of the world's leading economic powers years before World War II. The war contributed to a spectacular jump in U.S. economic leadership, putting it into a class by itself (Milward 1977; Rostow 1978). The example of aluminum procurement provides evidence that when a state exercises dominion over a large and dynamic economy, it can extract unmatched resources while negotiating an attractive compromise with leading corporations (Tilly 1990). In the prewar period, the U.S. state did not own significant manufacturing assets in this industry and played no direct role in guiding production. In fact, the Aluminum Company of America (ALCOA) maintained a monopoly position in the primary aluminum industry despite antitrust legislation and the Attorney General's repeated challenges (Stein 1952; Stone 1941; Wiltse 1946).

Although the Japanese state was far more intrusive than its American counterpart, the American state was far more powerful. United States firms accounted for a major share of world production in the 1930s and dwarfed their Japanese counterparts (Milward 1977). Before the war, the United States relied on domestic and South American (Surinam) sources of bauxite. The competition for transoceanic shipping and the effectiveness of German submarine warfare in 1942 and 1943 sharply reduced the supply and the reliability of bauxite shipments from Surinam. The United States enjoyed the alternative of turning to domestic supplies of bauxite that were abundant but relatively more expensive and consumed far more energy to process. Whereas Japan conquered other nations to gain access to strategic materials, the U.S. state financed the expansion of mining and smelting operations to exploit domestic supplies. While the Japanese conquered Malay and Indonesia to gain access to bauxite, the United States developed domestic sources concentrated in Arkansas, territory taken from American Indians 100 years earlier. Thus, by virtue of its earlier despotism, the American state was able to rapidly expand bauxite and aluminum production during World War II. The United States consumed approximately 126,000 tons of bauxite *per month* in the summer of 1941. However, in 1943, "Arkansas production reached a record level of more than 697,000 tons in August" and imports exceeded 300,000 tons per month (Wiltse 1946, p. 205). At the war's peak, the United States extracted from domestic sources more bauxite each month than the Japanese could acquire in a year. Consequently U.S. firms quadrupled the output of aluminum products, especially those needed for aircraft production (Wiltse 1946, p. 347).

While the United States government did not enter the war in a position to intervene in the production process, it could exercise authority over exports of raw materials and finished goods (Barnhart 1987). As tensions mounted in the 1930s, the U.S. state insured that sales of aluminum to Japan declined absolutely and relatively. Whereas the United States supplied over half of all Japanese aluminum imports in 1929, the U.S. share fell below 20 percent in

1931 and was negligible by 1933 as a result of a deliberate policy to control the flow of this strategically important resource to Japan (Barnhart 1987). All-out mobilization for World War II pushed the U.S. state beyond export controls and the extraction of this vital resource from private firms. During the course of mobilization, the government invested in such a staggering portfolio of capital equipment and factories that it owned an estimated 40 percent of the nation's capital assets by 1945, and actively participated in the production process (Hooks 1991, 1993; White 1980). In the aluminum industry, the state owned the majority of the assets by the war's end (U.S. Smaller War Plants Corporation 1946; Wiltse 1946). Private firms leased these plants from the state for a nominal fee to fulfill the state's munitions requirements.

This is not to suggest that World War II ushered in an era of statist management in the U.S. aluminum industry. In expanding aluminum production, representatives of the Federal Government met with the chairman of Alcoa behind closed doors and developed a plan that displayed a "strange solicitude for Alcoa's market position" and its profits (White 1980, pp. 42-3; see also *Fortune Magazine* 1941). During the war, Alcoa grew larger and more profitable by operating government-owned plants. At the war's end, the state sold emergency war plants to private firms at very attractive prices. In a successful effort to break-up Alcoa's monopoly, sales to Alcoa were restricted while sales to Kaiser Aluminum and Reynolds Aluminum were facilitated (Stein 1952). The state also reserved the authority to take control of privately-held aluminum facilities in future emergencies.

Negotiated accommodation emphasizes the positive sum character of state-led war mobilizations (Tilly 1990). This concept makes it possible to avoid myopic concentration on states or firms in isolation of one another. Clearly, mobilization for World War II gave birth to the military-industrial complex in the U.S. (Hooks 1991). For those who emphasize the nation's postwar militarism, mobilization initiated that militarization (see for example, Melman 1970, 1985). From this vantage point, the state's ownership of aluminum production facilities, its wartime control over the production and distribution of aluminum, and its influence over postwar aluminum manufacture are offered as evidence of increasingly statist economic governance. But an insistence on the growth of state power at the expense of the private sector obscures the very real benefits that flowed to leading businesses. In fact, many observers believe that the World War II mobilization and the creation of a military-industrial complex were carried out by and for the nation's largest corporations. In this tradition, the emphasis is placed upon the role of business leaders in federal planning agencies and on the great profits earned by leading corporations, including aluminum producers (Bernstein 1967, 1968; Domhoff 1992). However, the insistence on corporations winning at the state's expense obscures the important transformation of economic governance that entrenched state agencies in economic activities directly related to waging war. Rather than exaggerating either the power of the state or of corporations, negotiated accommodation allows for a positive sum outcome in which the state secures the resources and cooperation to pursue geopolitical objectives through the generous accommodation of leading corporations.

AIRCRAFT PRODUCTION

The following comparison of aircraft production develops two points. First, the lack of inputs to the aircraft industry, including aluminum, severely strained the Japanese planning effort, fueled infighting among the civilian government, military, and *zaibatsu,* and contributed to instability in administrative arrangements. Conversely, the far more favorable position enjoyed by the U.S. state and its aircraft producers facilitated the routinization of wartime planning agencies. This second point of contrast helps clarify how states and firms interact with each other. The increasingly overburdened Japanese state failed to exert effective centralized control over industrial planning. Instead, this despotic state had to depend upon the infrastructural power of the *zaibatsu* affiliated firms for aircraft manufacture. In contrast, the U.S. state dramatically expanded its ability to influence economic activity, especially in the defense industries. Aviation firms grew larger during World War II, but remained dependent on the state for capital and sales. As a consequence, in the course of creating a military-industrial complex, the United States was routinizing an unprecedented degree of state-led economic planning in the aircraft and other defense industries.

Japan

The Japanese government never played a direct role in manufacturing aircraft. The aircraft industry was not born until the 1920s, by which time large Japanese industrial firms were well established. Thus, the government was not obliged to jump-start the formation of an aircraft industry, it merely needed to encourage it. For example, Nakajima Aircraft was Japan's first aircraft production firm. Founded in 1917 and destined to be the largest Japanese aviation firm during the war (Table 4), Nakajima Aircraft sold most of its planes to the military and utilized the Mitsui Trading Company as a trading agent and a source of capital (Hadley 1970).

As Mitsubishi Heavy Industries and Nakajima Aircraft were the principal aircraft producers, the World War II Japanese aircraft industry was dominated

Table 4. Major Japanese Wartime Aircraft Producers

	Date of Founding	Military Connection	Maker of Complete Combat Aircraft	% Aircraft Production 1941-1945
Nakajima Aircraft[a]	1917	Army & Navy	Yes	28.0
Mitsubishi Heavy Industries	1920	Army & Navy	Yes	17.9
Kawasaki Aircraft Industries	1918	Army	Yes	11.8
Tachikawa Aircraft	1924	Army	Yes	9.5
Aichi Aircraft[b]	1920	Navy	Yes	5.2
Kyushu Airplane	1919	Navy	Yes	3.7
Japan Int'l Aircraft Industries[c]	1941	Army & Navy	No	3.1
Kawanishi Aircraft[a]	1928	Navy	No	1.9
Ishikawajima Aircraft Industries	1937	Army & Navy	No[e]	—
Fuji Airplane[d]	1939	Army & Navy	No	1.2
Showa Airplane	1939	Navy	No	0.9
Mitaka Aircraft Industries	1936	Army & Navy	No	—
Hitachi Aircraft	1939	Army (Navy after 1941	No	2.6
Army Air Arsenal	1941	Army	No	1.4
Navy Air Depots	1941	Navy	Yes	2.4

Source: Corporation reports of the U.S. Strategic Bombing Survey.

[a] These two firms were taken over by the Munitions Industry in 1945. [b] Began making planes in 1920 as Aichi Electric. Founded as Aichi Aircraft in 1943. [c] Merger of Japan Air Industries and Int'l Aircraft. [d] Spin-off of Nakajima Aircraft. [e] Except for one type of trainer aircraft.

by firms affiliated with two of the largest *zaibatsu*. These corporations recognized the economic potential in a new, high technology industry where government sales accounted for a significant percentage of their profit. In turn, the government, including the Army and the Navy, allowed these firms to take the initiative in developing the aircraft industry. "From the early days of the industry, the Army and Navy had placed primary responsibility for engine development and research upon the private manufacturing companies, and not the arsenals" (USSBS 1947b, p. 16). Indeed, the Army and Navy did not produce their own aircraft until 1941, and direct military production never accounted for a significant share of combat aircraft production (Table 4).

As the 1930s progressed and the war in China expanded, the demand for war material and government policies to stimulate production of these goods grew. The *junsenji keizai*, or "quasi-wartime economy" began in February 1936 (Cohen 1949). The government developed a five year plan in 1936, but it took two years before the implementation of this plan began. The delay in implementation was the result of various public and private sector interests demanding a consideration of their perspectives and in finalizing the plan (Inoue et al. 1989). The *junsenji keizai* did not challenge the prominence of the two leading industrial giants in aircraft production. Table 4 lists five corporations that were founded in the late 1930s in the aircraft industry. It is notable that these five firms a) accounted for only 4.5 percent of all aircraft production in Japan between 1941 and 1945, b) did not produce finished combat aircraft, c) were dependent on the government for capital and machinery, and d) supplied parts to the dominant aircraft makers. For example, Ishikawajima Aircraft received 30 percent of its machinery from the government as well as loans from government banks (USSBS 1947d), while Showa Airplane was founded by former Nakajima employees and produced subassemblies for Nakajima (USSBS 1947c). Both Showa Airplane and Nakajima Aircraft were tied to Mitsui interests (USSBS 1947e). Thus, even after the war with the United States began, the state stimulated aircraft production by mobilizing private sector subcontractors to allow the *zaibatsu* affiliated firms to expand their productive capabilities (USSBS 1946; Yamazaki 1991).

Japanese policies succeeded in expanding aircraft production. Nakajima Aircraft, the industry leader, rapidly increased its manufacture of airframes and engines during the war years (Table 5). The Japanese aircraft industry nearly doubled its production of planes and engines between 1942 and 1943, a remarkable accomplishment given the shortages of labor, materials, and heavy machinery. These increases notwithstanding, Japan could not keep up with the United States and the consumption of scarce raw materials by aircraft producers compounded raw material shortages and production bottlenecks throughout the economy. As Japan's military situation deteriorated, so did the

Table 5. Nakajima Aircraft Co. Ltd. Engine and Mainframe Production

Year	Engines			Airframes		
	Capacity	Ordered	Production	Capacity	Ordered	Production
1939	2,895	—	2,538	2,400	—	1,187
1940	3,680	—	3,195	2,220	—	785
1941	4,345	—	3,990	1,917	846	916
1942	5,990	—	4,897	3,008	2,635	2,215
1943	12,640	9,655	9,558	5,699	4,782	4,646
1944	20,100	21,175	14,014	10,634	9,896	7,896
1945	8,505	15,710	3,983	6,342	8,217	4,019

Source: U.S. Strategic Bombing Survey, 1947. *Nakajima Aircraft Co. Ltd.* (June), Corporation Report No. II.

debilitating competition among government ministries, between the Army and Navy, among firms, and between the public and private sector for access to raw materials and finished products. The struggle over war mobilization policy was particularly acute between the military and the *zaibatsu*, a struggle that centered on the creation and authority of the Munitions Ministry.

> The Ministry did not actually begin to function in the industrial sphere until January 14, 1944, when it designated the first set of munitions companies under provisions of the Munitions Company Act. Only then was it disclosed that the War and Navy Offices had been putting up a last fight behind the scenes before surrendering their administrative authority over aircraft production to the Munitions Ministry. . . . At the outset of the struggle, the Army and Navy Ministries were in a strong position by virtue of the administrative authority over aircraft production which they possessed. The primary issue, however, was that the two Ministries, in order to expand plane output, would have had to subject to their detailed control the great sectors of industry that were eventually mobilized to do the job in 1944. The size of the corporations involved, embracing the industrial giants of Japan, and the enormous political and economic power wielded by these combines, made them far too big a chunk for the military and naval leaders to swallow. . . . In the struggle, Japan's business interests did not in any way permit their determination to be swayed by the fact that their nation was confronted with the greatest military crisis in its history. . . . Higher profits for the *zaibatsu* represented one of the major issues at stake in the struggle over the Munitions Ministry (Bisson 1945, pp. 133-136, 139).

Developments in the Japanese aircraft industry run counter to the received view of the militaristic and despotic Japanese state forcing all its subjects to follow orders. Nor do developments in this sector conform to a vision of a unified military and *zaibatsu* working in concert toward the same goals. Rather, military and business interests competed for control. In the 1930s and the early 1940s, the military enjoyed great influence. However, even at the apex of the military's power, highly diversified industrial firms controlled aircraft production and distribution. Because these firms maintained infrastructural power, they could not be replaced. While it is true that a small number of firms, including Nakajima Aircraft, were eventually placed under nominal government control (USSBS 1947c), this was more a sign of a weakened state playing out its role in a disintegrating socioeconomic environment. Nakajima Aircraft was not taken over by the Munitions Industry until April 1, 1945, less than five months before the end of the war.

U.S. Aircraft Production

To shape economic development, the state must wield potent policy tools and private firms must be asymmetrically dependent (Pfeffer and Salancik 1978) on the resources at the state's command. The aviation industry represents a case in which the U.S. state's interests and resources were concentrated and the firms were demonstrably dependent upon the state for capital and for sales (Millis 1956, 306-07; Rae 1968, Chapter 9). In 1939, the aviation industry produced $244 million and generated $30 million in profits. During World War II, these figures were $8,204 million and $133 million respectively. However, in 1946 the industry produced only $711 million worth of equipment and lost $13 million (Finletter Commission [1947] 1972, pp. 187-88).

In aviation, as was the case in other defense industries, the Armed Services directly financed industrial expansion. Private lenders hesitated to fund the expansion of defense industries because the latter depended on Government orders. More important than the private sector's hesitancy, the military took advantage of the World War II mobilization to create a permanent munitions production capacity. The Armed Services feared a repetition of the post-World War I demobilization "which saw the complete scrapping of munitions plants. . . . Outright government ownership would furnish the best guarantee that specialized munitions capacity would be preserved" (Smith 1959, p. 497). The precedent of Government-owned munitions facilities was established well before World War II, i.e., the Navy's shipyards and the Army's arsenals. However, the scope of the military's investments and the commitment to maintaining a diverse munitions production base during peacetime changed dramatically during the Second World War. The military officers' distrust of market mechanisms led them to pursue statist solutions (Janowitz 1971). The military's desire for direct state control of defense production facilities extended beyond "traditional" defense industries such as ordnance production and shipyards to include the new and glamorous aircraft industry.

It is difficult to overestimate the importance of the World War II mobilization to the aviation industry (Hooks 1990, 1991; Rae 1968; USSWPC 1946). During World War II, the private sector supplied only 11 percent of the capital consumed in the 17-fold expansion of aircraft industry production. Further, the military used a variety of progressive payment mechanisms to provide wartime defense contractors with working capital (A.D. Little 1963). The long- and short-term financial instruments embedded in the procurement process offered far more attractive rates and terms than available in private capital markets. To gain access to these resources, aviation firms were obliged to successfully bid for and satisfactorily complete defense contracts. When the borrower is asymmetrically dependent for financing it is vulnerable to external influence and control. In this manner, the state developed enduring relationships with firms willing to forego autonomy in exchange for the opportunity to work on lucrative procurement contracts. The war enabled defense firms, especially aircraft producers, to become "big businesses" (USSWPC 1946). But in contrast to civilian sectors, this expansion was only possible if the firms accepted dependent and clientelistic relationship with the state, more specifically with the Pentagon.

Monopoly sector firms opposed direct Federal financing and successfully lobbied for a regulation that required defense contractors to exhaust private sources before turning to governmental financing (White 1980). In contrast, aviation firms energetically sought defense contracts and readily accepted the governmental dependence that went with them. As the Douglass Corporation official quoted below indicates, aviation firms resented the delays imposed while going through the motion of seeking private financing. "I don't give a damn about Government title. If the Government puts up the money it seems to me it ought to have title. As I see the situation, if the country is going socialistic when the defense program is over, Douglass can't stop it by contract. . . . As far as I am concerned, I don't give a damn what Congress does . . . if the Defense Commission will only let us go ahead . . ." (quoted in Durr 1952, p. 304).

The aircraft industry was at the core of the emerging military-industrial complex. During World War II, the value of aircraft assets increased by a factor of 17 and transformed the aircraft industry into the nation's largest by the war's end. In 1939 there were 49,000 wage earners in this industry, by 1945 there were 1,240,000. After World War II, a vast portfolio of industrial facilities were transferred to the Pentagon and provided the material foundation of the military-industrial complex. The Air Force was committed to maintaining the world's largest and most sophisticated aircraft industry in the postwar period (Smith 1970, p. 106). To that end, the Air Force took control of industrial facilities throughout 1945 and 1946 without formal approval. The "National Industrial Reserve Act legalized this program in 1947" and provided funding. By 1949, the Air Force controlled "some 50,000 machine tools and 26 Government-owned manufacturing plants" (Snyder 1956, p. 16). By 1955, the Air Force was in possession of 30 industrial facilities (U.S. Department of the Air Force 1956), and the Navy claimed another 14 aircraft factories (U.S. Department of the Navy 1956).

Thus, during the course of World War II, the Pentagon translated its authority to make wartime investments into a portfolio of munitions facilities that would provide a peacetime production capability. This did not constitute centralized control over the Federal bureaucracy and the private sector that overly monolithic views of the "military industrial complex" envision, but it does indicate how potent and self-sufficient the Pentagon became. After the war, aircraft firms not only continued to rely on the state, but this dependence was so extreme that between 1939 and 1955, "no aircraft company [sought] public financing," and "no airliner program of any size [had] been developed without some military aid" (Quinn 1960, pp. 324 and 330). In the early 1950s, the Department of Defense owned 63 percent of all plant and equipment, and it still owned over half of the industry's assets in 1961 (Stanford Research Institute 1963).

The Air Force had an overriding interest in maintaining an aircraft industry "that could do aggressive research and development work, produce the military aircraft essential for preserving peace, and expand quickly in case of war" (Snyder 1956, p. 14). However, if left to their own resources and civilian markets, the struggling aircraft firms could not produce aircraft in quantity, let alone pursue research and development. "Here is a rather different view of the 'military-industrial' complex, for instead of industry insisting on a large air force, the [USAF] planners were insisting on a large aircraft industry to insure that the anticipated mobilization and development needs in military aviation could be met by the aircraft industry" (Smith 1970, p. 106). Military planners not only had an agenda for this industry, they controlled resources indispensable to the survival of aeronautics firms.

The Pentagon's expansion into the aircraft industry did not spark protests from the private sector. Aircraft firms were much larger than they had been prior to the war, but they remained dependent on the Federal Government for their survival. They lacked the funds to purchase these plants after the war, as well as customers for aircraft. The acquisition of these plants by the Air Force and Navy did not run counter to the interests of these client firms, it represented a necessary but not a sufficient condition for their survival. When and if demand for military aircraft returned, these firms could hope to secure contracts in manufacturing facilities owned by the Armed Services. When assessing the relationship between the state and aviation firms in 1960, the Stanford Research Institute concluded that: The preponderance of bargaining strength in the [relationship] is clearly on the government's side. Its strength comes through control of funds, definition of goals, timing and technique, encouragement of competition, participation in management, the application of political pressures, and power to terminate contracts and retroactively to reduce prices and profits" (Stanford Research Institute 1963, p. 34).

Developments in the aviation industry draw attention to the statebuilding that occurred as the United States became the reigning hegemonic power. Although civilian agencies remained bureaucratically weak, military agencies grew more powerful over this period. The military was able to guide

World War II mobilization by directing the flow of investments and procurement contracts. This administrative insulation and budgetary authority permitted the Pentagon to gain control of a vast industrial portfolio at the war's end. The scope and diversity of these permanent acquisitions have been without precedent in the nation's history. Nevertheless, these acquisitions were made without securing new administrative authority and sparked little controversy. Even as the United States demobilized at the end of the war, the Pentagon acquired the production facilities at the heart of the military-industrial complex and the administrative authority to operate them in peacetime.

CONCLUSION

Examining warmaking is essential to developing a nuanced and holistic understanding of the state. World War II developments played a decisive role in the Japanese state's shift from an intrusive militaristic state to a less intrusive and commercially-oriented postwar state. The American Occupation aggressively demilitarized Japanese society after the war. More interestingly, although the various attempts to coordinate economic production in Japan had failed, they did create an environment that reinforced ties between governmental bureaucrats and business managers. In the course of destroying the formal *zaibatsu* organizational structures while revitalizing Japan's economy as part of its early Cold War strategy (Deyo 1987), the U.S. state made a major contribution to the rebirth of an activist Japanese state, geared towards the promotion of commercial, rather than military, economic development.

Conversely, the wartime and postwar U.S. state concentrated its intrusiveness in defense industries while avoiding commercially-oriented economic planning and criticizing "statist" intrusions in other nations. This rhetorical confusion notwithstanding, the U.S. state played a pivotal role in providing industrial finance and technological leadership, and guaranteeing demand for the output, especially at the critical early stages of growth in the aircraft and microelectronics sectors that served as the U.S.'s "sunrise" industries (Hooks 1990). Thus, to understand the distinctive and confusing character of the U.S. state, the wartime creation of the military-industrial complex and the U.S. state's postwar role as the hegemonic power must be central concerns.

The differences in the roles played by the contemporary Japanese and American states in their domestic economies, and in particular the presence of an articulated industrial policy in Japan, can not be understood without reference to their respective war mobilization experiences. Of course, the history of the active involvement of the Japanese state in promoting economic development began long before World War II. From the Meiji era onward, the Japanese state, in an attempt to play industrial catchup, encouraged investment and technology transfer in "key" industries, which for the most part came to be owned and managed by private capital. A direct consequence of war mobilization in Japan, including its ultimate failure and the loss of the war, was the civilianization of the Japanese political economy, with government bureaucrats and business managers playing a pivotal role.

In the United States, on the other hand, industrial policy has never been accepted by certain political elements as being ideologically acceptable. From the 19th Century on, private capital played the dominant role in forging economic development. Yet, mobilization for the Second World War served to militarize the American political economy, helping to create the military-industrial complex. In the decades that followed, a "wall of separation" was built that divides the economy between industrial sectors whose creation and growth have been heavily dependent on government financial and other resources, such as the semiconductor industry, and those where government involvement is eschewed, save in exceptional circumstances, such as the Chrysler bailout (Markusen and Yudken 1992).

The irony is that, despite the received notion of Japan being a strong state and the U.S. being a weak one, the effect of their participation in the Second World War has been to make them appear to be more similar. The power of the Japanese state, and in particular its despotic power, was severely weakened by this war. On the other hand, the power of the U.S. state, and in particular it's infrastructural power, was strengthened. The enormous cultural differences between these two societies notwithstanding, it appears that some convergence has taken place. Perhaps this is one factor that helps to explain the curious nature of the U.S./Japan postwar relationship, one that in many dimensions resembles sibling rivalry.

References

A.D. Little, Inc. 1963. *How Sick is the Defense Industry?* Cambridge, MA: Arthur D. Little, Inc.

Amemiya Shōichi. 1976. "Gaikō Chōsakai no rekishiteki kinō to ichi" (The historical function and position of the Foreign Policy Research Association). *Shisō* 622: 103-125.

Barnhart, Michael. 1987. *Japan Prepares for Total War. The Search for Economic Security, 1919-1941*. Ithaca: Cornell University Press.

Bernstein, Barton. 1967. "The Debate on Industrial Reconversion: The Protection of Oligopoly and Military Control of the Economy." *The American Journal of Economics and Sociology* 26(2): 159-72.

_____ 1968. "America in War and Peace: The Test of Liberalism." In *Towards a New Past: Dissenting Essays in American History*, ed. B. Bernstein. New York: Pantheon.

Bisson, T.A. 1945. *Japan's War Economy*. New York: The MacMillan Company.

Bisson, T.A. 1954. *Zaibatsu Dissolution in Japan*. Berkeley and Los Angeles: University of California Press.

Block, Fred. 1987. *Revising State Theory*. Philadelphia: Temple University Press.

Blum, John V. 1976. *V Was for Victory: Politics and American Culture during World War II*. New York: Harcourt Brace Jovanovich.

Campbell, John, and Leon Lindberg. 1990. "Property Rights and the Organization of Economic Activity by the State." *American Sociological Review* 55(5):634-647.

Caporaso, James. 1989. "Introduction: The State in Comparative and International Perspective." Pp. 7-16 in *The Elusive State*, ed. J. Caporaso. Newbury Park, CA: Sage.

Cohen, Jerome B. 1949. *Japan's Economy in War and Reconstruction*. Minneapolis: University of Minnesota Press.

Cuff, Robert. 1973. *The War Industries Board, Business-government Relations During World War I*. Baltimore, John Hopkins University Press.

Cusumano, Michael A. 1985. *The Japanese Automobile Industry*. Cambridge, MA: Harvard University Press.

Deyo, Frederick, C. 1987. *The Political Economy of the New Asian Industrialism*. Ithaca, NY: Cornell University Press.

Domhoff, G. William. 1992. "American State Autonomy Via the Military? Another Counterattack on a Theoretical Delusion." *Critical Sociology* 18:21-56.

Dore, Ronald. 1986. *Flexible Rigidities*. Stanford: Stanford University Press.

Durr, Clifford. 1952. "The Defense Plant Corporation." In *Public Administration and Policy Development*, ed. H. Stein. New York: Harcourt, Brace and Co.

Finletter Commission. [1947] 1972. "Survival in the Air Age." In *The Military-Industrial Complex*, ed. C. W. Pursell Jr. New York: Harper & Row.

Fortune Magazine. 1941. "The War Goes to Mr. Jones." December.

Friedman, David. 1988. *The Misunderstood Miracle*. Ithaca, NY: Cornell University Press.

General Headquarters Supreme Commander for the Allied Powers. 1951. "History of the Nonmilitary Activities of the Occupation of Japan 1945 Through March 1950." Volume 15; Part B.

Gerschenkron, Alexander. 1962. *Economic Backwardness in Historical Perspective: A Book of Essays*. Cambridge, MA: Harvard University Press.

Giddens, Anthony. 1985. *The Nation-State and Violence*. Berkeley: University of California Press.

Hadley, Eleanor M. 1970. *Antitrust in Japan*. Princeton: Princeton University Press.

Halliday, Jon. 1975. *A Political History of Japanese Capitalism*. New York: Monthly Review Press.

Hirschmeier, Johannes and Tsunehiko Yui. 1981. *The Development of Japanese Business*. London: George Allen & Unwin Ltd.

Hooks, Gregory. 1990. "The Rise of the Pentagon & U.S. State Building: The Defense Program as Industrial Policy." *American Journal of Sociology* 96:358-404.

_____ 1991. *Forging the Military Industrial Complex: World War II's Battle of the Potomac*. Urbana & Chicago: University of Illinois Press.

_____ 1993. "The Weakness of Strong Theories: The U.S. State's Dominance of the World War II Investment Process." *American Sociological Review* 58:1-17.

Hooks, Gregory and Gregory McLauchlan. 1992. "The Institutional Foundation of Warmaking: Three Eras of U.S. Warmaking, 1939-1989." *Theory and Society*. 21:757-788.

Huntington, Samuel P. 1957. *The Soldier and the State. The Theory and Politics of Civil-Military Relations*. New York: Vintage Books.

Inoue, Mitsusada, Nagahara Keiji, Kodama Kōta and Ōkubo Toshi. 1989. *Nihon Rekishi Taikei* (An Outline of Japanese History) Tokyo: Yamakawa Publishers.

Ishikawa, Junkichi. 1975. *Kokka sōdōin shi*. (A History of National Mobilization: Volume 1.) Tokyo: Shimizu Publishing.

Janowitz, Morris. 1971. *The Professional Soldier. A Social and Political Portrait*. New York: The Free Press.

Johnson, Chalmers A. *MITI and The Japanese Miracle*. 1982. Stanford: Stanford University Press.

Kennedy, Paul. 1987. *The Rise and Fall of Great Powers*. New York: Random House.

Krasner, Stephen. 1978. "United States Commercial and Monetary Policy: Unravelling the Paradox of External Strength and Internal Weakness." In *Between Power and Plenty*, ed. P. Katzenstein. Madison, WI: University of Wisconsin Press.

Lasswell, Harold. 1937. "The Sino-Japanese Crisis: The Garrison State versus the Civilian State." *China Quarterly* 2643-649.

_____ 1941. "The Garrison State." *American Journal of Sociology* 46: 555-68.

Lockwood, William W. 1954. *The Economic Development of Japan*. Princeton: Princeton University Press.

Mann, Michael. 1984. "Capitalism and Militarism." Pp. 25-46 in *War; State, and Society*, edited by M. Shaw. London: MacMillan.

_____ 1988. "The Roots and Contradictions of Modern Militarism." Pp. 166-87 in *States, War, & Capitalism*. New York: Basil Blackwell.

Markusen, Ann, and Joel Yudken. 1992. *Dismantling the Cold War Economy*. New York: Basic Books.

Melman, Seymour. 1970. *Pentagon Capitalism: The Political Economy of War.* New York: McGraw Hill.

_____ 1985. *The Permanent War Economy: American Capitalism in Decline.* New York: Simon & Schuster.

Millis, Walter. 1956. *Arms and Men: A Study in American Military History.* New York: Capricorn Books.

Mills, C. Wright. 1956. *The Power Elite.* New York: Oxford University Press.

Milward, Alan. 1977. *War, Economy and Society, 1939-1945.* Berkeley: University of California Press.

Ohkawa, Kazushi. 1969. "Phases of Agricultural Development and Economic Growth," in Ohkawa, Johnston, and Kaneda (eds.), *Agriculture and Economic Growth: Japan's Experience.* Tokyo: University of Tokyo Press, pp. 3-36.

Okazaki, Tetsuji. 1993. "The Japanese Firm under the Wartime Planned Economy." *Journal of the Japanese and International Economies,* 7:175-203.

Okimoto, Daniel I. 1989. *Between MITI and the Market.* Stanford: Stanford University Press.

Ozawa, Terutomo. 1994. "Exploring the Asian Economic Miracle." The *Journal of Asian Studies,* 53(1):124-131.

Pfeffer, Jeffrey, and Gerald Salancik. 1978. *The External Control of Organizations: A Resource Dependence Perspective.* New York: Harper and Row.

Polenberg, Richard. 1972. *War and Society: The United States, 1941-1945.* Philadelphia: J.B. Lippincott.

Quadagno, Jill. 1992. "Social Movements and State Transformation: Labor Unions and Racial Conflict in the War on Poverty." *American Sociological Review* 57:616-34.

Quinn, James. 1960. "Aircraft." In *Investing in American Industries,* ed. L. Plum. New York: Harper & Brothers.

Rae, John. 1968. *Climb to Greatness: The American Aircraft Industry, 1920-1960.* Cambridge, MA: MIT Press.

Reischauer, Edwin O. and Albert M. Craig. 1978. *Japan: Tradition and Transformation.* Boston: Houghton Mifflin Company.

Rice, Richard. 1979. "Economic Mobilization in Wartime Japan: Business, Bureaucracy, and Military in Conflict." *Journal of Asian Studies* 38(4):689-706.

Roberts, John G. 1973. *Mitsui.* New York: John Weatherhill, Inc.

Rostow, Walt. 1978. *The World Economy: History and Prospect.* Austin: University of Texas Press.

Rueschemeyer, Deitrich, and Peter Evans. 1985. "The State and Economic Transformation: Toward an Analysis of the Conditions Underlying Effective Intervention." In *Bringing the State Back In,* ed. P. Evans, D. Rueschemeyer and T. Skocpol. New York: Cambridge University Press.

Shiozaki Hiroaki. 1979. "Tōseiha no keizai seisaku ideorogii" (The economic policy and ideology of the Control Faction). *Nenpō: Kindai Nihon kenkyū 1: Shōwa-ki no gunbu.* 96-121.

Skowronek, Stephen. 1982. *Building a New American State: The Expansion of National Administrative Capacities, 1877-1920.* New York: Cambridge University Press.

Smethurst, Richard J. 1974. *A Social Basis for Prewar Japanese Militarism.* Berkeley: University of California Press.

Smith, Perry McCoy. 1970. *The Air Force Plans for Peace, 1943-1945.* Baltimore: Johns Hopkins.

Smith, R. Elbertson. 1959. *The Army and Economic Mobilization.* Washington: U.S. Department of Defense.

Smith, Thomas C. 1988. *Native Sources of Japanese Industrialization: 1750-1920.* Berkeley: University of California Press.

Snyder, Clifford. 1956. *History of Production Problems during the Air Force Build-up, 1950-1954.* Wright-Patterson Air Force Base: Office of Information Services.

Stanford Research Institute. 1963. *The Industry-Government Aerospace Relationship.* Menlo Park, CA: Stanford Research Institute.

Stein, A., and B. Russett. 1980. "Evaluating War: Outcomes and Consequences." In *Handbook in Political Conflict: Theory and Research,* ed. T. Gurr. New York: Free Press.

Stein, Harold. 1952. "The Disposal of the Aluminum Plants." In *Public Administration and Policy Administration,* ed. H. Stein. New York: Harcourt Brace and Company.

Stone, I. F. 1941. *Business as Usual.* New York: Modern Age Books.

Tilly, Charles. 1990. *Coercion, Capital and European States, AD 990-1990.* New York: Basil Blackwell.

Tsunematsu, Seiji. 1966. "The Development of the Japanese Economy and the Burdens Laid on Agriculture." *Rural Economic Problems,* 3(1):28-42.

Tsurumi, Shunsuke. 1986. *An Intellectual History of Wartime Japan 1932-1945.* London: KPI Limited.

U.S. Department of the Air Force. 1956. *Inventory of Military Real Property.* Washington: National Archives, Record Group 330.

U.S. Department of the Navy. 1956. *Inventory of Military Real Property.* Washington: National Archives, Record Group 330.

U.S. Smaller War Plants Corporation. 1946. *Economic Concentration and World War II.* Washington: Government Printing Office.

U.S. Strategic Bombing Survey. 1946. *The Effects of Strategic Bombing on Japan's War Economy.* (#53) Washington, D.C.: Government Printing Office.

U.S. Strategic Bombing Survey. 1947a. *Coals and Metals in Japan's War Economy.* (#36) Washington, D.C.: Government Printing Office.

94

U.S. Strategic Bombing Survey. 1947b. *The Japanese Aircraft Industry*. Washington, D.C.: Government Printing Office.

U.S. Strategic Bombing Survey. 1947c. *The Japanese Aircraft Industry: Nakajima Aircraft*. (#17) Washington, D.C.: Government Printing Office.

U.S. Strategic Bombing Survey. 1947d. *The Japanese Aircraft Industry: Ishikawajima Aircraft*. (#28) Washington, D.C.: Government Printing Office.

U.S. Strategic Bombing Survey. 1947e. *The Japanese Aircraft Industry: Showa Airplane*. (#27) Washington, D.C.: Government Printing Office.

Vogel, David. 1978. "Why American Businessmen Mistrust their State." *British Journal of Political Science*, 8:45-78.

Weir, Margaret, and Theda Skocpol. 1985. "State Structures and the Possibilities for 'Keynesian' Responses to the Great Depression in Sweden, Britain, and the United States." In *Bringing the State Back In*, ed. P. Evans, D. Rueschemeyer and T. Skocpol. New York: Cambridge University Press.

White, Gerald T. 1980. *Billions for Defense: Government Financing by the Defense Plant Corporation*. University, AL: Alabama University Press.

Wiltse, Charles M. 1945. *Aluminum Policies of the War Production Board and Predecessor Agencies, May 1940 to November 1945*. Washington, D.C.: Government Printing Office.

Yamazaki Shirō. 1991. "Taiheiyō sensō kōhanki ni okeru kōkūki zōsan seisaku" (The policy to increase production of aircraft in the final stages of the Pacific War). *Tochi seido shigaku* 33(2):16-34.

Zysman, John. 1983. *Governments, Markets, and Growth: Financial Systems and the Politics of Industrial Change*. Cornell University Press.

II. Total War and the Formation of Thought

The Spirit of Capitalism as Disciplinary Regime in the Postwar Thought of Ōtsuka Hisao

J. V. Koschmann

[T]he individual is interpellated as a (free) subject in order that he shall submit freely to the commandments of the Subject, i.e. in order that he shall (freely) accept his subjection. . . . There are no subjects except by and for their subjection. That is why they 'work all by themselves'. Louis Althusser[1]

As an economic historian whose primary research was focused on Western Europe, Ōtsuka Hisao devoted major attention to the transition to capitalism, with emphasis on the question of the historical motive force, or subject, that leads society into that revolutionary mode of production. Moreover, as a Christian who was deeply impressed with Max Weber's emphasis on the economic role of culture and religious ethics in the development of patterns of economic life, he was also vitally concerned with the quality of active subjectivity (*shutaisei*) that had characterized that historical subject. Therefore, his early post-World War II works formed a major component of what subsequently came to be called the "debate on subjectivity" (*shutaisei ronsō*).[2] In this essay, I will attempt to illuminate the notion of subjectivity that Ōtsuka espoused in the postwar era, and then consider continuities between that notion and some of his wartime interventions regarding "economic ethics."

Ōtsuka was born in 1907 and brought up in Kyoto. In 1927 he matriculated at Tokyo Imperial University, and six months later began attending the

Reprinted from J. Victor Koschmann, *Revolution and Subjectivity in Postwar Japan* (Chicago: University of Chicago Press, 1996), with the permission of The University of Chicago Press.

Sunday bible classes led by the Japanese Christian leader, Uchimura Kanzō, a habit Ōtsuka continued until Uchimura's death in 1930. Indeed, Ōtsuka remained a committed adherent of the Japanese Christian Mukyōkai, or Non-Church movement, throughout his adult life. After postgraduate study, he lectured at Rikkyō and Hōsei universities. Then, in 1939 he was invited back to Tokyo Imperial University, where he taught European economic history until his retirement in 1968.

By the end of the war, Ōtsuka had published several major works, including *Iwayuru zenkiteki shihon naru hanchū ni tsuite* [On the Category of So-Called Early Capital] (1935), *Nōson no orimoto to toshi no orimoto* [Rural and Urban Varieties of Textile Manufacture] (1938) and *Kindai Ōshū keizaishi josetsu* [Introduction to the Economic History of Modern Europe] (1944). Upon Japan's surrender, he brought his background in European economic history directly to bear on the urgent questions of agenda and method that were intrinsic to the process of democratic revolution in postwar Japan.

PRODUCTIVE FORCES: EAST AND WEST

Ōtsuka believed that postwar social and economic reconstruction had to be based on a correct understanding of how modernization had occurred endogenously in Western Europe. This was especially the case in view of his belief that in some ways Japanese rural society was considered to still be in a feudal absolutist state comparable to Europe two or three centuries earlier.[3] In one of his first postwar essays, he compared contemporary Japanese farmers with those in England in the 16th and 17th centuries, and drew certain conclusions regarding the proper priorities for democratic revolution in the economy. The very idea that English agriculture in the 16th-17th centuries could provide a useful comparison to Japanese counterparts in the mid-20th century might seem implausible in retrospect. Yet, the world view that made such comparisons seem reasonable—that is, the vision of a basically unilinear, world-historical march of progress through more or less prescribed stages—was reinforced from different angles in the early postwar period by both Marxist and bourgeois theories of history. Ōtsuka's essay introduced a number of the themes that would characterize his early-postwar line of argument.

According to Ōtsuka, a major objective factor differentiating English farmers "under the feudal-absolutist monarchy of the 16th and 17th centuries" from Japanese farmers at the end of World War II was the much larger scale of English agriculture. English yeoman cultivators, who were called "full villein," had typically occupied and tilled about thirty acres with draft animals and a heavy plow, and even lower-class "cotters" often farmed from two to six acres. However, from a Japanese perspective, the English farmers' product seemed extremely small in proportion to the land area they cultivated and the amount of seed they sowed. In other words, the productivity of English farm land was comparatively low in the 16th and 17th centuries, whereas in Japan it had been very high. Nevertheless, this did not seem to mean that the English farmers had been poor, at least not in comparison with Japanese farmers. Indeed, one was able to find plausible, contemporary accounts that commented at length on the prosperity of the English farmer, especially in the yeoman stratum. If their land had been so unproductive, why were they so prosperous? Ōtsuka's answer is that even though the productivity of land had been very low, that of the English farmers' labor was very high. This ratio was the result primarily of objective factors such as geography: In Western Europe, climate and soil quality had dictated livestock husbandry and extensive farming, while in monsoon Asia intensive, wet-rice agriculture had demanded only simple tools but was able to support a large population. Thus, in the former case the productivity of the individual farmer had been enhanced while in the latter it stagnated. English yeoman farmers were able to see a relationship between effort and prosperity, and this encouraged their development of a work ethic. The result, in direct contrast to the Japanese case, was the productive ethos of diligence and frugality that Ōtsuka associated with the "modern type" of human being, and it was this ethos that prepared the English "upper-level farmers and small to medium landlords" for their role as the subject—or motive force—of modernization. When tempered by the religious atmosphere of puritanism, the English yeomanry "gave birth from among their number to the stratum of modern industrial capitalists"[4] as well as to the industrial worker class.

Yet Ōtsuka rejected the conclusion that this difference between Japanese and English conditions constituted a geographic or climatic destiny that was incontrovertible. He believed that the legacy of objective conditions could be overcome, not only by means of land reform directed to the creation of a stratum of free, independent Japanese farmers but also through emphasis on the cultivation of a modern ethos among the ordinary people who would have to be the "subjects" of any viable liberal democracy. Therefore, a program of democratic reconstruction of the economy would have to include not only a reform of actual, "objective" ownership but also a comprehensive program of education targeted at the subjective mentality of the people.

Ōtsuka's essay raised a number of points which he developed further in other works, written both before and after 1945. These included an elaboration of the contention that the leading forces in the formation of modern capitalism were not to be found among the premodern merchants but rather among lower-level producers such as the English yeoman farmers; that not only objective factors, such as climate and technology, but such subjective factors as value orientation and ethos were essential to that formation; and, perhaps most important, that the transition to capitalism was a world-historical process whose fundamental pattern had been established in the Western European countries and the United States.

THE SUBJECT (SHUTAI) OF CAPITALISM

The upper stratum of the peasantry—yeomanry and small or medium-scale landlords—played a central role in Ōtsuka's theory regarding the indigenous origins of capitalism in Europe, especially in England. That is, his pre-war studies had led him to side with Weber rather than Lujo Brentano, Werner Sombart, or R. H. Tawney with respect to capitalism's human subject: rather than the merchant class and merchant capital, the petty bourgeois producers had led the transition to industrial capitalism. Ōtsuka's theory had immediate implications for the early-postwar program of democratic revolution because it bore upon the subjective dimension—the ethos—of capitalism and, by extension, of liberal democracy as well. That is, he held up the petty-bourgeois ethos of the 17th-century English yeomanry as the authoritative model of the kind of modern shutaisei that should be propagated in postwar Japan.

The basic coordinates for Ōtsuka's approach had been established by Marx:

The transition out of the feudal mode of production (toward the modern one) takes two different forms. The producers rebel against the natural economy of the farm or the guild-like medieval urban industry, and become merchants and then capitalists. This is the way that actually results in a revolutionary transformation. In the other, merchants directly take up production. Historically speaking, this latter way actually functions as a transition, but . . . in and of itself this method does not lead to a transformation of the mode of production, but rather preserves it, and maintains it as a prerequisite to its own survival." (Capital 3, chapt. 20)

Marx himself had not directly addressed the question of values or ethics in this connection. The issue for him was one of social class: which class was the subject, or agent, of early capitalism. Indeed, Marx resisted any suggestion that a particular entity or social group, especially the "capitalists," created capitalism. Rather,

The historic process is not the result of capital, but its prerequisite. By means of this process the capitalist then inserts himself as a (historical) middleman between landed property, or between any kind of property, and labour. History ignores the sentimental illusions about capitalist and labourer forming an association, etc.; nor is there a trace of such illusions in the development of the concept of capital.[5]

For Marx, capitalists as well as free laborers were the products of impersonal social forces. Nevertheless, he clearly implies that the social carriers of capitalism in its early stages should be understood to be, not the early merchant class, but rather ascendant elements of the producing class, that is, artisans and agriculturalists who dirtied their hands in the material formation of goods.

Ōtsuka agreed, but was not content to rely on Marx's authority in this respect. His own research in European economic development had convinced him that the "early-merchant" road to capitalism was ultimately incomplete, indeed "false"; it did not have thoroughly revolutionary implications for the social structure. Therefore, the latter, "producer-type" road was the true way to an entirely new form of society:

> Take late-15th century England, for example. The old, feudal landholding system (landlord system) was already prematurely breaking up and a stratum of free, independent, self-managing farmers (especially the yeomanry) was appearing. At the new stage, they were to become the agents of new productive forces, and in a corresponding manner were also emerging as commodity producers and accumulating monetary wealth. Thus the producing stratum—I will call it the middle-producer stratum—became prosperous and out of its midst gradually emerged industrial capital. . . . This is none other than the origin of the actual revolutionary transformation of modernization, and is the orthodox road to the historical formation of a modern social structure.[6]

In his earlier works on European economic history, Ōtsuka had argued, more precisely, that both capitalists and modern workers had emerged from this predominantly rural, "middle-producer stratum," and this insight was later confirmed independently by the English historian, Maurice Dobb.[7]

However, Ōtsuka was never entirely satisfied with purely economic analysis. In order to get at the question not only of the social subject of capitalism but of the particular mentality, or quality of subjectivity, that had to characterize that subject, Ōtsuka turned to Max Weber in search of a supplementary account of the superstructural dimension of capitalist development. In his *Protestant Ethic and the Spirit of Capitalism*, Weber had intimated that protestant faith and practice were conducive to a work ethic among employees as well as employers. Ōtsuka seized upon this consistency between Marx's conception of the authentic road to capitalism—that in which petty producers become merchants and eventually capitalists—and the Weberian account of the spread of the "spirit of capitalism" among petty producers and workers. Just as Marx's revolutionary route out of feudalism implied that the social agents of capitalism were to be found not among rich merchants but primarily among the petty bourgeoisie, Weber had given evidence for the spirit of capitalism among those who worked with their hands as well as among capitalists.[8]

THE 'SPIRIT' OF CAPITALISM

In a series of essays originally written largely during the Asia-Pacific War, between 1943 and 1946, Ōtsuka differentiated meticulously between Weber's concept of the "spirit of capitalism" and the similar term, "capitalist spirit," that was used by Brentano. Directed primarily against those who had criticized Weber from the perspective developed by Brentano, Tawney and Sombart, Ōtsuka's essays sought to show that such criticisms were premised on a fundamental misunderstanding of Weber's argument. According to Ōtsuka, Brentano had defined the "capitalist spirit" as "nothing but the '*Streben nach grösstmöglichen Gewinn*' ('aspiration for the greatest possible gain'), or in one word "*Erwerbsgier*" ('aquisitive-greed'), an expression used over and over again in [Brentano's] writings. . . ." Similarly, Tawney had described the bourgeois ethic as the "temper of single-minded concentration on pecuniary gain."[9] These definitions as such could not be considered wrong, but in Ōtsuka's view they had little in common with Weber's concept of the "spirit of capitalism."

First, these notions of capitalist spirit differed from Weber's in that they applied only to capitalist entrepreneurs and thus excluded wage earners, whose work ethic and calculation of wages Weber's concept of the "spirit of capitalism" had been designed to encompass. Here, of course, a parallel is strongly implied between the abortive, merchant-centered route from feudalism to capitalism mentioned by Marx and the merchant-capitalist centered "spirit" defined by Brentano, Tawney and others. Indeed, Ōtsuka describes Brentano's view in such a way as to make quite clear the parallel to Marx's two ways.

Second, Weber's spirit included an element of ethic, or ethos, while theirs did not. That is, for Weber, "profit-motivation per se becomes an 'ethical obligation' and assumes the 'character of an ethically colored maxim for the conduct of life'."

. . . Weber takes the stand that, while the '"spirit" of capitalism' certainly contains elements of profit-motivation, the structural element which acts upon that motivation to direct its impact toward the formation of modern capitalism, particularly rational industrial organization (*Betrieb*) supported by wage labor, is neither profit-motivation per se nor acquisitive-greed, but a particular 'Ethos' which embraces and gives direction to the profit-motivation.[10]

Ōtsuka does not neglect to cite Weber's ironic caveat that, in effect, the " 'spirit' " of capitalism" reaches maturity "just as the ethos of worldly asceticism (*die innerweltliche Askese*), having originally been formed in the ascetic Protestantism, begins gradually to lose its religious enthusiasm with 'acquisition' taking its place as the rallying force."[11] That is, in what amounted to an "inversion of values," mature capitalism had superseded the protestant ethic and was now driven by pursuit of profit for its own sake. But why had Ōtsuka been so concerned to differentiate between Brentano's purely profit-oriented "capitalist spirit" and Weber's ethical "spirit of capitalism" if, in the end, the latter was also to end up as merely a variety of "acquisitive greed"? Ōtsuka addresses this issue by arguing that Weber's own focus of concern went beyond the explanation of capitalism in the narrow sense. That is, in Ōtsuka's view, Weber's object of investigation is not merely capitalist economic relations but the "inner roles" played by the spirit of capitalism,[12] especially in catalyzing an "ethos which looks upon work in a worldly calling as a duty and prompts rational and organizational devotion, in short the 'ethic of a calling' (*Berufsethik*)."[13] That is, the kind of capitalist mentality that developed among producers through the mediation of the protestant ethic was an "inverted ethical order" in which externally people are devoted entirely to private acquisition while inwardly they firmly believe that by turning a profit they are "making a great contribution to the 'whole' (society, nation, and world). . . ."[14] Only such an ethic would contribute to the "task of building a '*Betrieb*' ('industrial organization') . . . or, a business enterprise based upon rational organization of labor."[15] Rather than "undisciplined liberum arbitrium"—an "attitude which sees and judges the world consciously in terms of the worldly interests of the individual ego—Weber (and Ōtsuka) believed that rational management could emerge only from disciplined individualism, forged through the ethos of worldly asceticism, and devoted to the social whole.[16] It was precisely the latter form of individualism that Ōtsuka renamed the "modern human type" and recommended as the ethical model appropriate to postwar Japan's era of democratic revolution.

Weber concludes his essay on a strikingly pessimistic note, evoking a contemporary situation in which "the technical and economic conditions of machine production" had come to dominate like an "iron cage" the lives of all who inhabited them. For his part, in a situation in which he was in effect prescribing an ethos of worldly asceticism as a fundamental component of Japan's postwar democratic revolution, Ōtsuka apparently felt constrained to suggest the possibility of a brighter future, in which that productive ethic that was part of the spirit of capitalism "may be called up again and may, under an entirely new guise, effect a great impact on the course of history."[17]

It is worth noting here that, despite his indebtedness to Marxian concepts and assumptions, Ōtsuka portrays "the process of the development of modern capitalism that had been taken up critically by Marx from the perspective of 'exploitation'" as "the 'smooth' and 'rapid' formation of 'a bright and abundant modern society (= modern productive forces)'."[18] Indeed, he seemed to look forward to a transition from capitalism to socialism that would be equally "smooth," by virtue of being mediated (as will be discussed below) by a new economic ethic that would deemphasize the profit motive and cause people to work directly on behalf of the social whole.

THE MODERN ETHOS AS DEMOCRATIC SUBJECTIVITY

Ōtsuka devoted a number of his early-postwar essays to the task of illustrating what he believed to be the essential aspects of a normative model of active subjectivity (*shutaisei*). As he did so, he often seemed to go beyond his earlier, supplementary appropriation of Weber to place primary emphasis on the formation of subjectivity in ideology: What was the most important element in the expansion of productivity in society? What qualities distinguished the subject of liberal, capitalist development, and in what sense was that subject equipped to lead the democratic revolution?

In one essay, he contrasted the "modern human type," as illustrated in the life and writings of Benjamin Franklin, against the prevailing social tendency in Japan which appeared to him to be dominated by "oyagokoro," or paternalistic concern. Quoting Franklin's reflections at the beginning of his autobiography to the effect that, "Having emerged from the poverty and obscurity in which I was born and bred, to a state of affluence and some degree of reputation in the world . . . ," Ōtsuka comments that, "From the time he was a poor youth [Franklin] seems to have known no servility and to have been equipped with an air of independence and freedom unaffected by established convention." When his works were read in the context of Japanese culture, however, Franklin seemed "strange and eccentric." That was because of the Japanese ethos of *oyagokoro*, which Ōtsuka describes as follows:

> Those above us in a leadership capacity are supposed to have the authority of parents. The people, or those "below," must be obedient to this authority. The leaders who have this authority as parents show "love and mercy" toward those below, who obey them. In any case, according to this pattern the people are treated as immature. Indeed . . . to be immature

is considered a virtue . . . [Therefore] it can be said that the people of our country have no inner originality (*jihatsusei*).[19]

In Ōtsuka's view, such an ethos would seriously impede democratic revolution. In England where, Ōtsuka believed, modern values had apparently emerged smoothly and naturally, "a decisive segment of the people was forged into the modern human type, and as that segment destroyed the old, feudal order it began at the same time to build a new, modern and democratic regime." The background for this natural emergence had been religious as well as economic:

It was none other than puritanism (ascetic protestantism) that began to spread like wildfire among the yeoman stratum and eventually forged them into the modern human type. The Reformation had instilled a deep modesty and thorough obedience toward God. Along with this, however, came the rejection of all servility and unreasonable, blind obedience to other human beings. The Reformation taught brotherly love of infinite depth—not sensual love, but rather the type of love made possible only by the thorough denial of sensuality—and at the same time, nay, for that reason, disseminated among the people a tendency to hold one's head high and always face others with powerful independence and freedom, thereby transforming their character.[20]

In the United States, the ethos of the modern human type had been best articulated by Benjamin Franklin, who showed that, "Inner originality (*jihatsusei*), rationality, consciousness of social solidarity and, pervading them, a realistic attitude of emphasizing economic life—if these are viewed very abstractly, they manifest the various attributes of the modern human type."[21]

In Japan, on the other hand, democratization was being imposed from outside rather than discovered from within. Far from a "decisive segment of the people becoming able to objectify its own views as a 'will of the people,'" in contemporary Japan there were virtually no "modern human types." Therefore, it was essential to initiate a broad program of education designed to instill modern virtues. When a "decisive portion of the people is molded into this modern human type, the results will be modern productivity and a potential for managerial construction, along with the endogenous formation of a democratic regime."[22]

Ōtsuka often portrayed the mentalité of this capitalist subject by means of another sort of contrastive strategy, one based on Marx's distinction between the two roads to capitalism, "early-merchant" and "producer." Ōtsuka took each road to imply a particular subjective type, or ethos, and in his early-postwar essays made it clear that the development of capitalism in Japan had not followed the "producer road" and therefore was in the thrall of values directly inimical to the truly modern ethos that the producer road had historically entailed.

One of Ōtsuka's illustrations is drawn from 17th-century Holland. He tells the story of the Dutch merchant Bijland who in 1638 openly supplied weapons and ammunition to his country's enemies because he felt justified in doing whatever would bring a profit. This merchant espoused an "ethos of naked egoism" which in principle, according to Ōtsuka, was by no means unusual in the European environment of the time. Such individuals ignored the welfare of the commonweal in pursuit of selfish gain.[23]

In order to relate this egoistic mentality to liberalism, he points out that occurring at about the same time in Holland was a religious dispute between the Libertines and the Calvinists. Ōtsuka points out that, although religious in essence, this dispute had ramifications that touched on various aspects of political, social and economic life. The Libertines, who were closely connected with the "rich, feudal—that is, aristocratic—merchant stratum that had its base in Amsterdam," believed in toleration with respect to the ethos of "naked egoism," and spoke out only weakly against its excesses. On the other hand, the Calvinists, who indirectly represented the "middle class of producers" including farmers and small to medium industrialists, openly and vigorously criticized unimpeded competition for profit, and instead, "professed strict self-control according to 'conscience.'"[24] Indeed, according to Ōtsuka, the "Calvin-type" people,

> . . . have within them true "freedom," a "freedom of conscience" that moves them from inside, and they discipline their thought, speech and behavior in accord with that free conscience. Also within the Calvin-type individual is always "original sin," and "thoughts of the flesh," that is, sensuous desires which incessantly tempt and draw him toward antisocial behavior. Nevertheless, such individuals "exhaust their heart, spirit and thoughts," and "chastise the body," in order to suppress those desires, striving to follow "conscience" and the inner voice of "freedom. . . ." In any case, only when a decisive segment of the people is forged into this human type, which possesses "freedom of conscience" and goes through a social "new creation," can liberalism of the true sort take shape.[25]

Clearly, in Ōtsuka's view, the liberalism of the Libertines and urban merchants (a liberalism he attributed to "Renaissance-type freedom") corresponded to what he had described in his historical theory as the "early-merchant road" to capitalism, while the ascetic Calvinist liberalism (based on "puritan-type freedom"), embraced by the "middle class of producers" and equivalent to the puritanism of the English yeomanry, corresponded to the "producer road."[26] In his view, only the latter could lead to the overthrow of the old regime and the establishment of an authentic modernity. Therefore, rather than the "freedom for egoism" of the Libertines, Ōtsuka sought to foster among the Japanese people (a secularized form of) the Calvinist ethos of individual autonomy based on freedom of conscience and suppression of selfish desire. The means was to be "education," in the broad sense, which would impact on "all sectors of social life." Such an education should not be limited narrowly to secular affairs, but should ideally result in "something deeper, like the attainment of the broadest possible religiosity or faith."[27]

Ōtsuka also found in Daniel Defoe's Robinson Crusoe a model of the mentality and mode of life he considered desirable, in this case illustrated with reference to the English early industrial bourgeoisie. Referring to the plot of the novel, Ōtsuka recalls Crusoe's father's injunctions that Crusoe should give up his life as a wanderer and settle down in the social stratum in which he was brought up, a stratum he described as "that middle State, or what might be called the upper Station of Low Life,"[28] which was the status "most conducive to human happiness." In Ōtsuka's view, Defoe believed throughout his life that the members of this stratum "carried on their shoulders the prosperity and welfare of their countrymen," and portrayed characters like Crusoe on the model of that stratum's values. This was also precisely the group that had become the historical subject of the English industrial revolution. Ōtsuka says,

In my view, the way of life followed by Defoe's Crusoe on that island was none other than that of the English early industrial bourgeoisie (the petty bourgeois stratum). That is, it could be said that once Robinson drifted to the island, he repented socially as well as religiously, and in accord with his father's admonitions returned to the lifeways of the English petty bourgeoisie. As I have said, this was the early industrial bourgeoisie that had already in Defoe's time emerged at the forefront of world history and had become the backbone of English civil society; it would eventually become the leading subjective force in the construction of the enormous, modern productive forces . . . in the industrial revolution, and in the process would split clearly to become both the great industrial bourgeoisie and the proletariat.[29]

Then, what values and way of life did this stratum (as represented in Crusoe) espouse? According to Ōtsuka, Crusoe "formed his life in an extremely rational, planned manner."[30] He showed "diligence, frugality, meticulousness; a consistently autonomous, rational organization of life . . . and a remarkably 'strong' and vigorous constructive ability." Ōtsuka goes on: "To borrow an expression from Max Weber, these comprised the very 'spirit of capitalism' that constituted the subjective motive force in the formation of expansive, modern production."[31] In the aggregate these values also represented major aspects of the modern "human type" (*ningen ruikei*), that Ōtsuka wished to instill in the Japanese people.

SELF-DISCIPLINE AND THE STATE

The modernist perspective elaborated by Ōtsuka is far from discredited even now among Japanese intellectuals. Nevertheless, its limitations are perhaps clearer now than ever before. Most noteworthy, perhaps, is his overriding concern to develop the "national economy" and, therefore, to promote such values as might be conducive to that development. His essays are suffused with references to the need to develop the productive forces, as well as with his contention that, rather than merely material, those forces should be understood primarily in terms of human resources. Unifying the goal of democracy with that of productivity he says, for example, that:

> The people must develop an internal consciousness of respect for the human being. Rather than having it bestowed upon them in the manner of premodern natural law, they must themselves become the kind of "free people" which, in a self-disciplined manner, will maintain a forward-looking social order and enhance the common welfare. Only such a "free people" can construct democracy from the bottom up and at the same time autonomously develop the productive forces that will provide the material foundation for democratic reconstruction of the economy. Such a "free people" is itself the decisive element in the formation of modern forces of production. Indeed, it is those forces.[32]

In this context, it is useful to recall Ōtsuka's anecdote regarding the dispute between the Dutch Libertines and the Calvinists, in which he favored the Calvinists on account of their profession of "strict self-control," their "ascetic and self-disciplined" outlook, "suppression of selfish desire," etc. Productivity, as well as true freedom, could only come through self-denial. In other words, Crusoe clearly represented for Ōtsuka something like those subjects of classical capitalist ideology, as described by Louis Althusser, who "work by themselves"—that is, without external sanctions—because they have internalized and identified with the Absolute Subject (God, the Father).[33] Thus,

Asada Akira is correct to characterize Ōtsuka's ideal capitalist subject as having "learned to supervise and motivate itself through discipline and training." He concludes that, "if we call this subject the adult, modernization is precisely the process of maturation."[34]

Moreover, in Ōtsuka's conception of national productivity, self-discipline is linked to the demands of the state. In order to illuminate this dimension of his approach, it is necessary to step from the early-postwar era back into the midst of the Asia-Pacific War. If we look at several of Ōtsuka's other wartime publications, written during the same era as all but the last of the essays on Max Weber and the "spirit of capitalism," referred to above (see note 9), we notice that his conviction of the importance of self-discipline is clearly linked to a focus on the level of "totality," that is, the state and its demands for expansion of productivity.

The essays in question constitute Ōtsuka's interventions in a wartime debate on "economic ethics."[35] Stimulated in part by the New Order movement, and especially the institutions and ideology with regard to labor that were instituted by the government between 1938 and 1940,[36] this debate focused on such questions as the role of the "profit motive" in workers' motivation, the content of a work-ethic that would be appropriate to Japan, and the role of private initiative and discretion in a centrally-controlled economy. To Ōtsuka, it was clear that any discussion of the relationship between ethics and the economy had to be premised on the work of the theorist who had most thoroughly investigated that relationship, Max Weber.

In the context of the wartime debate, Ōtsuka joined Ōkōchi Kazuo and others in arguing that Japan was on the brink of realizing a "new economic ethic," one that would transcend the "spirit of capitalism" as Weber had described it. Basically, Ōtsuka contended that the element of profit-making in the "spirit of capitalism" was in the process of being eliminated completely so that the Japanese people would soon work entirely on behalf of the social whole, i.e., the state.

Ōtsuka's argument follows Weber's to a certain extent. Recall that Weber had emphasized "the 'ethic of a calling' (*Berufsethik*)," which meant an ethos that "looks upon work in a worldly calling as a duty and prompts rational and organizational devotion." Moreover, Weber had pointed out that the kind of capitalist mentality that developed among producers through the mediation of the protestant ethic was an "inverted ethical order" in which externally people were devoted entirely to private acquisition while inwardly they firmly believed that by turning a profit they were "making a great contribution to the 'whole' (society, nation, and world) . . ." That is, even Weber had seen the importance of contribution to the whole, and it was in this inner commitment to the "totality" that Ōtsuka located the importance of the nation-state. Yet, at the same time, Ōtsuka reaffirms that even prior to its degradation the classical "spirit of capitalism" had been mediated by the profit motive. This was true despite the important role played in that "spirit" by the social community and the need to make a contribution to its welfare. More precisely, he says that in Weber's "spirit of capitalism" the individual bore responsibility for enhancing production on behalf of the social whole, but the measure and criterion of that contribution continued to be profit. High profit meant, ipso facto, that a sufficient contribution was being made.[37]

In the new economic ethics that Ōtsuka saw emerging during wartime, however, the mediation of profit was being rapidly overcome so that soon people would work directly on behalf of the state, accepting full responsibility for expanding the productive forces. Institutionally, this would facilitate the process of bringing all management under central control and allow it to be fully planned. In a 1944 essay, Ōtsuka clearly links an emphasis on ascetic self-discipline directly to the national task of expanding production. He says:

> World-historical reality now criticizes the supremely historical "spirit of capitalism" and overcomes its limitations, as a new "economic ethic" (ethos) gradually reveals itself. . . . Contrary to the "spirit of capitalism," the new form of "economic ethics" (ethos) transcends the mediation of "profit-making" and is now clearly conscious of the individual's "responsibility for production" in relation to the demand for expansion of productive forces that originates in the "totality" (state). . . . A new "economic control" ("economic plan") is expanding through transcendence of the "free" economics of old capitalism; moreover, management of specific enterprises—along with the "individuals" that carry out that management—is no longer mediated by "profit-making" but is rather brought directly within the "control" ("plan") of the "totality" and by virtue of that takes on sociality and a state character. . . . When viewed from the historical perspective, the meaning of "responsibility for production" can be fully understood only as the consciousness of this kind of "totality" (state) in the new "economic ethic."[38]

Self-discipline was necessary in order to expand the productive forces on behalf of the state. Yet Ōtsuka was not arguing for blind obedience. He emphasized that in order to be supremely *productive* in orientation and impact, the new economic ethic must contain within it the "structural moments" of "inner originality" (*jihatsusei*) and "instrumental rationality." In other words, even during the war, Ōtsuka was clearly talking about a kind of subjectivity that was to be self-disciplining, self-motivating and rational. It is also important to remember that Ōtsuka was not alone in this emphasis. Although differing from Ōtsuka on several points, Ōkōchi Kazuo and others associated with "productive forces theory" (*seisanryoku riron*) were also discussing the need for autonomous, self-disciplined participation on the part of workers during a time of mobilization for total war. A recent study of Ōkōchi notes, apropos of Ōtsuka's views, that:

> Ōkōchi certainly discusses the importance of subjective (*shutaiteki*) human activity, and says that in the absence of autonomous, self-disciplined participation on the part of workers, the long-term management of the wartime economy would have been impossible. . . . This kind of *shutaisei* and self-discipline was the essential psychological element in wartime economic mobilization. . . . Ōkōchi's conception was that in the historical era of wartime mobilization, the moment of democratic participation had to be activated to the highest possible level. However, for Ōkōchi the moment of democratic participation was certainly not at odds with state mobilization; on the contrary, he sought to encompass *shutaisei* and self-discipline within the war framework.

It is interesting that, because of their rejection of blind obedience, Ōtsuka's wartime works—especially the above essay—are often treated as acts of resistance, a judgment that, in the narrow sense, is not without some persuasiveness. Even more interesting is Ōtsuka's reputation for having bridged the transition from wartime to postwar without having to make any changes in his views. Ōtsuka was able to continue full-speed ahead from total war through democratic revolution.

Although the state as "totality" is much less prominent in his postwar writing (and to some extent is replaced by the notion of "national economy" [*kokumin keizai*]), the *shutaisei* that Ōtsuka advocates in the context of the postwar democratic revolution appears to be directly continuous with the proposals he made between 1942 and 1944. In part, this continuity simply enables us to see clearly the hidden complicity between totalitarianism and European-style liberalism with regard to how subject-formation is related to the nation-state. Centered on the quality of self-discipline, his conception of *shutaisei* immediately calls to mind Michel Foucault's demonstration that a whole range of disciplinary mechanisms emerged historically in parallel with the liberal-democratic state. Modern subjectivity—whether liberal or authoritarian—appears to be pervaded by the form of self-surveillance that results when people internalize the gaze of state authority.

In a manner more specifically related to the Japanese context, however, it also suggests the fertility of total-war mobilization as a source of the thought and institutions that became dominant in postwar Japan. Indeed, it appears that the wartime emergency, which called for rapid expansion of the productive forces and raised the question of "economic ethics" in relation to the productivity of labor, provided Ōtsuka with an initial, formative opportunity to develop his notion of modern subjectivity in relation to the contemporary Japanese context.

We are left, therefore, with the question of whether Ōtsuka's construction of subjectivity was in any sense adequate to the process of democratic revolution in early postwar Japan, and whether it still has relevance today. Ethnic groups, feminists, environmentalists and others persist in their efforts to extend politics beyond the state and beyond the notion of a unitary society whose needs—whether for productivity or for leisure—are capable of claiming precedence over private wants. As they politicize new spaces in the interstices of the state/society, these forces also challenge the applicability of supposedly universal ethical paradigms such as "modern subjectivity."

Notes

[1] Louis Althusser, "Ideology and Ideological State Apparatuses (Notes towards an Investigation)," *Lenin and Philosophy, and other essays*, trans. Ben Brewster (New York and London: Monthly Review Press, 1971), p. 182 (italics deleted).

[2] For an extended exploration of the post-World War II "debate on subjectivity," see Koschmann, *Revolution and Subjectivity in Postwar Japan* (Chicago: The University of Chicago Press, 1996).

[3] Ōtsuka Hisao, "Seisanryoku ni okeru tōyō to seiyō: Nishi-Ō hōken nōmin no tokushitsu" (May 1946); reprinted in Ōtsuka, *Kindaika no ningenteki kiso* (Tokyo: Chikuma Shobō, 1968), p. 203.

[4] Ibid., p. 206.

[5] Karl Marx, *Pre-Capitalist Economic Formations*, ed., Eric J. Hobsbawm and trans. Jack Cohen (New York: International Publishers, 1965), p. 109.

[6] Ōtsuka, "Kindaika to wa nani ka: kindaika katei ni okeru futatsu no michi" (February 24, 1947), in Ōtsuka, *Kindaika no ningenteki kiso*, pp. 137-38.

[7] Maurice Dobb, *Studies in the Development of Capitalism* (New York: International Publishers, 1947), e.g., p. 125. Dobb writes that the sixteenth century saw "a considerable growth of independent peasant farming by tenants who rented land as enclosed holdings outside the open-field system. Among these there developed . . . an important section of richer peasants or yeomen, who as they prospered added field to field, by lease or purchase, perhaps became usurers (along with squire and parson and local maltster and corn-dealer) to their poorer neighbours, and grew by the end of the century into considerable farmers who

relied on the hire of wage-labour, recruited from the victims of enclosures or from the poorer cottagers." Also see Kohachiro Takahashi, "A Contribution to the Discussion," in Paul Sweezy et al., *The Transition from Feudalism to Capitalism*, Introduction by Rodney Hilton (London: NLB, 1976), p. 88.

[8] Sugiyama Mitsunobu, *Sengo keimō to shakai kagaku no shisō* (Tokyo: Shin'yōsha, 1983), p. 79.

[9] Ōtsuka Hisao, "Makusu Uēbā ni okeru shihonshugi no 'seishin'," *Ōtsuka Hisao chosakushū* 8 [Kindaika no ningenteki kiso] (Tokyo: Iwanami Shoten, 1969), p. 24. These essays originally appeared in *Keizaigaku ronshū* 13/2, 14/4 and 15/1 (1943-46). English translation from *Max Weber on the Spirit of Capitalism*, trans. Kondō Masaomi [I.D.E. Occasional Papers Series No. 13] (Tokyo: Institute of Developing Economies, 1976), pp. 17-18.

[10] Ōtsuka, "Makusu uēbā ni okeru shihonshugi no 'seishin'," p. 27; trans. pp. 21-22.

[11] Ōtsuka, "Makus uēbā ni okeru shihonshugi no 'seishin'," p. 64; trans., p. 47.

[12] Ōtsuka, "Makusu uēbā ni okeru shihonshugi no 'seishin'," p. 95; trans., p. 72.

[13] Ōtsuka, "Makusu uēbā ni okeru shihonshugi no 'seishin'," p. 86; trans., p. 65.

[14] Ōtsuka, "Makusu uēbā ni okeru shihonshugi no 'seishin'," p. 93; trans., p. 71.

[15] Ōtsuka, "Makusu uēb ni okeru shihonshugi no 'seishin'," p. 96; trans., p. 73.

[16] Ōtsuka, "Makusu uēbā ni okeru shihonshugi no 'seishin'," p. 98; trans., pp. 74-75.

[17] Ōtsuka, "Makusu uēbā ni okeru shihonshugi no 'seishin'," p. 100; trans., p. 76. A contemporary who criticized Ōtsuka's use of Weber was Hayashi Kentarō. See Hayashi, "Rekishi ni okeru shutai no mondai," *Sekai* (April 1947).

[18] Ueno Masaji, "Keizaishigaku," in Chō Yukio & Sumiya Kazuhiko, eds., *Kindai Nihon keizai shisōshi* II [Kindai Nihon shisōshi taikei 6] (Tokyo: Yūhikaku, 1971), p. 210. Kan Takayuki writes that, "No matter how exploitative they were domestically, how aggressive overseas, or how violent their colonial administrations, the true modernization and true capitalism of England and the US were Ōtsuka's models.... [Moreover], according to Ōtsuka's logic, what was bad about Japan was its 'oldness', not that it invaded and set up colonies, massacred colonial peoples and, domestically, mobilized the Japanese proletariat through state violence." Kan Takayuki, *Sengo seishin: sono shinwa to jitsuzō* (Tokyo: Mineruva Shobō, 1981), p. 64.

[19] Ōtsuka, "Jiyū to dokuritsu" (August 1946); *Ōtsuka Hisao chosakushū* 8, p. 177.

[20] Ibid., pp. 179-80.

[21] Ibid., p. 184.

[22] Ibid., p. 184.

[23] Ōtsuka, "Jiyūshugi ni sakidatsu mono" (December 1946); *Ōtsuka Hisao chosakushū* 8, p. 190.

[24] Ibid., p. 193; also Ōtsuka, "Kindai ni okeru jiyū to jiyūshugi" (1946), *Ōtsuka Hisao chosakushū* 8, 208-209.

[25] Ōtsuka Hisao, "Jiyūshugi ni sakidatsu mono," *chosakushū* 8, pp. 197-98.

[26] For the "renaissance" and "puritan" distinction applied to freedom see Ōtsuka, "Kindai ni okeru jiyū to jiyūshugi," pp. 204-209.

[27] Ōtsuka, "Jiyūshugi ni sakidatsu mono," p. 200.

[28] Ōtsuka Hisao, "Robinson Kurūsō no ningenruikei" (August 1947); in *Ōtsuka Hisao chosakushū* 8 (Tokyo: Iwanami Shoten, 1969), p. 216. Original English wording from *The Life and Strange Surprizing Adventures of Robinson Crusoe, of York, Mariner*, ed. J. Donald Crowley (London: Oxford University Press, 1972), p. 4.

[29] Ōtsuka, "Robinson Kurūsō no ningen ruikei," p. 217.

[30] Ibid., p. 215.

[31] Ibid., pp. 219-220.

[32] Ōtsuka, "Kindaiteki ningen ruikei no sōshutsu," 169.

[33] Louis Althusser, "Ideology and Ideological State Apparatuses (Notes towards an Investigation)," pp. 180-81.

[34] Asada Akira, "Infantile Capitalism and Japan's Postmodernism: A Fairy Tale," in Masao Miyoshi and H. D. Harootunian, eds., *Postmodernism and Japan* (Durham and London: Duke University Press, 1989), pp. 274-75.

[35] Ōtsuka Hisao, "Keizai rinri no jissenteki kōzō—Makkusu Uēbā no mondai teiki ni kanren shite" (1942), *Ōtsuka Hisao chosakushū* 8, 305-316; Ōtsuka, "Keizai rinri to seisanryoku" (1943), *Ōtsuka Hisao chosakushū* 8, 317-323; Ōtsuka, "Seisanryoku to keizai rinri" (1944), *Ōtsuka Hisao chosakushū* 8, 324-338; Ōtsuka, "Saikōdo 'jihatsusei' no hatsuyō—keizai rinri to shite no seisan sekinin ni tsuite" (1944), *Ōtsuka Hisao chosakushū* 8, 339-344.

[36] See the essay by Saguchi in this volume. Clearly the debate on the "new economic ethic" was fundamentally consistent with several tendencies analyzed by Saguchi, including the post-World War I tendency to emphasize industrial workers' contribution state purposes, and also the later emphasis, under the *kinrō* (work) ideology, on workers' status as active subjects (*shutai*) and the appropriateness of a need-based rather than profit-oriented system of compensation.

[37] As Weber had written in his commentary on the works of the Presbyterian preacher, Richard Baxter, a calling was "measured primarily in moral terms, and thus in terms of the importance of the goods produced in it for the community." (Max Weber, *The Protestant Ethic and the Spirit of Capitalism*, trans. Talcott Parsons [London: Routledge, 1992], 162.) For Ōtsuka's explication of the relationship in Weber between private profit and contribution to the social whole, see Ōtsuka, "Keizai rinri no jissenteki kōzō," 305-316.

[38] Ōtsuka, "Saikōdo 'jihatsusei' no hatsuyō," 341.

[39] Yamanouchi Yasushi, "Senjiki no isan to sono ryōgisei," in Yamanouchi et al., eds., *Nihon shakai kagaku no shisō* [Shakai kagaku no hōhō III] (Tokyo: Iwanami Shoten, 1993), pp. 156-57. See Ōkōchi Kazuo, *Sumisu to risuto* (May 1942), in *Ōkōchi Kazuo chosakushū* 3 (Tokyo: Seirin Shoin Shinsha, 1969). For discussion of modernist approaches during the war to "productive forces theory," see the essay by Sugiyama Mitsunobu in this volume.

Civil Society Theory and Wartime Mobilization: On the Intellectual Development of Uchida Yoshihiko

Sugiyama Mitsunobu

Since the late 1980s, "civil society" has again begun to attract increasing attention in the social sciences. It is perfectly understandable that political scientists and economists in the eighteenth and nineteenth centuries should have granted it a central role in their theories, but why is the forgotten concept of civil society being taken up again now? It appears that the concept is referred to frequently in discussions of how to secure a social space that is not subject to intervention by the state or administrative organs, or to control by market forces; and, having secured that space, how to cultivate and expand within it autonomous associations, movements and active networks.[1]

In the background of the reemergence of "civil society" as a basis for political science discourse in the 1980s are the enormous political changes that have occurred in Eastern Europe and Russia. In these regions, single parties had penetrated and merged with the state and then, on the pretext of the "leadership role of the party," intervened in all aspects of social life. State/socialist regimes of this sort disappeared one after another in the 1980s, but Poland was the vanguard. Beginning in 1976, when the autonomous labor organization, Solidarity, was formed and became active in Poland, "civil society" also emerged as the theoretical concept that best described what seemed to be going on. At first, the movement stayed away from the state and the official system, working instead to organize and democratize society outside of those established structures. Then, on the basis of the pressures generated in the course of that organizational process, it finally aimed at structural transformation of the state and official institutions.

The emergence of civil society in Poland brought about the collapse of state-socialism and eventually played a major role in the process of

117

reconstructing a democratic society. Moreover, the theoretical concept of civil society proved to be suggestive for sociologists and movement organizers, not only in Eastern Europe but in the advanced countries of Western Europe as well. If in Eastern Europe the state, penetrated by the party, had closed off the social space where citizens might have been active, in the West huge capitalist enterprises had amassed great power and were having a destructive effect on market society. The result was to constrict the social space available for active citizen participation in the West as well. Of course, movements, groups and networks in the West protested against and challenged the forces that were disrupting the market; moreover, civil society as a perspective was connected to attempts to consolidate for these citizens' movements the forms and realms through which they could act entirely separately from the state and market society, and to protect and expand such movements (and also to secure regulation of them). That appears to be the background against which lively discussions of civil society have recently reemerged.

Yet, civil society also attracted concentrated intellectual attention in Japan in the 1960s. Indeed, it animated a wide cross-section of people far beyond the world of social science. Although the debates on civil society that took place in Japan in the 1960s are not completely unrelated to those of today, they were quite different in quality. Of course, at that time Japan was squarely in the midst of accelerated economic growth, and environmental pollution caused by industrial enterprises had reached life-threatening proportions; but only in the 1970s did that pollution call forth social movements and exercise the mass media. In the midst of the 1960s, most Japanese were still preoccupied with economic growth and Japan's expanding affluence. On the other hand, most Japanese scholars in the 1960s were under the influence either of the Marxism that had been revived after the war or of "postwar progressivism," and Marxism was also gradually changing. Indeed, the rise in concern related to civil society in the 1960s in Japan was deeply connected to changes in Marxist theory and attempts to reform it.

Some of those changes originated with advances in philological research on the works of Marx. It had long been unclear how the early philosophical explorations in the *Economic and Philosophical Manuscripts* were connected to the economic analysis of capitalist society that Marx developed later in *Capital*. However, the appearance of previously unpublished notebooks written by Marx during the 1850s, that is, the *Grundrisse*, stimulated rapid advances in thought as exegesis proceeded in the 1960s. Along the way, a number of viewpoints and arguments that had been left out of Marx's economic theory were rediscovered, and when Marxian theory was reformulated through the inclusion of these viewpoints and arguments, it became something quite different from what had been taught and understood up to that time.

At the forefront of that process were researches by Hirata Kiyoaki who, in *Shimin shakai to shakaishugi* [Civil Society and Socialism],[2] produced an intricate investigation focusing on terminology. In earlier Japanese Marxist writing no distinction had been made between "bourgeois society" and "capitalist society"; either they were treated as the same or, at most, bourgeois society was treated as an historical stage prior to capitalist society. But this practice was mistaken. "Bourgeois society" needed to be translated as "civil society," and the relationship between "civil society" and "capitalist society" had to be redefined. It is impossible to go into the details of Hirata's argument here, but the main points are as follows. The category that Marx called civil, or bourgeois, society referred, strictly speaking, only to Western Europe. As an ideal type it referred to the process by which, in conjunction with the dissolution of the various relations of feudalism, there emerges a free individual who produces and exchanges his products in the market. When we consider the form of ownership implied here, we find that what free individuals produce through their own labor remains their own property and as such is exchanged as a commodity in the marketplace. The development of capitalism, however, leads to an increasingly complex and expansive division of labor with the result that the individual no longer produces alone. Workers work as the employees of the capitalist, who is now the one who trades, as commodities in the market, what they produce. Once this is the case, the nature of ownership also changes. Whereas up to this point it had been the products of the individual's labor that had been traded in the market, what are traded there now are the products of the labor of others. Yet, the different forms of ownership that are reflected in this change do not occur historically in series, but theoretically reemerge continuously, day after day, in capitalist society. Hirata concludes that, "Actual society is a relation in which civil society is incessantly converted into capitalist society," and it was precisely this relation that Marx analyzed and sought to clarify. When individual property (*kotaiteki shoyū*) is distinguished from private property (*shiteki shoyū*), when the conversion from "civil relation" to "capitalist relation" is properly understood, and when such basic concepts of Marx's political economy are reread and reconceived as a system, Hirata argues, we find that Marx's vision of the society that would follow the destruction of capitalist society was also quite different from what had in the past been understood as socialism or communism. Capitalist society had negated the "individual ownership" of civil society and put "private property" in its place, so the new society that would reject "private property," in turn, would seek to reestablish "a union of free human beings" on the basis of "individual ownership."

What would be the result if this reformulated Marxist theory and vision of post-capitalist society were compared to the socialist societies that actually existed at the time? The result, in fact, was to raise the question of "civil society within the social system of socialism." Neither the Soviet Union nor the Eastern European countries seemed to have had such a thing as civil society, and when it finally did appear, the tanks of the 1968 Prague Spring snuffed it out. Hirata's arduous, philological analysis of civil society attracted people's attention because in the 1960s the liberal social atmosphere, and also the civil rights movements and student revolts that were typical of the advanced countries, occurred in Japan as well.

But Hirata's studies were not the only reason that theories of civil society aroused fervent interest in Japan in the 1960s. In fact, another civil-society theorist, Uchida Yoshihiko, was also writing during this decade, and he influenced a larger audience for a much longer period of time. Part of the reason is that, although Hirata Kiyoaki opened new vistas of thought, he limited his analysis to the *Grundrisse* and others of Marx's own works. Yet, ever since Marxism was imported to Japan, its adherents had struggled to provide an adequate Marxist analysis of Japanese reality. Such attempts had caused a major debate and left a unique corpus of writings by Japanese social scientists, but one can scarcely find in Hirata's work any connection to that previous set of issues. Uchida's arguments with regard to civil society, on the other hand, inherited the perspective of the Kōza-ha (Lectures School) scholars who had debated against the Rōnō-ha (Laborer-Farmer School), and evoked the experience of "quiet resistance" that had been undergone by Marxists and liberals when confronted with government repression in the mid-1930s, at the time of Japan's war of aggression in China. His analyses were also relevant to the debate over the "two roads" to the recovery of the Japanese economy after the war. Moreover, along with Maruyama Masao and Ōtsuka Hisao, Uchida Yoshihiko was a major proponent of the unique stream of scholarship and thought in postwar Japan called "modernism" (*kindaishugi*). "Modernism" appears to have lost its earlier influence in parallel with the end of rapid economic growth at the time of the oil shocks of the early-1970s. If that is the case, then can we not see Uchida's theory of civil society as modernism's final burst of brilliance?

The remainder of this essay will analyze Uchida's argument on civil society, which so captivated Japanese intellectuals in the 1960s. Such an analysis must begin with the deep connection between that argument and Japan's mobilization during World War II.

THE ADVENTURE OF PRODUCTIVE FORCES THEORY

In January 1948, the monthly journal, *Chōryū* (Undercurrent), published a special issue entitled "Nihon fuashizumu to sono teikōsen" (Japanese fascism and its line of resistance). At the time, only 2 1/2 years after the war, the democratization movement was reaching its apex under heavy influence from the revived Communist party. Under such circumstances, it was generally thought that between 1930 and 1945 virtually no one had resisted the rule of emperor-system absolutism except "the imprisoned Communists who refused to recant." But was that really the case? If that were so, it would be difficult to answer the question of, "What pre-existing Japanese social structures facilitated the postwar advance of democratization"? How could one explain, on the one hand, the connection between the systematic mobilization of the entire economic structure under the controlled economy of wartime (which at the time was interpreted as the establishment of state monopoly capitalism) and on the other the movements of postwar democratic forces? The special issue of *Chōryū* responded by trying to illuminate as an important legacy of the wartime economy the systematic integration of society, and the philosophies that provided its rationale. Of course, elsewhere in the early-postwar era that legacy was viewed negatively.

Uchida's contribution to the special issue was "Senji keizaigaku no mujunteki shinkō to keizai riron" (The contradictory development of wartime economics and economic theory).[3] Wartime economic controls and "civil society" would seem at first glance to be unconnected, but one of the "lines of resistance" that such a juxtaposition illuminates is the stream of productive forces theory, which was the point of departure for Uchida's theory of civil society and provided him with a constant reference point.

So-called productive forces theory was developed by Ōkōchi Kazuo and Kazahaya Yasoji in the late-1930s. According to Uchida, its major characteristic lay in the effort, "to actively contest the relations of production from the standpoint of strengthening the forces of production, and to do so while neither directly raising the question of class exploitation nor openly opposing the war, but rather taking these as 'given.'" Its basic thesis was that efforts to strengthen and expand the forces of production would force adjustments in the relations of production. Of course, this amounted to a reversal of the standard Marxist formula regarding the forces and relations of production; that such a reversal could be considered realistic in the context of an advancing war economy was an intellectually thrilling prospect, and it intrigued Uchida.

The emergence of what, from the perspective of Marxism, was a heretical proposal can only be fully understood against the background of the vision of the structure and character of Japanese capitalism that was projected by the Kōza-ha Marxists. The Kōza-ha people were at pains to describe the various types of capitalist economy which, if viewed in terms of national economic structures, were manifested in different parts of the world. It made a big difference whether, on the one hand, the bourgeois-democratic revolution swept away all the feudal elements, thereby allowing capitalist forces to gain complete power and giving rise to a new economic structure (the American model) or, on the other, the bourgeois revolution were incomplete, leaving feudal remnants. In the latter case, the capitalist forces would have to compromise with the feudal elements and therefore would be able to construct only a distorted form of capitalist economic structure (Prussian model). Uchida was heir to this Kōza-ha perspective, and considered Japanese capitalism to be a particular variant of the Prussian model. On the one hand, according to this image of the economy, were the imperial regime representing absolutism, a semi-feudal landlord system in the countryside and, in light industry, small and medium-sized enterprises with strongly premodern coloring. At the other extreme were the national industries established by the government, along with advanced monopoly-capitalist enterprises such as those grouped under the zaibatsu. Indeed, this image of economic structure was interpreted to be more similar to that of Russia under the Tsars than to Germany. Naturally such a distorted form of capitalism was believed to impose various constraints on development. Because of pervasive low wages resulting from Japan's rural tenancy relations, the domestic market was small and the formation of the productive forces extremely weak.

The Japanese capitalist economy continued to develop despite such structural and qualitative impediments, but internal contradictions accumulated. Finally, the Great Depression of the early 1930s brought this Japanese economic structure to the point of crisis. The Japanese government sought a solution to the crisis through encroachments on the Chinese continent, but this made war with East Asia inevitable. If war was unavoidable, then it was necessary to build the kind of heavy industry that modern warfare required. Beginning with the Japan-China war, this objective was pursued by instituting wage controls, promulgating an "employee regulation order" and a "national conscription order" under the "National Mobilization Law," and putting in place financial and investment policies. The institutionalization of this system of total mobilization occurred after even the "legal Left" was disbanded in 1937; labor unions were receding, and the "industrial patriotic movement" was promoted in their place.

Even in the era of the outbreak of war between Japan and China, Japan's economic structure was still interpreted as fundamentally consistent with the Prussian model. Nevertheless, war accelerated heavy industrialization. Thus, in order to consolidate the basis of the heavy-industrial structure that was generated in this manner it was necessary to produce a large number of modern, skilled workers. How did Japan compare to the Prussian model with respect to this factor? The answer was that, "The economic structure was stubbornly retained to the end, but this process of advancement within that structure inevitably eroded its foundations." Here is where the thesis of productive-forces theory—to the effect that expansion of the productive forces would cause favorable adjustments in the productive relations—could be seen to be working.

At this point, Uchida refers to Ōkōchi Kazuo. Ōkōchi had investigated the social policy theories of the German Historical School's economists and the theorists of the German Social Democratic Party, and had then proposed his own particular approach to social policy. The modern capitalist countries had carried out social policies designed to protect workers, including such aspects as wages, working conditions, and employment insurance systems, and he asked why they had done so. His answer was that individual capitalists and firms tended to pursue profit too avidly, lowering wages and allowing working conditions to deteriorate. Moreover, when viewed at the level of the nation as a whole, and from a long-term perspective, such behavior impeded the smooth reproduction of a country's economic activity and led to ruin. As a result, he concluded, there came into play at a level transcending the individual capitalists and firms, where all national economic activity was aggregated, a rational will of the whole—a "rationality of total capital"—and national social policy had emerged to give form and direction to that will.

In European countries, the "rationality of total capital" had been actualized by the state through social policy. However, in Japan, where still-numerous landlords charged high rents thereby undermining industrial wages, the state still tolerated premodern conditions. Therefore, according to Ōkōchi, because of Japan's backwardness, "social policy in the usual sense has fallen into crisis." However, since outbreak of the Japan-China war the situation had changed markedly under the policy of "expanding productive forces." Ōkōchi believed that the war had destroyed "Japanese-style" social policy and was at the same time bringing about a genuinely rational form of such policy. In the Western European nations, the expansion and reproduction of the capitalist economy itself had led to "increased intricacy and sophistication of the means of production and to emphasis on the formation of heavy and chemical industries in preference to light industry." In Japan's case, however, these advances were being accomplished by war. As such advances took place, there would have to be "increases in the productivity of labor in parallel with the increased sophistication of industrial technology; moreover, in response to the rapid development of technology, it would be necessary to cultivate socially the kind of labor power that could gradually refine itself and be able to come to grips autonomously (shutaiteki ni) with the new technology."[4] That is, heavy industrialization required the cultivation of large numbers of workers who were as "vigorous" intellectually as they were physically. Therefore, enterprises would be forced to pay higher wages and to guarantee improved working conditions. In the past, wages had always been pulled down by the feudal relations that survived in the rural economy, but now workers would have to be paid compensation equal to the "value of their labor power." In other words, the capitalist development of the Japanese economy had begun at the end of the 19th century, but compensation for labor at its fair value had come only in the era of the Japan-China War of the late 1930s. Value standards of a sort that had emerged at the outset of capitalist development in countries following the American model were only infiltrating Japanese society in the 1930s. That was the contention of the productive-forces theorists.

Moreover, it is necessary to point out that the Kōza-School Marxists also made a certain gesture toward the skilled workers in modernized heavy industry. This gesture originated in what they considered to be a foundational statement of their approach, Yamada Moritarō's *Nihon shihonshugi bunseki* (Analysis of Japanese Capitalism). Yamada granted to the skilled workers of the zaibatsu-run military production plants and heavy industrial facilities a leading role in the revolutionary movement that was supposed to develop in Japan. The skilled workers, who were able to operate lathes and other complex machine tools, could use the judgment and discipline they developed on the job to good advantage in a revolutionary movement.[5] Then, what is the result when we connect this gesture to the viewpoint that focused on the wartime expansion and strengthening of the productive forces?

The legal leftist parties and labor unions had been dissolved, and workers were being reorganized into the Industrial Patriotic Association, which formed part of the Imperial Assistance system. There remained virtually no resistance against the military and fascist elements that were launching the wartime adventure. Nevertheless, so long as the heavy industrialization of the industrial structure was progressing—even if for the purpose of making war—large numbers of modern skilled workers would be produced and, in the view of the productive forces ideologues, such workers would emerge as dissident elements in relation to the system itself and the forces around it that were moving toward war. In the event, looking for resistance among such workers was like "looking for fish in a tree." But Uchida's 1948 essay focuses enthusiastically on productive-forces theory as an intellectual venture that had begun with critical intent, calling it "a line of resistance against Japanese fascism."

Similarly, in the postwar period, Ōkōchi wrote that productive forces theory had been a form of resistance during the "era of darkness." But the works he and others wrote during the war are not necessarily explainable fully on the basis of such an assumption. He committed himself to the construction through war of a "productive-forces rational" economic order, and thus it is possible to view him as an active collaborator in the war effort. He held that the modern workers who were produced as a result of the wartime expansion of the productive forces, and who were in some ways at odds with the system, would strive mightily to secure the goals of the wartime order—that is, they would be loyal to the Industrial Patriotic Movement. Ōkōchi wrote that genuine social policy had nurtured autonomous workers, but "their autonomy will not be turned into energy in support of traditional class conflict, but rather will propel the workers toward active cooperation from below with the movement to construct subjects who would participate in the Industrial Patriotic Order."[6] That was so, Ōkōchi argued, not only because they supported the wartime economy but because, in line with his vision of a society restructured toward productive rationality, not only individual capitalists and enterprises but each individual Japanese national would now suppress the "profit motive" and "blind greed." That is, they were destined to become "rational beings" who would embody the "rationality of total capital." He portrayed an image of society in which the activities of these rational beings would spread beyond production to infuse their "lives as consumers" and "daily life as citizens"; indeed, they would come to consider each meal as merely a necessary means of acquiring the ability to work for the state. This amounted to the vision of a counter-utopia in which "the whole nation would control private life in deference to the supreme goal of expanding the productive forces." It was to be neither a socialist society nor a capitalist society but a society of productive rationality.

Nevertheless, it is possible to read Ōkōchi's vision in another way. In it, workers "become subjectively and actively aware that they are in charge of the necessary productive elements in economic society and they take pride in that." They have "status as industrial workers and as social beings." In other words, no society can survive if it neglects the fundamental necessity of reproducing the economy. Contrary to the historically-specific conditions that govern the stages of free competition or of monopoly capitalism, this principle was a constant across all historical periods. Social reality contained both historical dimensions and constant dimensions, and the need to preserve labor power was one of the constants. Ōkōchi held that preserving labor power through social policy could smooth out social reproduction, and argued that, "as an abstract principle, the preservation of 'labor power' is also a condition of all developmental stages of capitalist economy; it is historically originary as well as logically foundational."[7] In sum, Ōkōchi's argument includes some elements from an historical perspective and others from an a-historical, transcendent perspective, and he deploys each as he thinks appropriate, depending on the context. Indeed, from another angle, what we took above as a counter-utopic vision under a controlled economy can also be read as a relationship that recycles constantly, underlying and supporting historical change and development. That is how Uchida understood Ōkōchi's productive forces theory. This historically constant relationship was later understood as a process of "material metabolism between humans and nature."

It was in the above sense that Uchida Yoshihiko highly evaluated the wartime productive forces theory in his postwar essay in *Chōryū*. Even where capitalism had taken shape as a special variant of the Prussian developmental model, productive forces theory would enable its economic structure to be made into something more modern, that is, it might be changed so as to incorporate a "law of value." Uchida was not alone in understanding it in this way. Usami Seijirō, who contributed an essay to the same collection, was a more orthodox spokesman for the Kōza-ha than was Uchida, but Usami also argues that changes in the wartime economy "transformed the nature of the zaibatsu themselves." "Although they never rid themselves of their original, merchant-usurer qualities, didn't they strengthen their character as financial capital as a result of industrial expansion, especially in the means and sectors of production?"[8]

The prewar Kōza-ha failed to address "the infusion of laws of value" under Prussian-style capitalism. For them, the economic structure of capitalism in each country was fixed in its formative stage. Yet, in 1948, that structure was supposedly being "dismantled" through a "bourgeois-democratic revolution." Therefore, the exciting intellectual adventure launched in the special edition of *Chōryû* was criticized bitterly as one-sided and distorted. In the social atmosphere of the time, the predominant view was that productive-forces theory was wartime collaboration.

CIVIL SOCIETY AGAINST CAPITALISM

I said above that Uchida Yoshihiko, along with Maruyama Masao and Ōtsuka Hisao, was representative of the postwar Japanese intellectual stream of thought called "modernism" (*kindaishugi*). However, strictly speaking, it is incorrect to group them all under the label of "modernism," which as a category is not used much any more. The term originally referred to those who argued that Japan had engaged in aggressive war under a fascist system because it had failed to attain "modernity" in the true sense; that is, they held that in this Japan, which harbored anachronistic remnants of feudalism, the kind of "modern society" that matured in 18th and 19th century Europe had never taken root. Because underlying this argument was a tendency to idealize "modern society," it lost its influence once it became known that, historically, 18th and 19th century European societies had not lived up to that ideal. However, the arguments of Uchida and the others mentioned above were not so naive. Amidst the affluent society produced by the rapid economic growth of the 1960s, Japanese felt that they were living in world that was no different from those of Western Europe or the United States. Such feelings were only superficial. If one looked deeply into people's morals and spiritual life, was not the difference profound? Uchida's argument with regard to civil society was widely read in Japan in the 1960s because his way of thinking was quite widespread. Also, Uchida's rather flexible thought, which ranged from economics to literature, was very well suited to appeal to people's intuitive feelings along those lines.

Uchida's *Keizaigaku no seitan* (Birth of Economics), known as his major accomplishment, appeared in 1953. This work, which concerned Adam Smith's *Wealth of Nations*, neither situated Smith in relation to the development of the theory of surplus value, as Marxists were wont to do, nor followed the common practice of discussing the contrast between the standpoint of altruism in *Theory of Moral Sentiments* and the selfishness that formed the focal point of *Wealth of Nations*. Rather, in intellectual orientation Uchida's study paralleled Ōkōchi's *Sumisu to Lisuto* (Smith and List), which supported social policy for purposes of expanding the forces of production, and Takashima Zen'ya's works, including *Keizai-shakaigaku to shite no Sumisu to Lisuto* (Smith and List from the Viewpoint of Economic Sociology), which explained Smith's theories in relation to the system of productive forces. One can find the work's creativity in Uchida's view that Smith's conception of civil society provides a theory of division of labor and exchange and, therefore, of the productive forces; Uchida also posits that the division of labor builds social connections, and relates that proposition to Marx's theory of value. Uchida initiated a debate with Ōtsuka Hisao by contending that, in the context in which *Wealth of Nations* was written, Adam Smith was arguing against the monopoly system of the mecantilists; Uchida's argument here, in turn, connected up with Kamiyama Shigeo's theory of "double imperialism." But let's not go into the details.

I would prefer to focus on Uchida's argument that Smith used the term "civil society" to refer in a positive sense to the English society in which he lived, whereas in other countries that was not necessarily the case. According to Uchida, in France the equivalent concept functioned critically in relation to the actually-existing French economic society; that is, in terms of the dichotomy established by J. J. Rousseau, in France civil society was considered to be "natural" in contrast to the existing "civilization." In Germany, too, a role analogous to Smith's in England was played, not by those who introduced Smith's thought, but rather by Friedrich List, whose protectionism and encouragement of domestic industry conflicted with Smith's advocacy of free trade; indeed, a half century later, the equivalent figure was to be Max Weber. In terms of the discipline of economics, "civil society" meant a society that was penetrated thoroughly by the "law of value," that is, one where the products of individual labor were exchanged for their true value, "same thing, same price" (i.e., a society where prices are kept uniform regardless of the identity of parties to the exchange). Uchida's argument implies that society and social relations based on a uniform rate of exchange are anticipated and aspired to in all countries, even though the formative circumstances of capitalist economic structure differ from country to country, as does the extent to which feudal relations survive. Thus, the intellectual function of "civil society" varied according to these various criteria.

Clearly perceptible in the background of Uchida's approach are the thought patterns of Kōza-ha Marxism, especially the famous "Preface" to Yamada Moritarō's *Analysis of Japanese Capitalism*. There, Yamada argues that it is necessary to apply Marx's theory of reproduction in the analysis of national economic structure. He also holds that in order to clarify the particular quality of Japanese capitalism, one had to compare it against the types of capitalism that emerged in five other countries: England, France, Germany, Tsarist Russia, and the United States. The type of capitalism that existed in each of those countries reflected the particular stage of world history at which its economy emerged and developed, but if we look carefully at the "Preface" we find that in all five cases capitalist development began with some kind of bourgeois-revolutionary transformation against an absolutist monarchical order. The earlier that transformation occurred, the more far-reaching were its effects, and capitalism developed and expanded accordingly. Economies that emerged relatively late were not only subjected to the influence of their predecessors but, by virtue of the relative incompletion of their bourgeois-revolutionary transitions, were forced to put up with substantial feudal remnants, distorted economic structures, and fragile productive forces. That is the gist of Yamada's argument.

Because he inherited this viewpoint, Uchida Yoshihiko did not advocate that Japan's postwar development should merely follow an idealized, general image of Western European society. To the contrary, even Western European countries differed in the degree to which they had eliminated feudal elements, and their socioeconomic relationships also varied. Moreover, he emphasized that these differences, in turn, were reflected in the different forms assumed in each country by reflections on civil society. We can locate Rousseau's notion of civil society in the contrast he draws between "civilization" and "nature." But the concept of civil society emerged more clearly in Germany, where the economic structure of capitalism assumed the "Prussian form" of development. That was because, "there [the concept of civil society] emerged out of bourgeois opposition to the feudal base that was still a part of capitalism."[9] Accordingly, in Germany it was Max Weber who most clearly expounded the philosophy of "civil society." Why Weber rather than List? Uchida had been able to see in Ōkōchi's wartime theory of the productive forces the possibility that a "law of value" could penetrate a capitalist economic structure that had followed the "Prussian form of development," and he recognized the same phenomenon in the background of Weber's argument. Members of the 20th-century German Historical School had debated the issue of whether social policy should be directed towards distributive justice or rational expansion of the productive forces, and in this debate Weber had opposed Schmoller. In Japan, Ōkōchi, who advocated the conservation of labor power, was in a position equivalent to that of Weber, who was opposed by members of the old social-policy school who argued rather for low wages and morality. In sum, the permeation of a "law of value" into an economic structure produced by "Prussian-type development" took place in Germany during early-20th century imperialism whereas in Japan it finally occurred only in the late-1930s.

In Germany, the "civil society" perspective was in opposition to the laissez faire views of those who imported Smith's thought intact, and had a more nationalistic coloring. Nevertheless, it was clearly a perspective aimed at guiding capitalist development in the direction of civil society. How about in Tsarist Russia? Before the war, Kōza-School analysts had considered the economic structure of Tsarist Russia, in which an agricultural base premised on widespread serfdom was juxtaposed against the state and monopolistic capital, to be the closest parallel to Japan. The combination of serfdom in agriculture and, towering above the industrial structure, the huge, monopolistic enterprises distorted the relations of "civil society" and impeded their development. Therefore, concepts of "civil society" emerged in opposition to capitalism as it appeared in the Russian context. This is predictable given the circumstances, and in fact the same was true of civil-society arguments in Japan later on. However, Uchida's point diverges from this tendency, as he takes up the Narodniki as the bearers of Russia's version of "civil-society" thinking. The Narodniki placed their hopes for Russian social development in the continuation of the rural village community (*mir*) and, as is well-known, thought that such a continuation would allow Russia to go directly into socialism without out a capitalist stage. But the Narodniki associated capitalist development with the situation that would obtain if the serfs were liberated without being given any land. Without land, the freed serfs would either have to be employed by the landlords as agricultural laborers or again become debt-slaves. Indeed, even if the serfs were freed with land, the result might not have been much different given the circumstances in Russia at the time. But the two standpoints were very different. Those who advocated the liberation of serfs with land expected that it would lead to the capitalization of agriculture through the landlord's managerial initiatives and would therefore open routes to upward social mobility (American-type development). On this point, Uchida writes, "To the extent that the Narodniki were revolutionary, they actually advocated capitalism in the name of anticapitalism. But that is precisely where they should have seen orthodox capitalist development."[10] Here "orthodox capitalist development" should be interpreted as American-style development, which would give rise to the socioeconomic relations of "civil society." In Russian society under the Tsars, where capitalist development was late just like in Japan, the advocacy of civil society took the form of opposition to capitalism. That is what Uchida thought.

THE FUNCTION OF CAPITAL

The Birth of Economics was read mostly by scholars, and struck them as something new and different; in contrast, Uchida's little book, *Shihonron no sekai* (The World of *Capital*), was aimed at a broader audience. At the time it was written, Uchida was exploring the genealogy of concepts of civil society by writing on thinkers of the Meiji period. He was deeply involved in the group of intellectuals formed by the former actress of Tsukiji Little Theater, Yamamoto Yasue; also, he had by this time developed a devoted readership for his own plays and literary essays. Did he, perhaps, write *The World of Capital* because he wanted readers of his dramatic works to be aware that his intellectual starting point was still economics and that even his plays and literary works should be read with that in mind?

Most introductions to Marxist economics are written in dry prose and present definitions and concepts, one after another, along with explanations of how they all fit together in a system. This book, however, was different. That is partly because Uchida had the general reader in mind, but it is also because he focused largely on theories of the labor process and the production of relative surplus value—aspects that most works on Marxist economics either skipped entirely or dealt with only superficially. Of course, Uchida explains that capitalists produce by purchasing labor power and the means of production at full value, and sell their products for full value as well. He also shows that everything, including labor power, is bought and sold for fair value while, nevertheless, the value to the capitalist increased, and explains that surplus value results from the difference between "the working time necessary to produce labor power" and "the period of time the worker actually works in the factory." The point Uchida emphasizes is not that capitalism is a system of exploitation, although he admits that it is such; rather, he emphasizes that built into the system of capitalism is a logic of rationally organizing the productive process—through collective work, division of labor and manufacture, machinery and heavy-industrial production, and so on—

and, therefore, of developing the productive forces. Because he limits his coverage to a few issues, he is able to explore them thoroughly. Is it possible to expand the productive forces merely by introducing efficient new machinery and building heavy industrial plants? What does it mean for human beings to make things? By grappling with questions such as these, Uchida is able to show that in order to address such issues it is necessary to investigate the labor process. Moreover, in proceeding to do so, he is able to construct a unique vision of what results when capitalism is "cultivated in its pure form," that is, when there are no distortions originating in the remnants of feudal relations. Under such circumstances, capital was not "self-generating value"; rather, he presents its operation in terms of a theory of the labor process as it emerges when human labor is added to the means of labor in conjunction with a guiding conception.

Uchida revealed the origin of his vision in a postwar interview in which he remarked that, during the war, "The power of capital as property was especially strong in Japanese capitalism, obstructing the rational subjugation of nature."[11] Here again, he points out that even the nature of capital is determined by an economic structure that includes not only remnants of a semifeudal tenancy system in rural areas but monopolistic enterprises in heavy industry. But what, precisely, did he mean by saying that, "the power of capital as property was especially strong"? In the era he refers to, enterprises and factories were commonly merged in order to expand the productive forces. However, it was impossible to raise productivity merely through mergers and the rational positioning of industry. So long as the views of the technicians were not taken into account, there could be no positive results. In the era of expanding forces of production, a debate was underway as to whether the essence of technology is in the system of the means of production (system standpoint) or in the conscious application of the laws of nature (application standpoint). Uchida adhered to the latter view, and notes that in the background of that view was a movement of technicians who advocated the expansion of rationality. Conceptions of technology were intimately entwined with the theory of the labor process, and Uchida's concern for technology led him to an expanded conception of "capital that moves and functions"; that is, it led him to conceive of capital itself as the process of consciously applying laws of nature and rationally organizing the productive process. He ended up, therefore, with a conception of capital that recognized its exploitation of labor, but rather emphasized its positive function (and Marx's own references to this function) in promoting expansion of the productive forces.

Then, what notion of "pure" capitalism did Uchida's approach lead to? Capitalism was not merely a matter of converting liquid capital directly into a technological system, thereby producing goods and giving rise to profit. Even if the amount of capital were held constant, outcomes would vary widely depending on what was produced and by what methods. It was not sufficient just to buy machinery and put it into operation. What Uchida wanted to say was the following: In its conversion from currency to means of production and labor, and then to commodities, its total value expands. Because of its primary concern with the logic of capital's own movement, Marxist economics substitutes an abstraction for the capitalist as a person. However, if one were to focus on the capitalist as the agent of capital's movement, then the process of setting goals relating to what to produce and by what method (that is, the rational application of the laws of nature) would become crucially important. "In order to reach the goal, this or that mechanized system is necessary and such and such an amount of capital is required. It is essential that capital (i.e., a certain amount of currency) be combined with this kind of conceptual power (i.e., ability)." Nevertheless, in Uchida's view, this had not been achieved in the capitalism of most Western European countries (with the exception of England). In early-19th century France there were calls for this kind of combination between ability and capital in the proposals of some followers of Saint-Simon, but their rational, "civil-society" oriented approach to the productive forces calls attention to actual distortions in the French economy of the time.

Once one views capital not merely as ownership of a certain amount of currency but more broadly, as something that functions positively in combination with ability, the result will be a much more dynamic vision of capitalism than is prevalent among Marxists. The owners of big capital could certainly put in place highly-efficient installations of machinery. But if, through imagination and skill, small capitalists could cause their capital to function even more productively, they would ultimately outstrip big capital. Because of such competition, big capital had to strive incessantly to mobilize creativity and thereby improve its mode of production and system of mechanization. If it did so, the capital necessary for that purpose would increase accordingly. In other words, " competition and trust mediate in the functioning of the law of concentration"—big capital will find it easier to get credit from banks. Therefore, although in theory capital's functioning was limited only by the imagination of the capitalist, in fact big capital would ultimately gain the advantage.

Of course, if we look at competition among firms in the U.S. today, we find that a number of institutions are engaged in eliminating "monopolies" and insuring "fair competition," so it might be said that Uchida's viewpoint is biased in favor of "civil society"-type capitalism. Even so, it was distortion in the economic structure of Japanese capitalism that made Uchida think that way. What was unique about Uchida's argument was his next step: It was true, of course, that although "functioning capital" played a role in the competition, big capital would emerge victorious in the end. However, it was also important to recognize that, paradoxically, big capital's very victory "amounts to a victory for functioning capital and will give rise to rational management. It will also bring about the rational control of nature at the societal level. Ultimately, rational management will even render obsolete the existence of the capitalist as such."[12] Of course, the "pure" capitalism that Uchida portrays here greatly exceeds the reality of even its closest approximation, that of the United States. In *Nihon shihonshugi no shisōzō* (Philosophy of Japanese Capitalism), he writes that, "civil society is not a concept of historical reality but an abstract concept," and it is definitely a vision of a society that exists nowhere in reality. What Uchida calls rational management does not refer to profit-making. He is viewing it from a transhistorical perspective that he calls the material metabolic process between human beings and nature. One can think of his "functioning capital" that gives rise to rational management as something that does not exist in reality but provides a standard against which one could critically evaluate the capitalism that does exist in various countries.

As I noted above, Uchida explained the prewar failure of capitalists to make capital function rationally by saying that, in Japan, "the power of capital as property was very strong." In line with the wartime drive to expand the forces of production there had been a movement among technicians to gain greater influence; Uchida interpreted this movement as an effort to expand even slightly the room for active "functioning" on the part of capital, and attributed it to the transition, at the base of Japanese capitalism, from the category of rent to that of surplus value." The movement corresponded from the viewpoint of capital to what, for workers, was the exchange of labor power at its true value under productive forces theory. Both perspectives were deepened in Uchida's postwar thought as they flowed into and bore fruit in his civil-society theory of the 1960s.

I asserted above that civil society was heatedly discussed in the 1960s in Japan, and that Uchida Yoshihiko's notion of civil society provided the focal point of that discussion. It is true that Uchida produced no work equivalent to that of the other theorist I have mentioned, Hirata Kiyoaki, who addressed the issue of civil society directly in his *Civil Society and Socialism*. Yet, although he never took up the issue directly, observations regarding civil society are scattered throughout all of Uchida's works, from *Birth of Economics* and *The World of Capital* to his essays on theater and literature, so in that sense it can be said that his work in general related to civil society. He presented his vision of that society most directly in *Philosophy of Japanese Capitalism*, in the course of a discussion of Kubo Sakae's play, *Kazan baichi* (Land of Volcanic

Ash).[13] Clearly this is where Uchida is writing most forcefully, and readers have found it quite compelling.

Land of Volcanic Ash is set on a farm in rural Hokkaidō, and its main characters are farmers who work there and an agricultural technician. Here, it is important to note the Kōza-ha Marxists' way of situating Hokkaidō's agriculture. In contrast to the tenancy system that was prevalent throughout Honshū, Hokkaidō's agriculture was capitalistic. Farm workers were paid on a daily basis, even though their attitudes were still colored by the feudal relations that held sway elsewhere, and chemical fertilizer was supplied by monopoly capital with profit as the only consideration. Thus, it is not difficult to predict, on the basis of Uchida's argument, that in the context of this kind of capitalist economic structure, the civil-society orientation would develop in an anti-capitalist direction. Among farm workers heavily influenced by tenancy relations, exchange of labor power for its true value and recognition of the personality of the free individual would certainly clash with the existing framework of capitalism. In Kubo's story, the agricultural technician discovers that the makeup of the chemical fertilizer best suited to raising crops in soil heavily laced with volcanic ash differs markedly from that foisted off on the farmers by the monopolistic corporation. Yet, his voice is suppressed at the corporation's convenience.

Kubo himself asserted that the underlying concept of *Land of Volcanic Ash* was "the special quality of Japanese agriculture" which lay at the base of the absolutist system of power described by the Kōza-ha; he said he had tried to "unify scientific theory and poetic imagery." In terms of Uchida's theoretical apparatus, the drama combines two perspectives: that of the agricultural technician, who represents the metabolic process that links humans to nature (that is, the historically constant perspective of the rational organization of the labor process through conscious application of the laws of nature), and that underlying the way the farm workers are treated, understood in terms of the relations of production. This framework vividly captures the problems involved in the economic structure of Japanese capitalism as it has been illuminated by the Kōza-ha theorists, that is, the semi-feudal agricultural relations juxtaposed against monopoly capital, along with the fragility of the productive forces. To say that it vividly portrays all this must be taken to mean that it shows the direction toward a transformation of the system, and indeed, it clearly projects a vision of civil society, if only via the image of its opposite. *Land of Volcanic Ash* was published in 1937, the year the Japan-China War broke out, and Kubo, who was a playwright with the Tsukiji Little Theater, was at the time, like Uchida, not only seeking a line of resistance against Japanese fascism in the productive forces theory of the late-1930s, but was also no doubt expecting that in the changes accompanying the expansion of the productive forces there would occur "the permeation of a law of value" throughout Japanese capitalism. In sum, one could say that Uchida's "civil society" theory of the 1960s began in a concrete analysis of the expansion of the wartime economic forces in the late-1930s and then eventually circled back to the same issue.

In a sense, Uchida's theory of "civil society" consisted in the rethinking, several times over, of problems that arose in relation to the systematization of wartime mobilization. The final conclusion of this process was that, "Pure capitalism is a society in which property acquired through (self) labor is finally converted into capitalist ownership via the mediation of the law of value, and demands for earnings proportionate to ability are suppressed. That being the case, it is impossible to avoid the question of whether capitalist society can be called bourgeois society."[14] Perhaps one can say that evident in the first half of this quote is none other than what Hirata Kiyoaki, in the course of his reading of Marx's *Grundrisse* called "the conversion of the law of possession." However, Hirata does not connect ability (imagination) to his concept of capital. In Hirata's scheme, the negation of capitalist-type ownership is just abstractly posited as "restitution of individual ownership." Although they are both talking about "civil society," we can see why Uchida's works had the larger readership and longer-lasting influence.

I have attempted to interpret the main outlines of the thought of Uchida Yoshihiko, who was such a central figure in the heated debates over civil society that occurred in the 1960s. As I noted, it occurred as the Japanese people were becoming aware that they would have to pay a high price for the affluence brought by rapid economic growth, but the articulate expression of this anxiety did not emerge until later. Today's "new social movements" had not yet appeared. Rather, it was during the movement against the Japan-U.S. Security Treaty in 1960—even though it was "defeated"—that people began to devise an answer to postwar democracy, and this was the social atmosphere in which they apprehended the theories of civil society. If we remember that Uchida's thought was nurtured in the environments of the wartime discussion of productive forces theory and the postwar debates over how to rebuild Japan economically, and developed in close proximity to the rise of the postwar labor movement, we cannot but feel that a certain change took place. In the 1960s, Uchida's thought became more detached from these realities and he began to relate more directly to the cultured world of the intellectuals. This is evident in his membership in the circle of Yamamoto Yasue.

When we consider the degree to which today's global revival of theories of civil society is connected to movements to transform social reality, it is difficult not to feel that Japan's civil-society discourse of the 1960s was isolated from world trends. However, those who propound today's theories of civil society oppose the destructive influence of the state and its administration, and the markets ruled by the mammoth corporations, and seek to secure a space for free and autonomous citizen action. In effect, this would be the final realization of democracy. If we think along these lines, aren't we able to find something in Uchida's vision of civil society that connects it to today's movements?

Translated by Tok Hayashi

Notes

[1] For example, Jean L. Cohen and Andrew Arato, *Civil Society and Political Theory* (Cambridge; MIT Press, 1992).

[2] Hirata Kiyoaki, *Shimin shakai to shakai-shugi* (Tokyo: Iwanami Shoten, 1969).

[3] Uchida Yoshihiko, "Senji keizaigaku no mujunteki shinkō to keizaigaku" in *Chōryû* (January 1948): 37-42. Reprinted in *Uchida Yoshihiko chosakushū*, volume 10, (Tokyo: Iwanami Shoten, 1989), 109-118.

[4] Ōkōchi Kazuo, *Senji shakai seisakuron* (Tokyo: Jichōsha, 1940), 21.

[5] Yamada Moritarō, *Nihon shihon-shugi bunseki* (Tokyo: Iwanami Bunko, 1934, reprinted in 1977), 198-199.

[6] Ōkōchi, *Senji shakai seisakuron*, 27.

[7] Ōkōchi Kazuo, *Shakai seisaku no kihon mondai* (Tokyo: Nihon Hyōronsha, 1938), p. 174.

[8] Usami Seijirō, "Kokka shihon-shugi to sangyō kōsei no kōdoka" in *Chōryû* (January 1948): 34.

[9] Uchida Yoshihiko, *Keizaigaku no seitan* (Tokyo: Miraisha, 1953), p. 98.

[10] Uchida Yoshihiko, "Narodoniki to Marukusu-shugi" in Teikoku Daigaku Shinbunsha, ed., *Nihon hōken-sei no bunseki* (Tokyo: Teikoku Daigaku Shinbunsha, 1947), pp. 32-39. Reprinted in *Uchida Yoshihiko chosakushū* 10 (Tokyo: Iwanami Shoten, 1989), 74-80.

[11] Uchida Yoshihiko and Hirata Kiyoaki, "Rekishi no shutaiteki keisei to gakumon" in *Uchida Yoshihiko taidanshū* (Tokyo: Chikuma shobō, 1971), p. 219.

[12] Ibid., 221.

[13] Uchida Yoshihiko, *Nihon shihon-shugi no shisōzō* (Tokyo: Iwanami Shoten, 1967), pp. 79-101.

[14] Ibid., 93.

Women in the Motherland: Oku Mumeo Through Wartime and Postwar

Narita Ryūichi

INTRODUCTION

Japan's Fifteen Year War, fought from September 1931 to August 1945, was a total war that by its nature mobilized the entire nation and gave rise to a wartime social system. Women were also, of course, subject to its effects. For this reason, "women and total war" has constituted an important theme for research in women's history, yielding not only historical descriptions but a wealth of individual analyses as well.

A look at the *Nihon joseishi kenkyū bunken mokuroku* (Bibliography of Research in Japanese Women's History; edited by the General Research Center for Women's History),[1] reveals that there has been a steady proliferation of studies dealing with the topic of women and total war. In particular, in her overview of the "Modern and Contemporary Periods" segment of which she was in charge, Nagahara Kazuko notes an upward trend in published research between 1987 and 1990. She raises the issue of how to "understand as a totality women both as victims and as those responsible for aggression" during total war.[2] I would like now to take a closer look at the various approaches to the study of women in the context of the historical system of wartime mobilization.

First, past research in women's history can be classified according to its object of analysis. Studies in women's history covering the wartime period can be classified as to whether they focus on: (A) women's everyday lives during wartime, or (B) women's movements during wartime. Such works as *Onna to sensō* (Women and the War) edited by the Division for the History of Women's Movements of the Tokyo Historical Science Research Association[3] and "Sensō to onna no nichijō seikatsu" (War and the Everyday Life of Women) by Orii Miyako and Iwai Sachiko[4] are representative examples of type A.

137

Onna to sensō, with the subtitle of "Sensō wa onna no seikatsu o dō kaeta ka" (How did the war change the everyday life of women?), explores the interconnected issues of health, labor and labor policies, military support, motherhood, education and the mass media. "Sensō to onna no nichijō seikatsu" also focuses on women's life cycle, with particular attention paid to the domestic resourcefulness (*seikatsu kufū*) manifested by women during wartime.

In these studies, 1) the ontological status of everyday life is taken for granted; they contain no sense that everyday life is continually being formed historically. Life is taken as already there, fully formed, prior to being deformed and warped when "the dark shadow of war begins to loom."[5] Put another way, "the rhythm of daily life is destroyed by war."[6] Accordingly, 2) although such histories of daily life (type A) claim that "domestic resourcefulness" had the effect of "supporting the war in the end,"[7] they locate war outside of daily life. That is, everyday life is assumed to have been running smoothly before it lost its customary form as a result of war's intrusion.

While this type of research into the history of everyday life does not deny that women participated in aggression, its fundamental position is that women were victims of the war. These studies generally focus on such wartime experiences as rationing, mobilization, stocking up, air raids, and isolation, strongly coloring their portrayal of the war as a "hardship" for women.

Murakami Nobuhiko's *Nihon no fujin mondai* (Issues regarding Japanese Women),[8] however, adopts a different perspective from some of the other type-A studies. In his chapter "Women's Labor During Wartime," Murakami asserts that wartime brought about drastic changes in the previous order of everyday life, and emphasizes its entirely new dimensions. He sees the contradictions surrounding women under the wartime system as products of "patriarchy" and indicative of an "weakening of the family system." This standpoint allows him not only to point out the new "freedom of the young wife" in relation to the "national emergency" but to highly evaluate it: "Formerly confined within the narrow framework of the household, wives regained animation and energy through their home front activities."

Murakami's statements were greeted with criticism, eventually producing a debate on the question of whether the activity accompanying the war could really be seen as women's emancipation. That is, doubts were expressed with regard to Murakami's rather affirmative "documentary" (*tsuinin*) attitude toward women's activity during wartime.

Turning now to the type-B research, we see that it can be roughly divided into three categories by subject, that is, by social class and group: (a) proletarian women's movements, (b) civil/middle class women's movements and (c) officially sponsored women's movements and activities. Each camp has its own distinct point of view, and there is considerable debate in regard to interpretation. Ishitsuki Shizue, as a representative of the (a) category, analyzes the Social Masses Women's League formed in August of 1932 in her article "1930 nendai no musan fujin rōdō" (Proletarian Women's Labor in the 1930s).[9] Ishitsuki writes that the Socialist Masses Women's League continued its "struggle for the protection of everyday life," but notes that its influence "waned and finally disappeared altogether" before it could ever act on its "demands for peace and against war." Ishitsuki's portrayal of the impasse at which the proletarian women's movement found itself with its "demands for peace" belongs to the above-mentioned "hardship" vein.

However, type-B studies focus more often on groups (b) and (c), and include many analyses which adopt a wide range of positions. For example, in her book *Feminizumu to sensō* (Feminism and war), Suzuki Hiroko raises the issue of the "wartime cooperation" engaged in by such civil (*shiminteki*) women's movement leaders as Kora Tomi, Hani Setsuko, Ichikawa Fusae, Yamataka Shigeri, and Oku Mumeo.[10] Suzuki trains a spotlight on their wartime participation, that is, the manner in which they contributed to aggression.

Suzuki argues that "no matter what kind of intentions lay behind their actions," these women's "cooperation" with the war effort represented a "wrong turn," and she denounces their actions as "mistaken." Murakami Nobuhiko also criticizes such leaders. But, although she might deny it, in effect Suzuki "prosecutes" women for their participation in the wartime system. Meanwhile, representing group (c), we have Kanō Mikiyo's *Onnatachi no "jūgo"* (The Women's "Home Front"),[11] which explores the organization of the "home front" through a look at the Women's Association for National Defense and the Greater Japan Women's Association. Kanō unravels the logic which bound the "women of the home front" together through their "desire for emancipation." Women were so confined that the only way they could satisfy their "desire for emancipation" was by becoming "women of the home front."

Kanō further states that the "spontaneous service activities of women" "fanned the war spirit" of the soldiers. Laying bare the logic of women's "wartime cooperation" through category (c), she clarifies their roles as aggressors. Kanō's work raises the question, "Why did women so diligently fulfill their 'home-front roles' during the war of invasion?"

Nishikawa Yūko schematizes all of wartime women's movements ranging from group (a) through group (c).[12] Nishikawa herself focuses on the civil women's movements located in the interstice between the proletarian women's movement—upon which "an almost complete silence" was imposed—and the officially sponsored women's movements, which trod a "steady path of expansion." In her study, Nishikawa reveals the "women's logic" of "cooperative efforts to upgrade their position." Nagahara Kazuko also finds that the total war's "rational and progressive aspects" persuaded women to cooperate.[13] Fujii Tadatoshi, as well, traces the logic of "service" for women in relation to the practice of "national defense" in his study of the Women's Association for National Defense, which particularly focuses on class differences among women.[14]

Nishikawa, Nagahara and Fujii all examine the end result of "war cooperation" by women and the logic which leads to it. If we set aside fine nuances for the moment, we can roughly classify these writers' works into two categories: "documentation" and "prosecution." As more or less affirmative "documentarists," Nishikawa and Nagahara place greater weight on the logic of women's participation, that is, cooperation in the war. In contrast, the "prosecutors," Suzuki and Kanō, emphasize the collaborative aspects of such participation.

Research on military "comfort women," which has greatly increased in recent years, is also carving out a space from which to explore the relation between women and war. However, this research tends to display a two-part structure by examining the aggressive nature of the military, government, men in general, and Japanese as assailants in relation to military comfort women as war victims. Suzuki Hiroko's *Jūgun ianfu/naisen kekkon* (Military Comfort Women and Japanese-Korean Marriages) and Yoshimi Yoshiaki's *Jūgun ianfu* (Military Comfort Women)[15] exemplify this stance.

As seen in the above, research in women's history dealing with the wartime period includes a range of positions born of various combinations of concerns and perspectives, depending on whether the object of study is everyday life or women's movements, whether a "prosecuting" or "documentary" stance is adopted regarding wartime cooperation, and whether or not attention is paid to class differences. The following diagram illustrates the various possibilities.

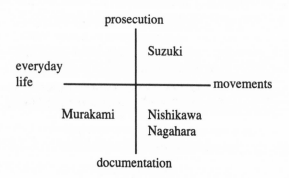

As the very fulcrum of these divergent positions or, more accurately, as someone who in one way or another manifested all of these standpoints, discussants love to bring up Takamure Itsue. Any discussion surrounding Takamure turns eventually to issues related to war and women, including everyday life vs. political movements, motherhood and equal rights, and participation vs. collaboration; and she provides the litmus test to illuminate the relative positions of the debaters.[16]

I would like to make four points concerning this field of research. First, the type-B studies all focus on the active adaptation or participation of women in relation to wartime circumstances, although their interpretations frequently differ from one another. Such studies seek to recover women as active subjects; through the "recovery" of women as subjects, it becomes possible to pursue their responsibility. Second, these studies all seek to grasp a "women's logic" (Nishikawa). However, there is a wide range of understandings regarding the contradictions and circumstances surrounding women. For instance, while Murakami focuses on the family system, Fujii emphasizes class differentials. On the other hand, while the interpretations of Nishikawa or Nagahara may differ from those of Suzuki or Kanō, they all share a focus on the wartime system (or the modernity which engendered it) as a mechanism governed by male principles.

Third, some scholars contributed to the project of situating the wartime era by examining the circumstances surrounding women and women's movements in the preceding era of the 1920s. For example, through an analysis of the League for Women's Suffrage, Kano Masanao uncovers the logic of "resisting while retreating and retreating while resisting."[17] The "documentary" stance sees relative continuity from the 1920s, while the "prosecuting" one emphasizes a radical break; nevertheless, both see some sort of "about-face" (*tenkō*) in the wartime period as compared to the movements in the 1920s.

Fourth, both the "documentary" and "prosecuting" camps locate the end of the wartime system at August 1945, marking it off clearly from the postwar. The history of women during wartime is separated from postwar women's history, and these are treated as different fields of study, each with its own set of issues and standards for critical judgement. In other words, women during the wartime period and, indeed, the wartime period itself are characterized as atypical.

Keeping in mind the above research concerning women and total war, I would like in the remainder of this essay to explore the writings of Oku Mumeo during the wartime and postwar periods. I have chosen to focus on Oku for two major reasons: (1) She continuously participated in women's movements from the 1920s on, and provides a wealth of material on this topic spanning the prewar, wartime and postwar periods. In particular, it is possible to analyze the connections between wartime and the postwar by comparing her wartime pronouncements with her postwar leadership in the Housewives' Federation. (2) Oku consistently spoke out on such topics as motherhood and consumption, elaborated a "women's logic," and opened up new horizons for women. Oku's own focus was on working women, so although she maintained close contact with middle-class women's movements, the movement she developed was inevitably in a relation of tension with her middle-class, civic counterparts.

Total war brought the "conversion of women into national subjects."[18] Accordingly, plans were drawn up to restructure the gender-specific division of labor, and policies were pursued on the basis of sexual discrimination. The significance of motherhood was stressed and efforts were made to integrate women as subjects on the basis of motherhood. I would like, then, to explore Oku's logic and practice during the period of this "motherland," and relate them to her postwar activities.[19]

WOMEN/EVERYDAY LIFE/COMMUNITY

Oku Mumeo was born in 1895 in Fukui Prefecture and married after graduation from the Japan Women's College. Possessed of great concern for social problems, she sought to experience for herself what it was like to be a female factory worker. In 1920, Oku, along with Hiratsuka Raichō and Ichikawa Fusae, established the New Women's Association, and from then on she continually participated in women's movements. In particular, in 1923, she established the Society of Working Women and poured her energy into dealing with problems related to "working women." The house journal for the Society of Working Women was initially published in June 1923 as *Shokugyō fujin* (Working Women), but the title was soon changed in April 1924 to *Fujin to rōdō* (Women and Work), and once again in September 1925 to *Fujin undō* (Women's Movements). These changes occurred at a dizzying speed, illustrating the process by which Oku's concern shifted from working women to the work which defined the working woman and finally to the women's movements which could point out and resolve related problems.

In this process Oku was also expanding the target of her activities "from the problems of working women to the problems of women in proletarian households."[20] Oku understood that "women's emancipation and proletarian class liberation" were "one problem, not two." In close contact with the proletarian movements of the latter half of the 1920s, Oku brought the directions and issues of women's emancipation and the proletarian movement together.[21] Her activities were not only part of, but helped propel what is known as the

Taishō Democracy movement of the 1920s; and she adopted a critical position aimed at the articulation and resolution of issues.

Oku's activities in the latter half of the 1920s have three distinguishing characteristics. First, she always spoke and acted from the stance of a woman who works. Oku defined herself as "a wife who, in the midst of the details of everyday life, experiences hardship as a proletarian woman."[22] While she welcomed a situation in which women worked and participated in society, she also saw them as housewives handling the time-consuming "domestic labor involving children and the daily necessities of food, shelter and clothing."[23] Oku characterizes a woman as someone who "purchases things, manages domestic affairs, and is endowed with the destiny of motherhood, that is, of pregnancy, birth and the raising of children."[24]

Accordingly, working women were trapped between two sets of demands: those related to working and those related to their social identity as women in charge of managing the household and raising children. For Oku, the crucial issue was how to resolve these dual demands. In other words, she (a) accepted the gender-specific division of labor which placed women in charge of domestic labor, and (b) had no doubts concerning motherhood, regarding it as women's fundamental nature.

Second, Oku was able to posit a space of "consumption" through her grasp of the reality of everyday life based on the points mentioned above. Oku argues that while "the most common and natural life style for women is to be confined in a house and surrounded by children," women should cultivate a sense of responsibility and participation in society without "withering away" in the midst of the daily routine.[25] That is, her goal was to have women who were "housewives for their households and good wives for their men" be "good mothers and housewives in social terms as well."[26] On the basis of these concerns, Oku actively participated in "the consumer union movement as one aspect of the social reform movement," since "consumption" belonged "within the housewife's realm of guarding the kitchen." She took part in the Western Suburban Working Couple Society, worked as a central committee member for the Kanto Consumer Union League, and in 1928 established the Organization of Women's Consumer Unions.[27] In the course of such activities, Oku developed a theoretical stance which located consumption in relation to production and proposed that the realm of "consumption" become a site of resistance.

In contrast to the value customarily placed on production as a public act, the "private" act of consumption was seldom given serious thought; a sharp line was drawn between the two categories. This was compounded by the asymmetric social organization of men/production and women/consumption. Oku attempts, on the other hand, (a) to give value to the act of consumption, and (b) to provide encouragement to women as the ones in charge of consumption. Moreover, (c) through her participation in movements organized around the act of consumption (consumer union movements) Oku both socialized consumption and built community through it.

From a woman's standpoint, even women "isolated in the household" were capable of participating in community and of gathering in solidarity through action in the realm of consumption. By way of the consumer union movement, Oku tapped into "the dissatisfactions and demands contained in their hearts as housewives and mothers," and tried to dispel feelings of "isolation."[28] The third characteristic of Oku's activities, then, is her concern with community. Oku's goal was community by and for women. In order to minimize consumption performed in isolation, not only did Oku promote joint purchase through consumer unions, but she also worked for the communalization of domestic labor, that is, for community kitchens, laundries and child care facilities.

In this regard, she had two main objectives: (a) to reduce the burdens borne by women because domestic labor is "troublesome and unscientific"[29] and (b) to avoid putting "our whole lives in the hands of profit-making enterprises"[30] because intermediary exploitation makes everyday life "unpleasant," "uneconomical" and "impractical." Her solution to these problems is the communalization of consumption.

The communal practice of consumption by women as proposed by Oku was realized first in 1930 in a women's settlement established in Honjo Ward, Tokyo, and then in 1935 via the "House for Working Women" in Ushigome Ward, Tokyo. These were places where women could gather together for activities and learning. For example, the women's settlement offered child care facilities, lodging, marriage counseling, pregnancy monitoring/counseling, and a night school for women as well as review courses for children. Of course, a communal dining hall and laundry facilities were also provided.[31]

In the latter half of the 1920s, Oku Mumeo concentrated on the domestic dimension of life as a working woman. She sought to minimize the burden of housework by means of communal consumption. Her attempt to grasp living patterns in terms of consumption and socialization was also linked to her claim that living patterns ultimately came down to making consumption rational and scientific. The horizons opened up by Oku corresponded to the development of consumer society in the latter half of the 1920s, pointing the way to a new fusion of the significance embodied in the linked concepts of women/living patterns/consumption with that of men/labor/production, with the former cluster of concepts serving as the axis. At the same time, however, Oku reinforced the links between women, daily life, and consumption, without examining the principles underlying this organization of consumer society. That is, she worked toward the resolution of the above problems without questioning the premises of male society.

Thus, while Oku organized "women as masses," and sought to create among them a "subjectivity,"[32] we must note that she never sought to "secure a position equal with men."[33] Rather than proposing "women's emancipation on the level of individuals," Oku argued for "women's emancipation as a group."[34] Her understanding of what constituted the identity of women included a gender-specific division of labor and motherhood.

Oku Mumeo under the System of Wartime Mobilization
Women as National Subjects

Oku described her own movement as "a rearguard movement to realize social reform,"[35] but when the vanguard crumbled, Oku temporarily lost sight of her goals. She even went so far as to write that a working woman was not happy and the more she worked the more she would lose "a woman's essential qualities," adding that "if possible, we would like to see women abandon the working life."[36]

However, in 1937 Oku regained her vigor with a piece in the September issue of *Women's Movements* called "Testing the Strength of Women in Times of Crisis."

In the background of her recovery were such drastic changes in the general situation as (1) the wartime demand for women to enter the workplace due to the departure of men for the front, and (2) the explosion of various problems in relation to the increasing numbers of working women. The system came to require the labor of the women for whom Oku served as an advocate; the nation was now confronted with the same problems that Oku had been working to resolve. Oku's issues were of national concern under the wartime system, so she turned once again to the problems of the working woman.

However, we can see a reversal of logic in Oku. First, she placed priority on the "dictates of the times," that is, on the needs of the state which were to govern women's management of the household. Under the wartime system, Oku repeatedly stressed that "personal feelings" should be suppressed during "this time of unparalleled crisis" and in light of "the great troubles faced by the nation." She exhorts her readers to give their all for the "sake of the whole," advising them that "we should contribute to home front production with the work of our hands, demonstrating exemplary strength in these times."[37]

Under the wartime system, consumption was "converted from a private to a public activity."[38] Since the nation was seconding Oku's claims, she had no problem working within the framework provided by the state. In the March 1941 issue of *Women's Movements*, under the banner of "Our goal! Advancing toward a Wartime Way of Life," Oku promoted "total savings" because "even when we lack material things, we are not poor; even when we have an income, we will keep advancing toward a wartime way of life with an unwavering heart." She called for people to "live within their means and to regulate consumption in line with national policies" while extolling the "minimal way of life of the wartime working woman" and the "way of life of the completely mobilized household under the direction of the wise housewife."

The socialization of consumption was given national priority under wartime circumstances. Oku worked within and contributed to this national discourse. Just as consumption in Oku's theories changed from a private to a public affair, so did the private realm become completely subject to the public/state. This trend grew even more pronounced in *Shin josei e no michi* (The Road to the New Woman, published in 1942),[39] where Oku argues that "even as today's wartime life comprises personal time, it also forms part of the nation's labor power" and that therefore matters related to it "should be decided, not at the level of the individual, but at the level of the state."

This is her second reversal, a move away from a position critical of the government to one of support and adaptation. No longer "making demands upon society," Oku now gave priority to the demands made by society (the state) and situated working women in relation to those demands. The wartime system promoted the advancement of women into the workplace and turned such work into "a virtuous act in accord with the demands of today's society." In the process, Oku's arguments achieved public recognition and lost their adversarial tone. Leading other women toward accommodation, Oku wrote that both "the ideals and virtues of women must change in conformity with the demands of society."[40]

Yet, there certainly was a strategic aspect to Oku's use of the wartime system: "We must make the most of the current crisis, as it provides a number of ways to protect and advance the lives of working women and to make great progress." Indeed, in an even clearer manner, she cautions in her argument for women to enter the workplace that this opportunity should not be "rejected" as a "reactionary phenomenon in time of crisis." She reasons that "even if it is for purposes of war," once the doors are opened to women, they can readily be made use of; she also advocates an "attitude" on the part of women that will enable them to respond to and expand such opportunities.[41]

As a member of various committees concerning national policy for women—for instance, as a labor survey committee member for the Imperial Rule Assistance Association (1941), a staff member of the Tokyo Military Support Central Counseling Division and a lecturer at the national savings promotion department of the Ministry of Finance—Oku spoke out and offered counsel and in this way actively contributed to the wartime system. Thus, for Oku, wartime was "a good time for women to advance and clear their own paths."[42] In her introduction to *Hana aru shokuba e* (A Workplace with Flowers), Oku exudes contentment tinged with some self-satisfaction as she comments, "These days, state and society are warmly and generously extending helping hands (to working women). Now I can just sit back; I don't have to say anything more."

The introduction to *Hana aru shokuba e* is dated "the year 2601," with the additional note, "on the date leaflets were handed out on the streets urging us 'to offer public service through the workplace to build a strong national defense state.'" In the latter half of the 1920s, Oku had attempted to transform women into active subjects and encourage their public participation, seeking at the same time to achieve official recognition for women's capacity for agency. Under the wartime system, her position did not change. Moreover, in the context of national policy these efforts to enhance women's subjectivity and direct them toward social action were tantamount to transforming women into national subjects. Oku argued that for women to have a public existence, "the household must be fused with society" and women "must live together with society, striving to become capable of contributing to social development."[43]

At a time when the "society" to which she refers is the "strong national defense state" confronting an "emergency," Oku's actions were directed toward "striving to construct the kind of national life called for by the state." She writes that she was "pleased and proud to be striving for the same goals as those of the state,"[44] and to be transforming women into "public persons," that is, national subjects. In *Shin josei e no michi*, too, Oku emphasized the need to be aware of "ourselves as national subjects," but her call for women to transform themselves into subjects of the nation was not a wartime innovation. Even in the latter half of the 1920s, the call for active identification with the nation was latent in her attempts to turn women into subjects. It was merely clarified under the wartime system as changing circumstances brought the national dimension to the fore.

Thus, although Oku can be said to have reversed the priority she accorded to the public vs. private spheres and shifted from a critical to a supportive position in relation to the government, her turnabout occurred in response to a reversal in the circumstances themselves. Oku's efforts for the socialization of women continued uninterrupted from the 1920s; even the call for "transforming women into national subjects" which seemed almost to come out of the blue, is best understood as an extension of her project to turn women into public actors. The causes for the dynamic of reversal and continuity in Oku's discourse lay in both Oku herself and the wartime system, but the wartime system should be given the most credit. As always, only after carefully determining the logic of the situation did Oku set her own direction.

The Logic of Wartime Life

When Oku's activities, which began as a critical movement in the 1920s, were redirected towards securing recognition and institutionalization from the state, the logic of her position changed internally so that the theme of "working women" reemerged in the form of "workers for the state." The sphere of daily life came to hold a strategic military importance as the "domestic front,"[45] and Oku urged the "drafting of plans for a new way of life for wartime." The main features of Oku's proposals for the "wartime way of life" were: (1) a search for identity in "home life," (2) a focus on domestic labor and its rationalization, and (3) an emphasis on community and equality. I would now like to turn to a closer examination of these three points.

Oku stressed that the "wartime way of life" required "a deeply felt commitment to the 'we'll win!' and 'we can do it!' frame of mind." As mothers, women could "keep up the spirits of national subjects" and provide a "bright wartime life" with a "calm state of mind."[46] Oku saw the household as a "blueprint for society," and sought an "authentic life" linked to "national goals." That is, these national goals were to determine the goals of the household and domestic life. While, on the one hand, her search for women's identity led her toward the state as public authority, on the other it pointed her toward the household; as a result, she connected household and state together. Women/household/state formed a "set" as the basis for identity; yet, Oku also sought identity in the household itself, even while trying to endow it with purpose and function.

However, the heart of Oku's program lies in the rationalization of daily life. Oku seized the opportunity presented by the wartime "domestic front" to call for "the rationalization of daily life" which "we should never stop pursuing even during peace."[47] In her article, "Blueprint for the Life of a Working Woman During Wartime," Oku underscores the need for "devices to facilitate efficient use of the time and labor" of working women,[48] advising the implementation of "an orderly, rational life style." She calculates that, if 8 hours are allotted for sleep, 8 hours for working and 1 hour for getting dressed and commuting, only "a mere 6 hours" are left for the "working woman" to do "the laundry, take care of clothing and foot gear, assist with the housework" as well as to "rest" and "study."

Oku continued to believe that domestic labor was a woman's responsibility, accepting the gender-specific division of labor; nevertheless, she argued that women also needed "pleasant moments" or "time for the heart to quietly reflect" while at home. For this purpose, she repeatedly stressed that it was crucial to "use the short time available to the working woman as effectively as possible." The "blueprints for the working life style" contained in *Shin josei e no michi*, deal in detail with the problems not only of time, but also money, material resources and labor. As for money, Oku urged (a) actively making efforts to increase income along with regulation of consumption, and (b) the accumulation of savings for the government through "domestic resourcefulness" and "economizing." In addition, (c) while she acknowledged that poor people were struggling just to raise enough to "cover the minimum necessary eating expenses," she urged everyone "during these times of war" to convert "coarse meals" into "enjoyable, delicious ones" through the application of "knowledge and nutritional information."

Measures related to curbing and minimizing expenses through economizing, resourcefulness and rational management were to be implemented in the name of the state and the wartime system; material resources were to be dealt with in the same manner. Since "everything contributes to the wealth of the country" careless treatment was to be avoided; moreover, "standards should be established" with respect to "the number of" kimonos and sashes, handkerchiefs, collars and socks "so as to reduce them to a minimum"—that is, she proposed that "family apparel was to be subjected to firm planning."

While complaining that many nutritious vegetables were still being thrown out as garbage, Oku noted that the war was in actuality "stripping away all waste and vanity from around us." With regard to labor power as well, "the whole day's time and labor power should not be expended in an aimless, disorderly manner," but rather it was necessary to achieve a "life revolution" that would involve drawing up "blueprints for a well-managed life."

Even in the context of the 1920s Oku had raised the issues of "life blueprints" and rationalization "to increase efficiency" as well as the necessity for rest. Her "peace time" goals had been couched in the language of their time, while in "wartime" she looked forward to the realization of her project under the dictates of "national goals" and the "recognition that the fate of East Asia hung in the balance at every moment." Oku argued that "work related to the daily necessities, housework and child care are in these times no longer merely private matters but play an important national role." As both producer and consumer, Oku vowed to "continue to pursue with unflagging effort the establishment of a proper domestic consumption."

As part of her overall program, Oku proposed increasing the level of communalization of daily life in order to "make the most efficient use" of the power embodied in material resources, personnel and money as well as to "strengthen the civilian ranks of national defense." This program included the communal stocking of goods, communal kitchens, communal sewing and repair of clothing, the establishment of child care facilities and promotion of group travel, observation tours, athletic meetings, recreational get-togethers and library facilities. Oku called for "life blueprints" based on a "social, national community" which went beyond the individual; her goal was "construction of a communal life through regulated, national organization."

Oku's statements were unquestionably intertwined inextricably with and actively supportive of the wartime system. However, I would like to make a couple points in this regard. First, because all shared the wartime situation, Oku's program included a concern for social equality. She argued that "with regard to all essential expenditures, everyone should adhere firmly to a minimum standard of life." Quoting the common saying, "Grieve not over poverty, but over inequality," she urged her readers to all strive for this spirit. Even Suzuki Hiroko, who judges the wartime Oku very harshly, writes that Oku "strove for a certain kind of equal society" during that period.[49] As Suzuki points out, in the 1920s, Oku worked for a more equal society by attempting to raise the position of working women, while during the wartime period, she tried to achieve this equalization by having the "wealthy leisured woman" also work. From the above reversal of terms, we can understand Oku's efforts for an "equal society" as a type of compulsory homogenization or *Gleichschaltung* (R. Dahrendorf) which transformed "nonworking women" into "working women."

Second, Oku strove for the modernization of the household. She disparaged "old customs as unyielding as stone" in reference to the ways of the people living in farming villages.[50] To combat this and modernize the household, Oku trumpeted such values as cleanliness, hygiene, and the rationalization of life style throughout the 1920s and the wartime period. Historical studies of the family in the modern period employ the concept "modern family," which, rather than some notion of a "feudal institution from the past," is used to describe the Japanese household (*ie*). Such research sees the development of the "modern family" as one key to understanding modern Japan.[51]

The definition of the "modern family" varies depending on the writer, but there is general agreement that its primary characteristics are: (a) a gender-specific division of labor turning on the axis of domestic labor, (b) the family's dual autonomy and exclusivity, (c) division between a domestic private space and a public communal space and (d) the existence of motherly love.[52] Oku supported all of these premises and worked toward their realization. Although up until this point in the essay we have not dealt directly with category (d), "motherhood" surfaces from time to time in Oku's arguments and eventually becomes one of her core concepts. For example, in *Tatakau josei* (Fighting Women), published by the Propaganda Department of the Imperial Rule Assistance Association, she maintains that "mothers constitute the ground which gives birth to and raises the next generation of the Japanese race." Accordingly, mothers must be "given the opportunity for warm rest and regeneration," that is, motherhood must be protected. From Oku's perspective, on the one hand, it was only natural for women to marry and give birth to children but, on the other, "motherhood" was equally self-evident and it was on that basis that she called on society to "cooperate" in protecting motherhood.

Oku's basic project was to resolve by means of communalization the contradictions and hardships which surrounded women and originated in aspects of the "modern family." Certainly, her proposed "communalization of life style"—the communal kitchens and communal laundries—seemed to diverge from characteristics (b) and (c). In the name of communality and sociality, she appears to direct her efforts toward overcoming the individualization and division of housework and child care and the isolation necessitated by the modern family.

However, because Oku's discussions overlook the problem of the management of housework at the top level of domestic labor and leave unquestioned the "communal life style," the concept of "domestic labor" is never in the least bit displaced, even if individual "domestic labor" is reduced. However, in her arguments the issue of management at the highest level of domestic labor is overlooked, and her notion of communal life is never subjected to questioning from that angle; the result is that, while domestic labor might be reduced in particular cases, the concept of domestic labor itself is never challenged. Moreover, since the idea of women as the bearers of responsibility (a) is seen as self-evident and in need of no further examination, the end result is to reinforce the logic of the "modern family."

In sum, Oku Mumeo's activities under the wartime system supported and contributed to that system, sought official recognition, and were directed toward modernization of the working class and especially the home environment of working women. Because she attempted to move the private self, which had been torn between the public and private realms, further in the direction of the public, it appears that she advocated a "transcendence" of the public/private split. In fact, strictly speaking, she left the split intact and merely sought to attach the self and its identity to the public side. Oku aimed to transform women into active subjects solely as the bearers of domestic labor and the possessors of motherhood. Because the social situation itself changed between the 1920s and the wartime era, in the sense that private entities of all kinds were converted into public ones, Oku's own logic reflected that change.

But throughout, she consistently adhered to the objective of modernizing the life circumstances of working women.

Claudia Koonz's *Mothers in the Fatherland* treats the participation of women in the wartime system of the "fatherland," Nazi Germany.[53] In the course of introducing various women, Koonz's study relates to the present one in its discussion of women as the "second sex" in relation to the Third Reich. According to her analysis, while women could not escape their second-class status, they could establish their own "sphere of control" in the margins of the men's world. Because Koonz argues that in the name of "elevating the status of women" the state intervened in such private realms as childbirth and consumption and "invaded" domestic life, she does not find any ambivalence in the actions of women in the wartime era. In that sense, the results of her analysis differ from those of the present study. However, in the context of wartime Japan's "mobilization of mothers," it was quite natural for Oku to employ the expression "hands of a social mother."[54] Moreover, because she herself viewed wartime Japan as a "fatherland," she sought to carve out a "women's realm."

Continuities in Life and Conception of Society

For Oku Mumeo, the loss of the war—the "cessation of the Greater East Asian War"—was the beginning of a new "dawn" for women. Seven years after the war, she wrote that "the signs of a new age offering a lifetime of daring and joy in exchange for sacrifice and endurance were making themselves known."[55] Oku drew a clear line between the wartime and postwar period, seeing an opportunity for women's liberation in the postwar. Oku added with passion that women "were given" "for the first time" a "guarantee of the fundamental human rights of freedom and independence," and that women should not let this "important key" rust in vain.

Yet, despite Oku's emphasis on a break between the wartime system and the postwar, I believe that Oku steadily maintained her former—1920s and wartime—problematic well into the postwar.

In the immediate postwar, Oku (1) urged the "recovery of the former prosperity of the ancestral country Japan" and pride in the "flower of culture." For this purpose, Oku (2) stressed "the heavy responsibility of housewives who hold the nation's economy in their hands." Oku also spoke of (3) "spurring the drive to produce among the working people" and noted the importance of household "economizing and rationalization" for the suppression of imports. The slogan "The housewife's hands which run the kitchen run the whole nation" highlighted the close ties between politics and daily life. Oku continued to pour effort into turning women into subjects on the basis of such logic, remaining an unfailing proponent of "economizing and rationalization." Immediately after the end of the war, on both a national and a more grass roots level, Oku continued her activities without a pause. She returned to co-operative movements and, in 1947, was a successful candidate in the first House of Councilors election. In particular, however, I would like to take a closer look at the activities of the Housewives' Federation (Shufuren) which Oku organized in 1948, making Oku Mumeo a household name. As is generally known, the inspiration for the founding of the Housewives' Federation was Oku's dissatisfaction with the great number of defective matches distributed under the rationing system. In September 1948, she opened the "Housewive's Rally to Abolish Defective Matches" by holding aloft a match that would not burn. Fourteen women's groups, ranging from the Women's Democracy Club to the New Japan Women's League, participated, and invitations were extended to staff from the Ministry of Commerce and Industry; various discussions were held. Many of the members of the women's groups were housewives. Oku was then working toward the organization of a group focusing on "household economic problems as a consumer" "because housewives are inextricably bound in a relationship to" the consumer life style of the home.

In this way and in the same month, the Housewives' Federation was established. "In a word" the Federation was said to be "a movement to promote a stable life style from the standpoint of consumer economics."[56] That is, the Federation was organized (1) among unorganized women (2) from the perspective of consumption (3) in the name of housewives. Here we find Oku, who had formerly focused on the "household life style" of "working women," now seeking to create a new subject, the "housewife." The very name, the Housewives' Federation, was only arrived at through a process of considering such other possibilities as "The Housewives' Association for the Lowering of Prices" and "The Tokyo Women's Price Movement Association." "The Housewives' Federation" was finally adopted in order to make it clear that this was "a movement in which housewives are becoming subjects."[57]

This movement, which "transmitted the voices of housewives" to the government, claimed to direct "a housewife's gaze" toward the "irrationality, trickery, profiteering and exploitation which abound in the daily life of the housewife." Except for the change in identity of the principal actor to the "housewife," this movement is reminiscent of the Society of Working Women in the latter half of the 1920s. Oku comes to once again occupy a critical stance. At the same time, the Housewives' Federation constituted "a common front by housewives who have been brought together by their concern with daily life." Oku's calls for "everyone to band together to protect their life style" and "to construct a cheerful life" clearly reiterate her concerns during wartime and the latter half of the 1920s, with the sole exception of her new focus on the "housewife."[58] In *Daidokoro to seiji* (The Kitchen and Politics), Oku describes the goals of the women's movement now embodied in the Federation as the "brightening" of household life, the "rationalization" of consumption, "in sum, the rationalization of everyday life." Thus, Oku established the Housewives' Federation movement as part of a project pursued under the wartime system as well.

What, then, should we make of Oku's new concern with "housewives"? I believe that when Oku pushed the issue of domestic labor to the forefront, the figure of the housewife, which until this point had been out of the lime- light, emerged as the appropriate focal point. Oku saw the changed circum- stances of the "postwar" as those in which women had "freedom," "basic human rights," and the "opportunity" and "ability" to participate. Women were coming into their own "with regard to the country and the family" in the process of being transformed into subjects aware of their responsibility. Oku's postwar understanding accorded priority, *first*, to steering women's attention to their responsibilities as managers of the household, and *second*, toward politics. The impact of the postwar "rationed life" may have been a signifi- cant factor, but the point remains that Oku's earlier efforts to grasp the dual aspects of women were finally reconciled in a focus on the one dimension of women as domestic managers, that is, as housewives.

Oku, here, (1) further develops the logic which reveals the outlines of the housewife role resulting from the gender-specific division of labor of the modern family; (2) attempts to deal with the isolating and individualizing processes inevitably found within the modern family through her logic favor- ing new political participation on the part of housewives as an alliance; and (3) placing the spotlight on women in their capacity as managers of consump- tion, Oku eliminates the premise that "work" must equal production and thereby clarifies the logic of her movement as being primarily that of consumption. Oku inaugurated the postwar Housewives' Federation movement on the basis of the wartime concept of "daily life" and of women (housewives) as subjects in relation to that concept. The metaphor of "the hands of the social mother" found use in the postwar as well.[59]

The symbol of the "rice ladle" (*shamoji*) adopted by the Housewives' Federation (a) indicated the status of housewives' rights, (b) represented the "skills needed for communal activities" since it is used to keep stirring food on the stove to prevent it from burning, (c) evoked "the housewife's dream" of bountiful food, and (d) suggested the meaning of "winning" through a pun on the word for food (*meshi*) and the word for the "spirit to hold on" (*meshitoru*).[60] The above constitutes a restructuring of the logic of Oku's activities based on the concept of "housewife"; moreover, points (a) and (d) mobilize folk culture concepts through their stronger representation of housewives.

Oku's activities included the establishment of the "Housewives' Hall" as a communal space which she described as a "house of concrete built by our ongoing efforts of collective struggle."[61] A direct descendent of the prewar "Women's Settlement" and "House for Working Women," the "Housewives' Hall" was completed in 1956. Located in Yotsuya, Tokyo, the Hall provided lodging, a wedding hall, counseling services including marriage counseling and family planning, and, in addition, offered classes in flower arranging and tea ceremony.

By 1963, the Housewives' Federation was sending staff members to twenty-nine inquiry committees, both national and regional, including the provisional government's survey committee, tax system survey committees, and insurance inquiry committees.[62] We can observe links with the wartime system since the 1930s in this achievement of the capability to speak and act effectively in such forums. The transfer of private acts, consumption in particular, to the public sphere effected under the wartime system continued in full force even after 1945; this trend and the activities of the Housewives' Federation mutually influenced and fed each other.

The "Housewives' Song" (lyrics by Noguchi Yasuyo) celebrates the strength and ideals of housewives and the Housewives' Federation: "Breaking traditions, old dreams/From households all over Japan/With bright hopes/Slender arms entwine/Victory for the undaunted housewives/Hooray for the housewives' victory!"[63] However, these ideals and issues did not suddenly emerge in the postwar, but were discussed and pursued from the 1920s on and were given a great opportunity for expansion during the 1930s under the wartime system.

Translated by Noriko Aso

Notes

[1] Joseishi Sōgō Kenkyūkai, ed., *Nihon joseishi kenkyūkai bunken mokuroku*, Vols. I-III (Tokyo: Tokyo daigaku shuppankai, 1983, 1988, 1994).

[2] *Bunken mokuroku*, Vol. III.

[3] Tokyo Rekishi Kagaku Kenkyūkai Fujin Undōshi Bukai, ed., *Onna to sensō* (Tokyo: Shōwa shuppan, 1991).

[4] Orii Miyako and Iwai Sachiko, "Sensō to onna no nichijō seikatsu," in Joseishi Sōgō Kenkyūkai, ed., *Nihon josei seikatsushi, daiyonkan: kindai* (Tokyo: Tokyo daigaku shuppankai, 1990).

[5] Ibid.

[6] Ibid.

[7] Ibid.

[8] Murakami Nobuhiko, *Nihon no fujin mondai* (Tokyo: Iwanami shoten, 1978).

[9] Ishitsuki Shizue, "1930 nendai no musan fujin rōdō" in Joseishi Sōgō Kenkyūkai, eds., *Nihon joseishi, daigokan: gendai* (Tokyo: Tokyo daigaku shuppankai, 1982).

[10] Suzuki Hiroko, *Feminizumu to sensō* (Tokyo: Marjusha, 1986).

[11] Kanō Mikiyo, *Onnatachi no "jūgo"* (Tokyo: Chikuma shobō, 1987).

[12] Nishikawa Yūko, "Sensō e no keisha to yokusan no fujin" in *Nihon joseishi, daigokan: gendai.*

[13] Nagahara Kazuko, "Josei wa naze sensō ni kyōryoku shita ka" in Fujiwara Akira, ed., *Nihon kindaishi no kyozō to jitsuzō*, Vol. 3 (Tokyo: Ōtsuki shoten, 1989).

[14] Fujii Tadatoshi, *Kokubō fujinkai* (Tokyo: Iwanami shoten, 1985).

[15] Suzuki Hiroko, *Jūgun ianfu-naisen kekkon* (Tokyo: Miraisha, 1992); Yoshimi Yoshiaki, *Jūgan ianfu* (Tokyo: Iwanami Shoten, 1995).

[16] Nagahara Kazuko, "Takamure Itsue kenkyū ni manabu mono" in *Rekishi hyōron*, Vol. 455 (1988).

[17] Kano Masanao, "Fuashizumuka no fujin undō" in Ienaga Saburō Kyōju Tokyo Kyōiku Daigaku Taikan Kinen Ronshū Kankō Iinkai, eds., *Ienaga Saburō kyōju tai-Tokyo kyōiku daigaku taikan kinen ronshō 2: kindai nihon no kokka to shisō* (Tokyo: Sanseidō, 1979).

[18] Françoise Thébeau, ed., *A History of Women in the West*, Vol. 5, 20th Century (Cambridge: Harvard University Press, 1994).

[19] For an introduction to aspects of this kind of "motherland" please refer to Nagahara Kazuko, "Josei tōgō to bosei" in Wakita Haruko, ed., *Bosei o tou*, Vol. 2 (Tokyo: Jinbun shoin, 1985) and Kano Masanao, *Senzen no "ie" no shisō* (Tokyo: Sōbunsha, 1973).

[20] Saji Emiko, "Oku Mumeo to musan katei fujin" in *Rekishi hyōron*, Vol. 359 (1980).

[21] Oku Mumeo, "Fujin wa musan kaikyū o shiji seyo" in *Fujin Undō* (March 1928).

[22] Oku, "Musan fujin undō no shinshutsu ni tsuite" in *Fujin Undō* (December 1927).

[23] Oku, "Omou kotodomo" in *Fujin Undō* (June 1925).

[24] Oku, "Shōhi kumiai fujin no shakai kaizen undō ni tsuite" in *Fujin Undō* (July, 1930).

[25] Oku, "Henshūshitsu nite" in *Fujin undō* (January 1931).

[26] Oku, "Fujin to shakaiteki kanshin" in *Fujin undō* (October 1928).

[27] For further details, please refer to Abe Tsunehisa and Narita Ryūichi, "Fujin undō no tenkai" in Kano Masanao and Yui Masaomi, eds., *Kindai nihon no tōgō to teikō*, Vol. 3 (Tokyo: Nihon hyōronsha, 1982).

[28] Oku, *Shōhi kumiai undō*, Vol. 10 (September 1928).

[29] Oku, "Kinji sandai" in *Fujin undō* (July 1927).

[30] Oku, "Fujin setsurumento e no koinegai" in *Fujin undō* (January 1932).

[31] Abe and Narita, "Fujin undō no tenkai."

[32] Oku, "Katei fujin to shite no hansei" in *Fujin undō* (May 1928).

[33] Oku, "Shōhi kumiai fujin no shakai kaizō undō ni tsuite" in *Fujin undō* (May 1928).

[34] Ueno Chizuko, *Onna to iu kairaku* (Tokyo: Keisō shobō, 1986).

[35] Oku, "Tooi yume/chikai yume" in *Fujin undō* (November 1935).

[36] Oku, "Hataraku fujin no tame ni" in *Fujin undō* (January 1935).

[37] Oku, *Hana aru shokuba e* (Tokyo: Bunmeisha, 1941).

[38] Yamanouchi Yasushi, "Senjiki no isan to sono ryōgisei" in *Iwanami kōza shakai kagaku no hōhō*, Vol. III (Tokyo: Iwanami shoten, 1993).

[39] Oku, *Shin josei e no michi* (Tokyo: Kinreisha, 1942).

[40] Oku, *Hana aru shokuba e.*

[41] Ibid.

[42] Ibid.

[43] Ibid.

[44] Ibid.

[45] Oku, *Shin josei e no michi.*

[46] Ibid.

[47] Ibid.

[48] Oku, "Hataraku josei no senji seikatsu sekkei" in *Fujin undō* (March 1941).

[49] Suzuki, *Feminizumu to sensō.*

[50] Oku, *Shin josei e no michi.*

[51] Ueno, *Kindai kazoku no seiritsu to shūen* (Tokyo: Iwanami shoten, 1994).

[52] Please refer to Ueno, *Kindai kazoku no seiritsu to shūen*; Yamada Masahiro, *Kindai kazoku no yukue* (Tokyo: Shinyōsha, 1994); and Ochiai Keiko, *Kindai kazoku to feminizumu* (Tokyo: Keisō shobō, 1989) among others.

[53] Claudia Koonz, *Mothers in the Fatherland* (New York: 1987). Himeoka Toshiko, trans., *Chichi no kuni no hahatachi*, 2 vols., (Tokyo: Jiji tsūshinsha, 1990).

[54] Oku, *Shin josei e no michi.*

[55] Oku, *Daidokoro to seiji* (Tokyo: Ministry of Finance Publishing Division, 1952).

[56] Oku, *Shufuren tayori*, Vol. 6 (March 1949).

[57] Ibid.

[58] Oku, "Tanoshii tatakai" in *Shufuren tayori*, Vol. 1 (December 1948).

[59] Oku, "Shufu no nerau mono," *Shufuren tayori*, Vol. 10 (1950).

[60] Shufurengōkai, *Shufuren 15 shūnen kinen, ayumi* (1963).

[61] Oku, *Shufuren tayori*, Vol. 8 (1949).

[62] Shufurengō kai, *Shufuren 15 shūnen kinen, ayumi* (1963).

[63] *Shufu tayori*, Vol. 1.

Desire for a Poietic Metasubject:
Miki Kiyoshi's Technology Theory

Iwasaki Minoru

The self-consciousness of early-postwar Japanese intellectuals is most clearly evident in the widespread attention they paid to the "postwar debate on *shutaisei* [active subjectivity]." The debate was touched off in 1946 by the publication in the journal *Tenbō* of "Ningenteki jiyū no genkai" [Limits of human freedom] by the unknown philosopher and Mito Higher School teacher, Umemoto Katsumi; it then spread rapidly as a variety of journals treated it as the illumination of a central question of the era.[1] This was the case despite the confusion caused by Umemoto's prose, and the marked ambiguity of the coined term *shutaisei*, not only among his interlocutors but in his own interventions as well.

Umemoto's challenge is in large part summed up in a question he himself posed: "How is it possible to achieve subjective [*shutaiteki*] human freedom in the midst of objective necessity?"[2] Orthodox Marxists heaped doctrinaire criticism on Umemoto's claim to have found a lacuna in the "scientific objectivity" of Marxism.[3] At the same time, Umemoto's query stimulated widespread discussion of "*shutaisei*" in a number of realms, including literature and science.[4] Taketani Mitsuo's theory of technology was hailed as a successful development of Umemoto's problematic in the realm of "epistemology," and for a time Taketani's three-stage theory—encompassing the "phenomenal," the "substantial" and the "ontological"—was praised as a promising new approach to materialism.[5] In any case, in the early-postwar era "*shutaisei*" was widely bruited about as a key concept for self-interpretation.

As Umemoto himself recollected later on, the honors bestowed upon him in the first two or three years after defeat must be seen in the context of an atmosphere best described as an "age of philosophy."[6] Nevertheless, the narrow path into which the "postwar debate on shutaisei" was forced by a certain

159

self-destructive tendency made it the prototype for a series of debates that followed it in the context of postwar thought.

The "postwar debate on *shutaisei*" has been taken to symbolize "discontinuity" in mentalité between the pre- and postwar eras. That is probably the result of the electrifying impact of the term, which cast a spell over intellectuals in the midst of abject defeat and, in effect, *brought about* historical discontinuity. Emphasis on the moment of "*shutaisei*" entailed a certain introspective attitude, leading to the realization that the experience of having one's resistance destroyed and being mobilized for a ruinous war meant that something had been missing in terms of internal confirmation and completion. Of course, at the present juncture, when the momentum of "postwar enlightenment" has so completely dissipated, it is simple to criticize the "postwar debate on *shutaisei*." A more difficult issue is how to deal with the general problematic of "*shutaisei*," especially in view of the immobilizing effect of the debate's own production of "discontinuity." The approach adopted here will be to look at the debate's prewar counterpart—that is, the interrogation of "*shutaisei*" that already was of central importance in the 1930s and early-1940s, especially in the form of "technological *shutaisei*"—in an attempt to show that the prewar discourse contained a certain awareness, in advance, of the defects that would plague postwar arguments. In such a perspective, the "postwar debate on *shutaisei*" emerges as merely a poor and emaciated repetition of discursive conundrums that had been engaged more fully in the thirties and early-forties. As Uchida Yoshihiko has pointed out, in that earlier context the discourse on "technology" and "*shutaisei*" was, in a sense, the technological version of the productive forces theory put forth by Ōkōchi Kazuo as a counterpart to the movement among labor bureaucrats.[7]

I will begin with a brief recapitulation of the discourse on technology as it developed under the wartime mobilization system (parts one and two), and then focus on philosopher Miki Kiyoshi's theory of technology, which attained its most creative formulation in Miki's "logic of imagination" (*kōsōryoku no ronri*) (part three). Against that background, I will consider the problems inherent in this "other" theory of *shutaisei* (part four), and suggest that it offers a useful perspective on our collective attempt to situate the wartime mobilization system as an object of study (part five).

THE SPIRIT OF TECHNOLOGY

At a time when the Asia-Pacific War had already encompassed the U.S. and Great Britain, Shimomura Toratarō spoke in the following manner in the course of the round-table discussion on "overcoming the modern." He was reacting against the other discussants' tendency to dwell fetishistically on what they believed to be essentially "Japanese" (*Nihonteki naru mono*):

> The character of the spirit that produced the machine is itself the issue. It is a new kind of spirit. It lives within us moderns as an indisputable fact, so simply to express dislike for it is to avoid the real issue. I don't think it can be treated merely as a matter of soul (*tamashii*) or inner resolve (*kakugo*). . . . It used to be that the soul was considered to be insubstantial spirit in contrast to flesh, but in the modern era the character of the body has changed. That is, *the modern body is a kind of organism that can be said to include the machine as one of its own organs*. The archaic soul can no longer rule this new body. A new kind of soul must be formed. The tragedy of modernity is that the archaic soul no longer fits the body . . . , the machine. Here, the problem is whether to go backward or forward; yet, of course, we cannot go back. . . . We need a new metaphysics of the mind/body relation. This is a problem of momentous proportions, impervious to the subjective (*shukanteki*), individual methods of the past, like soul-searching or discipline. *Social and political methods* are required, along with a new wisdom and a new theology[8] (emphasis added).

The participants in the round-table represented, variously, the Kyoto School of philosophy, the Japan Romantic Faction, and the group of writers around the journal *Bungakkai*, and on the whole they manifested a strong tendency toward Japanism (Nipponshugi). In opposition to that tendency, Shimomura tried to reorient the question of "overcoming the modern" toward the issue of how to accomplish a fundamental transformation of world view through technology. While he accepted the basic framework of "overcoming the modern," for him it was not a matter of opposing the modern but of internalizing the issues thrown up by modernity and developing them in conjunction with "social and political measures." Indeed, the mode of understanding latent in Shimomura's statements appears to parallel the consistently technological approach of those who actively came to grips with the wartime mobilization system.

The Shōwa Kenkyūkai (Shōwa Research Association), organized by Prime Minister Konoe Fumimaro's oracle, Gotō Kōnosuke, provided a central point of contact for such intellectuals. In terms of ideological stance, the Association's members were very diverse, but it cannot be denied that their major effort was directed toward dissolving the prewar social formation and, through the establishment of an efficient, controlled, "total-war system," to oversee the emergence of a homogeneous, national community.[9] Although as an organization the "Shōwa Kenkyūkai" was somewhat ponderous, and ultimately dissolved itself during the formative stages of the "Imperial Rule Assistance Association" (Taisei Yokusankai),[10] in selecting topics to investigate the Kenkyūkai ironically anticipated the political-economic and educational systems[11] that would dominate postwar society. Amid the waves of organization that gave rise to the Ultra Defense-Centered State (*kōdo kokubō kokka*), former Marxists and liberals channeled their urges for autonomy and influence into a frighteningly concrete form of rationalist involvement in the wartime mobilization system.

Miki Kiyoshi also became an active participant in the Kenkyūkai, especially in the latter part of 1938, when he was in charge of its Cultural Section. Through a series of pamphlets, including *Shin-Nihon no shisō genri* (Philosophical Principles for a New Japan) and *Shin-Nihon no shisō genri: zokuhen* (Philosophical Principles for a New Japan: Continued)(X VII-507 ff.), he sought to provide a theoretical basis for carrying out the renovationist bureaucrats' and intellectuals' mobilization plans. In doing so, he took on the dangerous task of trying to identify alternatives in an increasingly desperate era. For Miki Kiyoshi, the philosopher, these efforts dovetailed with his effort in his final work, *The Logic of Imagination*, to critically redelineate "logos and pathos." Therefore, while part of his theory of technology resonated loudly with other arguments being voiced at the time, it also contained a somewhat different intellectual perspective. For that very reason his philosophy suggests symbolically the internal characteristics and implications of the discourse of his time.[12]

THE CONFIGURATION OF TECHNOLOGY THEORY

The first stage in the development of a theory of technology in Japan took the form of a "debate on technology theory," in the narrow sense, among Aikawa Haruki, Oka Kunio, Tosaka Jun, Nagata Hiroshi, and other members of the Yuibutsuron Kenkyūkai (Materialism Study Group), formed in 1932.[13] However, it focused on the definition of "productive forces" that was prescribed in the orthodox "Marxism" of the Soviet Union, and did not go beyond doctrinal polemics. That is, participants remained preoccupied with the definition of concepts in accord with the "theory of the system of the means of labor." From the beginning, they suppressed any impulse toward a principled reinvestigation of "technology" in the midst of actual social dynamics, and thus remained mired in partisan dogmatics. That is why, in the postwar technology theory of Taketani and others, this early definition would be attacked as a materialist "objectivization" that refused the question of "*shutaisei*."

Later, as a result of continuing state suppression of the theorists who led the Materialism Study Group, they were unable to go beyond repeating the definition of technology according to the "system of the means of labor" theory, and the issue stagnated. At the same time, the focal point of this questioning of technology shifted to the discourse and activities surrounding organization of the wartime mobilization system. Ironically, it was precisely in this process that a "practical" moment was introduced into the definition of technology. From the "China Incident" of 1937 onward, references to "technology" in the context of discourse on "mobilization" multiplied explosively outside the confines of the Materialism Study Group.

For example, Aikawa Haruki, who originally proposed the definition of technology as "the system of the means of labor," shifted his position in his 1940 book, *Gendai gijutsuron* (Contemporary theories of technology),[14] so that, while "retaining to the end the definition of technology as the means of labor," he now declared that it was necessary to grasp technology not from a materialist perspective but from "the perspective of the practical actor." At the same time, he rejected the definition centering on "the system of the means of labor," which he himself had earlier proposed, and now defined technology in terms of "the means in process." The awkward (in Japanese) phrase "in process" was, according to Aikawa, the result of his recognition of the weak points in materialism; but it is also clear that he sought, amidst severe political oppression, to secure theoretically the unique position implicitly granted to technologists under the wartime mobilization system. In his "Futatabi *Gijutsuron* wo kaku dōki to natta futatsu no meta-nōto" (Two meta-notes on my motivation for writing *On technology*), he characterizes the flood of discourse on technology as follows:

In late-1937—that is, after outbreak of the present incident—a new inquiry into technology theory began in the context of national tension and reflection, and at the same time, [awareness of] the practical significance of technology emerged in state planning. A constructive theory of technology that was full of *practical* significance and dependent upon state planning moved to center stage in connection with economic controls and cultural policy[15] (emphasis Iwasaki's).

Under circumstances in which, beginning with Aikawa, theories of technology moved to the foreground in an era of urgent attention to construction of the defense-oriented state, the conception of "scientific industry" (*kagakushugi kōgyō*) propounded by Ōkōchi Masatoshi gained great theoretical influence in conjunction with that of the newly-formed "League for Industrial Technology" (1938)[16] and of the "new scientific-technical order" of

Cabinet Planning Agency (*Kikakuin*) vice-director Miyamoto Takenosuke. In contrast to the "capitalistic industry" advanced by the existing *zaibatsu*, which "gave priority to the logic of capital," the notion of "scientific industry" envisioned enterprise bodies that would be organized around the application of scientific principle and technological rationality. "As director of the Physical and Chemical Research Lab, Ōkōchi gave direct industrial application to the Lab's inventions, and conversely planned an enterprise organization that would recirculate the profits as research funds, leading to formation of the Physical and Chemical Industries Corporation (PCIC) in 1928. Against the background of expanding military production, this form of enterprise capitalized on the surplus farm population by putting them to work part-time, and expanded rapidly until it had generated a number of subsidiaries that were designed to give industrial application to various of PCIC's inventions. By 1940 it had grown into a new conglomerate (Konzern) with sixty-two companies and 121 factories.[17] The monthly journal that Ōkōchi began publishing in 1937, *Kagakushugi kōgyō* (Scientific industry), became a representative vehicle for wartime mobilization, and the articles that appeared there accurately reflected the demands for and reflections on an actually functioning, total war framework. Among the various articles and essays that were published in this journal, some that are worthy of special mention, including those discussed in Aikawa's *Gendai gijutsuron*,[18] are:

Saegusa Hiroto, "Gijutsu bunka to seishin" [Technoculture and mentalité] (1938), "Nihon gijutsushi obegaki" [A memorandum regarding the history of Japanese technology] (1938), "Gijutsu no rekishi to ningen no rekishi" [Human history and the history of technology] (1938), "Naze gijutsu wo iu ka?" [Why talk about technology?] (1939), "Gijutsu to wa kōsaku ka" [Is technology a matter of fabrication?] (1939), "Gijutsu to wa hataraku kikai ka?" [Is technology a matter of machines in operation?] (1939) and "Ningen to kikai no tōitsu" [Unifying people with machines] (1939).

Miki Kiyoshi, "Gijutsugaku no rinen" [The ideals of technology studies] (1937), "Gijutsu to bunka" [Technology and culture] (1937), "Kokuryoku to kagaku" [National strength and science] (1940), "Gijutsu to shin-bunka" [Technology and new culture] (1942).

Ikejima Shigenobu, "Gijutsu to geijutsu" [Technology and art] (1937) and "Kagaku to bungei" [Science and the humanities] (1938).

Moroi Kan'ichi, "Gijutsu to keizai" [Technology and economics] (1937) and "Gijutsuka to shakai" [Technicians and society] (1937).

Rōyama Masamichi, "Gijutsu to gyōsei" [Technology and administration] (1937).

Ōkōchi Masatoshi, "Shihonshugi kōgyō to kagakushugi kōgyō" [Capitalistic industry and scientific industry] (1937), "Tanō jukuren kikaikō to gijutsusha no yōsei" [Multi-skilled machine-tool operators and the cultivation of technicians] (1938), and "Kagakushugi kōgyō to rijun" [Scientistic industry and profit] (1940).

Satō Shin'ei "Atarashii gijutsuka" [The new technician] (1937), "Gijutsu kara kagaku e" [From technology to science] (1939) and "Soshiki aru gijutsu" [Organized technology] (1940).

Hayase Toshio, "Gijutsu no shakaiteki rinen" [The social ideal of technology] (1938).

Shinmei Masamichi, "Dōgu no shakaiteki rinen" [The social ideal of tools] (1938), "Kikai to te" [Machines and hands] (1940), and "Kikai to ningen to no kankei" [Relations between people and machines] (1938).

Funayama Shin'ichi, "Gijutsu no tetsugakuteki kadai" [Philosophical issues related to technology] (1938) and "Gijutsu to seikatsu" [Technology and daily life] (1940).

Fujisawa Chikao, "Gendai no bunka to gijutsu" [Contemporary culture and technology] (1939).

Tōbata Sei'ichi, "Nihon nōgyō gijutsu no tokushitsu" [Characteristics of Japan's agricultural technology] (1939).

Tosaka Jun, "Gijutsu seishin to wa nanika?" [What is the technological spirit?] (1937).

Ōkuma Nobuyuki, "Gijutsu genri to seikatsu genri" [Principles of technology, principles of life] (1939).

Miyamoto Takenosuke, "Seisan kakujū to tan'nōkō" [Technological diffusion and single-skilled workers] (1939).

Shimomura Toratarō, "Nihon bunka ni okeru kagaku no chi'i" [The status of science in Japanese culture] (1939).

Ōkōchi Kazuo, "Gijutsu to shakai rippō" [Technology and social legislation] (1940).

Ishihara Jun, "Kagaku to gijutsu no kankei" [The relationship between science and technology] (1940).

Aikawa Haruki, "Gijutsu no seikaku to gijutsu tōsei" [The character of technology and technological control] (1940).

Rōyama Masamichi's essay discusses the "technologization of administration," and proposes that technology be elevated to the level of technocracy. This process would ultimately bring technology into a close relationship with "the problem of the totality of the state itself," and through the reciprocal mediation of political ethics and technology, to give rise to a new "order as the totality of technology."[19]

This spurt of rich theoretical work on technology paralleled a process of concentrated study and translation focused on fundamental works on technology theory that were written in Western European languages, especially German. During this era, representative works such as the following were translated in full and absorbed: Friedrich Dessauer, *Gijutsu no tetsugaku* [Philosophy of technology] (Kagakushugi Kōgyōsha: Trans. Nagata Hiroshi, 1941), Oswald Spengler, *Ningen to gijutsu* [Human beings and technology] (Mikasa Shobō: Trans. Kamō Giichi, 1938), Werner Sombart, *Gijutsuron* [On technology] (Kagakushugi Kōgyōsha: Trans. Ahei Yoshio, 1941), and Eugen Diesel, *Gijutsuron* [On technology] (Kagakushugi Kōgyōsha: Trans. Ōsawa Mineo, 1942). We may conclude, therefore, that the rise of technological praxis from within the wartime mobilization system was not necessarily the result of Japanese peculiarities, but instead corresponded to similar tendencies elsewhere in the world.[20]

Let's look at another work that was translated and published, not surprisingly, by the Kagakushugi Kōgyōsha, that is, *Gijutsu no seishin* [The spirit of technology] (Trans. Tama Giichi, 1941, original title *Gijutsu no tetsugaku* [Philosophy of technology]) by Eberhard Zschimmer.[21] The first edition of this work had appeared in the era of World War I, but a third, thoroughly-revised edition was put out in 1933, complete with enthusiastic praise for the Nazis who had just seized power.

> We now witness the dawning of a new era. A truly healthy idealism filled with new will to power has moved into the vanguard. Only through this new idealism can we discover the way toward the ultimate significance of technological production and the authentic, fundamental principles of technology itself which will bring freedom and spiritual power in relation to the material world. Our task is to develop conceptual ideals and, through the spirit of our era, to make judgments concerning the meaning and significance of the various manifestations of the technological, sensual world that surrounds us.[22]

As a self-styled Hegelian, Zschimmer often repeats the view that creation through "technology" is itself the process by which the spirit and ideals of the "Volk" (*minzoku*) are realized. In his view, this ideal of technology as "Volksgeist" is impaired not only by an instrumentalized and fragmented conception of technology but also by capitalism's subordination of technology to economics.

> If it were to become the fundamental ideal for actual operations, the impoverished principle of economy would nullify not only technological

production but all courageous spirit and the full creative potential of technology.[23]

Zschimmer's Nazi tendencies, evident in his superficial attack on "capitalistic enterprise," are echoed in Ōkōchi's standpoint of "scientific industry." For people like Zschimmer, inasmuch as "all the ideals of spiritual life are organically united in an eternal power over nature," the nascent Nazi state itself could become, by way of technological creativity, "the most precious material produced out of the creative spirit of engineers."[24] Through metaphors of struggle and enthusiasm, Zschimmer connects the notion of self-realization in Hegel's "Volksgeist" to the anti-Semitic, anticapitalist propaganda of the Nazis.

It is true that in his *Gijutsu to tetsugaku*,[25] translated by Nagata Hiroshi and published by the Kagakushugi Kōgyōsha, Dessauer also enthuses that "by virtue of a peculiar genius, technology is the friend of mankind." In contrast to Zschimmer, Dessauer himself was cruelly persecuted by the Nazis and had to flee to Istanbul. For Dessauer also, however, any conception in which technology was instrumentalized and made into a function of economics had to be rejected as a most serious error. According to him, "technology is contact with God. Through technology, God's creative spirit is injected into the new dawn for mankind that is latent in the present."[26] The instrumental "fourth world" that was to be brought about through technology would supplement Kant's theory of three fundamental faculties and provide the key to a critical metaphysics that would unify the fragmented world and conquer agnosticism.

Mobilization required a practical theory of technology, and paradoxically this allowed the demand for technology's autonomy and uniqueness to generate a space in which a number of discourses could be connected to that demand as either its presuppositions or results. Of course, the obsessive demands for practicality and the multiplication of discourse extolling the significance of the technological subject can be explained with reference to the loud slogans related to establishment of a "total-war system." There is nothing especially surprising in the argument that for a Greater Japanese Empire "poor in productive resources," it was necessary to demand a one-dimensional system that would not only emphasize the significance of "technology" but develop, mobilize and control it in the most efficient manner. Moreover, the stance of the intellectuals who dared to throw themselves into this raging current arose not from mere opportunism but from a strategy fraught with ambivalence–that is, they were trying to produce an oppositional discourse that could counter the fanatical "Japanism" and "spiritualism" (*seishinshugi*) of the time. In opposition to the irrational stampedes of the military and the rampages of the patriotic rightwing, Marxists and liberals who were deprived of free expression, jailed, and from time to time brought face to face with death tried to find in thoroughgoing technological rationality the basis for a counterattack against established power relations. However, the ironic truth is that these very efforts at resistance provided a far more effective support for the wartime mobilization system than could any fanatical "Japanism."

TECHNOLOGY AS "FORM"

Miki Kiyoshi's *Gijutsuron* (On technology) was written as the third chapter of his longer work, *Kōsryoku no ronri*, and was published in the February, March and May 1938 issues of the journal *Shisō*. At the same time, another version was pulled together as part of the *Iwanami kōza: rinrigaku* (Iwanami lectures on ethics)[1941] and then published in 1942 as *Gijutsu tetsugaku* (Philosophy of technology) in 1942. Whether in the form of *Kōsōryoku no ronri* or *Gijutsu tetsugaku*, this work is clearly unfinished. Repetitive arguments and contradictions are numerous and it is difficult to reconstruct the inner order of the subject headings in any systematic way; they are best seen as expressing fundamentally the same content. In neither does Miki delve into the details of contemporary definitions of technology that were circulating in and around the Materialism Study Group. Rather, he criticizes them all together as forms of instrumentalism:

> When we ask what technology is, we usually get the answer that it is a means. Those who want a more detailed explanation are told that technology is the totality or the system of means. These answers seem to be quite correct, but are in fact incomplete. First, if technology is to be seen merely as a means, it must be said that it has no individuality (*dokujisei*). Something with individuality cannot simply be called a means. Something that is just a means has no individuality. That technology has been thought of simply as a means is one of the reason why until recently the problem of technology has been either ignored or taken lightly in philosophy. Indeed, if technology is to be simply a means, there can be no philosophy of technology. (VII, 302 ff.)

It goes without saying that, as outlined above, this kind of critique of the instrumentalist, or "means of labor," interpretation of technology was a staple element of discourse at the time in *Kagakushugi kōgyō* and elsewhere. What Miki aims at ultimately is a "total definition of technology" (VII, 212). In his view, whether technology was thought of as means, or as (means in) process, all such earlier definitions invited an overly objectivist understanding. Technology was certainly objective (*kyakkanteki*), but it was also at the same time subjective (*shukanteki*). Or, rather, it had to be something that transcended the subject/object dichotomy. Miki responds to this need by defining it in terms of "form":

> For all technology, a fundamental concept must be "form." Things made through technology all have form, and technological activity itself always has form. It can be said that to the extent one sees form, one is looking at technology (VIII, 227). Of course, all technology is based on natural laws, and accordingly must be premised on cause and effect. However, it is not just etiological but teleological. Technology is the unity of etiology and teleology. This unity is provided in form. One can probably say that the unity of etiology and teleology is morphology. Not simply a means, the totality of technological action is understandable only in this manner, that is, technology finds its complete definition in the definition of action (VII, 218).

No matter how many explanations were offered regarding relations between technology and science, or technology and skill, and no matter how many interpretations there might have been of the objectivistic definitions of technology, such as those of the Materialism Study Group, from Miki's standpoint they were all inadequate to the extent that they were conceived entirely within the framework of means and ends. It is true that Miki's own definition left much unexplained, but he did try to suggest a third theoretical dimension that avoided both the instrumentalization of technology and the consideration of it as an autonomous existence.[27] The view of technology that limited it to means-ends relations had a long history, extending from Aristotle's "techne" to the concept of technological/practical action in Kant. If technology was really to be considered independent of ends, then although one might point to appropriate, active intervention by a human being, technology itself would remain a neutral entity. In the theory of technology as "form," on the other hand, technology would not exist outside of the context that produces it. Moreover, rather than being limited to the mold of social production, such a concept would enable one to take a new look at life processes across the gamut of human phenomena. Technology as a fundamental phenomenon that is not limited by its connection to instrumental rationality but is the axis of world view—that is what Miki sought to capture through his definition in terms of "form."

Miki often substitutes "invention" for "form" in his definition of technology. Paraphrases like the following appear frequently:

To invent is to establish a relationship that did not exist previously. It is to constructively assimilate existing elements and construct a new behavioral Gestalt, a new form or configuration. That is, invention is creative in essence (VII, 224).

Some, who do not realize that Miki's technology = "invention" formulation is a variant of his argument that technology = "form," have criticized it as merely a warmed-over version of the argument put forward by Dessauer in *Gijutsu no tetsugaku*.[28] It is certainly true that Dessauer's theory of technology is full of idealistic, enthusiastic praise for "invention," but he ties it directly to a transcendental metaphysic. As I will show below, Miki's philosophy was not entirely free of an orientation to the transcendent. But for him it is located in the constellation surrounding imagination (*kōsōryoku*), and he intentionally avoids any tendency to posit a transcendent entity a priori. That Dessauer ultimately reduces his "Fourth Reich" to teleological one-dimensionality is evident even in his claim that ultimately technological form should be understood monistically in relation to its original function.[29] In his discussion of "form," or "invention," Miki, on the other hand, is able for the most part to avoid any direct appeal to metaphysics. Accordingly, his confirmation of the meaning of "form" involved criticisms of Dessauer, such as the following:

> If technological form exists in advance (*yoteiteki ni*), and if the inventor does not make it anew but rather simply discovers it, how is it that Dessauer is able to think of invention as the essence of technology, and speak even of creation? All creation must include the sense of creation from nothingness (*mu*). . . . That is, Dessauer fails to understand that technology is something historical, that technological form is historical and dialectical (VIII, 245).
>
> That the nucleus of the problem of technology is invention does not mean that invention can simply be considered the essence of technology. If we just remember that, in terms of the concept of technology, production is compositional (*kōseiteki*), it will from that fact alone be evident that invention cannot be considered the sole essence of technology. It is as something productive (*seisanteki*) that technology is rich in effects, that it is effective. Therefore, it can probably be said that the processes of adaptation, and of diffusion and dissemination, are already included in invention from the beginning (VIII, 229).

In order to avoid this misunderstanding and at the same time to grasp the transcendence of technology, Miki is forced to narrate "form" as the fundamental mode of expression of logos. In other words, he is forced to throw the problem back into the "logic of imagination," which is his original project. What he terms "invention" here relates to issues surrounding the term "ingenium" in classical rhetoric. In the theory of technology, its traces are barely apparent in the problem of the engineer, but in his theory of "invention" Miki retrieves it from derivative status. "Imagination" defines the nature of technology theory as follows:

> Technology is creative, and through it the world takes on new form. The transcendental character of imagination is recognizable in the materiality of the free products of imagination. The transcendentality of human existence is nothing mystical; it lies in the clear fact that things constructed freely are objective. Imagination is certainly not simply mental (*shukanteki*); rather, in the free operation of imagination what is mental becomes form and thus transcends the merely mental. The logic of imagination is recognizable precisely in technological action, action that is not merely a phenomenon of consciousness (VIII, 229).

> One cannot deny the role played in invention by the intuitive and the unintentional (*muishikiteki*), but modern technology is based more on rational supposition, calculation, and conscious planning. Invention does not follow merely from the intuition of genius, but now requires the kind of cooperative investigation carried on in research centers. The foundation of technology is still not just rationality but also imagination; it is just that imagination has become more conscious and compositional as it is increasingly mediated by science (VII, 233).

It must be said that, compared to this, postwar technology theory failed from the outset to come up to Miki's level. In the record of his wartime interrogation by the Special Police which was published after the war, Taketani Mitsuo says the following in relation to Miki's "invention" theory (or, perhaps, concerning the gamut of theories related to the "ideal of action," including those of Dessauer and Zschimmer):

> Looking at the technology theories of the idealists we find that they tend to situate technology in the concept of form. For example, in *Gijutsu tetsugaku*, Miki Kiyoshi defines technology as "the form of action." But the form of action appears as the result of action, and technology is not the result of action in this sense; rather, technology is the principle that makes action possible. In other words, Miki's definition of the concept of technology takes form, which is what gives action its phenomenal

character, and calls it technology, but this is little more than phenomenology.[30]

In his desire to avoid definitions that manifested the syncretic character of "phenomenological" description, Taketani countered with his famous "essentialist" definition, which was that "technology is the conscious application of objective laws in human praxis (productive praxis)."[31] Here, the rigid, formal logic of his three-stage theory becomes the premise of realism, and he does not touch at all on the specificity of the problem of "form" as elaborated by Miki. According to Taketani, Miki's definition and those of the Materialism Study Group were "logically" confused, and therefore, "the image of the technicians who are the bearers of technology does not emerge from these definitions."[32] Nevertheless, for Miki, at least—whether in *Kōsōryoku no ronri* or in *Gijutsu tetsugaku*—the term "form" (*katachi*) does not refer merely to the various effects of phenomena. Rather, he attempts through "form" to move the discussion to a level that escapes both the fixing of technology as an objective entity and its reduction to a mental (*shukanteki*) plan. Indeed, Taketani's own rigid view of "application" makes it impossible to investigate the circumstances that bring forth "form" contextually. For Miki "form" is not simply a way to confirm the subjective (*shutaiteki*) moment within the means-ends relationship, but has to be developed as the "originary logic" (*genshi ronri*) (VIII, 8) that generates the subject itself. This forces his theory of technology, or *Logic of Imagination*, to question consistently the most fundamental dimension of creativity.

In the text cited above, Taketani explains what motivated his "application" theory:

> Having, as a scientist, witnessed the technological failures and inadequacies that occurred under the supreme edict to "expand production" at the time of the China Incident, I decided that they arose from the failure among Japanese technicians and philosophers to truly grasp the concept of technology. That is, in attempting to assess the quality of Japanese technology they merely emphasized the elements of skill and such mental factors as so-called "*kan*" (intuition), along with the supposed "dexterity of the Japanese."[33]

But if that was the case, even without discussing Miki, how did Taketani's "conscious application of objective laws" differ in its logic from the general discourse of the "praxis" school that appeared in *Kagakushugi Kōgyō* throughout the 1930s and early 1940s? Of course, it is relevant that, although he published it after the war, Taketani was forced to write this as a "record of interrogation" during the war. Nevertheless, even Taketani's discussions of the facts of technology and technicians on behalf of postwar "democracy" leave no room for the penetrating thoroughness achieved in Miki's logic of imagination. "Now technicians have joined the workers and are fighting not for profits but for the national welfare,"[34] and "only in this manner can they stabilize their temporary status and affirm their social raison d'etre." Such a subject could be imagined only via technology theory as a standard for systemic reform on the part of technicians.

Taketani criticizes Miki for subjectivism, but charges that the Materialism Study Group theorists's definition in terms of the "system of the means of labor," was an objectivist understanding that detracted from technicians' subjectivity (*shutaisei*). Yet, whether in the "system of means" theory or the "application" theory, there remained a gap in their emphasis on the subject within the means-ends relationship.

It is true that Taketani was not unaware of the continuity in theories of subjectivity from prewar through wartime and postwar. In "Jissen no ronri" (*The logic of praxis*) he explains it this way:

There are those who act as if "the logic of praxis" or "subjectivity" are issues broached since the war, but only a moment's reflection will suffice to show that this is not so. To some extent this was because, as the wartime crisis became more serious and the pressure of fascism intensified, Marxist philosophy was suppressed leading inevitably to false recantations and outright ideological conversions. But even prior to that, neo-Kantian philosophy had been suppressed by Marxism, and as a result idealist philosophy turned from epistemological critique to the philosophy of praxis. Because some of these idealist philosophers resisted the storm of fascism while other went along with it, praxis philosophy became pervasive. Miki's philosophy also, while being pressured by fascism, trying somehow to resist, and also to hide that resistance . . . took the philosophy of praxis as its main topic. All these arguments with respect to subjectivity approached praxis from the side of the subject and in this way mystified and made it non-rational. . . . Our philosophy of technology strikes down this tendency toward "subjectivity" and the mystification and de-rationalizing of technology, and we have chosen a road that, although modest, should allow us to advance surely step by step. This is the road toward the demolition of the structure of praxis from the objective side, making it possible to approach it rationalistically.[35]

Taketani disposes of Miki's theory of *shutaisei* as "mystification," thereby positing the unique veracity of his own objectivist viewpoint. Yet it was precisely the generation of a logos of "rational praxis" that Miki had tried to critique. Miki broke through to the meta-level above subjective and objective in order to reconsider praxis as an issue that included the very ground of possibility of subject-object itself. In sum, he proposed a reflexive questioning that would include denial of the very existence of *shutaisei* itself.

EMERGENCE OF A CONSTRUCTIVE METASUBJECT

Therefore, one can say that the discourse of technology theory under the "political mobilization system" was already, in itself, a movement in search of an adequate theory of active subjectivity (*shutaisei*). Even in the imagination theory of Miki Kiyoshi, who was out ahead of the others in that he did not stop at the logic of the subject but delved down towards an incipient questioning of the subject's own generation and growth, we find the potential for overcoming the limitations of the postwar debate on *shutaisei*. If that theory radically questions heterogeneity in the very ontological possibility of subjectivity, perhaps "The Logic of Imagination" succeeds in showing that it could be further developed as the kind of alternative logos that Miki sought. Yet it appears that Miki failed, precisely at that point, to continue consistently along the line of questioning he had established. What he took was the "way of a 'transcendental subject' that corresponded to the presence of originality and totality."[36]

Thus far, I have intentionally limited my synthesis to background, but from the midst of Miki's difficult and complex prose there also emerges an aspect in which he himself abandons the way of "invention," which pared down the logic of "form" and presumed heterogeneity in the subject. That is because *the radicalism that underlies his questioning of "technology" as "imagination" is the same as the radicalism that leads him to the "technologization" of "imagination."* Even though the means/ends relationship is relativized and other phenomena are brought within its purview, at the same time, once they are defined as "technology," the category of "poietic" action slips in. For example, the "preface" to *The Logic of Imagination* was written only when the chapters up to and including that on "technology," which had been published earlier in the journal *Shisō*, were put together in book form; in it, Miki reviews the narrative process, and along the way has this to say about the function of the moment of "construction" (*seisaku*) or "poiesis":

> Through the logic of imagination I have attempted to think about the philosophy of action. Up to now, imagination has been thought of almost solely in relation to artistic activity; by the same token, form has been

conceived almost entirely in relation to contemplation. I have sought to avoid those constraints and to relate imagination to action in general. It is important in that connection to conceive of action not, as has been the case up to now, as an abstract matter of will in the context of subjective idealism, but rather as a matter of making things. All action is, in the broad sense, a process of making things, that is, it includes the aspect of construction. *Thus, the logic of imagination is a logic of construction.* All things that are made have form. To act is to act on things, to change their form, and to make new form. As something made, form is historical, something that changes historically. Form in this sense is not simply objective (*kyakkanteki*) but is a unity of the objective and the subjective (*shukanteki*), idea and existence, being and emergence, time and space. The logic of imagination is the logic of historical form. Although to act is to make something, if making did not at the same time include the meaning of becoming, history would be unthinkable. History becomes possible when construction also means emergence (VIII, 7, emphasis by Iwasaki).

When Miki criticizes the category of "contemplation" and emphasizes "praxis" and "action," his notion of "construction" as poiesis transcends its role as a partial definition of action and begins to determine the "logic of imagination" as a whole. What is present from the outset in this process of the self-actualization of imagination is a certain indifferent *something* that, as we noted above, is not understood as a subject in the context of means/ends relations but rather as a more versatile and free metasubject that has historical destiny. When he expresses this historical destiny as a challenge to the circumstances of the times through an effort to provide the principles of a new community in the midst of contemporary society, or develops and expands the definition of technology to apply to all human agency, he in effect brings forth a transcendental metasubject that, while connoting a critique of the subject, becomes omnipotent and omniproductive. For the present, let's call this quality of Miki's theory of imagination the "desire for a constructive metasubject." Precisely because the stirring of this desire is not exhausted in emphasis on the actively-subjective moment but from the beginning is narrated as possibility, it generates an even stronger logic of the subject. The most difficult aspect of Miki's "philosophy of technology" is his inability, ultimately, to escape the quickening of this "desire for a constructive metasubject."[37]

The concept of poiesis includes "myth," "institutional system," and "experience," so it was essential that Miki not limit "technology" to "production technology" (*seisan gijutsu*). To "art," "cognitive technology" and "conceptual technology," for example, he adds as another example of technology the notion of "social technology" (VII, 222). "Social technology" produces a variety of systems, through which "society gives itself form."

> Usually, when we say technology we are thinking in relation to material production, that is, natural-scientific technology. However, as a concept of technology this is excessively narrow; what we need today is rather an extension of the concept of technology. . . . Moreover, progress in social technology is urgently necessary. Social technology is implicated in what is usually called the control of contemporary technology, or its subjection to planning, especially the political control of natural-scientific technology (VII, 312).

As the result of such expansive moves, the inner politicality of Miki's own discourse is gradually dissolved in the quickening of "desire for a constructive metasubject," and he becomes unable to thematize "the political" as a specific realm of investigation. This smothering of "the political" in poiesis emerged concretely in his conception of community, specifically in relation to "cooperativism" and the "East Asian Community" (*Tōa kyōdōtai*).[38]

Writers who dominated a substantial portion of article space in *Kagakushugi kōgyō*, such as Rōyama Masamichi, Shinmei Masamichi, Funayama Shin'ichi and Ozaki Hotsumi, were at the same time major proponents of "East Asian Community." Moreover, *Kagakushugi kōgyō* itself periodically devoted special editions to the problem of the organizational development of technology in relation to "Manchuria" and the "East Asian Community." Miki also projected his "logic of imagination" horizontally across contemporary historical space and inevitably located it in the spatial representation of the bogus "multi-culturalism" of "East Asian Community." "Cooperativism" was structurally tautological with the "logic of imagination." In his representation of space, Miki rejects the level of extreme Volkism (level of the subject) while narrating the level of supposed multi-culturalism (level of the metasubject), but he returns to his starting point via the Japanese Volk's historical destiny (level of the ursubject).

> Fundamentally, environmental society and creative society should not be abstractly separated because what actually exists is a single society's self-formation and self-development; our own self-formation and self development are included in that. It is our duty to cooperate in this development of society. This society that develops through self-formation is none other than the historical world, and the historical world is formed

technologically. As something historical, our action is entirely technological (VII, 298).

If we consider this from the perspective of narrative form, we realize that the
rhetoric of *The Logic of Invention* is entirely metaphorical. The other possibilities contained in "ingenium," that is, metonymy, synecdoche and irony,
are completely excluded. Yet when this historical definition is developed in
its concrete aspect, the metasubject, which cannot limit itself solely to metaphor, takes on a regional identity. This is a form of existence which, while
being "technological" and historical, and encompassing all human action, also
presences precisely through the denial of that action.

Even the following words from Miki's little essay of 1939, entitled
"Chishikijin ni atau" (To the intellectuals), follow necessarily from his philosophy, even though Miki might have thought of them as strategic "concealment":

> What Japan needs at present is not a philosophy of interpretation but of
> action. Heretofore, virtually all studies of the Japanese spirit have been
> in the mold of hermeneutic philosophy. They all seek to discover Japa-
> nese particularity through a consideration of Japan's past. On the other
> hand, the philosophy of action begins not in the past but in the present.
> Because in itself it is something general, interpretation is preoccupied
> with particularity. Conversely, because action in itself is something par-
> ticular, it demands universality. Japan has to discover "world-historical
> meaning" through action and while confronting this vested meaning, to
> act dynamically. The philosophy of action must be a philosophy of his-
> tory. Reason in history is not originally something abstract, but rather
> appears concretely in a particular era, through and in a certain Volk. A
> Volk is not great merely by being a Volk, but is so by virtue of its world-
> historical mission (XV, 243).

Miki's discourse is not intended merely to demand mobilization for total
war. "In the mobilization of intellectual power it is important that the very
mechanism of mobilization itself should take into account the autonomous
views of the intelligentsia" (IV, 259). Mobilization has to produce mobilized
entities. It has to be voluntary, but must also include a mechanism to negate
subjects once formed. The objects of mobilization must be specified, evaluated statistically, and constantly renewed through the most efficient methods.
These are the sort of notions that contributed to the activity of the metasubject.

In other words, aside from the various factors that operated in each of
their personal lives, the proponents of technological rationalism were not only

quite friendly toward the wartime mobilization system but in some cases were thoroughly committed to it. Therefore, in attempting to assess the political valence of this discourse we must look first, not at "ideological conversion" (*tenkō*) and ambivalent forms of resistance, but rather precisely at the level where theories of *shutaisei* were generated.

IN PLACE OF A CONCLUSION

Yet, how important can such a task be now, at a time when the concept of *shutaisei* has been rendered so empty? I have argued that the wartime mobilization system and the theories of "East Asian Community" that were its spatial projection were, in and of themselves, theories of *shutaisei*. Yet, by arguing in this manner I certainly do not intend to draw positive meaning from the 1930s variety of rationality, which provided the fundamental framework for postwar system-integration; nor do I want to contribute to the now-conventional critique of the "postwar enlightenment." We need to reconfirm that the postwar Japanese socioeconomic system is itself squarely within the problematical purview of *shutaisei* theory as a form of the "desire for a constructive metasubject." Moreover, and quite apart from arguments based on *shutaisei*, we need to recognize that the concealment of "the political" is becoming increasingly serious even in the new system theory that claimed recently to be bringing about a decisive paradigm shift, away from the social science that embodied "postwar enlightenment." In such theory, the "desire for a poietic metasubject" has metamorphosed into "autopoiesis."[39]

It is said that the system-integration of postwar society is in crisis. Yet in the midst of such circumstances, we repeatedly witness intentional as well as unintentional reversions to representations typical of the 1930s. The perspective on the "wartime mobilization system" that underlies the essays in this volume opposes such a tendency. The effort here to understand the contemporary world in terms of continuities among prewar, wartime and postwar is not motivated by a desire to redeem the past but to criticize the present–to become, as it were, the Owl of Minerva to a crisis-ridden postwar social system. But it is still impossible to see what looms in the darkness beyond the twilight of the system-society.

Translated by J. Victor Koschmann

Notes

[1] Umemoto Katsumi, "Ningenteki jiyū no genkai," *Tenbō* (Feb. 1946).

[2] Umemoto Katsumi, "Mu no ronri to tōhasei," *Yuibutsushikan to dōtoku* (Tokyo: San'ichi Shobō, 1949): 103.

[3] For example, Matsumura Kazuto, *Yuibutsuron to shutaiseiron* (Tokyo: Nihon Hyōronsha, 1949).

[4] Usui Yoshimi, ed., *Sengo bungaku ronsō* 1 (Tokyo: Chikuma Shobō, 1972), 13 ff.

[5] Taketani Mitsuo, *Taketani Mitsuo chosakushū* 1 (Tokyo: Keisō Shobō, 1968).

[6] Umemoto Katsumi, "Daiichibu e no tsuiki," *Yuibutsuron to shutaisei* (Tokyo: Gendai Shichōsha, 1974), 325.

[7] Uchida Yoshihiko, Hirata Kiyoaki, "Gendai kenkyō e no keizaigakushiteki apurōchi," in Senshū Daigaku Shakai Kagaku Kenkyūjo, ed., *Shakai kagaku nenpō* 4, 208.

[8] Kawakami Tetsutarō, Takeuchi Yoshimi et al., *Kindai no chōkoku* (reprinted edition) (Tokyo: Tōzanbō, 1979), 216 ff. On this point, see Yamanouchi Yasushi, "Sanka to dōin: senjiki chishikijin no purofuiiru," in Tokyo Gaikokugo Daigaku Kaigai Jijō Kenkyūjo, *Chiiki funsō to sōgō izon* 3.17.

[9] Sakai Saburō, *Shōwa Kenky kai* (Tokyo: TBS Britannica, 1977) and Shōwa Dōjinkai, ed., *Shōwa Kenkyūkai* (Tokyo: Keizai Oraisha, 1968); also see Shiozaki Hiroaki, "Shōwa kenkyūkai to Miki Kiyoshi no kyōdōshugi," *Nihon rekishi* 542 (July 1993) and Yamaguchi Hiroshi, "TōA shin-chitsujoron no shosō," Parts 1 & 2, in *Meiji Gakuin Daigaku kiyō* 26 & 27 (Nov. 1990).

[10] Miki Kiyoshi opposed to the end the dissolution of the "Shōwa Kenkyūkai."

[11] Satō Hiromi, "TōA kyōdōtairon to kyōiku kagaku," *Jinbun gakuhō* 206 (1989) and Ouchi Hirokazu, "Inpei sareta kioku," *Gendai shisō* (Jan. 1995).

[12] For overviews of Miki Kiyoshi and his work, see Miyakawa Tōru, *Miki Kiyoshi* (Tokyo: Tokyo Daigaku Shuppankai, 1958), Arakawa Ikuo, *Miki Kiyoshi* (Tokyo: Kinokuniya Shoten, 1968), and Akamatsu Tsunehiro, *Miki Kiyoshi: tetsugakuteki shiso no kiseki* (Tokyo: Mineruva Shobō, 1994).

[13] Nakamura Seiji, *Gijutsuron ronsōshi* 1 (Tokyo: Aoki Shobō, 1975), 3 ff.

[14] Aikawa Haruki, *Gendai gijutsuron* (Tokyo: Mikawa Shobō, 1940).

[15] Ibid., 31.

[16] Ibid., 41 ff.

[17] Nakamura, *Gijutsuron ronsōshi* 1, 53.

[18] Aikawa, *Gendai gijutsuron*, 31 ff.

[19] Ibid., 37 ff.

[20] Also see Saegusa Hiroto, *Gijutsu no shisō* (Tokyo: Daiichi Shobō, 1941), Saegusa, *Gendai Nihon bunmeishi* (Tokyo: Tōyō Keizai Shinpōsha, 1940), Aikawa Haruki, *Gijutsuron nyūmon* (Tokyo: Mikawa Shobō, 1941), Aikawa, *Gijutsu no riron to seisaku* (Tokyo: Kigensha, 1942), Miyamoto Takenosuke, *Kagaku no dōin* (Tokyo: Kaizōsha, 1941), which were all published within the same short

period. For a consideration of reactionary modernism from a more inclusive angle, see Jeffrey Herf, *Reactionary Modernism: Technology, Culture, and Politics in Weimar and the Third Reich* (Cambridge University Press, 1984).

[21] Eberhard Zschimmer, *Philosophie der Technik, Einführung in die technische Ideenwelt* (Verlag der Jenaer Volksbuchhandlung, 1933).

[22] Zschimmer, *Gijutsu no seishin*, trans. Tama Giichi (Tokyo: Kagakushugi Kōgyōsha, 1941), 26 ff.

[23] Ibid., 63.

[24] Ibid., 95.

[25] Friedrich Dessauer, *Philosophie der Technik, Das Problem der Realisierung*, 1933.

[26] Dessauer, *Gijutsu no tetsugaku*, trans. Nagata Hiroshi (Tokyo: Kagakushugi Kōgyōsha, 1941), 52.

[27] Murata Jun'ichi, "Gijutsu no tetsugaku," *Iwanami kōza: gendai shisō* 13 [Tekunorojii no shisō] (Tokyo: Iwanami Shoten, 1994), 6 ff. After synthesizing a simple form of 20th century technology theory, Murata suggestively reconsiders the possibilities of the "form" theory (*katachi setsu*), as differentiated from the "tool theory" (*dōgu setsu*) and the "autonomy theory" (*jiritsu setsu*), in the context of recent scientific theory.

[28] Nakamura, *Gitsuron ronsōshi* 1, 60.

[29] Dessauer, *Gijutsu no tetsugaku*, 71 ff.

[30] Taketani, *Taketani Mitsuo chosakushū* 1, 132 ff.

[31] Ibid., 139 ff.

[32] Ibid., 140.

[33] Ibid., 133.

[34] Ibid., 126.

[35] Taketani Mitsuo, "Jissen no mondai ni tsuite," *Taketani Mitsuo chosakushū* 6, 231.

[36] Kimae Toshiaki, "Kōsōryoku-shinwa-katachi no ronri," *Shisō* (Sept. 1991): 41 ff. On "imagination" (*kōsōryoku*) also see the other essays in the special issue of *Shisō*.

[37] See Iwasaki Minoru, "Seisan suru kōsōryoku, kyūsai suru kōsōryoku," *Shisō* (Sept. 1991): 164 ff.

[38] Works from the 1930s discussing the "East Asian Community" include, in addition to Miki's *Shin-Nihon no shisō genri*, Kada Tetsuji, *TōA kyōdōtairon* (Tokyo: Nihon Seinen Gaikō Kyōkai Shuppanbu, 1937), and Takada Yasuma, *TōA minzokuron* (Tokyo: Iwanami Shoten, 1937). Note that Aikawa also explains his experience in the space of East Asia as having provided the occasion for a "conversion" (*tenkō*), and this agreement is not accidental.

[39] See Iwasaki Minoru, "Miki Kiyoshi ni okeru 'gijutsu,' 'dōin,' 'kūkan'— TōA kyōdōtai to kōsōryoku no ronri," *Hihyō kūkan* 2.5 (1995): 155.

Prewar, Wartime, and Postwar in Education: The Thought and Behavior of Abe Shigetaka

Ōuchi Hirokazu

Modern pedagogy was established later than the other social sciences in Japan. Even after World War I the idealist tendency toward a cultural pedagogy typical of Wilhelm Dilthey and the educational philosophy of the neo-Kantians remained strong. Japanese pedagogy in the 1920s was characterized more by a philosophical than a modern scientific quality. It was also in the 1920s and 1930s that a modern science of education based on American-style empiricism was introduced and began to develop. However, it must be said that research on this formative period is incomplete. The science of education that was created before and during the war continued as the basis for postwar Japanese pedagogy as well. Nevertheless, in the study of Japanese education, which from the Potsdam Declaration onward was institutionalized as a faculty within universities and equipped with scholarly foundations as an academic discipline, the preconception that the postwar era was born anew from the ashes of war—that is, an emphasis on discontinuity—has predominated. Analysis of connections among the prewar, wartime, and postwar has been neglected. The prewar science of education is most often either glorified as progressive without any attention to the contemporary social context or narrated as a history of resistance against the wartime system. In fact, however, the Japanese science of education that was established during the prewar period developed both as an academic discipline and as a movement of practice in conjunction with the rational educational planning and policy of the government during the 1930s, the period of the total-war system. With the realization of this fact, therefore, comes the issue of total war and modernity within education, hitherto unproblematized in educational studies.

This essay will focus on Abe Shigetaka, a central figure in the introduction and development in Japan of the science of education. It will analyze his

181

influence on the formation and development of a modern science of education and on the reform of the education system that was carried out during the prewar and wartime. This is to make clear, through education, the modernity and rationality of the prewar and wartime periods which are frequently depicted as ultranationalist and irrational. By showing that the postwar democratic reforms were on many points anticipated before and during the war, it contests the historical approach that insists on discontinuity between pre- and postwar.

FORMATION OF ABE SHIGETAKA'S SCIENCE OF EDUCATION

After graduating from the Education Department of the Literature Faculty of Tokyo Imperial University, Abe Shigetaka entered graduate school and joined the editorial staff of the Cultivation Society (Ikusei kai), which issued the magazine *Kyōiku jikkenkai* (The world of experimental education). Shortly after joining, he planned and managed the columns, "*Zasshi no zasshi*" (Magazine of magazines) and "*Kaigai kyōdan*" (Educational discourse abroad), which mainly introduced German-language materials related to education. As noted above, in this era, Japanese educational studies focused on cultural education under the influence of Wilhelm Dilthey and on the educational philosophy of the neo-Kantians. Therefore, Abe's interest in scientific research, especially experimental pedagogy, is quite significant. Experimental pedagogy based itself in the facts of education and employed empirical methods; it therefore differed from existing educational scholarship, which was based on a philosophical, idealist form of conceptualization. It had been introduced to Japan in 1906 and gathered momentum, but it was subjected to a variety of criticisms from the educational establishment and by 1910 was already beginning to fade.[1] Therefore, Abe's interest in experimental pedagogy was unusual within the Japanese education world of that time, and for that very reason his viewpoint stands out clearly.

Abe's early position on scientific pedagogy was clarified in a debate on aesthetic theory with Sasaki Kichisaburō, a representative contemporary educator. Sasaki, who had long asserted that education must be based on character and who was influenced while studying in Germany by Johannes Volkelt's *System der Ästhetik* and Ernst Weber's *Ästhetik als Pädagogische Grundwissenschaft*, developed an argument for "educational aesthetics," an aesthetic theory of pedagogy. His approach introduced aesthetic norms into the pedagogy of character, which emphasized the personality of the teacher in education, and sought to raise it to the level of a full-fledged theory. Abe criticized the aesthetic theory of pedagogy's premise that "the practice of education is an art," arguing that emphasis on the similarity between education and art would lead to neglect of truth and science and be prejudicial to the construction of a scientific pedagogy. Here is revealed the enormous passion and determination of the young (twenty-five) Abe toward the "construction of a scientific pedagogy."[2] Abe was in effect striving for the modernization of Japanese pedagogy as an academic discipline, and it can be said that, although belatedly, it was as the result of his efforts that a modern scholarly paradigm emerged in Japanese educational studies.

In July 1915, Abe left graduate school, while still involved with *Kyōikū jikkenkai*, and began to work for the General Educational Affairs Bureau (*Futsū gakumu kyoku*) of the Ministry of Education. There, he took part in a massive research survey whose results were published as *Education Materials Concerning the Current Situation* (*Jikyoku ni kansuru kyōiku shiryō*). The *Education Materials* took five years to edit, from 1915 to 1920, and ran to 7,500 pages collected in forty volumes (collections 1 to 34), including appendices and charts.[3]

Education Materials examined World War I, including the settlements that followed it, in what can perhaps be considered a study of total war in the broad sense. Satō Hiromi has periodized the work into early, middle, and late phases and analyzed them in detail.[4] The characteristics of these three phases can be briefly summarized following Satō's periodization. The early phase (collections one to ten), typified by volumes four, five, and eight, were primarily devoted to introducing the use of education to foster patriotic spirit in support of the war. By the middle period (collections eleven to twenty-four), however, the content of the materials changed. When the war ended, the countries of Europe and the United States looked to education to correct defects in their systems that had emerged in the course of the war and recognized the need for the rational reform of institutions. In the European countries in particular, social-democratic political parties appeared in parallel with the mass democracy that followed World War I. These political parties fostered unified school movements that sought equal opportunity and popular democratization in education, especially secondary education. The experience of total war had accelerated the trend toward the unification of national consciousness through education and the realization of educational equality, and Abe was keenly aware of that trend. Collection eleven introduced "British Education Secretary Fisher's Education Reform Proposal" and the "Education Reform Proposal of the Workers' Educational Association," which stressed child welfare and called for the extension by one year of compulsory education. Collection fourteen carried American President Woodrow Wilson's speech declaring war on Germany, introduced democratic thought, and examined the subsequent democratic and rational reforms in the U.S. and other countries. In the final phase (collections twenty-five to thirty-four), the presentation of American educational reforms predominated, reflecting contemporary attention to the U.S. as the leader in educational reform.

As a result of actually taking part in research on different national education systems and reforms, Abe Shigetaka shifted the focus of his scientific research from art education and psychology to education systems and administration. From this point on, Abe can only have solidified his critical consciousness toward contemporary idealist pedagogy. As he noted to Tomeoka Kiyoo, "Soon after graduating from college I worked at the Ministry of Education, and since I dealt with all sorts of budget and planning tasks while there, I realized that the old educational philosophy was quite worthless."[5] Furthermore, although research on patriotism and the exaltation of national prestige were central in the initial phase of compiling the *Education Materials*, from the middle phase on there was a shift toward European and American democratic and rational types of systemic reform, and this probably influenced substantially the later standpoint and characteristics of Abe Shigetaka's science of education. As spiritualistic ultranationalism spread during the years leading up to World War II and on through wartime itself, Abe consistently defended a rationalist position.

Education Materials was presented to the Provisional Education Council (*Rinji kyōiku kaigi*), an advisory organ on the contemporary education system directly under the cabinet. The Council undertook the formulation of fundamental education policy in response to the rapid economic development and flux in social structures during World War I. A broad range of issues was considered, but the plan to expand institutions of higher education, conceived to meet increasing secondary school enrollment and the demand for educated labor that resulted from the development of the industrial structure, drew the most attention. This was probably the first systematic educational plan in the history of Japanese education.

The submission of *Education Materials* to the Provisional Education Council was a turning point in Abe Shigetaka's life. Among the committee members on the council was Yoshida Kumaji, chairman of the Education Department at Tokyo Imperial University, and as a result Abe was invited to join that department. The expansion plan for institutions of higher education naturally called for increasing the number of instructors at such institutions. In 1917 the Provisional Education Council put out a report on teachers' education, stating that "education departments with fully-equipped facilities should be established" in the literature faculties of the imperial universities. As a result of this policy, the number of positions under Tokyo Imperial University's Education Department was expanded from one to five. Where Yoshida Kumaji had been the lone, full-time instructor, the Education Department now assembled a staff of three professors and two assistant professors. At the time, most departments in the Literature Faculty had only one or two positions, so Education became the largest department within the Faculty of Literature. Abe Shigetaka became an assistant professor, and taught educational administration as the occupant of the fifth line. There had long been a lecture course on educational administration at Tokyo Imperial University, and from as far back as 1908 Matsuura Chinjirō of the Ministry of Education had been in charge of it. With Abe's appointment, however, educational administration became an established professorial line under the control of the Education Department. In parallel with the expansion of the department, the Ministry of Education began to provide special funds for educational survey research. In all likelihood these funds were attached to the fifth line that was occupied by Abe, who had been in charge of survey research at the Ministry of Education. The new research technique of surveys required unprecedented levels of funding, but at the same time the government, in parallel with the rise of the administrative state, came to require such surveys as part of the policy science that would serve its own expanding needs. Thus, closer connections between the academy and the bureaucracy emerged not only in law and economics[6] but in education as well.

Abe Shigetaka lectured on education systems and education administration throughout his term at Tokyo Imperial University's Education Department. He also took part in various social surveys. In 1921, Abe led the Education Department in conducting an investigation of the "three grade/two instructor" system, in conjunction with the announcement of the Rationalization Plan for Local Education Costs (*Chihō kyōikuhi seiri-an*). As a result, "An Investigation of Otsuki and Three Other Elementary Schools" (*Otsuki shōgakkō-gai sankō gakkō chōsa*) was issued in 1922, and was considered "the most reliable investigation of the record of Otsuki Elementary School" by *Teikoku kyōikukai* (Imperial education association) and other magazines. Thereafter, the scientific investigation of schools in Japan expanded steadily. The methods and activities of Abe's pedagogical lab at Tokyo Imperial University greatly influenced Kaigo Tokiomi's research on the history of education, which used scientific investigative methods, and also the creation of the Okabe education laboratory, a social research group within the Tokyo Imperial University pedagogical laboratory.

Abe continued to develop his research. In 1923 he traveled to Europe and the United States to study education, while also publishing some general works from his original perspective, including *Chiisai kyōikugaku* (Introduction to pedagogy) in 1927 and *Kyōikugaku* (Pedagogy) in 1929. In 1930 he wrote what would be his major work, *Ō-Bei gakkō kyōiku hattatsu-shi* (A history of the development of school education in Europe and America), a study of reformist trends in European and American education systems from the standpoint of the comparative institutional history of education. He also turned his research activities toward reform in Japanese pedagogical science. Beginning in 1931, he participated in the publication of the Iwanami series *Kyōiku kagaku* (Educational science), which ran to twenty volumes. Other participants included such future leaders of the science of education movement as Kido Mantarō, whose empirical research was influenced by experimental psychology, and Tomeoka Kiyoo, who sought a scientific understanding of education while engaging with such practical issues as rural poverty and child welfare. Abe, in effect, was the organizer of the *Kyōiku kagaku* series, and even the title clearly reflects his orientation. In 1939, however, Abe Shigetaka, proponent of the science of education in Japan, died of illness at the young age of forty-nine.

The above outline of Abe Shigetaka's research activities is intended to expose the general characteristics of his science of education and clarify his position in contemporary educational circles in Japan by looking at the formative process of that science. The next section delves more deeply into its characteristics.

ABE SHIGETAKA'S SCIENCE OF EDUCATION

Three main features define Abe Shigetaka's educational science. First, he understood education as social fact (*shakaiteki jijitsu*). Therefore, he was critical of the speculative and idealist mainstream of contemporary pedagogy: "In my view, one of the criticisms of prevailing pedagogy that most merits our attention is that education has become overly dependent upon philosophy."[7] Against the strong bias in Japanese educational studies toward idealist philosophy, Abe advocated a realistic pedagogy based on facts. His orientation toward a policy science that utilized statistical data and employed investigative techniques resulted from this position. Abe paid particular attention to institutions within social reality.

> Most education histories up to now . . . do not seem to have given sufficient weight to the development of "institutionalized education." But what has truly determined national education is not simply educational philosophy, but institutions.[8]

The institutional view of education differed from contemporary normative (*sollen*; *tōiron*) pedagogy by treating education as a function integral to the social system. Abe Shigetaka's science of education, which grasped education not in isolation from other systems but through its various linkages to them, made possible the analysis of a system society, that is, one whose social institutions, although retaining relative autonomy, had begun to form organic connections.

Second, he supported the adoption of scientific research methods and sought to establish the independence of pedagogy. This orientation is readily apparent in his *Moiman jikken kyōikugaku kōyō*, a translation of Ernst Meumann's *Abriß der Experimentellen Pädagogik*, which Abe helped with during the early years of his research, and which influenced him greatly. This work contains a section entitled "Die Selbständigkeit de Pödagogik als Wissenschaft (The autonomy of pedagogy as science)." He presents two counter arguments against Herbartian and other currents of pedagogy that did not accept the independence of pedagogy as a science. The first addresses the argument that the subject matter of pedagogy lacked internal unity. The advocate of such a position would claim that pedagogy was an amalgamation of various sciences, pointing out that analysis revealed all sorts of materials among those of pedagogy, that the objectives of education were determined by ethics, and that subjects like arithmetic, language, and the sciences were best left to specialists in those subjects. In his counter-argument, Meumann held that in no science was internal unity sustained through the homogeneity of its subject-matter, but rather through the unity of the perspective from which it viewed that subject matter. Pedagogy, like the other social sciences, comprised a definite system of knowledge and maintained a consistent research perspective. His second argument countered the claim that pedagogy could not construct theory through its own unique methodology; in other words, the argument that because pedagogy invoked teleology from ethics and a psychological foundation from psychology it was subordinate to those two disciplines. Meumann argued in response that pedagogy did not simply invoke these other disciplines, but unified their subject-matter from a standpoint unique to pedagogy. Meumann's work also strongly advocated the adoption of scientific research methods, and its scientific aspirations for pedagogy were closely connected to the establishment of a specialized domain, that is the independent domain of pedagogy. This discourse on the "independence of pedagogy" was very influential in the postwar movement toward institutionalization of education as an academic discipline through the creation of education faculties in universities. Thus, the issue of autonomy that was raised in the postwar by various educators, including Katsuta Shuichi, had already appeared in the prewar and constitutes a significant element of continuity.

The third feature of Abe's educational science is the modernity of his thought in relation to such principles as the right to education, equal educational opportunity, and equality between the sexes in education. Concerning the right to education, Abe had the following to say in *Chiisai kyōikugaku*:

As I have noted, education is that which takes the individual to be educated and helps that person to become an even better person than before.

In saying this we tacitly accept a presupposition. We presuppose, in other words, that *people have the potential to receive education*[9] (italics added).

Expressions like "potential to develop" and "potential to be educated" occur frequently elsewhere in Abe's work as well, and they suggest the germination of a mode of thought that viewed education as a birthright. In his 1936 essay, "*Gimu kyōiku nengen enchō no mondai*" (The issue of extending compulsory education) Abe further develops this mode of thought.

In recent times compulsory education has ceased to be considered merely a duty unilaterally forced upon the people by the state. *All citizens have the right to receive this level of education*, because only when the state recognizes *children's right to education* and takes upon itself a certain responsibility can the so-called benefits of compulsory education be fully obtained[10] (italics added).

At this point, he is clearly expressing an extremely modern conception of education as a right of the people.

Abe discussed the meaning of equal opportunity in the entry "Kyōiku no kikai kintō" (Equal opportunity in education), which he wrote for the first volume of *Kyōikugaku jiten* (A dictionary of pedagogy), published in 1936:

School education has long been monopolized by the ruling classes of society. Historically, the education received by children and youths differed greatly according to the economic circumstances and social position of their parents. . . . Against the background of these historical facts, what has most recently been strongly advocated is *equal opportunity in education*[11] (italics added).

To realize equal opportunity in education, Abe called for not only compulsory education but secondary and higher education, as well, to be free of charge.[12] More noteworthy still is his argument in the same article on the school system's relationship to equal opportunity in education. This is an extremely interesting point that merits quotation at length.

Opportunities for education above primary school differ according to the form of the school system adopted by a country. In Europe before the World War the primary education system was separated from the secondary and higher education systems, and the lack of a connection between the two meant that secondary schools became class schools monopolized by the children of middle- or upper-class families. Ordinary people, no matter how great their ability, were unable in fact to advance to secondary education much less higher education. In countries adopting this kind of school system, children's opportunity for education varied greatly depending on the social class to which they belonged. On the other hand, in our nation and in the United States of America, primary schools are the common schools of the whole nation, and because secondary and higher schools are connected to them, as far as this system is concerned, the opportunity for education is provided equally to all children. In this sense, the unified school movement, with its motto of opening the path of educational advancement to those with promise and its call for equal educational opportunity, deserves our attention. After the world war, Germany's partial realization of the idea of unified schools was a step toward equal educational opportunity; however, the school systems of Britain and France are still unsatisfactory at present on several points related to equal educational opportunity. Nevertheless, both the unified school movement in France and the universal secondary education movement in Britain developed from the demand for equal educational opportunity.[13]

Abe identified the multi-track form of European educational systems as the origin of inequalities in educational opportunity based on class, and from this viewpoint approved of the single-track American and Japanese education systems. The points that appear here are those that caught his attention when he was researching the middle phase of the *Education Materials*, which dealt with the European unified school movement, and the later phase, on the American education system. They show his strong commitment to educational equality.

Abe Shigetaka also had a very modern outlook on the issue of educational equality between men and women: "All schools ought to be opened equally to both sexes, and all special privileges accorded with graduation from school abolished."[14] On higher education he stated:

One aspect of our nation's professional and university education in which we can take no pride in front of foreigners is that the path to higher education is not adequately open to women. This is most unfortunate; indeed, our country's system is indefensible on this point.[15]

Abe, moreover, had the educator and contemporary woman activist, Koizumi Ikuko, write the entry on "Coeducation" (*Danjo kyōgaku*) in *Kyōikugaku jiten*, which he co-edited. Incidentally, Koizumi's "*Danjo kyōgakuron*" (On coeducation) (1931) was translated into English by the GHQ and played a significant role in the postwar implementation of coeducation.[16] That Abe held ideas about equality between the sexes that were quite consistent with those of the postwar era can certainly be inferred from his work with Koizumi.

Abe Shigetaka's science of education thus had three distinguishing features: an understanding of education as social fact, a scientific approach to research in combination with aspirations for the independence of pedagogy, and modern thought. Abe's science amounted to a critique of existing idealist and philosophical pedagogy, but at the same time it also distanced itself markedly, in both methods and philosophy, from the contemporary tide of irrational, anti-scientific, Japanist pedagogy, which idealized a return to the wellsprings of Japanese spirit. Abe's science of education stood out from such notions by virtue of its modernity. Previous histories of education have narrated the wartime era of the 1930s and 1940s as a period when this kind of modern science of education was crushed by state repression. In this sort of history of resistance and defeat, many postwar, modernist educators have construed Abe's science of education as exceptional among wartime research and glorified its modernity as if it were dissociated from the war. But, although it stood out from contemporary currents, Abe's science of education was not merely an impotent heterodoxy. It constituted a social and intellectual force that was integral to the pedagogy of wartime but distinct from contemporary spiritualism. By exploiting its special qualities as a policy science, moreover, it was able to flourish under the wartime system through its connection to national policy.

Next, let's examine concretely what Abe Shigetaka did from the prewar into the wartime. Tracing the relationship between the wartime system and Abe's science of education—a relationship never fully problematized in prior studies—will help us to draw out the larger question of relations between the wartime period and modernity in education.

ABE SHIGETAKA, EDUCATION POLICY, AND THE PEDAGOGICAL SCIENCE MOVEMENT

Abe Shigetaka, researcher on education systems and policy, was also actively committed to the practical issue of education reform. In May 1930, with Gotō Ryūnosuke, Gotō Fumio, and Kido Mantarō, he formed the Education Research Association (*Kyōiku kenkyūkai*) to study proposals for institutional reform in education. In the 1930s, the slump that resulted from the world depression put Japanese society into a general state of crisis, with frequent outbreaks of social and agrarian problems. Various issues related to education presented themselves: college graduates had difficulty finding jobs, the influence of Marxism led to leftist tendencies among students, and an increase in applicants made it difficult to get into high school. Together, these trends suggested the collapse of a stable relationship between education and society and among the different levels of education. One stream that confronted this situation was a right-wing, nationalist one, which attributed it to the influence of Western liberalism and modernism since the 1920s, and sought to "overcome the modern" (*kindai no chōkoku*) by returning to "Japanese things" (*Nihonteki naru mono*). Against this, another force read the crisis as a failure of laissez-faire doctrine and sought to break out of it through the planned rationalization and organization of society. Representing the latter approach was the national-policy research group called the Shōwa Kenkyūkai (Shōwa Research Association), which was led by Gotō Ryūnosuke and the political scientist Rōyama Masamichi, and included many scholars, journalists, and bureaucrats.[17] The ideological character of the Shōwa Kenkyūkai was varied and cannot be simply summarized, but for the most part it was a liberal, reformist force composed of modernist democrats. Former Marxists, who had gone through one form or another of *tenkō* (conversion), also joined. The Education Research Association changed its name to the Education Issues Research Society (*Kyōiku mondai kenkyūkai*) and in 1933 became one of the research groups within the Shōwa Kenkyūkai. Abe Shigetaka played a central role as a specialist in educational administration. In 1937, this association developed into the Society of Friends of Education Reform (*Kyōiku kagaku dōshikai*), expanding its membership to eighty-eight.

While very active in a reformist national-policy research group, Abe also served during this period on many government councils. They included the Teachers' Education Research Committee (*Shihan kyōiku chōsa iinkai*; 1928), the Research Committee on Women's Secondary Education (*Joshi chūtō kyōiku chōsa iinkai*; 1929), the Cabinet Research Bureau Committee of Specialists (*Naikaku chōsakyoku senmon iinkai*; 1935), the Committee for the Promotion of Vocational Training (*Jitsugyō kyōiku shinkō iinkai*; 1936), the Education Council Committee (*Kyōiku shingikai iinkai*; 1937), and the University System Review Preparatory Committee (*Daigaku seido shinsa junbi iinkai*; 1937). He also served the Ministry of Education as its Director of Social Education (*Shakai kyōikukan*) from 1929. How can we explain Abe's appointment to so many government councils?

In 1928, a research department was formed in the Ministry of Education. Minister of Education Mizuno Rentarō believed that it was uneconomical for education research to be divided up among bureaus, as it led to duplication of effort. Therefore, he set up a research department which combined counterpart units from each bureau. This was only an internal arrangement within the ministry; neither an established research institution nor an official organization. In 1933, however, the research department was expanded to become the Education Research Division (*Kyōiku chōsabu*), and Morioka Tsunezō assumed the post of division head. With this development, research activities within the Ministry of Education became more serious.

Morioka described the three goals of the Education Research Division. The first was to compare the many educational reform plans put forward by the Seiyūkai party, the Minseitō party, the Imperial Education Association, and other organizations, and to determine comprehensively their similarities and differences. The second was to review the development of Japanese education, investigating the circumstances and reasons for all past revisions. The third was to examine the cases presented in foreign countries on behalf of education. After World War I, other countries had implemented various revisions in the content and systems of education, and Morioka identified these as valuable references for Japan.[18]

Finally, an authentic research organization had been established within the Ministry of Education. I suggested above that during this period the techniques of social research spread to pedagogy; now these techniques were also being used to support actual educational policy. In 1929, moreover, a reform group that was centered on young bureaucrats, called the Education Reform Research Association (*Kyōiku kaikaku kenkyūkai*), was organized within the Ministry of Education.

The Education Research Division and Education Reform Research Association were components of a movement that opposed the spread of ultranationalist thought control and extension of the police state, and sought to establish planned education policy aimed at the rational cultivation of human resources.[19] Abe Shigetaka's participation in a variety of committees can also be explained in relation to this movement. A representative of this reform group within the government, who was also a member of the Education Issues Research Association, was Miyajima Kiyoshi of the Ministry of Education. He published the essay "A Fundamental Policy for the Reform of the Education System" (*Kyōiku seido kaikaku no konpon hōshin*; 1934) in *Kyōiku* (Education), a magazine discussed below. The essential points of the essay were:

1) Education must always be planned. It is related to the total functioning of society, and thus a broad and comprehensive plan is essential. We keenly feel the need for this task to be undertaken by a kind of general staff for education.

2) Justice must be emphasized from the point of view of social policy.
   A. Universalization of secondary education (necessity of vocational education)
   B. Enactment of social legislation for education
   C. Fair distribution of education costs

3) School education
   This should entail the cultivation of comprehensive knowledge, not the transmission of rote learning.
4) Education administration
   A. Reform of administrative institutions in education.
   B. Education administration should be put completely under the control of the Ministry of Education (independence from the Home Ministry).[20]

Miyajima Kiyoshi's argument for rational planning had much in common with Abe Shigetaka's with respect to the necessity of universalizing secondary education, concern about education costs, and the independence of educational administration. As Miyajima was also a member of the Education Issues Research Association, he probably interacted with Abe personally as well as intellectually. The activities of policy-maker and researcher became closely intertwined as the two men maintained close contact. This helps explain how Abe Shigetaka was able to participate actively on so many government councils. Of course, it is not at all clear that views like Miyajima's were dominant within the Ministry of Education at the time. However, the image that has formed of 1930s and 1940s educational administration as being completely enveloped in ultranationalism is inaccurate. The kind of rationalizing force that was represented by Miyajima was one valid stream of thought in the government, and coexisted in tense interaction with spiritualist, ultranationalist elements. Moreover, the existence of a renovationist bureaucrat (*kakushin kanryō*) like Miyajima, who aspired to the planned management of education policy and engaged in scientific investigation, shows that the kind of educational planning and policy Abe advocated was realistic politically as well as intellectually.

Abe Shigetaka was also actively engaged in development and promotional activities in order to spread the pedagogical science he had molded. As noted above, Abe participated in the preparation of the Iwanami series, *Kyōiku kagaku*, which was initiated in 1931 and included, as a supplement, the pamphlet *Kyōiku* (Education). When the series was completed in March 1933, *Kyōiku* became a monthly magazine. The editor was Kido Mantarō, who had also participated in *Kyōiku kagaku*, and Tomeoka Kiyoo was his collaborator. Although Abe was not directly involved with editing, this magazine can be said to manifest Abe's conception of the science of education. The first issue, in April 1933, clearly articulated in an inaugural statement this periodical's concern for pedagogical science. First, because education could no longer be sustained on the basis of ideas internal to itself and since, moreover, contemporary education had not only to keep up with the rapid pace of society but participate in it at the front lines, the magazine resolved to grasp education in relation to society and to present trends of educational thought both at home and abroad. Second, it criticized unproven educational practices and techniques, pointing out the need for empirical research in the form of scientific investigation of schools and society. Finally, as journalists the editors promised to grapple with current issues affecting society and to emphasize educational reporting and commentary. Each of these three points was fundamental to Abe's science of education. By virtue of its strong interest in the realities of education policy, this magazine clearly differed from other periodicals on education, which were mainly concerned with educational philosophy and curriculum.

The magazine *Kyōiku* raised 'scientism' (*kagaku shugi*) and 'life-ism' (*seikatsu shugi*)[21] as slogans and gathered a broad spectrum of contributors: the educational science group around Abe Shigetaka, renovationist bureaucrats, educational activists involved with the "life composition" (*seikatsu tsuzurikata*)[22] and other movements, and social activists. Later, such leading postwar educators as Miyahara Seiichi and Munakata Seiya also participated. Ideologically, its character could perhaps be described as "people's front," as it ranged from liberal to left-wing. During the Takigawa Incident of 1933,[23] *Kyōiku* put together a special edition under the title, "The Mission of the University and the Kyoto University Issue," which lambasted the government and Ministry of Education from a liberal standpoint.

Kyōiku acquired a large readership, and from around 1936 researchers and practitioners began to gather together, organizing joint research societies. Subsequently, in 1937, these research societies were reorganized into the Science of Education Research Association (*Kyōiku kagaku kenkyūkai*), which became the organizational core of the pedagogical science movement. In the course of these events, *Kyōiku* became involved in practical organizational affairs. Moreover, in 1937 Miyahara Seiichi and Munakata Seiya began to participate in the Society of Friends of Education Reform, strengthening ties with national policy research associations. The Science of Education Research Association continued to develop under the wartime structure and in 1939, with the support of the *Kyōiku* editorial group and the Society of Friends of Education Reform, it sponsored the First Conference on Research in the Science of Education, a national event held at Hōsei University. As a result of this conference, the Science of Education Research Association strengthened its horizontal ties, becoming the vehicle of a national teachers' research movement that reached a membership of 1000 within a year. However, by this time, its political stance was completely different from that at the time of the Takigawa Incident; it had now shifted toward cooperation in constructing the "New Order in East Asia" (*Tōa shin chitsujō*).

How can this shift be explained? Existing historical studies attribute it to the suppression of such embodiments of modern thought as the Science of Education Research Association and the magazine *Kyōiku*, as a result of the expansion of ultranationalist forces in parallel with the advance of the wartime structure. It is certainly true that the Science of Education Research Association was driven to disband in 1940, and *Kyōiku* ceased publication in 1944. But how, then, should one explain the development of the Science of Education Research Association from the middle of the 1930s through 1940? Even in 1939-40, the Science of Education Research Association and *Kyōiku* had not abandoned their program of scientific planning in education. In other words, the relation between these entities and the national policy research associations and rationalist forces within government itself has not been adequately investigated.

A detailed account of war collaboration by *Kyōiku* and the Science of Education Research Association is beyond the scope of this essay.[24] Suffice it to say that *Kyōiku* and the Association were able to expand in the second half of the 1930s as a result of their connection with national policy research associations and other rationalist forces within government. This is precisely because the wartime structure required the rationalization and modernization of the social order. In the final section, I will examine concretely the reform of the educational system that was carried out in this period, with special attention to reforms in secondary education and education finance, which were of such concern to Abe Shigetaka. This will clarify the connections between wartime and the modernity of pedagogical science, and at the same time reveal continuity in the educational system throughout prewar, wartime, and postwar.

PRECEDENTS FOR POSTWAR REFORMS

Let's look first at reforms in the system of education finance. The shift from the Municipal Elementary School State Subsidy Law (*Shichō sonritsu shōgakkō kokko hojohō*) of 1900 to the 1918 Law for Provision from the National Treasury of Municipal Compulsory Education Costs (*Shichōson gimu kyōikuhi kokko futanhō*) (LPNTMCEC) clarified national responsibility to defray the costs of compulsory education. The intent was to correct inequities in education resulting from the differences among municipalities in economic resources; it was, thus, an important element in the equalization of education by the state. However, the second law was passed at a time of poverty in local public finances after World War I, so in practice it was used to reduce municipal tax burdens as a substitute for an adjustment of the tax system.[25] That is, the LPNTMCEC was burdened with the dual functions of subsidizing education and equalizing local public finances. In the background was increasing acceptance of the idea of equality in education and also of maintaining certain national minimums in local public finances. However, because of its limitations as a specific subsidy system the law did not function adequately as an equalizer. Moreover, because it provided support in a fixed amount it was easily affected by economic fluctuations and therefore of limited value in maintaining the stable provision of education expenses.

From 1923 to 1930 the LPNTMCEC was revised four times. Each time the amount of support was increased, and its role in equalizing local public finances was strengthened. The depression following the financial panic of 1929 put pressure on local public finances, however, and local outlays for education were reduced. The result in some places was the failure to pay elementary school teachers' salaries. Another problem that the government considered to be serious was the intellectual drift to the left among teachers that arose from their reduced standard of living. In sum, the rural depression opened further the economic gap between cities and countryside, so that the government was hard pressed to devise countermeasures. Abe Shigetaka commented on the education finance issue in his "A View on Education Reform" (*Gakusei kaikaku shiken*; 1935), which ran in the magazine *Kyōiku*.

> The extraordinary increase recently in the costs of municipal elementary schools has become common knowledge, yet even today neither facilities nor teacher training can be regarded as adequate. Not only are many children not in school these days, but it has gotten to the point where teachers are not even receiving their salaries. Up to now it has been considered proper and even most effective to have municipalities establish and maintain elementary schools. The customary method of meeting increasing public education costs was therefore to increase local taxes. Sixty years of experience with having municipalities establish and maintain elementary schools has shown that this produces extreme inequalities in education and in the burden of education costs among municipalities. The cause of this inequality, however, resides not only in the differing levels of wealth among municipalities, but also in their differing levels of enthusiasm for education. Placing education in the hands of municipalities presents serious problems for both education and education finance. . . . The state must therefore apply certain controls to education and endeavor to guarantee the equality of all forms of educational opportunity necessary for the development of the natural endowments of children. This is the essential significance of National Treasury provision of education costs and of state subsidies. The National Treasury has provided a portion of compulsory education costs in our nation from 1918, and although that amount has been increased gradually over the years, it has not necessarily

succeeded in guaranteeing equality of educational opportunity across municipalities.[26]

Abe criticizes the municipal provision of educational costs on the basis of the principle of equality of educational opportunity, and supports the guarantee of education costs by the state.

In the same essay, Abe refers to the rural-urban gap and calls for the correction of interregional disparities. In fact, the system of educational finance was later revised in the direction Abe advocated. The reform was propelled by the drive for strong national unity under the wartime system and interlocked with the need for a leveling of living standards and equalization of burdens across the nation. Indirect equalization through the LPNTMCEC was insufficient; demand mounted for a system whose central objective would be the equalization of local public finance. In 1936, the Temporary Municipal Public Finance Subsidy Regulation (*Rinji chōson zaisei hokyūkin kisoku*) was established as an adjustment system for local public finance. It was small-scale in the beginning, but gradually augmented. Finally, through the local apportioned tax system (*chihō bunyozei seido*) of 1940, a permanent general system for the adjustment of local public finance was established. As a result, a balance was achieved between the center and localities in the distribution of the national tax burden.

With the establishment of the local apportioned tax system it became possible to consider the burden of compulsory education costs apart from the adjustment of local public finances. In 1940, the Law for the Provision from the National Treasury of Compulsory Education Costs (*Gimu kyōikuhi kokko futanhō*) came into force. This law took the adjustment of local public finances that had fallen within the purview of the LPNTMCEC of 1918 and vested it in the local apportioned tax system, thereby restoring its original character as a specific subsidy system. This amounted to the realization of Abe's conception. First, through this law the compulsory-education portion of teachers' salaries that had been borne by municipalities and the central government was now shifted to prefectures and the central government. The transfer of the burden of education costs from municipalities to prefectures, which had greater financial resources, made possible more stable and flexible financing. Another factor was the conversion of the method of national treasury support from a fixed amount to a fixed percentage of costs, set at one half of actual salaries. This clarified the central government's obligation toward compulsory education costs, effecting a stable, national foundation for educational support that was immune to economic fluctuations.

Prefectural provision of compulsory education costs and fixed-rate subsidies were the basis of the education finance system from 1940 throughout the postwar period, except for a brief hiatus in the early 1950s. As time went on, the local apportioned tax system developed into the local public finance equalization subsidy system (*chihō zaisei heikō kōfukin seido*) in 1950, and the local transfer tax system (*chihō kōfuzei seido*) in 1954. The reform process from the enactment in 1918 of the LPNTMCEC through the enactment in 1940 of the local apportioned tax system and the Law for the National Treasury Provision of Compulsory Education Costs can be said to have prepared the way for postwar reform. The foundations of the egalitarian, administratively centralized education and local finance systems of the postwar were formed in the prewar and wartime period.

The universalization of the secondary education system was another such reform. In 1910, enrollment in primary education was 98.14% (Ministry of Education, *Nihon no kyōiku tōkei* [Japanese Education Statistics], 1971), or virtually 100%. Moreover, in the 1910s, particularly during World War I, the percentage of those continuing their education after elementary school rose sharply. At the time, the school system beyond the six compulsory years of elementary education consisted in a multi-track, socially stratified structure that included middle schools, which were elite institutions for the secondary education of those intending to continue further; various secondary schools, such as vocational schools and higher girls' schools; higher elementary schools, which were extensions of primary education; and technical continuation schools for working youths. Abe Shigetaka believed that secondary education was more open in Japan and America than in Europe, but he still found the structure of Japanese secondary education to be problematical in that respect. He was particularly critical of the goal that was set for middle schools by the 1899 revision of the Middle School Ordinance (*Chūgakkō-rei*), which was to provide "the high level of general education required by young men." Abe criticized the elite structure of secondary education based on the middle schools: "The structure of our country's system of education and the contents of school education at each level have been rationally arranged so as to benefit those continuing to higher-level schools," however, "from the point of view of the education of the nation's masses, we should certainly not be satisfied."[27]

In response to the increasing difficulty of entering high schools that resulted from the rapid expansion of middle schools in the 1920s, the so-called type-one curriculum (*dai-isshu katei*) was established in middle schools for students intending to work afterward rather than continuing their education. This was a planned, quantitative adjustment between levels of education which, insofar as it opened the door to middle schools for those students not necessarily intent on continuing their education, can also be considered the realization of the popularization policy that Abe supported. Popularization of the elitist middle schools continued, and by 1935 the number of middle schools with a type-one curriculum (457 schools) had reached about 80% of the total.

Secondary education was also expanded at lower levels. In 1926, at the strong urging of the Army Ministry, youth training centers (*seinen kunrenjo*), which emphasized military training, were established as educational institutions for young workers. Like the technical continuation schools, the youth training centers were educational institutions for ordinary young people who had graduated from primary school and were employed. As a result of the overlap between the two types of institutions and the increased municipal burden that resulted, proposals to merge the two into a single educational institution appeared in the 1930s. The adjustment was difficult because of the clash of views between the Ministry of Education, which stressed vocational education, and the Army Ministry, which emphasized military education. A compromise was finally achieved in 1935, and youth schools (*seinen gakkō*) were formed by merging the technical continuation schools and the youth training centers.

Abe Shigetaka was interested in these youth schools. The June 1936 issue of *Kyōiku* carried a round-table discussion entitled "educational reform" that focused on Abe's "Personal Proposal for the Reform of the Education System" (*Gakusei kaikaku shian*). One of the points in Abe's "Proposal" had to do especially with the reform of secondary education. Specifically:

III. Reform of the Education System

. . .

  3.) Middle Schools
    i. The complete course of middle school shall be six years divided into first and second terms, each of three years.
    ii. In the first year of the first term the primary object shall be to educate according to the individual character of the pupils, local conditions, and so forth. From the second year the curriculum shall be differentiated so as to meet the needs of both those intending to advance to an upper level school and those who [upon graduation] will directly enter society. Education in the second term shall be directed toward completing the education of the first term.

. . .

  6.) Youth Schools
    i. The complete course of youth school shall be six years divided into first and second terms, each of three years.
    ii. A minimum of 400 hours shall be devoted to instruction during the first term, with heavy emphasis on civic and vocational education.

7.) Compulsory Education
  i. Compulsory education shall be carried out according to a primary and a secondary plan.
  ii. In the primary plan, compulsory education shall last until the age of fifteen, and may be fulfilled at either a middle school or a youth school. However, for those students who drop out of middle school, youth school education shall be compulsory until the age of fifteen.
  iii In the secondary plan the first term of middle school shall be compulsory, but those unable to advance to middle school may be exempted from this obligation by graduating from a youth school.[28]

Abe proposes a policy of compulsory secondary education with the object of equalizing educational opportunity. One means of achieving that was to fully implement the youth schools. By raising the status of youth schools, which were designed to be supplementary educational institutions for working youths, to the level of secondary education, he intended to expand national participation in secondary education. Abe's division of middle and youth schools into first and second three-year terms is also noteworthy, in that it is identical to the postwar 6-3-3 system of primary and secondary education. Later, in the postwar period, Kido Mantarō would assert that the postwar conversion to a 6-3-3 system was based on Abe's youth-school proposal.[29] At the very least, we have to recognize that the postwar 6-3-3 system was conceptually prefigured in the mid-1930s. The Society of Friends of Educational Reform, including Abe, also began to grapple with this problem of universalizing secondary education. A Compulsory Youth-School System Research Association was set up within the Society of Friends of Education Reform, and with the participation of key members of the Science of Education Research Association and *Kyōiku* writers it took a firm stand for making youth schools compulsory.

The actual establishment of compulsory youth schools was not long in coming. On 13 January 1938, at the second general meeting of the cabinet's Education Council (*Kyōiku shingikai*), Minister of Education Kido Kōichi reported on the cabinet's decision to implement a compulsory youth-school system for young men. That this was a sudden decision is clear from the recorded complaints of Education Council members that they had been ignored. Previous research has explained this decision as one part of an Army-initiated government policy of "embracing" (*kakoikomu*) youths in order to prevent any drop in youth-school enrollment that might result from the elimination of the draft exemption provision in the revised Military Service Law (*Heieki hō*).[30] At the same time, however, the influence of Abe Shigetaka and the Society of Friends of Education Reform, who called for the universalization of secondary education, cannot be ignored. The proposal and decision to make youth school compulsory originated with Prime Minister Konoe, who had close relations through the Shōwa Kenkyūkai with members of the Society of the Friends of Education Reform. In fact, the Ministry of Education's "Outline Plan for the Implementation of a Compulsory Youth School System" duplicated on many points the "Outline Plan for a Compulsory Youth-School System" that had been put out the same year by the Compulsory Youth-School System Research Association, including seven years (one year more than in Abe's conception) of compulsory education after elementary school, that is, until age nineteen. Thus, the realization of compulsory youth schools linked the Army's demand for education, driven by the need to improve military technology and the intellectual capacity of personnel—essential components of modern warfare—with the proposals of Abe Shigetaka and the educational-science reform group, who strove to equalize educational opportunity through the universalization of secondary education. From 1939, therefore, the 80% of male youths who joined the working class were required to complete seven years of postprimary schooling, a drastic extension of compulsory education.

Certainly, many problems remained in the quality of teachers, facilities, and the curriculum, and the strong military coloring of youth-school education cannot be denied.[31] Nevertheless, compulsory youth schools greatly expanded educational opportunity for working youths who had graduated primary school. The implementation of this system also meant that almost all of the country's youths were in school under the surveillance of the state throughout the entire period from elementary school through enlistment. It should not be overlooked, however, that this development occurred within the context of modernization in education, that is, the expansion of educational opportunity. Under the wartime system, it was as modern subjects that Japanese nationals were subjected to discipline and training.

The Education Council, which approved of the Ministry of Education's compulsory youth-school system, discussed the homogenization (*ichigenka*) of secondary education, which had also been incorporated conceptually into the Education System Reform Plan (*Kyōiku seido kaikaku-an*) produced by the Society of the Friends of Education Reform. Arguments in favor of homogenization were that the equal valuation of all secondary schools within the system would correct the overemphasis on middle schools and the tendency to view vocational schools as "subsidiary"; it would improve facilities and raise student and teacher "morale" at vocational schools; and it would help realize equal opportunity in secondary education and promote homogeneity in the credentials of graduates.[32] Opinions within the Education Council were divided, for and against, and although homogenization was not implemented, in 1943 the Secondary-School Ordinance (*Chūtō gakkō-rei*) did increase the systemic commonality of secondary school education. The multi-track, socially stratified secondary education structure was being equalized into a single-track system.

The preceding survey of the reforms that were carried out in secondary education and educational finance under the wartime regime shows that in both respects these reforms amounted to realizations of Abe Shigetaka's vision. Insofar as the reforms were all directed at breaking through the class-based stratification and inequality of European education systems, they can be said to have aimed at "transcending" (*norikoe*) European modernity. However, they did not seek to overcome modernity in the sense of rejecting modern values. Indeed, by opening secondary education to the whole nation and striving for equal opportunity they showed themselves to be more modern than was the rule in contemporary Europe. Abe's approach to securing equality through centralized authority was a more far-reaching effort to promote equal rights to education than what was possible in the decentralized American system. And it was through reforms under the wartime system that Abe aimed at equal rights in education. To the extent that these wartime educational reforms—directed toward a modernity more thorough than that of either the U.S. or Europe—eroded class stratification and made possible wide-ranging social mobility, they signify the beginnings of a "system society" capable of giving stable organization to the emergence of mass society.

From the perspective of postwar social norms, according to which increases in social mobility are an index of democratization, the reforms under the wartime system constituted an advance in the "democratization" of education, regardless of the extent of state control involved in their implementation. It was in the course of pursuing this "democratization" that Abe and his group of educational scientists cooperated with the wartime regime. Moreover, this "democratization" that was begun in the wartime period was inherited and fully developed under the postwar "system society." The single-track, egalitarian, educational system that had been anticipated in the prewar and wartime periods formed a fundamental condition for the development of education and society in postwar Japan. Pre-1945 developments undergirded postwar, social-democratic reforms, including the Constitution and the Fundamental Law of Education, and completed themselves through those reforms. As a result, after the war education spread rapidly throughout the nation, as enrollment rates rose rapidly from compulsory middle school through high school and college. Many have noted that, when combined with organized economic mechanisms, this supported the development of the postwar Japanese economy.

On the other hand, the problems engendered by this education system ought not to be overlooked. The 6-3-3-4 system, whose archetype was prepared during wartime and which was finally established in the postwar, separated secondary education into middle and high school and, furthermore, weakened the systemic connection between secondary and higher education. In fact, in this system all that now bridges the gap between middle school and high school and between high school and college are the entrance exams. This may be considered one factor behind the formation of Japan's mass, meritocratic structure, conspicuous even among the advanced nations. The problematical character of modernity, including such elements as the penetration of education by disciplinary and training power [Michel Foucault] and the emergence of new types of class domination rationalized through education [Pierre Bourdieu], has become clearly evident in this structure.

Although in the early-postwar period the advocates of a modern pedagogical science opposed the Ministry of Education, which was promoting a return to the prewar, their support of democratization and equalization led them to attempt to increase educational opportunity even further without coming to grips with the problematical nature of modernity itself. This is evident, for example, in the 1970s movement to universalize enrollment in high school. The paradox that such "modernization" promotes a schooled society [Ivan Illich] that deprives children of any space or experience outside of school must not be taken lightly. At present, educational institutions at each level are increasingly taking on the character of preparatory organs for higher levels, and in the process the substantial content of their educational contribution has shrunk, while their formal-rational character as mere mechanisms of selection has been enhanced. Since the 1970s, when the high school enrollment rate surpassed ninety per cent and a steep increase in college matriculation occurred, pathologies such as violence in schools and refusal to attend have proliferated and are assuming increasingly serious forms. It is time to call fundamentally in question not only the educational reforms that were conceived during wartime, but also the actual postwar institutions that took those earlier reforms as their historical point of departure. What pervades both of these is, of course, none other than the problematical character of modernity itself.

Translated by Adam Schneider

Notes

[1] Mitsuishi Hatsuo, "'Kagakuteki' kyōikugaku kenkyū no seiritsu to jikken kyōikugaku," in *Kyōiku kagaku kenkyū* 2 (1983): 97-98.

[2] Hirata Katsumasa, "'Kagakuteki kyōikugaku' no kensetsū to geijitsu kyōikugaku" in *Kyōiku kagaku kenkyū* 2 (1983): 89.

[3] Satō Hiromi, "Abe Shigetaka to 'jikyoku ni kansuru kyōiku shiryō chōsa'" in *Kyōiku kagaku kenkyū* 2 (1983): 109.

[4] Ibid., 113-17.

[5] Tomeoka Kiyoo, "Abe Shigetaka sensei ni sasagu," *Kyōiku* (July 1939): 67.

[6] "It is worth noting that considerable human talent left the bureaucracy for academia at around this time. From the Ministry of Finance Ōuchi Hyōe, Morito Tatsuo, Maede Chōgorō and Itoi Yasuyuki moved to the Faculty of Economics at Tokyo Imperial University. The law faculty as well was joined by Tanaka Kōtarō, Nambara Shigeru, and Takagi Hasshaku, who abandoned their bureaucratic posts." Yamanouchi Yasushi, "Senjiki no isan to sono ryōgisei" in Yamanouchi Yasushi et al., eds., *Kōza shakai kagaku no hōhō daisankan: shakai kagaku no shisō* (Tokyo: Iwanami Shoten, 1993), 140.

[7] Abe Shigetaka, *Kōza kyōiku kagaku dai-nijū satsu: kyōiku kenkyū hō* (Tokyo: Iwanami Shoten, 1933), 3.

[8] Abe Shigetaka, *Ō-Bei gakkō kyōiku hattatsu-shi* (Tokyo: Meguro shoten, 1930), 1.

[9] Abe Shigetaka, *Chiisai kyōikugaku* (Tokyo: Ōkura Kōbundō, 1927), 21-22.

[10] Abe Shigetaka, "Gimu kyōiku nengen enchō no mondai" in *Kyōiku kaikaku-ron* (Tokyo: Iwanami Shoten, 1936), 25.

[11] Abe Shigetaka, "Kyōiku no kikai kintō," in Kido Mantarō et al., eds., *Kyōikugaku jiten* I (Tokyo: Iwanami Shoten, 1936), 464.

[12] "Free secondary and higher education, however, does not of itself guarantee the equality of educational opportunity. The income procured by youths supports family finances, and many families cannot afford to live without it. To guarantee the equality of educational opportunity, the state must provide financial support to those families that have promising youths but which, because of poverty, cannot allow them to continue their education. Therefore, in this provision of expenses must be included a family sustenance allowance in addition to scholarship money." Ibid., 464-65. Abe's view on state financial support for equal opportunity in education, holding as it did a social policy objective, was quite far-reaching.

[13] Ibid., p. 464.

[14] Abe Shigetaka, "Gakusei kaikaku" in *Kyōiku kaikaku-ron* (Tokyo: Iwanami Shoten, 1936), 14.

[15] Abe Shigetaka, *Kyōiku seido* (Tokyo: Teikoku Kyōikukai Dai-nanakai Sekai Kyōikukaigi Nihon Jimukyoku, 1937), reprinted in *Abe Shigetaka chosakushū* 5 [Kyōiku seidoron: kyōiku zaiseiron] (Tokyo: Nihon Tosho Sentā), 42.

[16] Shimizu Yasuzō, *Ishikoro no shōgai: sūtei obirin monogatari* (Tokyo: Kirisuto shinbunsha, 1977), 250.

[17] For detailed discussion of the Shōwa Kenkyūkai, see Shōwa Dōjinkai, ed., *Shōwa kenkyūkai* (Tokyo: Keizai ōraisha, 1968) and Sakai Saburō, *Shōwa kenkyūkai* (Tokyo: Chūō kōronsha, 1992).

[18] Morioka Tsunezō, "Kyōiku chōsabu no chōsa hōshin," *Kyōiku* (January 1934): 109-110.

[19] Suganami Shigeki, "1930nendai no kyōiku kaikaku kōsō," *Kenkyū shūroku* 12 (Sendai: Tōhoku Daigaku Kyōiku Gakubu Kyōiku Gyōseigaku Kyōiku Kanri Kyōiku Naiyō Kenkyūshitsu, 1981), 20.

[20] Miyajima Kiyoshi, "Kyōiku seido kaikaku no konpon hōshin," *Kyōiku* (January 1934): 111-13.

[21] "Seikatsu shugi" sought stability in the lives of the people by securing their right to livelihood. It was also used in place of terms like "communism" and "socialism" which were forbidden at the time.

[22] "Seikatsu tsuzurikata" refers to an educational activity in which children wrote and presented compositions about their own lives and the things that they felt or thought in order to cultivate their own and their peers' self-awareness, capacity for sympathy, and ability to discover the difficulties of daily life.

[23] The Takigawa Incident arose when the Minister of Justice found the lectures of liberal legal scholar and Kyoto Imperial University law professor Takigawa Yukitoki to be communist in substance; Minister of Education Hatoyama Ichirō had Takigawa's works banned, and demanded that university president Konishi Shigenao suspend him.

[24] I have examined this in *Senzen-senjiki ni okeru kyōiku no keikakuka to gōriteki shakai hensei* (Master's thesis, Tokyo Daigaku Daigakuin Kyōikugaku Kenkyūkai, 1994).

[25] Kokuritsu kyōiku kenkyūjo, *Nihon kindai kyōiku hyakunen-shi II: kyōiku seisaku* 2 (Tokyo: Kyōiku kenkyū shinkōkai, 1974), 164.

[26] Abe Shigetaka, "Gakusei kaikaku shiken," *Kyōiku* (March 1935): 11-12.

[27] Abe Shigetaka, "Gimu kyōiku nengen enchō no mondai," *Kyōiku kaikaku-ron* (Tokyo: Iwanami Shoten, 1936), 34.

[28] "'Kyōiku kaikaku' zadankai," *Kyōiku* (June 1936): 54-55.

[29] See the statement of Kido Mantarō in the exchange between Gotō Ryūnosuke and Gotō Fumio, "Atarashii kyōiku puran," in Shōwa dōjinkai, ed., *Shōwa kenkyūkai*, 181.

[30] Miyahara Seiichi, *Kyōiku-shi* (Tokyo: Tōyō Keizai Shinpōsha, 1962), 298.

[31] Terasaki Masao and the Senjika Kyōiku Kenkyūkai, eds., *Sōryokusen taisei to kyōiku* (Tokyo: Tokyo Daigaku Shuppankai, 1987), 250.

[32] Kokuritsu Kyōiku Kenkyūjo, ed., *Nihon kindai kyōiku hyakunen-shi* 5 (Gakkō kyōiku 3) (Tokyo: Kyōiku Kenkyū Shinkōkai, 1974), 1051-52.

III. Total War and Social Integration

Self-Renovation of Existing Social Forces and Gleichschaltung: The Total-War System and the Middle Classes

Amemiya Shōichi

Research around the world has now demonstrated quite conclusively the drastic effect of the total-war systems of World War II on the states and societies of the nations involved, Allied nations included.[1] As one of the editors of this volume, Yamanouchi Yasushi, has pointed out, with the exception of such pioneering figures as Ralf Dahrendorf, research on these transformations has appeared "simultaneously" around the globe only in the late 1980s.[2] Whether the researchers involved have been conscious of it or not, the spontaneous simultaneity of this global research effort is probably no accident; rather, it most likely reflects increasing awareness that the system of social and political arrangements established during World War II has already reached its peak of effectiveness and the limits of its continued usefulness have become increasingly obvious. The mid-1980s, of course, were the years when the Reagan, Thatcher, and Nakasone administrations beat their drums for neo-conservatism and neo-liberalism. The Democratic Party in the U.S., the Labour Party in the U.K., the Social-Democratic Party in Japan, and labor unions everywhere came under attack for their attachment to "big government," but on the basis of presently-available research it seems fair to say that such attacks were a direct expression of changes occurring in systems based on the total-war regimes of World War II. The policies of the Nakasone government differed from those of the English and American administrations by virtue of two main themes. First, Nakasone continued to espouse an Anglo-American type, "small government" ideal. Just as in other countries, this "small government" argument was characterized as a "taxpayer's revolt," and especially as a "revolt of the middle-class." Moreover, he pursued the theme

209

of "settling accounts with the postwar system" (*sengo taisei no sōkessan*).[3] This meant that he strove to make Japan, which was still bound by the "peace clause" (Article Nine) of the postwar Constitution, more like the NATO countries in the realms of security and foreign affairs.

By 1990, Reagan, Thatcher, and Nakasone were all out of power, replaced by governments that leaned towards relatively bigger government, especially in the form of the welfare state. Nevertheless, these new administrations did not simply return to the "big government" of yesterday. That is, we have entered a new era which cannot be so easily described through the old dichotomies of large vs. small government and socialism vs. liberalism.

Why, in this new age, is it important to return to an analysis of the total-war systems that originated in World War II? Yamanouchi has argued that we should do so from the standpoint of "overcoming the modern" (*kindai no chōkoku*). That is, in his view, the wartime mobilization system was hardly a "departure" from modernity, but was rather its ultimate realization, and he believes that an analysis of total-war regimes can contribute to overcoming that manifestation of modernity.

For my part, I am not inclined to follow Michel Foucault in emphasizing how increased organization under modernity has led to dehumanization and even permeated inner norms; I would prefer to argue along with Alberto Melucci that the very same process has led to autonomy in social organization and prepared the way for new political and social spaces,[4] or with Matsushita Keiichi, who contends that industrialization, democratization, and increasing emphasis on educational qualifications have given everyone the leisure time, economic margin, and capacity for self-determination that are the foundation of democracy.[5]

While noting the characteristics of total mobilization that are shared cross-nationally, in this paper I will look primarily at the peculiar contributions of Japan's total-war regime. Specifically, in Japan the objective conditions that Melucci and Matsushita enumerate have been "achieved," but the corresponding type of social actor, or subject, has not always been evident. It is certainly true that Japan accomplished high economic growth under a regime based on the total-war system, and that globally speaking, Japan is "economically strong, culturally rich, politically democratic, and socially free and stable."[6] On the other hand, it is often said that clientism and paternalism remain strong. Whether or not such charges are legitimate, the material and institutional conditions for autonomy are in place, even though the Japanese people still manifest tendencies typical of what Lenin called the "natural-born bourgeois," that is, tendencies to consider the local community, politics, and institutions of rule as Other, merely forms of external interference. Initially, I will consider these issues from the angle of the middle class (*chūkansō*).

THE MIDDLE CLASSES, PAST AND PRESENT

A great deal of research indicates that the middle strata played a decisive role as the social base for forces that brought about the Nazi and fascist regimes. In *Escape From Freedom*, Fromm located the social-psychological basis of Nazism in the *ressentiment* of the old-middle strata caught between big capital and the organizational power of the working class. On the other hand, Ralf Dahrendort argued that the new-middle classes formed the social basis of Nazism.[7] In Japan, Maruyama Masao identified two major categories of middle class. The first included the so-called old-middle class of landlords, small factory owners and shopkeepers; the second encompassed the so-called white-collar stratum. The first type was the more numerous, and according to Maruyama its members helped establish the social basis for emperor-system fascism by ensconcing themselves as "miniature emperors" within their local regions or business domains, and establishing social structures that survived into the postwar era. The second type of middle class was not only less numerous but relatively isolated in the context of society as a whole.[8] Later analyses of the "middle stratum of the emperor system" generally retained this scheme.[9] Maruyama Masao and Fujita Shōzō have pointed out that when the emperor system physically collapsed during the postwar reforms, this middle class lost its norms and lapsed into "hedonistic materialism" (*yokubō shizenshugi*). Matsushita Keiichi has observed that the Japan of 1960 was a "village society," pointing to the central importance of the old middle class in the urban, block-associations and rural communities.[10] Incidentally, Matsushita would also later argue that the white-collar class, whose ranks had swollen as a result of postwar industrialization, had accepted and taken to heart the "sentiments of the Peace Constitution," and he believed this common commitment would provide the basis for "citizen autonomy."[11]

Japan's New Middle Class by Ezra Vogel focuses on the white-collar, corporate employee, or "sarariiman." Vogel includes in this category such different types as specialized and technical workers, managers, and clerical workers. He points out that their numbers increased rapidly during the war, and especially during the 1950s and 1960s, and argues that in some ways they conformed to the "samurai" model established during the Tokugawa period (1600-1868). Husbands, wives, and children belonged to separate communities, in that the wife was devoted to supporting her husband, the husband was tied primarily to his place of employment, and the children were occupied with education, which was granted prime importance. In contrast to the old-middle classes, which held control in local communities, the "sarariiman" husband was politically cynical, and other than voting, hardly participated in his local community at all. Vogel believed that this sort of political (non)engagement was spreading, and that the privatism of "my-homeism" was expanding with it.[12]

The above might be summarized in terms of four points: First, during the Nazi period or, in Japan, during the period of emperor-system fascism, the old and new middle classes played a structurally constitutive role in forming and maintaining the system. Second, in Japan the old-middle class played an important role during this period, while the new-middle class expanded. Third, after the war, the new-middle class increased further, and its culture spread throughout the society. Fourth, in contrast to the old-middle class, the new-middle class was only weakly inclined toward community participation and self-determination.

For purposes of comparison, let's look at the middle classes in the United States. American works on the subject are quite numerous, beginning with Tocqueville's *Democracy in America*, and extending down to Hofstadter and Walter Lippman. Tocqueville had warned that American society in the formative stage of the American republic, consisting in the communities and independent individualism fostered by the old middle stratum that centered on the independent farmer, would fall into crisis when beset by industrialization and the development of major organizations. His prediction seemed to have become reality when theories of mass society were propounded in the 1950s by David Riesman, C. W. Mills and others. Reisman observed in *The Lonely Crowd* that amidst the influence of large organizations and mass media, the "inner-directed personality" that had mediated between public and private was being replaced by what he called the "other-directed personality"; and in *The Power Elite*, C. Wright Mills portrayed the masses as powerless and manipulated by the elite groups within large organizations. It is probably safe to assume that those whom Reisman and Mills refer to as the "masses" are the new-middle classes centering on white-collar employees of large organizations.

Robert Bellah's collaborative work of 1985, *Habits of the Heart*, argued that rather than culture or consciousness rooted in the working class or race, it was the middle class itself that from the beginning had formed the characteristic core of American society.[13] According to this work, an authentic public life had been achieved in American society through active participation premised on the intellectual legacy of individual success, freedom, and justice bestowed by the independent farmers who had founded the nation. With industrialization, this legacy was increasingly borne by entrepreneurs, managers and therapists, and eventually by the contemporary white-collar stratum. Throughout, however, the individual is linked with participation in the public realm or community. Bellah and his collaborators portray the changes that have occurred in the bearers of the American character, but it is rather the continuities in the American case that stand out when comparison is made to Japan. This is true even now, as Americans participate in local communities, environmental protection groups that are strongly anti-corporate, and many other organizations, including those for the defense of human rights.[14] They also tend to oppose government-sponsored national insurance plans on the grounds that they detract from equal opportunity. For example, a certain town of about 25,000 people on the outskirts of Boston has some 19 committees (leaving education aside) and many more ad hoc groups composed of volunteers to deal with all kinds of issues, including the elderly, cable television, etc. The residents hold that such volunteer participation is essential to prevent the town authorities from raising taxes.[15] Moreover, most of the residents are white-collar employees. It is often said that American society is actually supported by volunteers, and the example cited here suggests that the ideals, values, and behavior patterns of the community that formed part of the original rural society centering on the old middle class still survive today, even though the objective conditions and participants have all changed. The form of "self-determination" that leads one to maintain the local community by means of one's own labor power has survived, despite the transition to third-stage industrialization, the development of massive organizations, and the shift to "big society" caused by the rise of the mass media.

By way of contrast to the Japanese case, then, we can sum up the characteristics of the local community in the U.S. as follows: First, the values, prestige, and practices of the old-middle class that were the agents of self-determination in agricultural society were in more recent times transferred as a whole to the new-middle classes. Second, in the U.S. public space, including the local community, has always been paired with private space. Third, there is always room for autonomy, even if one belongs to a huge organization. Fourth, the ideology of equal opportunity is very strong. Therefore, fifth, entities and forms of ideology unique to the middle class have retained their power in American society. In order to reinforce the comparison to Japan, if we take the second point, what stands out is the lack of participation in all domains of Japanese public life, including the local community. Whether they depend upon the community or criticize it, Japanese interpret local community, administrative organs, and politics as the Other, pressuring them from outside. Consequently, they try to minimize the labor, money, and time they relinquish to them. The other side of this defensiveness is a social structure of "extortion," according to which, as a "natural-born bourgeois," one attempts by all means to fatten one's own private realm. In regard to number three, there is a tendency in Japan to commit unconditionally to a large organization and to bury oneself within it; as to the fourth point, there is a strong tendency to perceive as legitimate the absence of any differences among classes or strata. Fifth, for all these reasons, entities and ideologies peculiar to the middle class are extremely weak in Japan. More concretely, this is the result of the belief that everyone is a member of the middle class, that is, of the thorough saturation of Japanese society by middle-class values.

In the background of all these factors is the difference between American society, where space is left for autonomous activities on the part of religions, communities, and families that operate according to a logic other than economic efficiency, and Japanese society, which is "advanced" in the degree to which the increasing efficiency of industrial society has dissolved all such autonomy. But in this essay I will not reconsider the above contrasts along a developmental axis, because a significant level of interpenetration between the two societies has already been brought about by a variety of "achievements" in Japan-U.S. relations. In other words, the two systems largely share a space of simultaneity. Rather, what I would like to do here is clarify the historical background of Japan's special characteristics. In order to do so, I will examine in the Japanese case, and especially in relation to the total-war system, the matter I raised as the first American characteristic above, that is, the various continuities and connections between the old and new middle classes. Politically, this amounts to looking from the perspective of the middle classes at the interwar system of party politics, the Imperial Rule Assistance regime, and the 1955 system of party politics. I will begin by looking at the middle classes in relation to local community in both rural and urban contexts.

THE MIDDLE CLASS AND LOCAL COMMUNITY IN THE 1920s

I would like to avoid using the terms *Gemeinschaft* and its equivalent, *kyōdōtai*, that have acquired meanings and been situated historically in various ways. Instead, in the interest of relative neutrality, I will use the English term "community." My definition of community is close to Bellah's: the community is a group of people who depend on one another, participate together in debate and decision-making, and share in the execution of those decisions; community also imposes certain limits in a manner consistent with the group's past, or at least its memory of the past.[16]

In a 1962 work, Fukutake Tadashi wrote with regard to the local community of prewar Japan that within the group "peace and unity" were taken as the supreme values, that no outward expression of individual class or occupational interest was permitted, that the individual was a slave to traditional communalism, and that probably individuals would democratize such communities by means of free, spontaneous cooperation.[17] Shared by many, including Ōtsuka Hisao, Maruyama Masao, and Kawashima Takeyoshi, this

view defines the community as a vestige of premodern times. Murayama
Yasusuke, Kumon Shunpei, Satō Seizaburō, Kashiwabara Eisuke, and Noguchi
Yukio have divided the traditional organizational principles into two types,
the logic of the household (*ie*) and the logic of the village (*mura*). According
to these scholars, the household contains a structure of hierarchy and class
difference as a result of demands from the community, but also manifests
strong solidarity by virtue of its functional role in community management
and its self-conscious identity as part of a larger clan (*dōzoku*). In principle,
the village rejects the validity of representation in decision-making and equality
of results; yet, although personal benefits and interests could not in principle
be expressed within it, the village was in fact the locus of intense competition.
In prewar years the family stood for the "household" (*ie*) proper, while modern, fictive versions of the household were reproduced in corporations and
government organs; the state was presented as a "family state," and the infra-
structure of the whole system was provided by the village. After the war, the
village replaced the household as the basis for social orthodoxy, but despite
the postwar reforms under the Allied Occupation, the logic of the household
remained alive in corporations and government bureaucracies and promoted
rapid economic growth. However, by the 1970s the household model was
becoming bankrupt, and the village principle took over entirely. These scholars contend that the "village" model, which is a management style suited to
small-scale agriculture, does not function well in the context of large-scale
industrial enterprises, much less at the level of an entire nation.[18]

In response to Maruyama and Ōtsuka's depiction of the "village" as typical of premodern community, Satō Seizaburō and his collaborators posit it as
a fundamental and trans-historical principle of Japanese society. However,
both sides agree that it is a form of community that outwardly affirmed the
equality of individuals and frowned on the expression of individual interests.
Moreover, neither theoretical framework is adequate for the analysis of community in urban society.

Surely, ever since antiquity, communities based on the principles of common interest and equal participation, on the one hand, and organizations based
on the principle of bureaucratic hierarchy, on the other, have coexisted in
separate realms and on different social levels. With this as my basic hypothesis, I will proceed to examine, not ideals and principles, but rather the real
situation as it obtained in farming villages, towns that were half commercial-
industrial and half agricultural, provincial cities, and urban metropoles.
While attempting to avoid the "old-middle class as the enemy" thesis and the
opposite "pro-old middle class" thesis, both of which emerged from community and village studies, I will examine changes in the situation of the middle
class in relation to the community, and, in interaction with them, the political

transitions from the liberal system of the 1920s to the Imperial Rule Assistance system of the 1930s and 1940s, and then to the postwar system after 1945. Thus, my overall method will be historical analysis of social change mediated by systemic changes in politics.

Prior to formation in 1954 of the present-day city of Enzan, Yamanashi prefecture, the site was divided among a number of villages, including Nanasato-mura (which in 1928 became the town of Enzan-chō), Matsusato-mura, Okunota-mura, Kamikane-mura, Oofuji-mura, Tamamiya-mura, and a few others. Excluding the Kamiozo hamlet, which accounted for some 60-70% of the secondary and tertiary industry in all of Nanasato-mura, this was an agricultural region in which silkworm production occupied more than 70% of the agricultural population. Let's take a look at the circumstances of this local community, not from outside but rather through materials kept by people who were actually involved in it, focusing on such indispensable elements of village life as the Seinendan (young men's group), the district (*ku*), and the village (*mura*).

The records kept between 1921 and 1932 by the second branch of the Okunoda-mura Seinendan tell us a great deal about the routine operation of such organizations.[19] All the young men of the village, from their mid-teens through late-twenties, belonged to this or some other village Seinendan, and through it performed such functions as shrine rituals, clearing snow from the local roads, escorting elementary school children, keeping trash off the roadsides, making repairs, and planning and taking charge of events such as Respect for the Aged day, athletic meets, and speeches. Moreover, in cooperation with the local Veterans Associations they held send-off and welcome-home events for draftees and veterans, delivered newspapers and collected donations to raise money for such events and, for themselves, planned and carried out evening schools, training sessions, and recreational activities such as travel. These were all essential functions, but we find from internal documents that they were carried out and controlled autonomously, without any compulsion from outside or above. It was self-evident to the members that they should take care of and manage their own region through their own activities and labor.

Activities of organizations like the Seinendan were not self-contained, nor did individuals' interests or opposing views have to be papered over in the interest of harmony. Lectures and evening classes provided by teachers from outside the village attest to the community's openness. And not only did conflicts surface on a daily basis regarding how to manage events and other matters, but in the drive to secure the autonomy of the Seinendan such confrontations were often very salient. The Seinendan were still commonly led by someone like the elementary school principal, the village head, or the town mayor, even though in the latter half of the Taishō period a nationwide movement arose against such arrangements.[20] The Okunota Seinendan was no exception, and in February 1923 it developed a movement to expel the "president" (*sōri*) of the group, who was the school principal and also a night-school teacher. The reasons had to do with the principal's new educational policy which stressed music and physical education, what might best be termed his "urban attitudes" towards women and pleasure, and his drunkenness at night school classes. In addition to manifesting older standards of morality and provincialism, the Seinendan's reaction reflected a demand for autonomy. The group held meetings, where they called for the principal's resignation. Then, later the same year, a "bargain" was struck, which stipulated that both the principal and the Seinendan should "reflect" on their behavior. However, reverberations from the incident spread. According to the records of the Seinendan of Kumano district, Okunota-mura, between 1923 and 1926, this group at first took a stance opposed to the Seinendan headquarters and the second branch's position, recording that, "It is ridiculous that young men should presume to speak out on such matters as the elementary school." The Okunota-mura group was expelled by the Seinendan headquarters as a result. However, as mentioned above, these groups took charge of all sorts of activities in the local community; therefore, in 1923 a new Seinendan that agreed with headquarters policy was formed in the same district, and by 1926 it had merged with the former group. This incident demonstrates that, rather than being hidden, conflict was openly and autonomously expressed and finally "resolved."

The most serious conflicts in rural areas at the time occurred around the landlord-tenant relationship. In the 1920s and 1930s, tenant unions appeared in each of the villages and hamlets of the Enzan region, and various major and minor tenancy disputes arose. Naturally, one would expect such conflicts to have an impact on the Seinendan, to which all young men belonged, and also on the districts, which I will discuss below. Nevertheless, no such conflicts are recorded by either type of group. The only reference is a single entry in the record of the above-mentioned second-branch Seinendan to the effect that on that day the committee and night school activities were "cancelled on account of the union gathering." Rather than a case of covering up conflict, this should be viewed rather as a result of the practice of treating social and political conflicts as specific to the organizations in whose purview they fell, and compartmenting them from the functioning of local community.

Next, let's take a look at inside documents that reveal the circumstances of the districts. In the Enzan region, as in others, what was called a district brought together many hamlets, but in general it was more or less equivalent to the region served by a single elementary school. According to records of Shimoyunoki district of the former Matsusato-mura, dated April 14, 1913,[21] there was a confrontation between the district officials, who favored building a branch school, and the village authorities, who refused. There emerged a movement to hold meetings at local levels in order to determine the views of the district as a whole, and then if the opinion of the district still did not convince the village leaders, to unofficially support candidates for the village assembly. Existing documentation includes ballots and a joint proposal from the school district's Veteran's Association and the local Seinendan. These groups had suggested that send-offs for draftees be simplified, and were now proposing that the issue be decided by vote of a committee made up of members of the school district's seven organizations.[22]

The involvement of the district—in this case the Kumano Seinendan's parent organization, the Okunota-mura district—in the modernization of life was also clearly revealed in another movement. The electrification movement in the Enzan area was led by village assemblies (Nanasato-mura) and the Shimoyunoki and Kumano district administrations, but in Kumano also, virtually everyone became involved. Here the district officials played a central role, gathering the opinions of the district's residents after long debate and carrying out frequent, complex negotiations with power companies. District residents cut the electric poles themselves and set them up so as to serve every household; they also bore the substantial cost of these activities.[23] If we consider this process in relation to the profit-making assumptions of the power companies under the conditions obtaining at the time, it seems fairly clear that without the labor and economic contributions of the people in the district and the management provided by the district officials—that is, without the involvement of local community—the "modernization" of life in the form of comprehensive electrification could never have taken place.

Such a process of decision-making to solve regional issues and of execution involving both local and outside participation is hardly unique in modern societies. At the same time, the case related above also inevitably has certain peculiarities that cannot be generalized. Take, for example, the background of social inequality manifested in the landlord-tenant relationship. Although ambivalence always surrounded such matters, in order to maintain the local community it was necessary to have leaders, and most were from upper levels of the old-middle class, especially landlords who both resided and farmed in the villages. Also, of course, such people represented the upper level of a stratified social order. The movement that sought to reform that order emerged in the form of the expansive tenancy disputes that occurred in the Enzan region. The first such conflict in Enzan in the 1920s occurred in Shimoozo hamlet. It broke out in 1921, against the backdrop of rising land rents occasioned in part by the reactionary tendencies and economic panic that accompanied the end of World War I, but it was caused more directly by the rising land values that accompanied the rapid urbanization of neighboring Kamiozo hamlet. The dispute pitted the upper stratum that were economically defined as landlords, socially defined as paternal caretakers (*oyabun*), and politically loyal to the government-affiliated Seiyūkai party, against the lower stratum who were economically defined as tenants, socially relegated to the symbolic position of "child" (*kobun*), and politically loyal to the Kenseikai party. The dispute occurred when the latter rose up against the former, driving a major landlord from his position as lay head of the local shrine-worshippers' organization (*jinja ujiko*), and securing a majority for the Kenseikai in the village assembly, thereby precipitating a major change in local politics and society.[24] The movement spread throughout eastern Yamanashi county (*gun*), and in 1921 a *gun*-level tenant union was formed. The ideology evident in its declaration was scarcely socialistic, but rather argued that in order for Japan to become an international great power (*kokusaiteki yūshōsha*) and in order to develop the "national political essence" (*kokutai*), it was necessary to achieve domestic equality, respect the humanity of tenants, overcome the conventions of paternalistic relations of *oyabun*/*kobun*, and so on.[25] In other words, it called for imperialism abroad, social reform and equality at home.

In the background of such events was an important movement with respect to political organization. This was the formation a year prior to the Shimoozo dispute of the Kyōtō Rikken Seinentō (Kyōtō Constitutional Youth Party). This party was formed to achieve social equality and stamp out unequal social conventions (like *oyabun*/*kobun* relations) by the tenant movement leader and lawyer Furuya Sadao, along with other young men from the tenant class, a few from the landlord class, and independent farmers. It enjoyed the support of Nakano Seigō, a member of the House of Representatives who was active in the first movement to protect the Constitution. Under the restricted suffrage of the time, this party represented the political tendency in support of imperialism abroad and equality at home that mediated between the national Kenseikai, based on the urban and rural middle class and above, and the proletarian movement. The party also represented and attempted to promote the political and social advancement of the old middle classes— local landlords and independent farmers—as well as the classes beneath them (since very few tenant farmers depended solely on sharecropping, and because they were, after all, agricultural managers, one could say that the tenant farmer class made up the bottom of the old middle classes). In other words, the party signified self-renovation. Just before establishing the new party, the future members held a seminar on young men's self-government, at which they discussed how to manage regional affairs so as to prevent them from being dominated by landlords and the elderly, that is, so as to reform the gerontocracy that was based on the socially-unequal relationships that were currently dominant and allow the young men to become the leaders.[26] It was movement to criticize and improve the status quo, premised on the assumption that they themselves should be responsible for self-government in the local community.

From this point onward, tenant unions were organized openly in all the hamlets and villages of the region, and prior to the early 1930s, tenancy disputes, large and small, were launched either independently or through the mediation of court systems. At the same time, the village assemblies in the area were split neatly into two factions: one supporting the Seiyūkai, more or less representing the interests of the upper stratum of the old-middle class, and the other supporting the Kenseikai, which represented the interests of those in the middle class and below. This was what happened at the base of the "two-party system" of the time.

Thus, as social groups were becoming active in the Enzan region centering on the tenant stratum, the political parties were striving to incorporate these movements into their own mechanisms, and village assembly members and other local authorities were using them as a springboard to office; individuals were becoming involved in all this, while at the same time, at a different level, the Seinendan and local community continued to operate in the districts. These movements are also documented in records from Ibaragi Prefecture's Goka-mura (presently Mitsukaidō City).[27] They continued to spread until the early-1930s but, as I will show below, were transformed under the internal and external impact of the Great Depression and war.

Towns whose population were engaged partly in agriculture and partly in commercial-industrial enterprises shared the experiences related above. In Manabe-chō, Ibaraki prefecture (now the City of Tsuchiura), an organization called the Sekishunkai was established primarily by young men. The leaders of this organization were youths whose fathers had since the Meiji era held such positions as town mayor, mayor's assistant, or chamberlain and were mostly resident landlords or businessmen who had graduated middle school, volunteered for a year of military duty as an officer, and led the local Veterans Associations and Seinendan. The organization had some 600 members, including sons of tenants and proprietors of tiny businesses from an area that transcended any single town. They promoted local organizational autonomy by participating in the day-to-day, hamlet-level activities of such groups as Seinendan, fire brigades, and Veterans' Association branches, etc. They also are said to have promoted young men's participation on the acquisitions committee of the Tsuchiura City Library, reform of the activities of the Tsuchiura City investigative organ, which was reputed to provide "honorary positions for the wealthy," establishment of night-school facilities at the middle and college levels, and so on. Moreover, with respect to improving tenancy relations the members of the Sekishunkai clearly recognized opposing class interests, but urged that conflicts be settled in a "straightforward" manner within the local, social context rather than depending on the authorities or pre-existing organizations. They called themselves the "*Seinentō*" (Youth Party), but they were also members of the regional Kenseikai's party organization.[28]

Now let's turn to the city level. As the administrative seat of Ibaraki Prefecture, the provincial city of Mito had both an Army regiment and one of the prewar national higher schools. The population were 50% commercial-industrial and 20% agricultural, with the remainder falling in categories such as transportation workers, officials, soldiers and students. In light of its overlapping functions as administrative center, college town, military post, and commercial-industrial center, Mito was probably best termed an administrative and service-industry city. The city's south side, as demarcated by the Jōban train line and station, came to be known as "downtown," and the north side of the tracks "uptown." Each side was divided into several neighborhoods (*chōnai*), which were led by neighborhood committees. On the downtown side, the chairmen of these committees included proprietors of businesses dealing in pharmaceuticals, fertilizer, soy sauce distilling, and so on, and also self-employed entrepreneurs, doctors, postmasters, etc. After the Sino-Japanese war of 1894-95 these public-spirited local leaders ("*yūshi*") formed the "Night of the Full Moon Association" (*Jūgoyakai*), with its own meeting hall and funding, and set about through their own labor and resources to improve roads, staff neighborhood administrations and, in the Taishō era, to maintain city precincts. Of course, contrary to the situation in rural areas, they had no choice but to operate through the already highly-structured environment of city government, so from the outset they sought to advance their own regional interests by deciding in advance through their own preliminary selection process who would stand for city council, prefectural assembly, and the House of Representatives. This practice did not survive intact beyond expansion of the suffrage in the 1920s, as in the new situation people could be elected without their "recommendation"; yet, as the so-called "downtown faction," they retained considerable influence in the city council down to the early-1930s. In the late-1920s they expanded their membership to include entrepreneurs in the expanding industries of bicycles, real estate and construction, glass, printing, electric power, and electric appliances, and on the basis of such support were able to take over the chairmanship and governing board of the Chamber of Commerce as well as the post of mayor. In the meantime, using their own funds and labor, they continued to manage affairs in the various city neighborhoods. The situation changed only when downtown was split up in conjunction with the consolidation of neighborhood associations (*chōnaikai*) around 1940. Under the administration of the doctor who, in the 1930s, succeeded the seed dealer who had been the group's political representative, there was a spurt of industrialization and infrastructural construction in the city which strengthened the local influence of those in real estate and construction trades.[29]

What was the situation in metropolises like Tokyo? The Meiji government had abolished the system of *goningumi* ("Five-family groups") that had been prevalent in both urban and rural areas during the Edo period and in its stead established the city and village system. Therefore, from mid-Meiji onward the "ward self-government system" that had been central to the urban *goningumi* network—a network comprised only of household heads and landlords—lost its former role as an administrative organ. However, actual regional communities existed and had to be managed, so the managerial role was assumed by the independent businessmen based largely in traditional industries. During the period from late-Meiji to mid-Taishō, that is, the period of approximately from 1900 to 1920, there occurred an explosive expansion of the urban working class, and enhancement of social diversity in general, as a result of industrialization and urbanization. Urban issues became serious, and gave rise to mass phenomena such as the rice riots, labor unions and disputes, and the suffrage movement. The old urban neighborhood society, that is, the local community structure of the city, was disintegrating, and in many areas there was no local community at all, despite massive concentrations of population. Such circumstances stimulated the formation of fraternal organizations among public-spirited locals, most often self-employed businessmen. In the 1920s and 1930s these fraternal organizations opened their doors to all the households resident in their region or neighborhood, and the result was the formation of neighborhood associations (*chōnaikai*) that aspired to comprehensive membership. The city authorities were keenly aware of the need for such organizations, and in the early 1920s recognized the neighborhood associations from the angle of social education, that is, as contexts for "training in self-government."

In this era, the metropolis contained three types of local society. One was the traditional "downtown" (*shitamachi*) pattern that was formed when local community broke down as a result of business/residential differentiation between areas and the emergence of commercial districts, which caused the old leaders to step in and organize neighborhood associations. Also clearly evident was the suburban, *yamanote* (surrounding foothills) pattern, in which neighborhood associations were formed by "successful," stable businessmen and industrialists who had moved into these areas in the Meiji period. Third, in suburban regions outside the original fifteen city wards, which were being converted from agricultural to residential in a process of urban sprawl, the lead in forming neighborhood associations was assumed largely by an old, landed class that was primarily agricultural in orientation and followed older frameworks for organization.

Metropolitan authorities eventually became involved in neighborhood associations, not only to promote social education, but to carry out social welfare policy and introduce the welfare committee system (*hōmen iinkai seido*) in the 1920s, and as part of the development of comprehensive metropolitan administration, which included crisis management in relation to disasters and the military, along with the rearrangement of ward boundaries that followed the Great Kantō Earthquake of 1923.[30] In contrast to rural examples of "small government," where there might be only a few officials in addition to the village head, his assistant, and the chamberlain, the big cities and metropolises considered "big government" a daily necessity in the 1920s, so it was only natural that the city authorities and urban technocrats would become involved in community affairs. However, in all the patterns outlined above, it was primarily the old-middle class, consisting of business and industrial proprietors and landowners, that actually formed and ran these local communities.

Of course, metropolitan interests were very diversified, and organizations and movements proliferated in the form of labor unions, trade associations, and Chambers of Commerce along with political parties and administrative organs. Of course, members of the old-middle class belonged to their own social and political organizations in a realm separate from their involvement in local community, and gradually relinquished to other strata their leading role in community management and leadership.

How, then, might we summarize the tendencies detailed above with respect to the operation and leadership of local community at the various levels of agricultural village, commercial-industrial as well as agricultural town, provincial city, and metropolitan center? We have noted the compartmented, functionally-differentiated existence, throughout the 1920s and into the early-1930s, of 1) diverse social and political interests, 2) local communities managed on the assumption of equal, comprehensive participation in debate, decisions, and activities, 3) associations organized and operated for the express purpose of advancing the class or occupational interests of their members, and 4) political parties, which represented those groups politically, as well as the political and administrative organs they influenced. Such local communities tended to be led and managed by farmers and proprietors of commercial and industrial enterprises, that is, by members of the old-middle class. Of course, these communities confronted a variety of problems, which included landlord-tenant relations in rural areas and, in urban environments, the problem of the role to be played by classes and strata outside the old-middle class. Moreover, as we have seen, despite the communities' at least formal compartmentation from such issues in terms of level, they attempted to address and solve problems of, in the first case, inequality and in the second, participation, by approaching them from within local society in an autonomous manner. This might be called the self-renovation of the old-middle class as a pre-existing social force within the villages and cities.

Japan in the 1920s was certainly an unequal society, in which rights were denied to women and workers, and clear gaps separated landlords from tenants, large corporations from small enterprises, and the rural context from the urban. Yet, movements for redress emerged within that very society among workers, farmers, and women; efforts were also made by the reconstruction faction (*Kaizō-ha*) of the Kenseikai and in government bureaucracies, especially the social bureau of the Ministry of Home Affairs and parts of the Ministry of Agriculture and Forestry. Such efforts spread despite fierce resistance from the mainstream in big-business (*zaikai*), the non-proletarian political parties, and other sectors of the bureaucracy.

THE FIRST GLEICHSCHALTUNG AND COMMUNITY: THE MIDDLE CLASS UNDER THE TOTAL-WAR SYSTEM
Gleichschaltung and National Reorganization

Without external interference, the process of self-renovation centering on the old-middle class would probably have developed smoothly, that is, it would gradually have been passed on to the new-middle and working classes who were themselves becoming more differentiated amidst heavy industrialization and were projecting their behavior patterns and value systems increasingly onto society at large. Yet, needless to say, Japan in the 1930s already participated in a web of global relationships, even though it had not yet truly reached the stage of industrial capitalism. Because of those global connections, the Great Depression dealt a serious blow to Japanese society. Recovery could occur only through further rationalization and expansion of capitalism, more specifically, further heavy and chemical industrialization. Japan's international relationships also brought it into intense competition with the great powers for markets. The result was heavy industrialization that centered on rapid, short-term expansion of military production in preparation for war. Thus, in order to increase productive power, it became necessary to transform the existing industrial structure, including production, distribution and consumption. Large-volume production according to uniform standards also required the "rational" organization of labor power. This meant that labor power had inevitably to move from nonindustrial sectors, like agriculture, distribution and service industries, into the heavy industrial sector. It also meant that anything that impeded this process, including organizations independent of state power, whether "old" or "new," "authoritarian" or "democratic," had to be dismantled. This, then, was Gleichschaltung at the hands of the state (I will call this the first Gleichschaltung, and that carried out by large corporations and other social organizations the second).[31]

This process also appeared in the form of "national reorganization" in various areas such as occupation, geographical area, gender, and age. More specifically, in the political realm this meant the dissolution of the parties in 1940, formation of the Imperial Rule Assistance Association and then the New Political Order, in addition to the formation in 1942 of the Greater Japan Industrial Patriotic Association, the Agricultural Patriotic League, the Commercial Patriotic Association, the Naval Patriotic League, the Greater Japan Women's Association, and Greater Japan Young Men and Youth Association, and the one-dimensional incorporation of the hamlet and neighborhood associations under the umbrella of the Imperial Rule Assistance Association as "organ of the state." This marked a qualitative change from what had been accomplished as a result of the organizational efforts in civil society during the 1920s. Thus, the formation in Japan of the total-war system, that is, the Imperial Rule Assistance system, did not go smoothly.

Four Political Tendencies

In the 1930s, four influential tendencies, or groups, emerged in the wake of the Great Depression and engaged in bitter confrontations with each other and other groups at the national political level. First, the "reactionaries," including the Army's Imperial Way faction (*Kōdō-ha*), the Navy's Fleet faction (*Kantai-ha*), the landlords, and the ideological rightwing, emerged to snatch away the rights that had been won in the course of, for example, disarmament and the tenants' movement. Second, the "national-defense state" group, made up of the Army's Control Faction (*Tōsei-ha*) and the renovationist bureaucrats (*kakushin kanryō*), especially in the economic realm, aimed at organizing a state-centered, total-war system and a controlled economy from above. Third, the "social-nationalist group," who were more autonomous from the state than the above two, included influential forces around Konoe Fumimaro during formation of the Imperial Rule Assistance Association, that is, the reconstruction faction of the Minseitō, those in rural areas who were based in the industrial union movement, labor union leaders, officials in the social bureau of the Home Ministry and a wing of the Agriculture and Forestry ministry; these entities espoused an ideology of cooperativism as the basis for a total-war system and promoted equality, modernization and rationalization in Japanese society. The fourth group comprised the "liberals," including the mainstream elements of the established political parties, big-business leaders (*zaikai*), certain forces in the imperial court, etc. The reactionaries and the liberals were generally from the upper and upper-middle strata of Japanese society, while the social-nationalists came from the middle and lower classes and had roots especially in the new and old-middle class groups that had been engaged during the 1920s in the self-renovation process described in Part 2 above. The real driving forces in the transition from the "liberal" 1920s to the Imperial Assistance/total-war structure of the early 1940s were the "national-defense state" group and the social-nationalists.

Yet, the local society that we surveyed in Part 2 was not always passive in relation to the one-dimensional organizational efforts of the state.

Total-War System and the Old-Middle Class's Second Self-Renovation

In some ways, the particular realities and orientations of local society actually encouraged the tendencies toward one-dimensionality mentioned above. However, first I would like to mention a case in which the element of naked coercion was dominant, that is, the imposition by the Ministry of Commerce and Industry of provincial industrialization, including the deployment and dispersion of factories, in line with the construction of the wartime economic system. Although moved to the countryside, these war-production factories were not relocated to uninhabited areas, but were rather plunked down in the midst of rural society. Prefectural bureaucracies, the military-production enterprises, the police, and the military brushed aside opposition from local farmers, especially landlords, and locals involved in commerce and industry, and went so far as to consolidate towns and villages to facilitate land purchase and in other ways cater to the "convenience" of commercial and industrial enterprises. The result was to destroy the independence and autonomy of local social forces and ultimately of the regions themselves.[32]

That said, let us turn to changes within local society, focusing especially on areas that by and large did not experience coerced industrialization. In purely agricultural zones, in the midst of tenancy disputes following the Depression, there was a nationwide movement for rural economic renewal. Such villages in the Enzan area as Ofuji-mura, Tamamiya-mura, Kamikane-mura, and Okunota-mura were included in this program. The aims of the movement included trying to encourage diversification in place of exclusive reliance on sericulture; whole local units, whether hamlets or villages, participated. On the other hand, even after the May 15 Incident of 1932, some villages were split politically and others ravaged by tenancy issues, so there was a strong tendency within local society to try to overcome these divisions and to advance economically.[33]

The economic renewal movement was carried out in the former Gokamura as well, but there it led to the formation in the various hamlets of farmer's unions, especially the so-called industrial unions (*sangyō kumiai*), and aimed at reforming patterns of daily life, inculcating a stricter observance of time schedules, and rationalizing the processes of production, sales, purchasing, and finance. The leading elements in this effort were the upper segment of the old-middle class, that is, the local landlord-farmers, but even landed tenants rose to become officials at the hamlet and village levels, so some equalization was taking place. In other words, in local communities the management prerogative was diffusing downward. In terms of the framework employed above, it might be said that by means of the renewal movement the orientation toward self-renovation that was evident in the 1920s was further developed and expanded into the realms of economy and daily life. However, once the industrial unions that were central to that movement were reduced to links in the wartime system after the outbreak of war with China in 1937, such orientations in the local community changed markedly. The local old-middle class that had manifested such orientations now actively participated in the wartime system. Moreover, that system brought further social and economic equalization.[34]

In the half-commercial-industrial, half agricultural town of Manabe-chō, the Sekishunkai played a central role in introducing the economic renewal movement at all levels in the various hamlets, Seinendan, industrial unions, and so on, but at the same time the Sekishunkai members involved in commerce and industry also organized a commercial-industrial association for small enterprises, a Commercial-Industrial Patriotic Association, and a Men's Association (*Sōnendan*). The leaders of these organizations became officers in the city, county and prefectural level Imperial Rule Assistance Association and supported the system that resulted.[35]

In the provincial administrative and commercial-industrial center of Mito, it was the old-middle class centering on proprietors of established shops and enterprises who, as members of the neighborhood committees and–after the change in 1942 from the neighborhood committees to neighborhood councils and standing committees in conjunction with each elementary school district– as neighborhood council chairmen, ran the local community, even though over time there was some diffusion of authority downward. It is especially worthwhile to look at the second movement among the powerful merchants and shop proprietors. Right after the great financial panic in February 1932, and under the additional impact of incursions by department stores and industrial unions into the local distribution system, a sense of crisis drove some forty "young entrepreneurs" and "sons of the city's first-rank commercial houses"[36] to form the Ibaragi Comrades League of Young Entrepreneurs (Ibaraki Seinen Jitsugyō Dōshikai) and, through it, to try to improve management by cooperating in advertising and related tasks such as layout, offering each other reciprocal discounts, etc. Finally, in order to survive, League members moved toward specialization in their businesses in order to differentiate themselves from the department stores: in 1938 they joined the Japan Speciality Shop Association, which was the motive force in the Commercial Patriotic Movement, and changed their name to the Mito Speciality Shop Association. In their efforts to move toward a "scientific," "efficient form of small retailing," they were said at the time to be "leading the existing small retail shops in a horizontally-linked civil control organ."[37]

It was almost exactly the same group who in 1940 formed the "Eastern Imperial Society" (Tōtenkai), which professed the ideals of the Edo-period Mito School. Regardless of what they intended, their move in the direction of the Mito Speciality Shop Association was quite consistent with construction of the total-war system, which involved reorganizing small retail industry, changing and closing businesses, establishing institutions for the rationing of goods, etc. In other words, the horizontal "civil control organ" they formed soon incorporated itself into the vertical control system imposed by the government and prefectural administrations. Meanwhile, the Tōtenkai hastened this process in the political realm. In 1941, in connection with, or perhaps led by, the prefectural bureaucracy, Imperial Rule Assistance Association, bank executives, military, and neighborhood council chairmen, and on the basis of the claim that a "mayoral dictatorship" had been established by the doctor who was mayor and the City Council majority that had pursued infrastructural expansion under the domination of the construction trades, the Tōtenkai was instrumental in destroying the former coalition by securing the dissolution of the City Council and replacement of virtually all its members, the resignation of the mayor, and his replacement by a military officer. With these events, the city's transition to the Imperial Assistance regime became complete.

In the metropolitan area of Tokyo, classes outside the old-middle class, including the new-middle and the working classes, certainly increased in the 1920s and 1930s, but in contrast to other areas, in Tokyo the old-middle class continued to run local communities right down to the 1940s. If we look at occupational data concerning neighborhood association heads throughout all Tokyo wards for June 1942, we find that 31.5% were commercial, 10.1% were industrial (small and medium-sized enterprises), and 7.3% agricultural, while salaried company employees representing the new middle class amounted to only 11.1%.[38] The old-middle class was thus overwhelmingly dominant. In the 1920s, members of the old-middle class tried without any coercion from the state to broaden and deepen representation of lower classes in community leadership positions, but by about 1940 the state was exerting pressure to bring all residents into the neighborhood associations. Matches and sugar began to be rationed in 1940, and the rationing system expanded steadily from then on; once administration of this system fell to the neighborhood associations, the new-middle and working classes, which up to that point had stayed away from local community activities, had no choice but to get involved. Of course, the old-middle class that dominated the neighborhood associations employed not merely coercion but also the close neighborhood contact involved in mutual aid, joint purchase of staples, etc., to secure the cooperation of members of other classes.[39] However, it is also true that some coercion was employed to bring into the neighborhood association those who did their best to stay aloof, like those with "individualistic" or "liberal" attitudes who tried to maintain a "cultured" existence, the "upper class" and the "rich." This was also true of those perceived to be of the lower classes. The desire to overcome various forms of segregation among the "upper class," the "middle class" and the "poor" existed within the state as well, especially in the Home Ministry. The Home Ministry tended to want to dismantle the more or less autonomous groups that had emerged during the 1920s and 1930s—such as the existing neighborhood associations, hamlet associations, shrine lay-associations, and various local groups (*kō, kumi*) that had been formed to expand credit and promote recreation, religious worship, etc.—and to replace them with homogeneous local organizations that in principle included everyone and in which social lines were blurred. Because the "upper class" and the "poor" were more or less equivalent in size, the rationing system tended over all to detract from the status of the upper stratum; also, the broadening of the neighborhood associations beyond the old-middle class, to include other middle and upper strata, also had the effect of homogenizing society in a downward direction,[40] and thereby equalizing power and authority de facto. This broad process of coercive participation, which sought to "equalize" the "individualistic" new-middle and upper classes by bringing them into the neighborhood and hamlet associations, and which also amounted to downward homogenization at the hands of the old-middle class, was in the background of many of the books and essays of the time which extolled the village and excoriated the old-middle class.

I have tried to make it very clear that between the 1920s and the early-1940s there occurred a sharp, qualitative change in relations between the local community and, especially, the old-middle class. From the 1920s through the early-1930s, the old-middle class participated in local community, social groups, political parties, and the organs of politics and administration whose interests were expressed in those parties. By compartmenting their participation so as to keep these various levels separate, they recognized, in effect, a plurality of organizational entities in the same region. On that basis, the old-middle class moved in the direction of broadening the leadership of local community to include those who were different, and those who were relegated through unequal treatment to the lower class. However, in the late-1930s, the state turned rapidly to the establishment of a total-war regime, and adopted a policy that recognized no compartmentation of organizational realms or social oppositions, but moved instead toward one-dimensionality; as a result, local community was reoriented from a horizontal structure to a vertical one. Moreover, the community was not merely coerced from above but in fact complied voluntarily, solving its own social-stratification problems by means of the state. The old-middle class, which was oriented toward self-renovation, began politically to follow the lead of the social-nationalist and defense-state factions, which provided the impetus for the total-war system. Therefore, the movements "from above" and "from below" were mediated at the social base. The 1920s dynamic of self-renovation, through which the old-middle class sought to expand the management of local community in a fundamentally horizontal direction, was now converted through the agency of the state to a vertical process aimed at homogeneity, and this shift was facilitated by links between the local, old-middle class and the two national-level factions mentioned above. This may be called the old-middle class's second self-renovation. In this process, social integration de facto through heavy and chemical industrialization and vertical homogenization was paralleled by the establishment of norms which opposed segregation of the "upper classes" and the "poor," promoted the "achievement" of social equalization of the sort typified in "comprehensive national [health] insurance,"[41] and pursued rationalization in the interest of efficiency. These transformations were irreversible in their impact on Japanese society.

Of course, much was sacrificed along the way. First, economic independence and autonomy were lost through the process of coercive, short-term heavy and chemical industrialization, which involved closing or transforming small businesses and establishing vertical integration through subcontracting. Second, although it is true that aside from differences in form this was the kind of process that might occur in any country, of greater importance for Japanese society specifically was the loss, through dependence on the state, of the values, behavior patterns and prestige that had attended the management of local community, and the loss, also, of the opportunity to achieve equality, not through compulsion from above, but autonomously from within the existing social fabric. Social legitimacy was compromised through the coercive imposition of legal legitimacy from above. Third, and even more tragically, far from a situation in which the above-mentioned value orientations, behavior patters and prestige of the old-middle class might be inherited by the new-middle class (something that was still possible in the 1920s), the coercive enforcement through state power of new-middle class participation turned the two strata of the middle class into enemies. The forms of "individualism" and "liberalism" that refuse involvement in local community are not necessarily worth cultivating, but it is undeniable that compulsion from above nipped in the bud the special culture, and the "cultured life" (*bunka seikatsu*), of the new-middle class. The new-middle class of the 1920s was indeed a "privileged" minority of company employees, university and higher-school teachers, and officials at various levels of bureaucracy. However, the new members of that class who emerged in large numbers under the wartime system were entirely creatures of the state whose normative orientation not only did not favor autonomous participation in community but considered any social independence or plurality to be wrong. Members of this new-middle class belonged to the expanded state institutions and military-production industries from the beginning and had been forcibly molded into "organization-men," thoroughly devoted to military production and the total-war system.

Thus, in Japan, neither the autonomous old-middle class that had formerly taken responsibility for local community nor the new-middle class that was capable of inheriting such norms existed any longer. Their demise was another important "result" of the Japanese total-war system, which also produced heavy and chemical industrialization, equalization and rationalization.

In Place of a Conclusion: The Second Gleichschaltung and Upward Homogenization

Against the background of such irreversible developments, let's look at the situation from the postwar era down to the present. In 1945 and 1946, the neighborhood and hamlet associations continued to function just as before the war, handling distribution and allocation of goods. Then, in 1947, they were made illegal. Yet, the overall effect of the defeat and postwar reforms was to expand the scope and leadership of local community. Especially by the 1950s, there existed communities of workers that had developed against the background of fundamental labor rights, farming communities that included former tenants now liberated through land reform, associations of teachers now freed from state control, a diverse local society, children beyond the purview of adults or school, etc. Political forces, especially the "progressive" forces such as the Japan Communist party (JCP), the Japan Socialist party (JSP), and the labor federation, Sōhyō, paid attention to various communities in connection with "local people's struggles" (JCP), and "all-region" (*chiiki-gurumi*) and "all-workplace" (*shokuba-gurumi*) struggles (JSP, Sōhyō's Takano faction); that is, they made an effort to encompass workers, the old and new middle classes, housewives, etc., in their organizational strategies. These various communities were also the foundation of the "national movements" that burgeoned in the 1950s, which included the anti-nuclear and peace movements, the campaign against the Police Duties bill, and others. By the 1950s the Japanese were not only free of Occupation "Enlightenment" but in possession of a democratic system guaranteeing fundamental human rights, and also of multiple, autonomous spaces and communities beyond the state and big capital. It was a unique society with no equal before or since. Nevertheless, this era of multifaceted, decentralized society ended after a few years, just as had the era of one-dimensional, centralized society during the Pacific War. If Japan's first total war was the Russo-Japanese conflict of 1904-05, and the second was World War II, then it was Japan's third "total war," the accelerated economic growth of the 1960s, that destroyed these diverse communities. The preconditions for that destruction were already latent within and outside the communities of the 1950s.

At first, Occupation policy, especially in its early stages, did not promote industrialization but focused on 'forging a strong middle class and building a stable society," a policy which it carried out via dissolution of the zaibatsu and land reform. These policies converted tenants into independent farmers and revived the fortunes of small and medium enterprises, bringing about a resurgence not only of the middle class but especially of the old-middle stratum within it. In other words, this amounted to expanding and strengthening precisely those strata that would be relatively disadvantaged and rendered powerless in the course of the further development of heavy and chemical industry that would be the aim of rapid postwar growth. In the agricultural sphere, the mid-1950s brought a shift from the regulated production of staple grains to the production of agricultural commodities. This meant that farmers would have to deal in the free market, and government aid was necessary to help them prepare for that in terms of both productive base and standard of living. Already this marked the beginnings of a new form of "direct links to the center." In the meantime, working-class society lost its independence as a result of management's drive to regain control of the workplace, and education made the transition to centralized control according to uniform national standards that were designed to enhance industrialization.[42]

This productivity-first drive, which in extreme form produces people with standardized values oriented solely to commodity production and distribution, again drove communities toward disintegration. It was typically the new-middle class, or "sararii-man," who embodied such values, which, reinforced by the wartime canards about the "old-middle class as the enemy" and a postwar tendency to attribute war responsibility to the neighborhood associations, lent new legitimacy to non-participation in community and thus objectively helped reproduce the "natural-born bourgeois." Overall, this amounted to the mass-production of one-dimensional company-men who inherited the total-war propensity to submerge themselves entirely in an organization. It was the civil equivalent of Gleichschaltung at the hands of the state. Accelerating this tendency were enhanced links among leaders in the political, financial, and bureaucratic realms that were designed to promote industrialization according to a revived wartime pattern, and the so-called 1955 system that was established largely via the Sōhyō-JSP mainstream (led by Iwai Akira, who in 1954 replaced Takano as secretary-general of Sōhyō) and marked a shift in emphasis toward the size of the economic "pie" and how it was distributed.[43]

From the perspective of local community, the neighborhood associations were first abolished under the Occupation, then were treated with a great deal of suspicion as a result of being tarred with war guilt and consigned to the status of premodern remnant. Having by this time lost both legal and social legitimacy, the local communities were again being run by the farmers and commercial-industrial proprietors who flourished as a result of the Occupation, but who were now being dispersed through the effects of accelerated economic growth—that is, the old-middle class. This class provided the power base for the conservatives, that is, the Liberal-Democratic party, and formed the "structure of extortion" that provided it with financial support. Therefore, the postwar Japanese middle class includes this stratum plus the above-mentioned "company men."

This is the system that made Japan's rapid postwar growth possible, thereby increasing the size of the economic pie. Moreover, because the way of dividing that pie up was constructed under the wartime system, and conformed to the norms of equalization that were further extended during the postwar reforms, it amounted in effect to upward homogenization. That is, it might be said that upward homogenization was premised upon downward homogenization. Equalization was the result of ironing out regional disparities through the structure of extortion, instituting the comprehensive national health insurance system that sacrificed the independence of the doctors and others who comprise the upper level of the old-middle class, and encouraging the belief that everyone was a member of the middle class. That Japan, unlike the European countries, developed a welfare state without a social-democratic administration is largely a result of the processes outlined above, beginning with the wartime system.

Once rapid economic growth ended in the 1970s, citizen's movements emerged in reaction against the environmental problems caused by that growth.

In the beginning these movements, led by the new-middle class, conflicted with neighborhood associations, but in the 1980s some were able to bring together the old and new middle classes in the name of "community development" (*machi-zukuri*). With the full "achievement" of industrialization, the ideology of Production First began to be reevaluated, as first the wives of "company men" and then the new-middle class men as well, began to "discover" local community. They now began to put at the service of horizontally-structured, local communities the knowledge, specialized skills, and organizational/managerial abilities that they had acquired from the vertically-structured educational and enterprise systems. They did not always accept the neighborhood/hamlet associations as the only embodiments of community, but developed a variety of innovative organizational forms under new-middle class leadership, including regional councils, community committees, etc. Yet some movements also tried to retain the neighborhood associations as one organizational form among others.[44] This might very well be called an "historical rapprochement" between the old and new middle classes, premised on the first and second processes of Gleichschaltung and the "achievements" of industrialization, the welfare state, and social equalization brought about by erasing distinctions among "upper class," "middle class," and the "poor." The political result of these "achievements" has been the collapse of the 1955 system.

As a particular, historical process of adjusting to what Melucci calls the new societies and political spaces of the postmodern, post-industrial era, the realities I have attempted to describe must differ markedly from those obtaining in other countries, especially the United States, where elements and values peculiar to the middle class remain very strong.

Translated by Guy Yasko

Notes

[1] For a study that includes Germany, Japan and the U.S., see Yamanouchi Yasushi, "Senji dōin taisei," Shakai-Keizai Shi Gakkai, ed., *Shakai-keizai shigaku no kadai to tenbō* (Tokyo: Yūhikaku, 1992). Shiba Kensuke introduces German work on the subject in, "Nachi senji taisei ni okeru dōin to tōgō," *Rekishigaku kenkyū* (1993 convention issue) (1994). For detailed analysis of the Japanese case in the political realm, see Amemiya Shōichi, "1940 nendai no shakai to seiji taisei: han-Tōjō rengō o chūshin to shite," Nihonshi Kenkyūkai, ed., *Nihonshi kenkyū*

(1987 convention issue) (April 1988). In the field of economic history, see Okazaki Tetsuji, *Gendai Nihon keizai shisutemu no genryū* (Tokyo: Nihon Keizai Shinbunsha, 1993), and John W. Dower, *Japan in War and Peace* (New York: The New Press, 1993.

[2] Yamanouchi Yasushi, "Nihon shakai no henyō to Nichibei kankei puroguramu shiryō," November 2, 1993.

[3] Amemiya Shōichi, "Tokushū shakai kagaku no genzai: seijigaku no baai," *Mirai* (November 1986).

[4] Alberto Melucci, "Minshushugi saikō," trans. Nagai Kōichi and Yamanouchi Yasushi, in Yamanouchi Yasushi and Murakami Jun'ichi, eds., *Shakai kagaku no hōhō: nijusseiki shakai kagaku no paradaimu* (Tokyo: Iwanami Shoten, 1993). Also see Yamanouchi Yasushi, "Shisutemu shakai no gendaiteki isō, 1 & II," *Shisō* (June 1991, July 1991), especially part II.

[5] Matsushita Keiichi, *Gendai Nihon no seijiteki kōsei* (Tokyo: Tokyo Daigaku Shuppankai, 1992), and Matsushita Keiichi, *Shōwa kōki no sōten to seiji* (Tokyo: Mokutakusha, 1989).

[6] Albert M. Craig, "Tradition and Transformation in East Asian Civilization: Japan," *1994-95 Courses of Instruction*, Harvard University (1994), 9.

[7] R. Dahrendorf, *Society and Democracy in Germany* (Garden City: Doubleday and Co., 1967). For a summary and comments see Amemiya, "Taisei ikō to shakai: Doitsu, Itaria, Nihon no senzen to sengo," *Ibaragi Daigaku kyōyōbu kiyō* (March 1989).

[8] Maruyama Masao, *Gendai seiji no shisō to kōdō* (Tokyo: Miraisha, 1964).

[9] Fujita Shōzō, *Tennōsei kokka no shihai genri*, Revised Edition (Tokyo: Miraisha, 1976).

[10] Matsushita, *Gendai Nihon no seijiteki kōsei*, 17-19.

[11] Matsushita, *Shōwa kōki no sōten to seiji*.

[12] Ezra Vogel, *Japan's New Middle Class* (Berkeley and Los Angeles: University of California Press, 1991), 6, 98.

[13] Robert N. Bellah, ed., *Habits of the Heart* (Berkeley and Los Angeles: University of California Press, 1985), especially the Preface and 29, 35, 47.

[14] Several American white-collar workers interviewed by Amemiya between July and September 1994 were each active in three or four national organizations intended to "Stop Teenage Addiction to Tobacco," help victims of family violence, etc., and contributed between $10 and $20 each month. For a comparison of the U.S. and Japan with regard to local community, religion, big versus small government, etc., see Amemiya, "Boston tayori" 1-6, *Nyū-Ibaragi* (September 1994-May 1995).

[15] *Belmont Citizen Herald*, June 30, 1994.

[16] Bellah, *Habits of the Heart*, 333.

[17] T. Fukutake, *Man and Society in Japan* (Tokyo: The University of Tokyo Press, 1962), 100.

[18] Kashiwabara Eiji, Noguchi Yukio, "Okurashō, Nichigin ōchō no bunseki," *Chūō kōron* (August 1977).

[19] Daily record of the Okunota-mura Seinendan, second branch, 1921-23 (kept in Hanazono-ku, Okunota-mura). On materials related to the Enzan City area and Mito City area, see Amemiya Shōichi et. al., "Taishō-Shōwa zenki kaisetsu," and the materials collected in *Enzan-shi shi: shiryōhen* 5 (Sept. 1995), and chapter five section one, and chapter six section one, *Mito-shi shi* II.2 (August 1995).

[20] The analysis below of Japan in the 1920s also bears upon the content of the tradition of self-rule in Japanese local communities. See Amemiya, "Chō-son reberu no seiji katei: Ibaraki-ken, kyū-Gokamura wo chūshin to shite," *Nihon gendaishi kenkyūkai: gendaishi tsūshin* (Nov., 1982), and Amemiya Shōichi and Arakawa Hajime, "Keizai kōsei undō to kitei ni okeru seijiteki henka," *Ibaraki daigaku kyōyōbu kiyō* (March 1989).

[21] "Sonkai ni fugi o shinsei suru ni tsuki gochō kaigi o shōshū suru yōkyūsho," April 14, 1913 (owned by Yamada Tamotsu, Kyū-Matsusato-mura).

[22] "Heishi sōgei ni kakarishi kahi hōmonsho," February 23, 1919 (Shimoyunoki-ku shorui tsuzuri—owned by Yamada Tamotsu, Kyū-Matsuzato-mura).

[23] "Dentōsen hikikomi," February 1921 (Kumanoku-shiryō, owned by Nakamura Hitoshi).

[24] Nōmukyoku, Nōshōmushō, ed., "Kosaku sankō shiryō kosaku sōgi ni kansuru chōsa" (1922), in *Yamanashi-ken kengikaishi* 3 (Kōfu).

[25] "Kosaku kumiai gundōmeikai" (1921-22), in *Yamanashi-ken kengikaishi* 3.

[26] *Yamanashi nichi-nichi shinbun*, series of ten articles in October 1920; also see sources noted in footnote 24 above.

[27] See source mentioned in footnote 20 above.

[28] Amemiya Shōichi, "Taishō makki: Shōwa shoki ni okeru kisei seiryoku no 'jiko kakushin' 'Seikishunkai' no keisei to tenkai," Nihon Gendaishi Kenkyūkai, ed., *Nihon no fuashizumu* 1 [Kokka to shakai] (Tokyo: Otsuki Shoten, 1981). Beginning with Maruyama Masao's well-known observation that the major characteristic of the development of Japanese fascism was that, "pre-existing political forces such as the military, bureaucracy, and political parties gradually brought about the maturation of a fascist regime from within the state structure itself," I attempt to show in this essay that preceding or paralleling that process, there occurred within each of those political forces themselves a process of fascization, especially in connection with their economic base, and that this process might be called the "self-renovation of existing political forces." In the present essay, I have extended that argument to include the old-middle class.

[29] Kaneko Chikusui, *Meiji kōhanki to Taishō jidai no shimo-ichi kaikoroku* (Mito: personal publication, 1963); also *Ibaraki minyū* (Sept. 1 and October 1, 1921); and *Tokyo nichi nichi shinbun* (April 8, 9, and 29, 1925).

[30] Amemiya Shōichi, "Sōryokusen taisei to kokumin saisoshiki: chōnaikai no ichizuke o chūshin toshite," in Banno Junji, ed., *Shiriizu Nihon kindaishi: kōzō to hendō* (Tokyo: Iwanami Shoten 1993), especially 359-362, which includes a survey of research focused on sociological studies.

[31] Gleichschaltung is usually translated into Japanese as "forced uniformity" (*kyōseiteki kakuitsuka*) or "forced homogenization" (*kyōseiteki kinshitsuka*). It has historically been used in two ways: 1) Maruyama Masao and scholars in the former East and West Germany have used it to refer to the suppression and dissolution of political parties, labor unions and other modern organizations, and 2) Ralf Dahrendorf uses it to refer to the dismantling of premodern, authoritarian groups. Gleichschaltung has been seen as what Dahrendorf called the "unintentional revolution," and its leading force has always been taken to be either the wartime state or the Nazis. However, in the course of studying the Japanese case I have redefined the term as follows: First, I have included as its object all autonomous groups and organizations, whether "modern" or "premodern," "old" or "new." (See Amemiya, "Sensō to toshi: kyōseiteki kakuitsuka to toshi keisei," in Narita Ryūichi, ed., *Kindai Nihon no kiseki* 9 (Tokyo: Yoshikawa Kōbunkan, 1993). Second, I have argued that there existed a powerful current of intentional social change that included the content of the social revolution pointed out by Dahrendorf. See references in footnote 28 to Amemiya (1981) and footnote 1 to Amemiya (1988). For a survey of recent German studies with a similarly "intentionalist" viewpoint, see the reference in footnote 1 to Shiba (1994). Third, the leading force in this movement included not merely the state and the Nazis, but should be broadened to include business enterprises and other social groups. See Amemiya, "1950 nendai Nihon shakai no ichi sokumen," *Mirai* (October 1990), and Amemiya (1993).

[32] On these four tendencies, see Amemiya (1988), footnote 1.

[33] "Nōsanson keizai kōsei buraku oyobi kojin keikaku jirei" (1934), in Yamanashi kenritsu toshokan, ed., "Matsusato-mura keizai kōsei keikaku shiryō" (1937), in Kyū-Matsusato-mura Shiryō. "Okunota-mura keizai kōsei keikakusho" (1939), in possession of Hirose Kazuo. "Okunota-mura mura heiwa shingōcho" (Nov. 13, 1932), in Kyū-Okunota-mura shiryō.

[34] See footnote 20 for Amemiya (1982) and Amemiya, Arakawa (1989).

[35] See footnote 28 for Amemiya (1981). Also, Amemiya Shōichi, "Yokusan taisei no ichisokumen: Ibaraki-ken o chōchin to shite," *Shiryō Nihon gendaishi geppō* (Tokyo: Otsuki Shoten, March 1981).

[36] *Ibaraki shinbun*, February 14, 1932). *Chihō keizai* May 1, 1936).

[37] "Mito shōgyō no hana, senmontenkai no dōsei to genkyō," *Sangyō no jidai* (June 1938). Hasegawa Kozō, ed., *Tōtenkaihō dai-ichi* (June 1942). On dissolution of the city council, etc., in 1941, see *Ibaraki shinbun* (June 14, 1941), and "Mitoshi jimu hōkokusho" (1941).

[38] See footnote 30 for Amemiya (1993). Information on the occupation of neighborhood association heads is from Akimoto Ritsuo, *Sensō to minshū* (Tokyo: Gakuyō Shobo, 1974), 67.

[39] See footnote 30 for Amemiya (1993).

[40] See footnote 1 for Amemiya (1988).

[41] On the movement for "comprehensive national health insurance," which was in accord with the intentions of the Welfare Ministry and the military, through the standing committee/council system of Koga-chō (presently Furukawa City), Ibaraki prefecture, see footnote 30 for Amemiya (1993).

[42] Amemiya Shōichi, "55-nen taisei no keisei," and "1950-nendai no shakai," in Nakamura Masanori, Amemiya Shōichi and Kibatake Yōichi, eds., *Nihon dōjidaishi* 3 (Tokyo: Aoki Shoten, 1990). Also see footnote 31 for Amemiya (990).

[43] Ibid.

[44] See footnote 31 for Amemiya (1993) and footnote 30 for Amemiya (1993). Related in personal conversation with members (housewife, employee of Hitachi Heavy Industries, designer, and city government employee) of the community liaison council of Hanayama district, Hitachi City, on October 1, 1992. For the argument that Japanese "agricultural villages" are at a trans-industrial, trans-urban stage, see Amemiya Shōichi, "Shakaiteki konjū, konjū shakai no rironteki shatei o megutte," *Ibaraki daigaku chiiki sōgō kenkyū no nenpō* (March 1995), and "Jichitai bunri o meguru shinkyū chūkansō no dōkō ni tsuite."

The question regarding recognition of the neighborhood associations has come up repeatedly since the war. From the perspective of the development of local community from the 1920s as dealt with in this essay, I think that it should be reconsidered with respect to the main issue of whether its legitimacy should be recognized by the state, or whether it should aim at mutual recognition within society—that is, whether it should be officially recognized within society.

The Japanese Wartime Economy and the Development of Government-Business Relations: An Overview

Okazaki Tetsuji

A high level of international interest has recently been focused on the experience of the Japanese economy as a model for developing nations and for the former socialist nations now converting to market economies.[1] At the same time, attention in the field of economics is being directed toward the new approach of comparative institutional analysis as a framework for the theoretical comparison of economic systems.[2] The basis of this approach is summarized in two principles: institutions matter, and history matters.

Concerning the first point, while all economies generally operate by coordinating the actions of multiple actors, variation occurs in the mechanism of that coordination. An economy completely coordinated by a pure market mechanism of the sort postulated in neoclassical economics does not exist. Instead, the task of coordination is achieved through the combination of a variety of institutions. In other words, the market itself is but one institution; organizations, such as the government, firms, and banks, as well as the relations among organizations also contribute to the coordination function. The particular mix that obtains among such institutions varies across both country and era.

Relating to the second point, large, fixed costs are typically involved in putting a new institutional system in place, and complementarity emerges among multiple institutions. Thus, when an economic system receives a large, exogenous shock and produces a certain combination of institutions as a result, even after the shock has disappeared it is possible that those institutions will continue to exist. In such cases, the existence of the prevailing system may justifiably be attributed to "history." The phenomenon of an exogenous

239

or chance historical event irreversibly altering subsequent processes in this way is called path dependence.

With these postulates in mind, this essay will focus initially on the wartime transformation of government-business relations in Japan. The relationship between government and business forms one important component of an economic system. Moreover, total war is likely to deal a powerful, external shock to an economy, creating the possibility of irreversible change in the economic system. Wartime is therefore potentially a very significant era in relation to the historical foundations of the Japanese economy. Of course, after the war the system established in wartime did not simply remain unchanged, as Japan went through a transition from a planned to a market economy. Therefore, the second question for examination below is how and to what extent the various institutions that relate government to business were revised during the transition to a market economy. Such an examination might help explain Japan's "soft landing" in the market economy and illuminate the institutional foundations of postwar industrial policy.

THE PREWAR GOVERNMENT-BUSINESS RELATIONSHIP[3]

Deliberative councils, sponsored and led by the government, commonly act as mediating institutions between government and business, and are by no means limited to postwar Japan. Therefore, comparative study of the role of deliberative councils offers an effective means of understanding the nature of government-business relations. Here, deliberative councils will help us examine the special characteristics of government-business relations in prewar Japan. The first deliberative council in Japanese economic history was the High Council on Agriculture, Industry, and Commerce (*Nōkōshō kōtō kaigi*), which met from 1896 to 1898. Later, in the wake of the great change in the scale and structure that the Japanese economy experienced during World War I, many deliberative councils were set up to explore responses to that change. The Financial System Investigative Committee (*Kin'yū seido chōsakai*), formed in 1926 to cope with financial instability whose immediate cause was the collapse of the bubble of 1919-20, was one such council. Industry also saw the establishment in succession of the Economic Investigative Committee (*Keizai chōsakai*; 1916-1917), the Council on Commerce and Industry (*Shōkō shingikai*; 1927-1930), and the Provisional Council on Industry (*Rinji sangyō shingikai*; 1930-1935), all deliberative councils that addressed industry as a whole.

The composition of these three industry-related deliberative councils is shown in Table 1. It is evident first of all that in general they were made up of a small number of committee members, although the Economic Investigative

Table 1. Deliberative Council Membership (Prewar)

	Econ. Inv. Comm.[a]		Council on Com. and Ind.[b]		Prov. Council/Ind.[c]	
Gen. Econ. Organizations	13	1	4	1	5	1
Trade Associations	1	1	8	0	2	0
Zaibatsu	6	0	3	1	2	1
Financial Institutions	3	1	1	1	2	1
Industrial Firms	16	6	3	1	3	0
Public Corporations	3	1	1	1	0	0
Newspapers	2	0	5	0	0	0
Labor Unions	0	0	0	0	0	0
Academics	7	0	3	1	2	2
Diet Representatives	10	10	3	3	0	0
Bureaucrats	9	0	0	0	0	0
Other/Unknown	2	0	2	0	0	0
Total	72	20	25	9	16	5

Source: Okazaki (1933a)

[a] Economic Investigative Committee. [b] Council on Commerce and Industry. [c] Provisional Council on Industry.

Note: Figures on the right in each column are the number of Imperial Diet Representatives included in the figures on the left.

Committee was somewhat larger than the others. Representatives from general economic organizations (interindustry economic groups), especially regional Chambers of Commerce, and from the zaibatsu accounted for the core of these committees. This is an important point in considering the character of prewar government-business relations. To grasp its significance requires an understanding of the function of these representatives in the prewar Japanese economy.

The representatives of Chambers of Commerce and other general economic organizations in the prewar coincided almost exactly with the leaders of the business world, known at the time as *zaikai sewayaku*. One important function of these business leaders was to participate in the launching of new firms by becoming large stock holders and using their social credibility to induce investment from other capitalists.[4] They were leaders, in other words, in the capital market. They performed the roles of producing and mediating information about firms and industries, and providing it to investors gathered in the capital market. The zaibatsu, on the other hand, functioned as internal capital markets. The main company absorbed and redistributed the cash flow of affiliated firms, while its directors, who represented the zaibatsu on the deliberative councils, were in a position to control the distribution of funds in this internal capital market by deciding among investment proposals that were presented by member firms. In contrast to the postwar, when indirect financing through banks became the norm, in the prewar era capital markets, understood broadly to include internal capital markets (zaibatsu), were an important channel for the flow of funds.[5]

Prewar deliberative councils thus collected information on industries and firms, and because they were composed of talented individuals from the private sector, were able on the basis of that information to influence significantly the distribution of funds through capital markets. The basic assumption was still that capital markets were capable of effectively screening industries and firms, selecting out those worthy of loans or investment. Thus, prewar industrial policy both presumed and functioned to supplement the screening of industries and firms by capital markets, and the deliberative councils facilitated those processes as information brokers between the government and capital markets.

THE EXPERIENCE OF THE WARTIME ECONOMY[6]

In the era of the Japan-China War and the Pacific War, there emerged a relationship between government and business that differed greatly from the prewar relationship described above. In response to the international balance of payments crisis of late 1936, the government began in January 1937 to practice trade control de facto in the form of foreign-exchange controls, and after the outbreak of war between Japan and China, imposed expanded economic controls through the use of the Import/Export Provisional Grading Measure Law (*Yushutsunyūhin nado rinji sochihō*) and Provisional Funds Adjustment Law (*Rinji shikin chōseihō*).[7] Economic controls implied the cessation or limitation of the market mechanism and were imposed in accordance with various economic plans drawn up by the government. In other words, the economic plans of the government and the economic controls based on them came to replace the market in performing the basic function of resource allocation.

The first wartime economic plan was the 1938 Materials Mobilization Plan (*Busshi dōin keikaku*). Starting in fiscal 1939, a Trade Plan (*Bōeki keikaku*), Labor Mobilization Plan (*Rōmu dōin keikaku*), Transport and Electric Power Mobilization Plan (*Kōtsū denryoku dōin keikaku*), and Funds Control Plan (*Shikin tōsei keikaku*) were drawn up. Together with the Materials Mobilization Plan, they were generally referred to together as National General Mobilization Plans (*Kikka sōdōin keikaku*). Moreover, following the initiation, also in fiscal 1939, of the Four-Year Plan for Productive Forces Expansion (*Seisanryoku kakujū yokkanen keikaku*), a long-term production and investment plan, drafting began on an annual breakdown of this plan, the Productive Forces Expansion Operating Plan (*Seisanryoku kakujū jisshi keikaku*), essentially completing the system of economic planning. These economic plans strove for a predetermined and artificial balance in international payments (Trade Plan, Materials Mobilization Plan), the labor market (Labor Mobilization Plan), the financial market and macro-level investment-savings balance (Funds Control Plan), and the micro-level goods market (Materials Mobilization Plan).[8] Just to draft, let alone to implement, systematic plans like these so that they would conform to each other and be effective required abundant information and work. In order to meet those requirements, a new mechanism was introduced that produced great change in government-business relations.

In the early wartime economy, economic planning had for the most part been carried out exclusively within bureaucratic organizations. In 1937, the Planning Board was set up as a bureaucracy with jurisdiction over planning. It drew up the plans discussed above based on the requirements of the military and in cooperation with the Ministry of Finance, the Ministry of Commerce and Industry, and others.[9] This planning process had a serious shortcoming in that it did not take into account information that was scattered among individual private-sector firms. Moreover, the material aspects of plan implementation were consigned to industrial groups that resulted from the reorganization of existing cartels, and implementation by the firms that ultimately received production quotas was inadequately monitored. Although implementation in finance was based on the Provisional Funds Adjustment Law, the functioning of that law was primarily restrictive. That is, the main purpose of that law was to constrict the flow of funds to sectors with low priority in the war economy. It did not function to actively supply funds to munitions-related sectors.

The outbreak in 1939 of World War II in Europe had exposed the limitations of the early-wartime economic system. The government responded by freezing the prices of manufactured goods, but when costs related to imported raw materials and wages rose, the relative price structure changed radically, and the profitability of firms declined. The incentive for firms to increase production weakened as a result, and the rate of fulfillment of production plans declined. In response to this situation, the government (Planning Board) decided to put in place a command-style, planned economy, billed as the "New Economic Order" (*Keizai shintaisei*), that would both raise the effectiveness of economic plans and strictly monitor their implementation by private firms.[10]

The institution devised for this purpose was the control association (*tōseikai*), an essential component of the New Economic Order. The control association was a compulsory organization that was established in each industry by imperial ordinance (Important Industries Association Ordinance; *Jūyō sangyō dantai rei*) and to which, in principle, all the firms in that industry belonged as members. The result was to establish strong, encompassing authority by firmly linking government, control associations, and member firms. The control associations participated in the government's economic planning process and at the same time handled the implementation of the plans by portioning them out to firms, as well as monitoring implementation. In other words, the control associations were devised as mechanisms that would effectively utilize information scattered at the firm level in the drafting and implementation of plans. From 1941 on, starting with the Steel Control Association (*Tekkō tōseikai*), they were set up in twenty-two industries (Table 2).

The Steel Control Association illustrates well the function of such associations in general. With the formation in August 1941 of the Steel Control Association, the government immediately assigned it many tasks, such as reworking the government-drafted Steel Supply and Demand Plan (*Tekkō jukyū keikaku*), one part of the Materials Mobilization Plan, and improving the efficiency of the Marine Transport Plan (*Kaijō yusō keikaku*). The New Economic Order's call for including control associations in economic planning was not mere lip service. The Steel Control Association participated actively in the drafting of the Materials Mobilization Plan.

In the drafting process, the Planning Board first notified the Steel Control Association of the shipping capacity that could be allocated to steel production. Shipping capacity was rationed because it was the scarce resource that

Table 2. Control Associations and their Postwar Successors, with date of establishment

Control Association Name	Date Est.	Postwar Successor	Date Est.
Steel Control Association	11/41	Japan Steel Council	12/46
Coal C.A.	11/41	Japan Coal Mining Association	5/46
Mine C.A.	12/41	National Mine Association	3/46
Cement C.A.	12/41	Cemept Industry Association	
Rolling Stock C.A.	12/41	Railway Car Ind. Association	11/45
Automobile C.A.	12/41	Automobile Council	11/45
Precisiton Machinery C.A.	1/42	Japan Machine Tool Association	1/46
Electric Machineis C.A.	1/42	Japan Electric Machine Product Association	2/46
Industrial Machines C.A.	1/42	Industrial Equipoment Indus. Association	3/46
Metal Industry C.A.	1/42	Japan CableAssociation, etc.	11/45
Trade C.A.	1/42	Japan Foreign Trade Council	5/47
Shipbuilding C.A.	1/42	Fed. of Shipbuilding Association	10/45
Rail C.A.	5/42	Japan Railway Association	12/45
Light Metals C.A.	9/42	Light Metals Council	10/46
Wool C.A.	9/42	Japan Textile Association	12/45
Leather Tanning C.A.	9/42	Leather Tanning Control Union	12/45
Jute C.A.	9/42	Japan Textile Association	12/45
Silk and Rayon C.A.	10/42	Japan Textile Association	12/45
Cotton Yarn C.A.	10/42	Japan Textile Association	12/45
Oils and Fats C.A.	10/42	Oils Fats Proc. Union, etc.	1/46
Chemical Industry C.A.	10/42	Chemical Industry Federation	3/46
Rubber C.A.	1/43	Rubber Control Union	12/45

Source: Okazaki (1993a).

presented the most significant bottleneck at the time. Using the shipping quota that it received from the Planning Board, the Steel Control Association calculated the most appropriate distribution by mode of use and region, and on that basis drafted steel production plans that it then reported back to the Planning Board. The Planning Board weighed these steel production plans against conditions in other industries as well as changes in the general situation following the previous notification and then notified the Steel Control Association of a revised shipping quota. The Steel Control Association revised the steel production plans on the basis of that quota and reported them back to the Board. The process was repeated ad infinitum, an iterative solution to the planning problem in a situation where shipping was the restricted shared resource.[11]

As the above explanation makes clear, the concrete drafting of steel production plans was almost completely entrusted to the Steel Control Association. What made this possible was that association's power as an organization run by several hundred capable, full-time staff assembled from steel companies. Such members enabled detailed information relating to member firms to be concentrated in the Steel Control Association, where it was used in drafting and implementing plans. That is, in essence, the participation of the Steel Control Association made it possible to take local information that had been scattered throughout individual firms and incorporate it into government-level planning. Information concerning firms was concentrated by industry and transmitted to the government for incorporation into production plans. The government could then formulate economic plans by coordinating among industries.

At the same time that the distribution of the bulk of resources was being determined according to economic plans drafted in the above fashion, important financial institutions were reformed significantly by means of the "New Financial Order" (*Kin'yū shintaisei*). The financial system was called upon to supply funds in coordination with the economic plans, but the capital market, which before the war had provided firms with their major source of funds, had been cut back in capacity as part of the shift to the New Economic Order. First of all, the New Economic Order tried to address the fall in the rate of fulfillment of production plans by further extending the planned economic system rather than by reviving the rate of company profitability by revising fixed prices. The result was an even more serious decline in profitability. Second, and in relation to this, the theory of the New Economic Order included the notion that stockholder influence on the management of firms should be eliminated. In the Planning Board's perception, the fall in rates of profitability obstructed increased production because stockholders were forcing managers to maximize profits. It thus believed that it could raise the rate of production-plan fulfillment by eliminating this influence. It goes without saying that this sort of policy posed a threat to investors in the capital market, and they became very reluctant to move funds into stocks. From 1940 on, the decline in stock prices and stagnation of capital expansion became increasingly serious, so that in 1941 the government was forced to adopt a comprehensive policy of purchasing stocks in order to shore up their prices. The situation can be interpreted as signifying the investors' opposition to the New Economic Order.[12]

Banks were expected to replace the capital market as suppliers of funds, but they were also hesitant. First of all, the falling rates of company profit made it more risky for banks to act as financiers. Second, the banks did not have a great deal of prior experience in long-term financing; in fact, in their view the avoidance of long-term commitment was a criterion of sound banking. Moreover, as described above, the Provisional Funds Adjustment Law did not function to actively compel financing. To address this situation, a new form of financing was introduced. A National Finance Control Association (*Zenkoku kin'yū tōseikai*) was formed around the Bank of Japan, and through its mediation syndicated financing was promoted among banks. The main bank of a financing consortium would assume the role of investigating and monitoring the investment plans of individual firms from a financial perspective on behalf of the financing group. This spread out risk and made it possible to economize by cutting back on investigative organs.[13] Shortcomings in the main bank's capacity to organize a loan consortium were compensated for by the National Finance Control Association and the Bank of Japan.[14] In the wartime economic system that was completed in this manner, the economic plans drawn up by the government and control associations set the fundamental direction of resource distribution, and the economy was managed through the coordination of bank financing by the National Finance Control Association, the Bank of Japan, and the main banks of loan syndicates.

GOVERNMENT-BUSINESS RELATIONS UNDER POSTWAR ECONOMIC RECONSTRUCTION

The postwar government-business relation was shaped by two factors: the experience of the wartime economy, discussed above, and changes produced by the postwar economic reforms and inflation. The postwar reforms and inflation broke up the zaibatsu as internal capital markets and at the same time accelerated the equalization of income and asset distribution that had progressed during wartime. These processes dissolved the institutional and substantive foundations of the capital market as it had functioned before the war. The prewar system to which things otherwise would have returned, therefore, was destroyed at its foundations by the postwar changes. Since circumstances eliminated the option of reinstating the prewar system, a substitute system that had been in place, that is the wartime economic system, was adopted for the period of economic reconstruction. From 1945 to 1948, broad economic controls were implemented, and a planned control economy almost unchanged from the wartime was left in place. The well-known priority production system was a symbolic example of this.

Priority production was a policy that strove to resuscitate the entire economy using as a lever the restored production in a small number of strategic industries, primarily coal and steel. It gave priority to these industries in allocating material resources and funds and simultaneously provided favorable conditions via price and subsidy policies. After the war ended, mining and industrial production, especially in chemical fertilizers and machines, experienced relatively smooth recovery, but in the second and third quarters of fiscal 1946 they went into decline. Mining and industrial production were at only twenty to thirty per cent of prewar levels and were sustained at all only by eating into stocks of both raw materials and facilities. Consequently, it became clear that under contemporary conditions the existing inventories would dry up completely by fiscal 1947, resulting in a sharp drop in production. This was how the Economic Stabilization Board and the Ministry of Commerce and Industry perceived the situation.

It was the famous radio broadcast, "The Economic Crisis and Crude Oil Imports," by Arisawa Hiromi, University of Tokyo professor and participant in an advisory organ to the prime minister (The Coal Subcommittee), that clearly identified the cause of stagnation in raw materials production, and formed the background to the reduction in inventories that was viewed with such concern.[15] In the broadcast, Arisawa stated that "because of the shortage of steel materials, expanded production of coal is being held back. Because of the shortage of coal, the production of steel materials in turn has declined, and, as a result, the supply of steel materials to coal mines is further reduced. This is truly a vicious circle." The vicious circle identified here was the result of a failure in coordination among industries, and it was hoped that government-regulated coordination would eliminate it.

How was government coordination in priority production implemented in practice? The Materials Supply and Demand Plan (*Busshi jukyū keikaku*) and the Provisional Materials Supply and Demand Adjustment Law (*Rinji busshi jukyū chōseihō*) became the means for ensuring the prioritized investment of material resources. In the former, the government estimated the appropriate supply levels for specific materials and then allocated them to each sector of demand. This was the same procedure as had been followed under the Materials Mobilization Plan, which provided the basis for wartime economic operations. The wartime plan had been drawn up by the Planning Board and later the Munitions Ministry; after the war it was taken over by the Ministry of Commerce and Industry. This ministry drew up plans for the third quarter of fiscal 1945 and for the first three quarters of fiscal 1946, but after that the Economic Stabilization Board took over. The measure for reciprocal priority investment in steel and coal is well known in relation to priority production, but it could be implemented only by increasing the "weight" assigned to these materials as strategic sectors within the Materials Supply and Demand Plan.[16]

The Provisional Materials Supply and Demand Adjustment Law formed the legal framework for the implementation of the Materials Supply and Demand Plan. This law came into force at the same time that the National General Mobilization Law went out of use in October 1946, and its role, carrying over from wartime, was to provide the government with broad powers to control materials. In order to secure the implementation of fundamental policies and plans as determined by the head of the Economic Stabilization Board, it allowed the responsible ministers to order: allocation and distribution of materials; restrictions on the use of scarce materials; production, shipping, and construction involving scarce materials, as well as their restriction and prohibition; the transfer, delivery, and loan of idle facilities and scarce materials.[17]

The Materials Supply and Demand Plan/Provisional Materials Supply and Demand Adjustment Law framework was basically the same as the Materials Mobilization Plan/National General Mobilization Law framework that operated during wartime. A relationship of continuity with the wartime economy is also discernible in the trade associations as mechanisms supporting the drafting and implementation of plans. Right after the end of the war, the government planned to transfer authority to the control associations and the trade associations that had been formed from the former's reorganization. In September-October of 1945 the Ministry of Commerce and Industry decided to promote a "law concerning the improvement of economic stability" to replace the National General Mobilization Law and a policy to reorganize the control associations into groups based on this law. Because these measures would have transferred control from the government to autonomous, private groups, they contravened the antimonopoly policies of the Occupation authorities and could not be put into effect. However, business groups with origins in the control associations were continued in reorganized form (Table 2).

In the case of the steel industry, the Steel Control Association cooperated in the drafting of the Materials Supply and Demand Plan and in the distribution of materials until its dissolution by order of the Occupation authorities in May 1946. Furthermore, after the dissolution of the control associations, the

Japan Steel Council (*Nihon tekkō kyōgikai*) was established as an autonomous group. Until its dissolution as a result of the revision of the Provisional Materials Supply and Demand Adjustment Law in May 1947, this council engaged in "production allocation, brokering of raw and secondary materials, linking of producers and buyers, compilation of statistical materials, and investigation and research."[18] In the early days of postwar economic reconstruction, the control associations and the business groups that were their successors after reorganization cooperated with the government almost exactly as they had during wartime in both the drafting and implementation of plans.[19]

Continuities with wartime are also discernible in the second element of priority production, the mechanism for priority allocation of funds. Plans relating to funding began to be drawn up in the fourth quarter of fiscal 1946. The Funds Plan (*Shikin keikaku*), which called for industry to plan the allotment of industrial funds, was drawn up with the purpose of holding the demand for fiscal and industrial funding within the limits of increases in savings and currency issue. It was fundamentally of the same character as the Funds Control Plan and the National Funds Plan (*Kokka shikin keikaku*) that the Planning Board and Munitions Ministry had drawn up during wartime.

The Funds Plan was implemented through the Reconstruction Finance Bank, the Financial Institution Funds Accommodation Regulation (*Kin'yū kikan shikin yūtsū junsoku*) that was based on the Emergency Financial Measures Ordinance, and the loan mediation system of the Bank of Japan.[20] Different versions of the plan were drawn up for the Reconstruction Finance Bank and for private financial institutions, and the version for the Reconstruction Finance Bank was implemented only after it had been subdivided and made concrete by the Economic Stabilization Board, adopted by the cabinet, and approved by the Reconstruction Finance Committee (*Fukkō kin'yū iinkai*). However, because only limited financing was available from the Reconstruction Finance Bank, it became necessary to pour private funding into strategic industries. The Financial Institution Funds Accommodation Regulation called for: 1) each financial institution, through independent arrangements worked out under Bank of Japan guidance, to hold increases in outstanding lending below fifty percent of increases in ordinary free deposits; 2) using the balance for such things as holding national bonds, making payments on primary frozen deposits (*daiichi fūsa yokin*), and purchasing Reconstruction Finance Bank debentures; 3) financing in accord with the priorities of the Industrial Funding Loan Priority Schedule (*Sangyō shikin kashidashi yūsen jun'ihyō*) contained in the Financial Institution Funds Accommodation Regulation.[21] The Industrial Funding Loan Priority Schedule classed 460 types of industry in four ranks of decreasing priority: A1, A2, B, and C. Funding of industries in rank C was discouraged, and permission from the Minister of

Finance via the Bank of Japan was required for: 1) funding for new or expanding firms in B industries, 2) funding for restoration, repair, or improvement in C industries, and 3) operating funds in excess of ¥100,000 for C industries. This was precisely the same method as that by which funds were controlled during wartime through the Enterprise Funds Adjustment Standard (*Jigyō shikin shōsei hyōjun*), based on the Provisional Funds Adjustment Law. The direct effect of finance control was to inhibit the supply of funds to B and C industries. Postwar financial controls were also similar to controls based on the Provisional Funds Adjustment Law in that they did not function actively to direct private sector financial institutions to supply funds to A industries.[22]

The above funding limitations were compensated for through loan mediation by the Bank of Japan. In this system, the Bank of Japan mediated in the formation of financing syndicates and loan consortia for firms in strategic industries, thus actively promoting the supply of funds to these firms.[23] Again, this had the same character as mediation by loan syndicates carried out in wartime by the National Finance Control Association (*Zenkoku kin'yū tōseikai*). If one considers that the National Finance Control Association was, in fact, the Bank of Japan itself,[24] the continuities with wartime become even clearer. Thus, the wartime experience and system were fully exploited in the implementation of the priority production policy. This was an important factor leading to success in the difficult tasks of government-coordinated production and the recovery of production after 1947.

THE SHIFT TO A MARKET ECONOMY AND GOVERNMENT-BUSINESS RELATIONS

A planned/controlled economic system that was in many ways similar to and continuous with that of wartime was employed after the war until around 1948. It goes without saying that this system did not stay in existence up to the period of high-speed growth. The American government forced a rapid shift to a market economy via the Dodge Line, which began in 1949, and most economic controls were abolished in that phase. The task facing Japan then was the same as that faced by the former socialist countries today. Looking at the results, there can be no doubt that Japan successfully accomplished the task of converting to a market economy. However, it did not shift to the sort of pure market economy postulated by neoclassical economists and contemplated by Dodge; indeed, it should be emphasized that it was precisely this divergence from a pure market model that made Japan's "soft landing" into market economics possible.

One plan that displayed long-term vision and anticipated the transition to a market economy was the "Report of the Economic Reconstruction Planning Committee" (*Keizai fukkō keikaku iinkai*) of May 1949. This report was premised on the assumption that dependence on textile exports, that is, the sort of policy Japan had pursued in the prewar, could no longer be continued given the industrialization policies of the formerly colonized nations. It presented in the form of a quantitative plan a long-term vision for Japanese industrial structure that was weighted toward heavy and chemical industries.

It is highly significant that the Economic Reconstruction Planning Committee that came to this conclusion was composed of representatives of various industries and banks. It comprised a general committee and eight sections: mining and industry, foodstuffs and daily necessities, trade, transport, building and reconstruction, employment, national income, and technology. The mining and industry section was further divided into five subcommittees: general affairs, power, metals and machines, textiles, and chemicals. Many individuals from the financial world, such as the chairman of the National Association of Banks (*Zenkoku ginkō kyōkai*), the vice-president of the Industrial Bank of Japan, and the president of Teikoku Bank, participated in the national income section, giving it the character of a finance section. In each industry that had a control association predecessor, the posts of subcommittee chair of the various subcommittees in the mining and industry section were filled by chairmen of the trade associations (the Japan Coal Association, the Japan Iron and Steel Association [*Nihon tekkōkai*], the Japan Spinners' Association, and the Japan Chemical Industry Association, respectively). In the composition of membership as well, unlike the prewar deliberative councils, the share of representatives of general economic groups and the zaibatsu was small, while the representatives of trade associations occupied a larger share (Table 3). Through this mechanism information scattered among firms was concentrated according to industry in the trade associations and coordinated with information on other industries in the deliberative councils. As suggested above, the concentration and transmission of information through trade associations was a method introduced via the establishment of the control associations during wartime.[25]

Although a consensus formed around this long-term vision for the industrial structure, the rapid implementation of a market economy through external pressure brought to light a serious coordination failure in the Japanese economy.[26] Under the fixed exchange rate of US $1.00=JP ¥360 established by the Dodge Line, machines and steel, in which hopes were invested as export products, lacked international competitiveness. The cause lay for the most part in the interrelation between industries: expensive iron ore and coal meant expensive steel, and expensive steel meant expensive machines. Furthermore, expensive iron ore was the result of high transport costs, which in turn stemmed from expensive ships. Similarly, economies of scale in the steel industry were limited by the small scale of the machine industry. Thus the high price of goods in various interrelated industries formed a vicious circle. As long as these interrelated industries were not simultaneously rationalized, individual industries were prevented from becoming internationally competitive. It was therefore impossible for individual industries or firms to escape this vicious circle through their own efforts.

Table 3. Deliberative Council Membership (Postwar)

	Econ. Reconst. Plan Comm.[a]	Ind. Rat. Coun.[b]	Ind. Structure Council[c]
Gen. Econ. Organizations	8	3	13
Trade Associations	77	30	108
Zaibatsu	0	0	0
Financial Institutions	2	0	24
Industrial Firms	46	48	179
Public Corporations	28	8	39
Newspapers	0	0	19
Labor Unions	3	0	0
Academics	39	4	53
Diet Representatives	10	0	0
Bureaucrats	141	18	4
Other	23	7	66
Total	377	118	505

Source: Okazaki (1933a).
[a] Economic Reconstruction Planning Committee (1948).
[b] Industrial Rationalization Council (1949).
[c] Industrial Structure Council (1970)

The Industrial Rationalization Council (*Sangyō gōrika shingikai*), established in December 1949, gave top priority to achieving an escape from this vicious circle. The Council was made up of twenty-nine industry sections, a coordinating section, and a general section. Numerous representatives from trade associations and major firms in each industry participated in the industry sections (Table 3). It began by devoting concentrated study to policy for the rationalization of the steel and coal mining industries. The steel and coal sections each drew up a rationalization plan that was then adjusted by the coordinating section, and onward in an iterative pattern. In the course of this repetition, a consensus developed that the steel industry could become internationally competitive if the coal and steel industries were rationalized through simultaneous investment. Moreover, the expected price of steel derived by the Industrial Rationalization Council satisfied the price conditions on steel materials that had to be met if the shipbuilding industry were to become internationally competitive. The latter calculations were made by the Research Association for Steel Materials in Shipbuilding (*Zōsenyō kōzai kenkyūkai*), a body formed from the Ministry of Transport, the Economic Stabilization Board, and major shipbuilding firms.[27]

As a consequence of coordinating their requirements and expectations through the Industrial Rationalization Council, firms and industries developed a vigorous interest in investment. The prospect of breaking out of the above sort of vicious circle probably enhanced the willingness among financial institutions to provide funds for the industries involved. Added to this was direct policy coordination of funding by financial institutions and of firms' investment plans.

First, the proportion of public funds (the United States A.I.D. Counterpart Fund and Japan Development Bank financing) devoted to investment in industrial rationalization was relatively high in the early 1950s. Moreover, financing by the Japan Development Bank signaled the direction of industrial policy and the results of Japan Development Bank screening, thereby encouraging financing by private banks as a result of the well-known "cow bell effect."[28]

Second, loan mediation by the Bank of Japan continued on a large scale until April 1950, augmenting the coordinating function of main banks in loan syndicates. Bank of Japan mediation also occurred sporadically for a few years thereafter. It is worthwhile to call attention again to the frequently cited example of Bank of Japan opposition to providing operating funds for the Kawasaki Steel Corporation's Chiba factory: the main bank (the Dai-Ichi Bank) was able to organize a loan consortium only after receiving Bank of Japan loan mediation.[29]

Finally, the Industrial Rationalization Council itself played a coordinating role between the financial and industrial sectors. In April 1950, a funds subcommittee was set up under the general section of this council. Representatives from the Bank of Japan, the Industrial Bank of Japan, and the big three city banks participated in this subcommittee, along with members from major industrial firms.[30] The subcommittee heard explanations and appraisals of plans for fund procurement and for plant and equipment investment at 1500 or so major firms (researched by MITI's Industrial Finance Division) in industries under MITI jurisdiction and then debated fund procurement policy. The presentation of plant and equipment investment plans, along with a MITI appraisal of those plans, to a committee on which major financial institutions served can be viewed as a way of closing the information gap between financial institutions on the one hand and industrial firms and the government on the other, thus reducing the risk to financial institutions.[31]

The Industrial Rationalization Council's coordinating role was institutionalized further through the establishment in 1957 of an industrial finance section. The membership composition of the industrial finance section at the time of its formation is presented in Table 4; participants included the secretary-general (*jimukyokuchō*) of Keidanren as well as representatives of trade associations, major industrial firms, and financial institutions. The actual work of coordination was shouldered for the most part by MITI's Industrial Finance Division; this division, in cooperation with other concerned MITI bureaus (*genkyoku*), the Financial Bureau of the Ministry of Finance, and the Financial Institution Funds Council (*Kinyū kikan shikin shingikai*), which had been set up under the Ministry of Finance, undertook the adjustment and screening of plant and equipment investment plans for industries under MITI jurisdiction. The industrial finance section provided the final adjustments and at the same time functioned to obtain approval from representatives of the financial world for these equipment and plant investment plans and the industrial policy of MITI that they reflected. The deliberations and conclusions of the industrial finance section were passed on to the Federation of Bankers Associations of Japan, in particular its funds adjustment committee. This committee played a coordinating role among banks to achieve the level of funds from private financial institutions that was called for in the plant investment plans.[32]

CONCLUSION

In postwar Japan, the government, trade associations, firms, and banks participated in a mechanism that coordinated the distribution of resources, and this mechanism constituted an important dimension of government-business relations in postwar Japan. Interestingly, this mechanism took root in the midst of efforts to cope with the inadequate results of the Dodge Line, which had tried to convert Japan to a pure, Anglo-Saxon type, market economy. The market mechanism that began to function with the removal of economic controls under the Dodge Line could not resolve the coordination failure among related industries like coal, steel, machines, and shipping that mutually constrained their international competitiveness. Furthermore, the collapse of the prewar capital market as the result of changes during wartime and the period of postwar reform prevented the Occupation authorities from succeeding in their reform of the financial system, through which they had sought to make the capital market into the main institution for long-term finance.

Table 4. Industrial Rationalization Council Industrial Finance Section Membership
(April 1958)

Members	
Horikoshi Teizō	Sec'y. General, Japan Fed. of Economic Organizations
Usami Makoto	Managing Director,The Mitsubishi Bank
Enjōji Jirō	Editor in Chief, The Nihon Keizai Shimbum
Tsuchiya Kiyoshi	Chairman, Japan Chemical Fibers Association
Nakayama Sōhei	Editorial Writer, TheAsahi Shimbun
Hirata Keiichirō	Vice-President, The Industrial Bank of Japan
Hirayama Takeshi	Vice-President, The Japan Development Bank
Fukura Toshiyuki	Managing Director, Mitsui Petrochemical
Matsune Sōichi	Editorial Writer, The Tokyo Shimbun
Saku Hiroshi	Managing Director, Fed. of Electric Power Companies
Yamamoto Takayuki	Vice-Chairman, Fuji Steel
Prov. Members	
Nomura Sueichi	Vice-President, Tōyō High-Pressure Industries
Arai Hiroshi	Managing Director, Nippon Oil Corporation
Tech. Spec. Members	
Magōri Iwao	Div. Chief, Ind. Fin. Div., Bus. Affairs Bureau, MITI

Based on Okazaki (1994c).

Efforts to address this situation resulted in the reestablishment of various institutions that had developed during wartime to handle resource distribution in place of the market, even as those institutions were revised so as to make them compatible with a market economy. Foremost examples include the mechanism for the implementation of interindustry coordination, which was based on the mediation by industry groups of information exchange between the government and firms, and the mechanism for the coordination of the financial and industrial sectors which was premised on the main bank system of the government and the Bank of Japan. Indeed, some of the various functions, such as coordination, screening, and risk management, that had in pre-war Japan been performed by the market and which the Occupation authorities believed the market ought to perform were in fact carried out through a non-market system in which the government, trade associations, firms, and banks participated, and which originated in the wartime economic system.

In conclusion, let's try from a broader perspective to explain why many wartime institutions were preserved and continued to function in the institutional foundation of the postwar economic system. First, in relation to the fixed costs involved in building a new system, it is highly significant that during the war relations including those among firms, between firms and banks, and between firms and their employees were determined by the government.

As a general principle, a given relationship will be endowed with relation-specific assets only if it is expected to be continuous. During the war the government's enforcement of continuity in relationships encouraged the formation of relation-specific assets; thus, from the postwar vantage these became sunk costs which most likely gave parties an interest in continuing the relationships autonomously even after the wartime controls were dissolved. Second, the institutions and practices introduced during wartime were mutually complementary. For example, complementarity prevailed among such factors as the reduced role of capital markets, the government's performance of a coordination function and the distribution of risk, the enhanced role of banks in corporate finance and governance, and the reduced role of stockholders and the expanded status of employees in corporate governance. Moreover, this structure of corporate governance was reinforced by the employees' accumulation of firm-specific skills and knowledge. Third, in their fundamental orientation the postwar reforms were broadly consistent with those that were carried out in wartime in that both sought to dismantle entirely the institutional foundations of the prewar economic system. The result was to close off decisively the possibility of a return to the prewar system in the postwar era. The Japanese economic system is therefore unique in that, although it is a market system, its institutional framework includes important elements that were introduced as part of the planned, controlled economy of wartime.

Translated by Adam Schneider

Notes

[1] World Bank, *East Asian Miracle* (Oxford and New York: Oxford University Press, 1993).

[2] On comparative institutional analysis, see Aoki Masahiko, *Nihon keizai no seido bunseki* (Tokyo: Chikuma Shobō, 1992); Aoki Masahiko "Shisutemu to shite no Nihon kigyō," *Kikan: riron keizaigaku* 43.5 (1992); and P. Milgrom and J. Roberts, *Economic Organization and Management* (New York: Prentice-Hall, 1992).

[3] Based on Okazaki Tetsuji, "Nihon no seifu/kigyō-kan kankei: gyōkai dantai–shingikai shisutemu no keisei ni kansuru oboegaki," *Soshiki kagaku* 26.4 (1993).

[4] Miyamoto Matao, "Sangyōka to kaisha seido no hatten," in Nishikawa Shunsaku and Abe Takeshi, eds., *Sangyōka no jidai* 1 (Tokyo: Iwanami Shoten, 1990).

[5] Okazaki Tetsuji, "Senji keikaku keizai to kigyō," in Tokyo Daigaku Shakai Kagaku Kenkyūjo, ed., *Gendai Nihon shakai* 4 (Tokyo: Tokyo Daigaku Shuppankai, 1991).

[6] Okazaki Tetsuji, "Nihon: seido kaikaku to keizai shisutemu no tenkan," in *Shakai keizai shigaku* 60.1 (1994).

[7] Hara Akira, "Nitchū sensōki no gaika kessai" (1), *Tokyo daigaku: keizaigaku ronshū* 38.1 (1971), 18-19.

[8] See footnote 6 for Okazaki, "Nihon: seido kaikaku," 1994.

[9] Yamazaki Shirō, "Seisanryoku kakujū keikaku no tenkai katei," in Kindai Nihon Kenkyūkai, ed., *Kindai Nihon kenkyū nenpō* 9 (1987).

[10] Okazaki Tetsuji, "Senji keikaku keizai to kakaku tōsei," in Kindai Nihon Kenkyūkai, ed., *Kindai Nihon kenkyū nenpō* 9 (1987).

[11] Okazaki Tetsuji, "Dainiji sekai taisenki ni okeru senji keikaku keizai no kōzō to unkō," *Shakai kagaku kenkyū* 40.4 (1988).

[12] Okazaki Tetsuji, "Kigyō shisutemu," in Okazaki Tetsuji and Okuno Masahiro, eds., *Gendai Nihon keizai shisutemu no genryū* (Tokyo: Nihon keizai shinbunsha, 1993).

[13] Teranishi Jūrō, "Meinbanku shisutemu," in Okazaki Tetsuji and Okuno Masahiro, eds.

[14] See footnote 12 for Okazaki, "Kigyō shisutemu" (1993).

[15] Arisawa Hiromi, ed., *Keisha seisen to sekitan shōiinkai* (Tokyo: Tokyo daigaku shuppankai, 1990), pp. 150-152.

[16] Okazaki Tetsuji and Ishii Susumu, "Sengo Nihon no sangyō seisaku-yakuwari to seidoteki kiso," in *Tsūsan kenkyū rebyū* 4 (1994).

[17] Ōkurashō Zaiseishi Shitsu, *Shōwa zaiseishi: shūsen kara kōwa made* 10 (Tokyo: Ōkurashō, 1980), 299-300.

[18] Nihon Tekkō Renmei, *Sengo tekkōshi* (Tokyo: Nihon Tekkō Renmei, 1958).

[19] See footnote 3 for Okazaki, "Nihon no seifu kigy kan kankei" (1993).

[20] See footnote 6 for Okazaki, "Nihon: seido kaikaku" (1994).

[21] Finance limits were changed from independent arrangements to legal restrictions by the July 1947 reform of the Financial Institution Funds Accommodation Regulation (Ōkurashō Zaiseishi Shitsu [1976], 216; Zenkoku Ginkō Kyōkai Rengōkai, *Ginkō kyōkai 20 nenshi* (Tokyo: 1994).

[22] See footnote 16 for Okazaki and Ishii (1994).

[23] Okazaki Tetsuji, "Sengo keizai fukkōki no kin'yū shisutemu to Nihon ginkō yūshi assen," *Nihon ginkō kin'yū kenkyūjo itaku kenkyū hōkoku* 3.6 (1994).

[24] Nihon ginkō, *Nihon ginkō hyakunenshi* 4 (Tokyo: Nihon Ginkō, 1984).

[25] See footnote 3 for Okazaki (1993).

[26] On coordination failure and the theory of industrial policy, see Itō Motoshige, Okuno Masahiro, Suzumura Kōtarō and Kiyono Kazuharu, *Sangyō seisaku keizai bunseki* (Tokyo: Tokyo daigaku shuppankai, 1988).

[27] Okazaki Tetsuji, "Sengo keizai fukkōki no seifu-kigyōkan kankei: sangyō gōrika seisaku to kigyō," *Tokyo daigaku keizaigakubu: Discussion Paper Series* 94-J-6 (1994).

[28] Higano Mikinari, *Kin'yū kikan no shisa nōryoku* (Tokyo: Tokyo daigaku shuppankai, 1986); and A. Horiuchi and Q. Sui, "Influence of the Japan Development Bank Loans on Corporate Investment Behavior," *Tokyo daigaku keizaigakubu Discussion Paper Series* 93-F-4 (1993).

[29] See footnote 27 for Okazaki, "Sengo keizai fukkōki no seifu-kigyōkan kankei" (1994).

[30] On the composition of the committee, see ibid.

[31] Ibid.

[32] Tetsuji Okazaki, "Evolution of the Financial System in Postwar Japan," *Tokyo daigaku keizaigakubu Discussion Paper Series 94-F-2* (1994); and see footnote 16 for Okazaki and Ishii (1994).

The Historical Significance of the Industrial Patriotic Association: Labor Relations in the Total-War State

Saguchi Kazurō

The Industrial Patriotic Association (*Sangyō hōkokukai*, or Sanpō) was the most important Japanese organization concerned with industrial relations during World War II. This paper attempts to clarify the historical significance of that organization, from the following perspective. That is, it seeks to transcend the question merely of the degree to which "relations surrounding labor" under the total-war system "continued" into postwar Japan. Rather, it relies on the hypothesis that wartime labor relations powerfully constrained postwar labor-management interaction, wage systems, and employment systems in several countries, and analyzes the Japanese case as an example of that process. A glance at the U.S. case suggests the advantages of such an approach. It has been argued that the American war experience played a decisive role in the spread of seniority and compensation systems, and one can say much the same of the mediation system. Moreover, it can be argued that these systems not only brought about quantitative increases in the rate of unionization but largely determined the character of industrial democracy as a postwar American institution.[1]

However, it is a bit more difficult to evaluate the impact of the war in countries like Japan and Germany, which rejected industrial democracy. For example, among labor-relations theorists the German Works Council is widely seen as a typical example of the so-called "decentralization" of decision-making, but studies of its historical development have not necessarily paid adequate attention to role of the war.[2] In the case of Japan's Industrial Patriotic Association (Sanpō), the dominant historical interpretation presents it as the end point of a process of "fascization," and treats its organization as an inoperative, empty shell. Very few studies have used Sanpō as the starting point for a consideration of postwar labor relations. Specialists have largely agreed that one should look for the origins of a "living," or need-based, wage (*seikatsu kyū*) in the wartime experience. Yet, no studies have focused in any depth on connections between the wage system and the labor-relations system more broadly.

Ōkōchi Kazuo's work has always been exceptional in this regard. In his treatments of the wartime period he sought to understand the ways in which total war, although in itself peculiar and irrational, paradoxically offered "various opportunities for rationalization and modernization." With respect to Sanpō, Ōkōchi emphasized the experience under it of mandatory and universal membership on the part of enterprises and industrial associations, arguing that without considering that experience it is impossible to understand the rapid growth of enterprise unions after World War II.[3]

Against the background of Ōkōchi's arguments, this paper will take up the following questions: First, it will consider not only how universal issues generated by the total-war state found their way into the "relations surrounding labor" but also whether in some cases they might have been dealt with in a manner peculiar to Japan. It is difficult to say that Ōkōchi's arguments have ended debate on these questions. Second, it will look at issues related to organizational experience. Rather than merely confirming the existence of organizations as such, it will stress how social actors became involved in them and what they believed ought to be accomplished within the framework of such organizations. Accordingly, it will emphasize the role in labor relations of ideology, something Ōkōchi could only see in a passive role. Third, it will focus on the gap between Sanpō policy and the ideology underlying it, on the one hand, and, on the other, what it actually accomplished. Needless to say, the Sanpō fully realized neither the policy objectives of its framers nor the ideology that guided them. This essay will try to suggest what it accomplished and what it did not, and to assess the implications of the shortfall for the postwar process.

The discussion below begins with a significant element of historical background, that is, the consultation system of labor relations (*rōshi kondan seido*, or "joint consultation system") that developed after World War I. On that basis, it will then distinguish between two stages of Sanpō policy, contrasting the early Sanpō, which emerged as a countermeasure anticipating an early end to the Sino-Japanese War of the late-1930s, against Sanpō as the total-war policy that followed reorganization. It will pay special attention to the *kinrō ideologii* ("work ideology," or ethic) that was the centerpiece of Sanpō policy after reorganization, analyzing it in detail along with the institutions and concepts that corresponded to it. That will lead to a consideration of how workers responded to the reorganized Sanpō, and how its relationship to policy changed. It will conclude with a somewhat hypothetical attempt to show how the wartime experiences of social actors affected "relations surrounding labor" in the postwar era.

HISTORICAL BACKGROUND

The question of the character and quality of workers as a social group arose after World War I, which had greatly increased the number of workers in the advanced sectors of the economy. Ultimately, what this meant was that the universal issue of whether labor unions ought to be recognized, in either a social or legal sense, had now arisen in Japan as well. Moreover, it was in response to this issue that the labor relations consultation system developed, even before labor unions became an influential social force. Accordingly, it is necessary to understand the organizational characteristics and ideological background of the consultation system because of its importance as a standard by which to evaluate the Sanpō as a wartime system of labor relations. In other words, in order to assess the degree of Sanpō's originality, it is necessary to go through the preliminary process of comparing the Sanpō, especially the post-reorganization Sanpō, to the post-World War I consultation system.[4] Three points bear mentioning in reference to the ideological and organizational peculiarities of the consultation system.

First, workers' demands brought forth under the consultation system tended to favor vague, all-encompassing demands for recognition of workers' dignity and value as human beings in preference to concrete demands for wages or recognition of labor unions. It is well known that the great influx of workers (mostly unskilled) during World War I had disrupted the structure of workplace hierarchies. Under these new circumstances—in for example, mining—rising education levels among workers and the development of mechanisms for labor management led unskilled workers to begin attempting to raise their own status. Moreover, skilled workers were attempting to resist the decline in their status in military factories and elsewhere. Common to all these efforts was the demand for a more equitable position within the workplace and the firm. Workers could no longer put up with the capricious discrimination and punishment meted out by managers and others.

Of course, these demands necessarily led to issues related to labor unions. Mechanisms such as mutual aid among privileged workers, paternalistic benevolence on the part of management, and the system under which high-ranking workers and employers consulted informally on problems of the workplace were all showing signs of having reached their limit as a result of qualitative and quantitative changes in the working class. There was a need for some kind of system for interest mediation and adjustment—a system that was official and clearly representative. Yet, whether the subjects involved are conscious of it or not, such a system inevitably raises the question of what kind of workers' group should send representatives, that is, the question of a union.

Second, it is necessary to look at organizational characteristics. Organizations took many forms, but provisionally, one can say the following: First, it is important to note that the topic of working conditions was included on the consultation system's agenda. This means that the necessity for adjustment of interests between worker representatives and management was at least minimally recognized. On the other hand, the issue of what sort of worker collectivity would choose such representatives was left vague. Furthermore, even though these structures were supposed to mediate conflicting interests, they provided only for consultation and lacked any procedures for dealing with situations in which interests stood fundamentally opposed.

A typical example of the consultation system in this era can be found in the company unions in zaibatsu-affiliated mines. For example, Mitsui's Miike Mine Workers' Benevolent Society included not only the miners but, as quasi-members, the administrative staff as well. Included as an important component of this organization was a purchasing union designed to procure life necessities at low cost for the members (relying on funds collected from members as well as the company). Also included was a system for consultation on labor-relations issues, called the consultant society (*sōdanyaku-kai*). Worker representatives, legitimized by vote of their fellows, were able to engage in discussion with management on issues that included working conditions. However, this system could neither bind both sides in formal agreements nor make other decisions, and there was no explicitly recognized forum in which workers and their representatives could discuss ahead of time the issues that they would bring before management under this system. That is why the status of the workers' organization was ambiguous, as I noted above. On the other hand, pure consultation systems did exist, as in the case of the Kure Naval Arsenal's Employees' Council (*Shokkō Kyōgikai*). In that such councils included only a relatively small number of management delegates and allowed "autonomous decisions" (*jihatsuteki ketsugi*) by workers, they were quite different from the consultation arrangements within enterprise unions. Nevertheless, neither made any provision for a clearly defined deliberative body whose membership would be limited to workers and which would be capable of deciding policy in advance of consultation with management. In terms of organizational form, most examples of the immediate post-World War I Japanese consultation system left the question of labor unions very ambiguous.

Third, we have to address problems related to underlying ideology. Here, it is significant that, in the process of developing the consultation system, both parties adopted the term "recognition as a human being" (*jinkaku shōnin*). In other words, the consultation system was viewed as a means of realizing such recognition, and it is fair to say that labor-management conflict arose over different interpretations of this concept. The ideology of "recognition of humanity" was by no means peculiar to Japan and, indeed, as an approach to the general problem of securing the social status of workers as a group, it had a degree of universality. The problem was rather in the way this ideology surfaced in Japan. If we examine the development of the consultation system, we can abstract from it two main trends. First, one notices a tendency to work towards "recognition as a human being" by reducing industrial relations to interaction among real human beings who are homogenized in the process. This tendency was especially strong on the management side, but workers adopted it as well. For example, in the enterprise unions of zaibasu mining companies, administrative and other personnel as well as miners participated in the consultation system and were eligible to receive whatever fringe or welfare benefits the company provided. Second, the search for "recognition" often involved a connection with the goals of the state. This tendency was particularly evident among workers in the state-operated enterprises, but was shared by employers as well. At the Kure Naval Arsenal, for example, the employer legitimized the consultation system by emphasizing the importance of smooth cooperation between workers and employers in order better to serve the state.[5] As we shall see later, this became a fundamental premise of the reorganized Sanpō.

What needs emphasis here is that in no case were the interests of labor and management viewed as fundamentally opposed. In other words, in this period the Japanese labor-management consultation system embodied the contradiction that, on the one hand, the system was conceived as a way of mediating the interests of labor and management in order to avoid labor unions, while on the other it was bound by an ideology that denied the existence of conflicting interests. This contradiction inevitably contributed to the instability of labor-management relations after World War I. By the latter half of the 1920s, the labor movement had become more active and both labor and management recognized that a labor union law might be imminent, so surrogate measures were increasingly adopted in the direction of actual unionization. For example, there was a new willingness to recognize workers' organizations that clearly stopped short of asserting "the right to strike," which was a bone of contention at the time, and to incorporate these organizations into the consultation system. However, this tendency was short lived because it called attention to the above-mentioned contradiction and the instability that arose from it. If workers' organizations were too weak they were ineffective as surrogate unions, but if they became too active management would adamantly reject them. By the 1930s, as the social environment changed as a result of the Great Depression and the semi-wartime situation precipitated by the Manchurian Incident, institutions that had begun to recognize the particular interests of workers, inadequate as they might have been, came to be seen as obstacles to be overcome. In other words, along with slogans such as "labor-capital unity" and "patriotic labor" came the search for a new ideology and a system to implement it.

THE FORMATION OF SANPŌ POLICY: COUNTERMEASURES FOR THE "POSTWAR" PERIOD

The Conceptions of Major Actors

After the outbreak of war with China in 1937, the bureaucracy, employers' associations, and representatives of labor unions began to discuss a new system of labor relations. The motive force behind these discussions was not the bureaucracy itself, but the semiofficial Conciliation Society (*Kyōchōkai*). In February 1938, a Countermeasures Committee (*Jikyoku Taisaku Iinkai*) was established, providing a common forum for the parties involved in labor issues.

The Committee was not actually established to deal with the labor disputes of the time. Its mission was rather to discuss how the current situation in labor relations, in which disputes were very infrequent, could be extended into the period after the Sino-Japanese War of 1937, which was expected to be over quickly. Taking as an object lesson the rise of the European labor movement after World War I, the Committee felt an urgent need to establish a "postwar" labor policy.[6] In other words, in this period Sanpō was conceived as a basis for countermeasures aimed at the period that would follow the Sino-Japanese War. As everyone assumed that the war would soon be over, the Committee did not take up the problem of current mobilization as an immediate policy concern. Moreover, as noted above, labor conflicts had in fact subsided, and even if we look at nominal wages and labor mobility, we find that they had only begun to change in comparison with the post-1939 period. The relatively unproblematical contemporary situation is also reflected in the prominence of the Kyōchōkai rather than the government as the driving force behind the early Sanpō. In any case, the early-Sanpō, in the form of the Industrial Patriotic Federation (*Sangyō Hōkoku Renmei*), was formed in July 1938 as a centralized but private organization.

The main issues that arose in the process of conceptualizing the new system of labor relations were how to formulate a "guiding spirit"—in other words, how to legitimize the new system ideologically—and how to organize Sanpō's operating units at the enterprise level. As discussions proceeded, they revealed differences in opinion between bureaucrats and employers' organizations regarding the "most desirable system of industrial relations." The organizational form envisioned by bureaucrats included a consultation system in which duly-elected workers' representatives would consult with management, especially in the area of "rationalizing" (*tekiseika*) compensation," thereby producing agreements that would bind both sides.[7] Indeed, according to this view, in some circumstances the Sanpō units could be equated with institutions for labor-management consultation. Leaving aside the issue of "guiding spirit," in the post-World War I period this was generally thought to be a more or less effective means of establishing a consistent and stable system of labor relations, centering on the Ministry of Interior. In the background of this conception was the view that, as a response to the drive to establish labor unions, the new system of labor relations should mirror as closely as possible the system that would obtain if unions had officially existed. The idea of founding Sanpō units on a consultation system oriented to the "rationalization of compensation" shows that even at the end of the 1930s elements in the bureaucracy were thinking along these lines.

However, the conception of a "guiding spirit" evoked something new— the "ideology of dedicated work (*kinrō*)." In this connection, it was said that "all Japanese nationals (*kokumin*) are equally dedicated workers (*kinrōsha*)" and that employees "are not the private property of the employer but children (*sekishi* = 'infants') of the emperor," suggesting that relations of command and subordination in the workplace were not absolute in the context of overriding loyalty to the state. At this juncture, however, although the word "*kinrō*" was prevalent, it had not yet been elaborated into a systematic ideology. Moreover, it was still unclear how the notion of "work" in the sense of labor dedicated to the state would relate to ideas regarding the adjustment of interests in an organizational framework.

By way of contrast, the employers' conceptions of organizational framework faithfully reflected the situation of company unions in the 1930s by proposing a scaled down consultation system and more robust corporate welfare programs.[8] In an extreme case, one employer rejected even the expression, "tea time conversation," out of fear that any permanent system would inevitably invite further demands for meetings. This reflected the way of thinking of employers who, even while recognizing the need for mutual understanding, always insisted that it be pursued informally. Note that Japanese employers had always thought that it was desirable to achieve mutual understanding through informal consultation, but they had no idea how to activate such consultations so as to include rank-and-file workers. They were never able to overcome the tendency for exchanges of views to drift away from issues related to the shopfloor. Therefore, they actively promoted reliance on existing corporate welfare facilities instead, arguing that the new organizational framework should place as much emphasis on corporate welfare as it did upon organs for reaching mutual understanding. Concerning the "guiding spirit," the employers' organizations resisted the bureaucrats' belief that the needs of the state should be placed above those of the individual corporation. Even the suggestion that the program of the central Sanpō organization should be included in the charters of the branch units met with their strong resistance.

Reaching a Compromise and the Situation of Sanpō Units

The discussions aimed at agreeing on a system of employment relations for the period following the China War in the late-1930s did not lead to consensus, but instead called attention to differences of viewpoint. Accordingly, the "guiding spirit" and organizational form of Sanpō branch units that did emerge were merely the results of empty compromise. Indeed, the proposal for Sanpō units merely united a half-baked consultation system with welfare facilities, while ignoring the issues of "guiding spirit" and work ideology.[9]

Especially noteworthy is the relationship to existing labor unions. In short, it was forbidden to forcibly disband labor unions on the pretext of forming Sanpō branch units. That is, in this era the Sanpō conception was not premised on the outright rejection of unions. In fact, even in 1939, Sōdōmei (a national center of labor unions) was able to legitimize itself in the following manner.[10] First, it advanced the premise that, with reference to cooperation with the state, Sanpō and labor unions were on the same level, and on that basis argued that Sanpō was necessary precisely because the unions, which alone could bring industrial peace, were underdeveloped. Accordingly, it was natural for Sanpō and the unions to supplement each other, and the cooperation of labor unions was indispensable if Sanpō was ever to reflect the general will of employees. Clearly this conception of Sanpō, which deemed it possible for corporate associations, a pure consultation system, and existing labor unions all to coexist, could not become the norm that would give rise to a new labor-management relationship.

The central Sanpō organization, or Industrial Patriotic Federation, was a private institution, and had no concrete function aside from "encouraging" the establishment of Sanpō units at the enterprise level; for this and other reasons, it actually became an obstacle to the realization of the Sanpō conception. Even after agreeing to guidelines for the establishment of Sanpō units in September 1939, the All-Japan Industrial League (Zensanren), an employers' organization, put out an interesting pamphlet on Sanpō. In this pamphlet, the

League interpreted Sanpō's "guiding spirit" as an extension of "warmly paternalistic [labor] relations" (*onjō kankei*), and offered its own, original guidelines for the establishment of Sanpō units that would differ from those of the Federation. The pamphlet mentions that the consultation system is not a decision-making organ, and adds the cautionary note that sometimes introducing issues of how labor is treated could cause "unnecessary disputes."[11]

Beginning upon formation of the Sanpō Federation in July 1938, over 200 Sanpō units were formed each month, and the movement began to operate normally in November. Looking at a survey that the Sanpō Federation took in April 1939, one immediately notices that more than thirty percent of the units had subordinate departments (*bukai*).[12] Departments concerned with specialized issues, like Safety Committees and Mutual Aid Departments, were by far the most numerous. Moreover, the survey includes the remark that it is inappropriate for subcommittees to substitute for the consultation committees. This suggests that in a number of Sanpō units the existing departments, like safety committees, were made to take on extraneous tasks in the realm of consultation. For example, let's look at the Mitsubishi Heavy Industries' Nagoya Engine Works.[13] There, organizations such as a Safety Committee, a Salaried Employees' Consultation Committee, and a Factory Committee were already in place, and the Sanpō unit merely brought them under one roof. Moreover, the unit did not supervise their activities, but instead simply redefined them as the activities of the Sanpō unit. In other words, only the name was new.

As this example shows, Sanpō in this era was incapable of generating a new framework for labor relations with regard either to the character of the central organization or to the institutional forms of the Sanpō units. Yet, in this same period, an active search for a new form of labor relations was already underway, at Nihon Steel's Yawata Works.[14] The central actors were certain Personnel Department officials who were favorably disposed towards "totalism" (*zentaishugi*). They struggled to reconcile the propagation and practice of an ideology of "complete fusion of capital and labor," with the objective of "making sure that decisions on the treatment of workers reflect the general will of employees at all levels." Their answer was a complete system of consultation at the workshop level that would "determine the fate of Sanpō." Specifically, this function was to be assumed by workshop sections chaired by assistant managers (*kakarichō*). The resultant consultation system would provide a framework for "face to face" (*hiza to hiza wo tsukiawasete*) consultation on a variety of issues, beginning with the improvement of conditions in the workplace, and would also establish various subgroups (for example, the Safety and Hygiene Group) whose membership would include white-collar as well as blue-collar employees. The idea of "face to face" consultation is consistent with the logic of reducing labor relations to the homogeneous level of personal relations, but the objective at the Yawata Works was rather to destroy the empty shell of the existing consultation system and activate a new one capable of channeling workers' labor toward state goals.

Of course, at the stage the Yawata Works had reached in April 1939, the practice of "labor-capital fusion" at the workshop level and the adjustment of disagreements over compensation at higher levels were still pervaded by ambiguity. Yet, consultation systems were commonly malfunctioning throughout virtually all Sanpō units,[15] and it cannot be said that the Sanpō Federation's guidelines had solved the problem of how to unite the "guiding spirit" with an appropriate organizational form. In this respect, Yawata Steel Works' problems were common to other Sanpō units as well. The need for a thorough reorganization of Sanpō was not simply in the minds of bureaucrats, but was also evident in the realm of practice.

THE TURNABOUT IN SANPŌ POLICY: SANPŌ AND TOTAL WAR
Origins of Reorganization

Three conditions underlay the early rise of the Sanpō movement in the form of half-private, half-public organizations. First, no one imagined that the war between Japan and China that began in 1937 would be a lengthy one; second, labor disputes were rare; and third, the economic changes brought by the war, particularly in the labor market, had stopped at an early stage. Ironically, soon after Sanpō was formed, these conditions began to erode. First, by 1938, it began to seem that the war in China would be a longer one. This was especially apparent after the limits of Japanese mobilization were reached during the Guanzhou and Wuhan offensives in October. Therefore, Sanpō's initial concern to establish a "postwar" arrangement was soon supplanted by the search for a system of labor relations that could meet the needs of a protracted, total-war. Moreover, in 1939 and the first half of 1940, labor disputes began to increase. These were not merely peripheral disturbances, but arose in important factories such as the Kawasaki Shipyards, and the Fuji Nagata Shipyards. Moreover, because many disputes arose in factories filled with inexperienced workers, and because these disputes threatened the Japanese military position, none of the parties involved could dismiss them as passing or temporary phenomena. The increase in labor disputes in this period resulted directly from a decline in real wages and the consequent instability of workers' living conditions. The increase also revealed that the early Sanpō, which was designed as a means of preventing such disputes, was not functioning as planned. In addition, the wartime changes in the labor market that were merely nascent in 1937 were now accelerating. Even in the context of a general rise in nominal wages in this period, the increase in entrance wages was extraordinary, and the Ministry of Welfare and others took special note of the expanding gaps among wage levels as well as the dramatic increase in worker mobility. Wage controls that aimed especially at regulating starting wages were instituted in March 1939, and in April the government began direct control of labor via the Employee Hiring Control Directive (*Jugyōin Yatoiire Seigenrei*). Such measures inevitably affected labor relations. Paralleling these changes was a great influx of young workers and an increase in worker mobility, not to mention a significant outflow of older, higher-ranking workers (*yakutsuke rōdōsha*) as a result of the draft. Compared with the period around 1942, these phenomena were only in their initial stages, but in any case, the rise in worker turnover raised the question of a new order at the workplace.

Against this background, the reorganization of Sanpō began in April 1939 with the establishment in various prefectures of local Sanpō organizations headed by prefectural governors. With this move, government direction of Sanpō began.[16] This provincial Sanpō federation advanced a number of policies, but it exerted its most substantial influence by encouraging the formation of Sanpō units even among small firms. In the Tokyo area, it established the model of the "all-inclusive, employer-centered standing discussion group (*kondankai*)." The reorganization had the effect of increasing the nationwide number of Sanpō units tenfold.[17] Nevertheless, in terms of organizational form, it relied on the old model of the Sanpō consultation system, and in this respect, it still remained within the bounds of the bureaucrats' designs in the early period of Sanpō. Drastic change would come only after the Cabinet issued the "Guidelines for Establishing a New Order for Labor" (*Kinrō Shintaisei Kakuritsu Yōkō*).

The Ideology of Dedicated Labor

The "Guidelines" provided the first indication of the kind of ideology and institutions that would form the basis for a reorganization of Sanpō at the government's initiative, and this document had great impact on the various actors concerned with labor relations by virtue of its newness alone. As the very name (*Kinrō Shintaisei Kakuritsu Yōkō*) of the provision suggested, a new ideological focal point was to be "dedicated labor" (*kinrō*). Moreover, this new ideology was not just for the edification of employees, but applied to employers as well. That is, blue and white collar workers and employers, too, could become true members of the Japanese nation (*kokumin*) only as "workers" (*kinrōsha*) serving the state by means of their dedicated labor, and in that sense they were all equal. Moreover, these dedicated workers were not to be understood as employees divided among various individual firms. Sanpō now took on new significance as a "movement uniting all workers," which transcended the existing framework of firms and organizations. Note that the "work ideology" should not simply be conflated with the program of expanding the productive forces. "Work" in the sense of "*kinrō*" was honorable—that is, insofar as a person was the autonomous subject (*shutai*) of his or her work, he or she ought to be respected. This is how the older ideology of recognizing the workers' "humanity," the demand for which had played such an important role in labor relations after World War I, was refashioned in the era of the reorganized Sanpō.[18]

The real significance of the new work ideology lay in its premise that the worker is actively and purposefully engaged. As a lofty pursuit that "expresses one's full personality" and has public significance as service to the state, "work" could not, of course, be considered drudgery, but was rather to be understood as "creative" and "spontaneous." Inasmuch as the worker was "recognized as a human being" by the state on account of his subjective identity, he or she was also situated in relation to the productive process as an active subject who exercised "creativity" and "autonomy." And what activated this mechanism of recognition was to be the "work organization" (*kinrō soshiki*). The "Guidelines" did not spell out the precise nature of this organization, but did specify that "as a cooperative unit it will promote the highest level of productivity." If we refer to what is also called the "work organization" in the proposal made by the Planning Commission at about the same time, we find that it envisioned the establishment at various levels of "Production Cooperation Councils" (*Seisan Kyōryoku Kaigi*), which would facilitate discussions of daily workplace issues.[19]

These work organizations were not intended to function as surrogate labor unions but rather were conceived as a means of transcending and overcoming unions. Moreover, as organizations rooted in the production process, they were complementary to the new work ideology. This meant that the mismatch between organizational forms and bureaucratic visions of "guiding spirit" that had plagued Sanpō's early period was now to be dissolved. Of course, the consultation system, which had previously been emphasized as a means of harmonizing the interests of workers and employers, was not clearly defined in the "Guidelines," and at the operational level it was often situated in a supplementary role.

However, the work ideology was logically connected to a specific view of the wage system. When "work" was understood in the above sense, it could not be motivated by a desire for wages as compensation and, accordingly, could not be assimilated to a system in which wages were believed to be a powerful stimulus to efficiency. Insofar as the worker's "honor" was worthy of respect, it became necessary to see that his or her livelihood was stabilized. This gave rise to the notion of a stipend that would provide for the workers' livelihood, aside from all considerations of labor supply. Of course, this development was also related to the nature of the work organization. Such organizations were fundamentally connected to the process of production, and were much less concerned with mediating conflicts over conditions of employment. Issues related to such conditions were settled with reference to a standard that was relatively independent of the adjustment of interests between capital and labor, and came increasingly to rely on the principle of a "living wage" settled on the basis of workers' living expenses. What undergirded this "living wage," or need-based, principle was the logic that stabilization of the worker's livelihood made possible his daily work and thus also constituted recognition of the worker's humanity. In juxtaposition to the ideological dimension in which the worker was recognized as an active subject in the productive process, this logic situated him or her as an entity whose service to the state had to be maintained via a stable livelihood.[20]

The work ideology was certainly innovative in comparison with previous ideologies of labor relations. However, in bureaucratic circles at the time it was considered indispensable for the purpose of forming a new pattern of labor relations. In light of the Japanese experience in the 1920s, when a variety of labor union surrogates had been introduced, it was clear that coercive measures alone would be inadequate means of avoiding labor disputes and gaining the cooperation of workers in the total-war effort. There had to be some mechanism capable of generating spontaneous cooperation among workers, and it had to go beyond earlier conceptions of labor union substitutes and interest mediation. In this respect, Japan was not at all exceptional. One could say that in the countries that had adopted industrial democracy, this alternative was found by giving labor unions their say, while in those that rejected industrial democracy, labor had to be invested with quasi-public significance. However, it should be recognized that in the Japanese case the latter alternative was adopted under the rubric of "recognizing the workers' humanity," just as it had been after World War I. That is, in analyzing the elaboration of the "work ideology" in the form of an institutional structure we ought not ignore the elements that were peculiar to Japan.

The Greater Japan Industrial Patriotic Association

Central Organization. In November 1940, the reorganized Sanpō was established as the Dai-Nippon Sangyō Hōkokukai (Greater Japan Industrial Patriotic Association). This new organization differed from the earlier Industrial Patriotic Federation (Sanpō Renmei) in many respects. First, the Greater

Japan Sanpō was a national organization under the presidency of the Minister of Welfare. It encompassed all the existing Sanpō units and took the provincial federations as its branch organizations. It was still a loose federation of allied groups but, unlike the Federation, which had been an essentially private organization, it was clearly designed to give the central headquarters comprehensive powers. Second, included in its list of functions was a "clause concerning cooperation in the control of labor." As I noted above, by this time direct state control of labor had already begun, but the Labor Management Department of the Greater Japan Sanpō central headquarters was to be involved in mediating occupational changes and studying the allocation of labor resources.

Whereas discussions leading up to the Sanpō Federation had attempted to form a consensus among the organizations representing the various actors related to labor relations, this was not at all the case with the post-reorganization Sanpō. On the question of labor unions, by July 1946 the dissolution of the Sōdōmei (mainstream faction) had become inevitable. The work ideology had considerably narrowed the grounds on which it was possible to argue that labor unions retained their raison d'etre as adjuncts of state policy. For their part, employer organizations criticized the centralized Sanpō for aiming to become a "totalistic organ of labor control" (*zentaishugiteki kinrō tōkatsu soshiki*), but their revisionist views were not at all reflected in the final form of the reorganized Sanpō.[21] Zensanren (the employers' federation) was disbanded in May 1942.

Military-Type Organizations and Five-Person Groups. According to the document, "Concerning the Establishment of Industrial Patriotic Association Organizations in Factories and Enterprises" (Ministry of Health and Welfare, Home Ministry), the "work organization" was actualized in August 1941 in the forms of military-type organizations and the five-person groups. That this took so long after the initial establishment of the Greater Japan Sanpō shows the difficulty that was experienced in bringing these entities to fruition. At about the same time, the "Outline of an Emergency Labor Policy" (*Rōmu Kinkyū Taisaku Yōkō*) was enacted and a full-scale policy of reallocating labor power was put into effect. These factors should be kept in mind as a basis for the following discussion.

The new, military-type structure corresponded to workplace divisions, with the "battalion" (*daitai*) at the department level, the "company" (*chūtai*) at the section level, and the "platoon" (*shōtai*) at the office level; the five-person group was at the most basic level of all. Supplementing this military-style hierarchy were the previously emphasized consultation groups (*kondankai*). It is worth noting that although the military-type structure mirrored the existing workplace hierarchy, it was not identical with it. And indeed, precisely because they were different, it became necessary to face the question of their respective jurisdictions. Greater Japan Sanpō's central office formally delineated those jurisdictions, and among the responsibilities of the Sanpō unit it mentions "functioning as the central organ for administering labor" (*kinrō kanri no chūyō kikan to shite no jigyō*), which included "overall direction of labor administration" (*kinrō kanri no sōkatsu*). Although the facts are unclear, we are led to wonder if this did not result in a dual structure within the enterprise between the administrative structure of the "work" section and the military-type organization of the Sanpō unit. If so, managerial authority must have been in question. Indeed, in some cases the boundaries among elements became confused, making structural reform unavoidable.[22] Later on, there were criticisms to the effect that the existence of the Sanpō unit alongside the administrative structure led to inefficiency, and this also suggests a dual structure.

Although the military-type structure had a certain degree of independence from the workplace hierarchy, it was expected to provide more complete control over the workers, and in this sense it directly reflected the policy goals of the "Outline of an Emergency Labor Policy." In contrast, the five-person groups[23] were expressly designed as organizations that would "activate autonomous labor power." It is important to note that, organizationally, the five-person group did not correspond to any equivalent level in the workplace hierarchy. The groups included from five to ten workers of the same shop, and because their leaders were supposed to be chosen without regard to status in the workplace hierarchy, they did not automatically have authority over the other members of the group in the context of the daily work schedule. Their actual functions were subsequently decided among all members of the five-person group in the course of regular meetings (*kumijokai*). In concrete terms, it was hoped that these groups would stimulate workers to spontaneously improve workplace operations, in the sense of repositioning tools and machinery, etc. It was also expected that the groups could meet at any place and any time—in a corner of the workshop, if necessary. These expectations marked a conscious departure from the earlier consultation system, which had been rather distant from issues that arose on the shop floor.

As I have suggested, the ideology of "recognition as a human being" that had developed in Japan after World War I was manifested via two major elements: a tendency to try to reduce labor relations to personal relations between individuals presumed to be equals, and a tendency to link labor relations to the goals of the state. The five-person group, with its regular meetings, was conceived as a site where workers could informally discuss job arrangements in a familiar environment and consult when necessary on the basis of intimate, personal relations (*aidagara*), thus effectively carrying out their service to the state. Clearly, this conception relied substantially on the Japanese ideology of discipline in labor relations, and was the product of a reinterpretation of that ideology that sought to elicit active participation from workers. As noted above, at the Yawata Steel Works there was an attempt to "merge labor and capital" by exhausting the potential of consultation groups; and, indeed, it is possible to see the five-person groups as an extension and further deepening of that reformist effort.

Wage Controls and Family Stipends. The close connection between the principle of a need-based wage and the "work ideology" was clarified in the Wage Control Order (*Chingin Tōseirei*) of 1940, which announced the need for limits on the incentive pay and steeply-graduated overtime increments that had been intended to stimulate greater productivity. In its study of wages in the previous year, the Ministry of Welfare had correlated the high proportion of piecework wages with the equally high level of absenteeism, and argued on that basis for a need-based wage that would stabilize workers' livelihood. Moreover, although this was for the coal mining industry alone, in October 1942 the Ministry of Welfare recommended a basic wage whose clear intent would be to "guarantee a stable livelihood for workers of a certain age and thus secure more continuity in labor."[24]

However, the need-based wage was actually instituted in the form of the family allowance. In terms of policy, family allowances were in the process of losing their temporary and limited nature. The Wage Freeze Directive of September 1939 had outlawed changes in or establishment of family allowances, but this prohibition had gradually loosened to the point where after 1940, and especially by 1942, a broad expansion was planned with respect to the objects of payment, definition of dependents, and amount of allowance. In actual fact, in "industrial" and "transportation" companies with more than 1000 employees, almost 100% of the workers were receiving such allowances by July 1942. It is estimated that the level of allowances as a percentage of total wages rose to about 10% for adult male workers.[25] In the past, the family allowance had been a substitute for a minimum wage, and was considered by some to express the "merciful and benevolent character" of Japan's labor policy. What I would like to emphasize here is that the full development and spread of the family allowance occurred in parallel with the reorganization of Sanpō. Accordingly, in this period such allowances cannot be attributed entirely to the arbitrary whim of managers. In fact, managers were prohibited from manipulating wages in accord with their perception of worker diligence.

Then, in September 1941, policies dictated that any wage increases should be minor, and should include the establishment of a standard wage, along with maximums and minimums. Previously, most wage increases had been issued as "about xx *sen*," and therefore left considerable room for arbitrariness on the part of management. The 1941 policy put a stop to that. The above measures, which moved in the direction of a need-based wage, presumed a "recognition of humanity" and conformed to the aims of the state. They also provided the occasion for the state gradually to make clear its view regarding what constituted a fair wage. Put simply, this came to be a wage that provided stability in income and did not produce large differentials between high and low. This standard had an unmistakable effect on workers.

REORGANIZED SANPŌ
Problematical Situation in the Workplace

The period of late-1941 to 1942 was crucial for both the ideology and structure of the reorganized Sanpō. However, during this same period, conditions on the shop floor began to depart from the situation of 1940, when Sanpō was reorganized. The problems of 1941-2 were a widespread labor shortage, a great influx of unskilled workers in the form of new labor conscripts, rising absenteeism, and declining will to work. In contrast to the period when a certain level of productivity was taken for granted and the main problems were worker cooperation with the war effort and the need to smooth out the labor mobilization process, now the maintenance of productivity itself was called into question.

The 1942 plans for national mobilization clearly indicate that the sources of labor power were drying up. It was extremely difficult in any case to respond to the demand for industrial labor power while also guaranteeing that sufficient labor was left in agriculture to maintain the food supply, and heightened military mobilization only exacerbated this difficulty. The policy adopted at the time attempted to make up for declining numbers through a program of increasing efficiency, but this was frustrated by rising absenteeism. One survey showed that absenteeism had been about 10 per cent in 1940, but by 1942 it ranged from 12 per cent to highs of 30 per cent. That the Ministry of Welfare considered even the 10 percent figure to be too high shows the seriousness of the situation.[26] It is speculated that the main cause was the increase in conscripted labor and, in fact, not only did the labor conscripts' influx coincide with the increase in absenteeism but, indeed, their own absentee rate was found to be unusually high. Furthermore, a study conducted by the Osaka metropolitan government found that the inflow of conscripts created an atmosphere that led other workers to think that job changes were now a simple matter. There is also some evidence that many absentees were skipping work to earn supplemental income as day laborers. Moreover, among managers the labor conscripts were notorious for their lack of enthusiasm. They were not only conscious of receiving worse treatment since their conscription, but were often ill-suited to the jobs they were given. In the Tokyo metropolitan area, the most common previous experience for conscript workers was commodity retailing; the conscripts had also gotten steadily older, so that by 1943 their average age was 35.[27]

The "Work Organization" and the Workers' Response

How did such changes in the workplace affect the establishment of the five-person groups and the military-type units? According to the results of a survey in November 1941, the average worker expected from Sanpō such things as "a steady supply of goods" and "establishment of welfare facilities."[28] Of course, one must take into account that the poll was taken only three months after the announcement of the government's plans for the establishment of the groups, but the above responses, along with "renovate operation of the consultation groups," suggest that workers' expectations concerning the reforms were very low. We can surmise that from the workers' standpoint, the existing Sanpō functioned neither as a site where workers could unreservedly discuss the problems of the workplace nor as a means of activating worker's "spontaneity" (*jihatsusei*) and "creativity" (*sōisei*) through "work" (*kinrō*). There was also little hope that it would do so in the future. Moreover, in the 81st Imperial Diet of February, 1943, one politician charged that "workers misunderstand Sanpō as an organization that suppresses their spontaneous will;" others contended that in the Sanpō units "they just listen to the sermons of the boss," and that Sanpō organizations outside the enterprise were all "under the control of the police."[29]

I have noted above that managerial authority was a central problem in the effort to operationalize the "work organization." If the military-type units and the five-person groups were to function as planned, managerial authority had to be limited. Naturally, management resisted such moves, and the question arose as to whether it would be possible to find a modus vivendi by which managers could consent to the new situation and workers could also agree to participate.[30] However, if one considers the actual situation in this era in terms of the marked class difference between employers and employees, their keen awareness of this difference, and the pervasive power differential, it becomes clear that any hopes for such a compromise were unrealistic. It was impossible to alter the framework in terms of which the actual Sanpō units were considered by the workers to be oppressive organizations. The proposal, advanced by Nishio Suehiro in the 81st Diet, for a "Committee on Countermeasures for an Urgent Expansion of Productivity," which would investigate daily levels of productive efficiency and identify causes when they were low, was in tune with the rationale for the military-type organizations and the five-person groups. However, an organization that could function in this manner in accord with the will of the workers did not appear until the postwar period.

The five-person groups were proposed because of a new fluidity that eroded the workplace order and thereby made it possible for them to be conceived as independent from existing workplace hierarchies. On the other hand, the groups depended on existing forms of organization at the workplace, and in that sense, were weakened by that very fluidity. For example, the document that provided for the five-person groups stipulates that group members should be familiar with each others' personalities and be able to consult with each other on family matters. It also says that the group leader ought to be a respected, older worker. These ideas were taken from the patterns typical of traditional workplace organization, but at that very moment the great influx of labor conscripts and increasing worker turnover were making such patterns anachronistic. Moreover, in this period the proportion of veteran workers (*yakutsuke*) was decreasing, and the inability of younger leaders to direct older labor conscripts was becoming obvious.[31] Such were the obstacles standing in the way of proper functioning on the part of the "work organization."

In spite of all this, even for workers who expected little from it, Sanpō was not totally meaningless. We can surmise that a number of workers supported the "work ideology" of reorganized Sanpō once they reinterpreted it in their own way. As evidence for this, we can cite the occurrence even in 1942 of labor disputes in which workers appropriated this ideology as a basis for legitimating their demands. For example, at the Kawasaki Heavy Industries Sheet Metal Factory or Nikkō Electric's Copper Works, workers supported their demand for a pay increase by pointing to the need for stability in living conditions in order to guarantee the productive efficiency that the state required. At the Hitachi Kameido factory, workers included in their demands not only a wage increase but the elimination of inequality in pay hikes and bonuses.[32] Arguably, the Kawasaki Heavy Industries and Nikkō workers formulated their demands according to the logic of wage-determination based on social need, while those at Hitachi cited the work ideology's standard of fairness. As noted above, in September 1941, government policy sought to limit pay increases that had produced large disparities in wages and left considerable latitude for arbitrariness on the part of assessors. In fact, pay raises leading to wide income disparities were inconsistent with the work ideology from the standpoint not only of its standards of income stability but of the quasi-official character it gave to work. Thus, one can assume that workers' demands for the elimination of inequality were based on these criteria as set forth in the work ideology.

In the same period, a headquarters official of Greater Japan Sanpō noted that employers, despite their outward support for national goals, actually tagged as extremists any workers who devoted themselves to national goals, and that in response such workers became despondent.[33] He further points out that because venting their anger had no effect, workers were beset by feelings of powerlessness, and this in turn led to high rates of absenteeism and a drop in efficiency. Of course, we should keep in mind that these are the impressions of an official charged with promoting Sanpō, but in combination with the above-mentioned disputes and the repeated criticism from Sanpō headquarters of uncooperative attitudes on the part of enterprise managers, we can surmise that the work ideology was becoming an influential standard for workers' conceptions of fairness, and that the gap between that standard and their treatment at the hands of employers led to widespread despondency.

Meanwhile, the idea of a need-based wage that also formed a part of the work ideology was gradually spreading throughout society as a principle that no major actor could easily contest. I have already mentioned that process in conjunction with the family allowance as it emerged around 1942, but towards the end of 1943, the regional Work (*kinrō*) Councils, which included many members with connections to the old Regional Industrial Federation and personnel office workers, endorsed "without hesitation" (*kōko no ureinaku*) "a wage system based on living costs" as the system that would best "promote work."[34] Moreover, the "Application for Change in Wage System" that Toshiba Electric submitted to the Minister of Munitions in April 1945 proposed a base wage that was graduated according to age, and supplemented with increments based on seniority. Yet, in this case the age-based wage would constitute eighty per cent of the total. In addition, with respect to wage increases, the proposal not only specified maximums and minimums along with a standard wage, but was to be applied to all workers with only very few exceptions. We can already see emerging here the notion of "all within a narrow range" that would spread widely in the postwar era as the guiding principle for wage increases. 1944-45 also brought the tendency to lump white collar and blue collar workers together, and this was undeniably the result of the common identity, attributed to them during the war, of workers dedicating their labor to the state (*kinrōsha*). For example, according to the "Research Report regarding the Reconfiguration of Workplace Organizations" (January, 1944), which was produced by people connected with Japan Steel Tube Corporation, "Heretofore, we have been dominated by a conceptual distinction in regard to status that honors administrative employees and disparages workers," but now "such concepts should be struck down, and distinctions should be based solely on function."

Of course, we should keep in mind that what brought such moves to the fore was the unprecedented fluidity in the workplace. It can also be said that conscription exposed the illogic of the existing distinction between white and blue collar workers by creating a situation in which technical secondary school graduates became blue collar laborers while elementary school graduates had become administrators. The work ideology and unprecedented fluidity in the workplace promoted the kind of equality that extended even to fundamental questions of status and qualification. This tendency did not spread widely throughout society until well into the postwar period, but it was clearly different from the post-World War I form of equality, defined merely as common membership in the employee's organization.

Sanpō in Crisis

By late-1943, labor policy had to confront the new situation precipitated by establishment of the Munitions Ministry, whose mission was to expand air power and promote the unification of military production. With this development, Sanpō lost some of its jurisdiction, and even the Ministry of Welfare, which had directed Sanpō, lost a great deal of its autonomy in dealing with labor policy. The duties of military procurement officials under the new ministry included many of the functions originally intended to be performed by the Sanpō units. Under this new arrangement, Sanpō was left with the responsibility of "insuring the supply and smooth distribution of goods and uplifting patriotic spirit."[35]

Not only was Sanpō's operational jurisdiction reduced, but it began to be said in workplaces that Sanpō was an obstacle to productive efficiency. Indeed, critics charged that "any entity extrinsic to the workplace system is an impediment," and the five-person groups were also said to "interfere with the organic functioning" of the workshop as a whole. Even within the government, consideration was being given to policies that would involve rejection of the work ideology. Some began to argue that uniformity in the wage system would not increase production and that therefore a system of strong incentives for efficiency should be adopted. In fact, although it was limited to a few industries, a wage structure was beginning to take form that would recognize temporary supplemental wages designed to spur production.[36]

Nevertheless, these new moves were not capable of providing an alternative to a labor policy centered on the reorganized Sanpō. This was because the conditions for establishment of a system of large-volume production did not exist in Japan at the time. It is often pointed out that Japan lagged in standardization of both products and the productive process, and, above all, suffered a serious shortage of specialized machine tools. Subjective conditions were inadequate as well, in the sense that the training of technicians who could manage production was in its early stages, and as a result of the military draft and difficulties in the training system there was an inadequate supply of "lead workers" who would be able to direct workshop activities, then and in the future.[37] Moreover, the move toward a different arrangement at the workplace was not considered in relation to the sort of labor relations most suitable to it. On the other hand, the policies of the reorganized Sanpō had run into insurmountable barriers at the level of implementation. Even Sanpō's policy leaders had difficulty explaining what Sanpō had to offer beyond just being a conscious-raising movement or an organization for supplying materiel. Such were the confusions and contradictions in the realm of labor relations that beset the government on the eve of defeat.

However, even in this situation, guidelines concerning labor relations produced jointly by the Munitions Ministry and the Ministry of Welfare argued for a wage system that included a stipend based on a worker's age and family. Thus, even if not recognized in pure form, the principle of a need-based wage was not rejected even at the policy level. Moreover, since the guidelines specified that "workplace hierarchies" (shokkaisei) were for the purpose of clarifying the chain of command, one can interpret them as having narrowed the purview of the five-person groups and their standing committees. On the other hand, in so far as they specified equal status based on the common "job classification" method for both blue and white collar workers, one may also interpret such moves as tending toward elimination of the distinctions between ranks. Thus, this tendency dovetailed with efforts at the workplace, as mentioned above.

CONCLUSION: TOWARD THE POSTWAR

The policies of the reorganized Sanpō and its work ideology were not simply the unrealistic plans of a few bureaucrats. They were put forward in answer to both the accumulation of policies toward labor unions and the responses to those policies at the workplace in the wake of World War I, and also to the unavoidable question of how to achieve the spontaneous cooperation of workers under the total-war system that emerged on the basis of that earlier accumulation. Moreover, the workers who chimed in with the work ideology were not merely overcome by temporary enthusiasm. They supported it because it was premised on essential elements of the ideology that governed labor relations in Japan, and because it did result in a system that, although inadequate, did give some credence to the principle of the need-based wage.[38] Although the work ideology found a certain level of support among workers, it could be only partially realized institutionally. One can only suppose that this gap between goals and achievements provided significant motivating energy for the postwar labor movement. It is also reasonable to suppose that this energy was intensified by the experience of having been granted the status of an active subject serving the state.

It is impossible to explain adequately the various events in the period called the "postwar crisis" without taking into account the experiences of the parties involved in the wartime Sanpō. Japan's newly-legalized labor unions were able to establish themselves as economic subjects without going through an ideological baptism as "free bargaining agents." Moreover, it is worthy of special emphasis that the demand for a need-based wage, known as the "Densan wage," that became the symbol of the postwar labor movement was not perceived as a legitimate end in itself but was legitimized as a necessary means of promoting Japan's economic reconstruction. It is not difficult to recognize continuity here with the work ideology of wartime that positioned workers as subjects actively contributing to the state and defined the stabilization of their lives as means to that end. Moreover, the movement in favor of the "democratization of management" that emerged in this period was oriented toward the abolition of discrimination between white and blue collar workers. In this case, as well, the basis for legitimacy was the logic that all workers were active subjects in the process of economic reconstruction, and that as Japanese nationals (*kokumin*) in that sense, they should be considered equal. In the immediate postwar period, both the government and enterprise managers suffered a significant loss of control over the productive process, while labor unions, as organizations of solidarity among all "workers" (*kinrōsha*), both blue and white collar, gained considerable initiative. And it is quite reasonable to interpret that behavior pattern as having been powerfully conditioned by the latent image of the organization formed during the war, which included all three levels of workers, managers, and the state.

Postwar activism on the part of labor was to lead as far as the production control movements, but eventually compromised with a co-opted system of industrial democracy. However, even in the "relations surrounding labor" that followed that compromise, it is possible to cite elements that are best explained with reference to the experiences of the various actors during the war. The principle of a need-based wage provides one such example. Although the extreme, Densan form of the need-based wage was rejected, most observers agree that the need-based wage remained a powerful element of the Japanese wage system. It is not simply a matter of wages being closely linked to workers' age; clearly the principle of "everyone in a narrower range" was operating even in the system of regular pay hikes. I do not deny that measures to assess and stimulate efficiency played a significant role with respect to competition among workers, but they were always premised on an underlying principle of equality manifested in the guarantee of minimum living standards and stability. It is worth repeating that during the war fairness was sought, not in detailed comparison among jobs, but rather in wage raises of a sort that would lead to stability and not create large gaps between low and high levels.

Second, let's look at the post-World War II manner of deciding on the level of wage raises through the mechanism of annual *shuntō* (Spring offensive). In concrete terms, this mechanism provides a way for labor unions to legitimize their compromises by appealing to the principle of conformity with the national economy. This tendency is evident not only in the "managed *shuntō*" (*kanri shuntō*) of the post-1970 period, but even in the mid-1960s, when the "Spring offensive" system was in full stride. The behavior pattern of legitimizing demands according to the logic of conforming and contributing to the national economy (rather than engaging in thorough confrontation to the end based on one's own particular interests) can be interpreted as the reproduction under new conditions of the wartime logic of receiving a guarantee of stability as quid pro quo for contribution to the state.

Third, there is the question of worker participation in the workplace, and here careful scrutiny and analysis are essential. Nevertheless, if one accepts that the products of Japanese industry are of high quality, it is difficult to account for this without allowing for the existence of some sort of active involvement on the part of workers, informal accommodation of views between workers and managers on the shop floor, and, based on these, assiduous efforts by workers to maintain quality. Efforts to clarify the origins, functional conditions, and limitations of this kind of commitment to the productive process are also important as means of preventing mystifications of Japanese behavior. Such clarification would be advanced by further comparison of current organizations on the shop floor with the five-person groups and their standing committees that failed, even though they formed the nucleus of the Sanpō units.[39] In addition, in the realms of both practice and ideology, Japanese workers became all the more sensitive to those differences that remained as a result of having experienced the wartime narrowing of differences between blue and white collar workers. It is therefore possible to analyze the postwar Japanese employment system from the perspective of how it has dealt with difference between blue and white collar workers.

Translated by Guy Yasko

Notes

[1] On this subject see, for example, Nelson Lichtenstein and Howell Harris eds., *Industrial Democracy in America* (London: Cambridge University Press, 1993). For recent inquiry in the Japanese context, see Kawamura Tetsuji, *Pakkusu Amerikana no keisei* (Tokyo: Tōgō Keizai Shinpōsha, 1995).

[2] For example, see Joel Rogers and Wolfgang Streeck, "Workplace Representation Overseas: The Works Councils Story," in Reichard Freeman ed., *Working under Different Rules* (New York: Russel Sage Foundation, 1994).

[3] Ōkōchi Kazuo, "Sangyō Hōkokukai no mae to ato," in Chō Yukio et al., ed. *Kindai Nihon keizai shisōshi*; also in *Ōkōchi Kazuo-shū*, vol. 3.

[4] For a description and evaluation of the post-World War I industrial relations consultation system, see Saguchi, *Nihon in okeru sangyō minshushugi no zentei* (Tokyo: Tokyo Daigaku Shuppankai, 1991).

[5] As the foundation of this tendency, it is necessary to understand the formative process of the managerial and working classes. My *Nihon ni okeru sangyō minshushugi no zentei* includes some preliminary investigations in this area.

[6] *Kyōchō* (the organ of the Kyōchōkai), no. 13, June 1938.

[7] On the designs of the bureaucrats, see the reports of the deputy ministers of the Ministry of Welfare and the Home Ministry, entitled "Rōshi kankei chōsei hōsaku yōryō," August 1938; Ministry of Welfare, Labor Bureau, "Rōshi kankei chōsei hōsaku yōryōan," June 1938; Current Policy Committee, 2nd Sub-Committee, "Sangyōjin no kokoroe, jigyōshu no kokoroe, jugyōin no kokoroe," 1938.

[8] On the employers' plan, see the Kantō Sanren's "Sangyō Hōkokukai kiyaku sankōrei," August 1938; Kansai Sanren "Kantō Sanren Sangyō Heiwa I'inkai, Sangyō Hokokukai kiyaku sankōrei ni taisuru senmon iinkai no iken," 1938.

[9] Sangyō Hōkokukai Renmei Rijikai, "Sangyō Hōkokukai kiyaku rei, kiyaku sakuseijō no chūi jikō," September 1938.

[10] Nihon Rōdō Sōdōmei, "Sōritsu 28-nendo taikai narabi ni gian," November 1939. Between November 1938 and August 1939, there were 37 companies where Sōdōmei affiliated labor unions and Sanpō branches existed side by side.

[11] Zensanren, "Sanren panfuretto 13, Nihon sangyō seishin to Sangyō Hōkokukai Undō," December 1938.

[12] Sangyō Hōkokukai Renmei, "Sangyō Hōkokukai ni okeru kondankai no un'ei, sono ichi," July 1939.

[13] See Mitsubishi Jūkō, "Shashi shiryō."

[14] Nihon Seitetsu Sangyō Hōkokukai, "Shōwa 13 nen nikki bassui (Sanpō kankei bun); Nihon Seitetsu, "(Sangyō Hōkokukai ni tsuite no) Setsumei," 1939.

[15] About 10 percent of the organizations adhered to the Sanpō standard of at least one meeting a month, and less than 5 percent held elections in which workers chose their representatives from among themselves. These figures come from Sangyō Hōkokukai Renmei, "Sangyō Hōkokukai no soshiki katsudō jōkyo," September 1940.

¹⁶ By the time of the formation of the Sanpō Federation, there were already debates within the bureaucracy about a central organization with branches in each of the prefectures. On the basis of such details, we can assume that the reorganization of Sanpō began as early as 1939.

¹⁷ Tokyo Chihō Sangyō Hōkokukai Renmeikai, "Sangyō Hōkokukai Undō gaiyō," September 1940.

¹⁸ On this topic, in addition to "Kinrō shintaisei kakuritsu yōkō," see also Minami Iwao's *Nihon kinrō kanri ron* (Tokyo: Yagumo Shoten, 1944); and Kikakuin "Kinrō Hōkokukai kōsō," 1940.

¹⁹ Kikakuin, "Chūō kikō soshikizu B an," 1940.

²⁰ On the theoretical groundings of a socially determined wage, see Ōnishi Seiji and Takimoto Tadao, *Chingin seido* (Tōyō Shokan, 1944).

²¹ Sangyō Hōkokukai Undō Kyōka I'inkai, "Sangyō Hōkokukai Undō ni kansuru iken," November 1940.

²² On the question of the allocation of tasks between the two, see Dai Nippon Sangyō Hōkokukai, "Sangyō Hōkokukai to jigyōba ni oite okonaubeki jikō no han'i," 1942. For the confusion that this issue generated, see the case of Nippon Hassōden discussed in Dai Nippon Hōkokukai's *Sanpō*, October 1942.

²³ On the content of the five person work units, see Dai Nippon Hōkokukai, "Goningumi setchi yōryō," 1941 and Nakamura Megumi, *Shokuba no jōkai*, 1941.

²⁴ *Rōdō jihō*, October 1940.

²⁵ *Rōdō jihō*, March 1943.

²⁶ *Rōdō jihō*, February 1942; Naimushō Keihōkyoku, "Shōwa 17 nen ni kansuru shakai undō no gaikyō."

²⁷ Osaka-fu, "Akushitsu chōyō kōin shiō torishimari ni kansuru ken," November 1942; Keishichō Kinrōbu, "Kinrō gyōsei gaikyō," July 1944.

²⁸ Dai Nippon Hōkokukai Chūō Honbu, "Sangyō Hōkoku Undo ni kansuru kibō chōsa," November 1941.

²⁹ On this topic see *Sangyō jihō*, 6-5, May 1943.

³⁰ On the employer's opinions of the five person work units, see Dai Nippon Hōkokukai, "Sanpō un'ei ni kansuru shokanshû," April 1942.

³¹ "Rōmu kanri no jitsujō wo miru," in *Tōyō Keizai Shinpō* 2105, January 1944.

³² Naimushō Keihōkyoku, "Gaikyō."

³³ Dai Nippon Hōkokukai, "Jūdai kikyokka kinrō kikō seibi no kyūmu," November 1942.

³⁴ Dai Nippon Hōkokukai, "Kinrō konponhō seitei ni kansuru kakuchihō kinrō kyōgikai no iken," 1943.

³⁵ Gunjushō Sōdōinkyoku, "Gikai ni oite mondai to narubeki jikō."

³⁶ For example, in the steel and aluminum industries, an imperial proclamation was issued. (See *Kinrō jihō*, March 1943.)

³⁷ Of course, this process created the outlines of a system of inserting school graduates into the labor force. This new structure paved the way for the postwar

287

system of introducing (chiefly middle school) graduates to jobs through government employment agencies. On this subject see my "Nippon no naibu rōdō shijō," in Yoshikawa Hiroshi ed., *Keizai riron e no rekishiteki pāsupekutibu* (Tokyo: Tokyo Daigaku Shuppankai, 1990).

[38] Also, the unprecedented fluidity in the workplace had the effect of rendering irrational the existing hierarchy of jobs, which presumed vast differences between occupations.

[39] On the active subjectivity (in the broadest sense of the term) of Japanese workers, Takeuchi Hiroshi has made some valuable contributions from the perspective of educational sociology. See his *Nihon no meritokurashii* (Tokyo: Tokyo Daigaku Shuppankai, 1995).

The System of Total War and the Discursive Space of the Thought War

Satō Takumi

INTRODUCTION: "A CLOSED DISCURSIVE SPACE"

Historical studies of the modern Japanese media generally leave a large gap between the wartime and Occupation periods. Without any sense of incongruity they set forth such generalizations as, "the first step in the formation of postwar national consciousness was liberation from the fetters of wartime propaganda,"[1] and treat the prewar and postwar discursive spaces as if they were completely separate.

On the other hand, studies of postwar media control and censorship under the American Occupation have become popular of late, revealing interest in the formation of the postwar Japanese information system. The point of departure for such studies is Etō Jun's contention that under the Occupation "democracy" and "freedom of speech and expression" were the objects of extreme fetishism and reverence while actual discursive space was not only restricted and unfree but completely closed.[2] Etō critically examines the American Occupation's censorship system as the origin of this condition, and portrays the Occupation plan as follows. "First, Japan was to be enveloped in 'an efficient censorship net,' completely cutting its expressive space off from the outside world. Moreover, this closed space for speech was to be remade later in accord with the will of the occupying power through a 'wide ranging' censorship 'offensive.'"[3] Etō argues that, in line with this plan, the occupying army forbade the use of the term "Greater East Asian War" and systematically imbued the Japanese people with the historical perspective of "the Pacific War," while keeping the existence of the censorship apparatus a secret. Etō also concludes that censorship under the Occupation was of a completely different nature from censorship in prewar Japan. Whereas prewar censorship elicited common values by prohibiting any mention of taboos, Occupation censorship was designed to lure people into complicity through contact with those taboos.

If this view is correct, we may say that censorship under the Occupation had an extremely "modern" character in the sense that it mobilized subjectivity and autonomy as system resources.[4] If the distinguishing characteristic of modern power is to be found in the transition from violence and public discipline to regulation and concealment, then modernization in "propaganda" is not openness but the formation of a "closed discursive space" along with surveillance (invisible censorship). But does this kind of modern discursive space actually have its origin in the postwar/Occupation period? Etō states that "the visible war ended, but an invisible war, a war of annihilation against thought and culture had begun."[5] But in fact, "thought war" was the slogan loudly proclaimed throughout the period of total war in Japan. If one calls censorship under the Occupation "hidden" in contrast to the "blatant" censorship before the war—or else calls it an "offensive" policy on speech as opposed to a "defensive" speech policy—then one supposes that this supervisory power was clearly conceived under the system of wartime mobilization. Further, the key fact that the various media—the wire services, newspapers, broadcasters, publishers and so on—organized under the wartime mobilization system continued in the postwar with hardly any changes has been ignored by historical narratives which attempt to locate an actual termination or a point of departure at the end of the war.[6]

Attempts to critically problematize the "closeness" of the contemporary Japanese media system—in fact, the entire social system—cannot overlook the thought war that was conceived under the wartime mobilization system. In this essay, I will attempt to demonstrate this "continuity" through an introduction and analysis of this "envisioned thought war."

THE CABINET INFORMATION DIVISION AND THE "THOUGHT-WAR SYMPOSIUM"
Activities of the Cabinet Information Division

Various changes occurred in the wartime information system over the 13-year period that began with the National Emergency Association (*Jikyoku Dōshikai*) that was formed in the wake of the Manchurian Incident in May 1932: in September of the same year, the Information Committee (*Jōhō Iinkai*) was established outside the bureaucratic system; this was followed in 1936 by the bureaucratic Cabinet Information Committee (*Naikaku Jōhō Iinkai*) and in 1937 by the Cabinet Information Division (*Naikaku Jōhōbu*); finally, the Information Bureau (*Jōhōkyoku*), established in 1940, lasted until December 31, 1945, when it was abolished by Imperial Order 733. These changes have been seen as "a process of guaranteeing 'government by conformity' in the formative period of Japanese fascism." In addition, "if we look only at the decision-making apparatus for mass communication policy," these changes may also be seen as "the broadening and strengthening of active propaganda, and the tightening of a control network for the passive regulation of mass communication."[7] However, since studies of the history of media control have focussed on the war between Japan and the U.S. after Pearl Harbor, the period of the Information Bureau has been studied but relatively little attention has been paid to the "Cabinet Information Division" period from 1937 to 1940 (during which the total mobilization system was solidified).

The Cabinet Information Division was formed out of the Cabinet Information Committee on September 24, 1937, about two months after the outbreak of the Japan-China War and exactly one month after the adoption of provisions for the enactment of a National Spiritual Mobilization. Through this reorganization, the Division was given, in addition to its existing tasks of facilitating communication among the various related ministries and the overseeing of the "national" Dōmei News Agency, the tasks of "collecting information not available in the various ministries and agencies and disseminating information and enlightenment propaganda," thus becoming an independent propaganda institution. In addition to continuing the publication of the former Committee's *Shūhō* (Weekly Report), *Shashin shūhō* (Pictorial Weekly Report), *Tokyo gazetto* (Tokyo Gazette) and so on, it also sponsored the Thought-War Symposium, the Thought-War Exhibition, the National Emergency Research Association and the Regional Emergency Support Associations. Its staff included about 150 people, seconded from the various ministries. Corresponding with this change, the relative weight of the office increased. Twelve full-time "information officers" were employed in place of the previous "administrators" and a "councillor" system was introduced to obtain the cooperation of private media.[8]

Councillors included, from the newspapers, Ogata Taketora (Managing Director and Editor-in-Chief of the *Asahi shinbun*), Takaishi Shingorō (Managing Director and Editor-in-Chief of *Daimai* and *Tōnichi*), and Ashida Hitoshi (President of the Japan Times Ltd.); from the news services, Furuno Inosuke (Managing Director of the Dōmei News Agency); from broadcasting, Kataoka Naomichi (Managing Director and Chief of the Operations Bureau of the Broadcasting Corporation of Japan [NHK]); from publishing, Masuda Giichi (President of Jitsugyō no Nippon, Ltd. and Chairman of the Print Culture Association) and Noma Seiji (President of Kōdansha); from film and theater, Kobayashi Ichizō (President of Tōei Pictures) and Otani Takejirō (President of Shōchiku Inc.); and as someone with scholarly qualifications, Fujinuma Shōhei (Chairman of the former Information Committee). These men continued to dominate the political and media worlds after the war, with Ashida becoming Prime Minister, Ogata the Deputy Prime Minister in the fourth Yoshida cabinet, Kobayashi a minister of state and President of the National Reconstruction Board under the Shidehara cabinet, Fujinuma the Chief Secretary of the Tokyo Metropolitan Government, Takaishi a member of the Organizing Committee for the Tokyo Olympics, and Furuno a board member (*riji*) of the Kyōdō News Service.

The media system that continued into the postwar was rapidly developed during the period of the Cabinet Information Division in the name of organization and unification.[9] In film, the consolidation of the four newsreel companies was considered from the fall of 1938. On April 5, 1939 the "Film Law" was enacted and the newsreel companies were consolidated into the Japan News Film Corporation on April 15, 1940.

In broadcasting, a "National Emergency Broadcast Planning Conference" was established within NHK in July of 1937 and broadcast programming itself was moved to the Information Division. In January 1938 the "National Emergency Radio Reader" (*Rajio jikyoku tokuhon*), produced by the Information Department, went on the air and the broadcasting control system was completed when the "Regulations for Private Broadcasting, Wireless and Telephones," were expanded to include the right to give broadcasting orders when necessary.

According to an Information Division document titled "On Policy for Guiding Newspapers," dated February 13, 1940, "the key to newspaper policy is bringing newspaper operations under control," to which end they planned to strengthen the system by which the supply of paper was nationally managed. The Division also planned to extend its influence over newspaper advertisements using the Dentsū Agency, half of whose stock was owned by the Dōmei News Agency, which, in turn, was directly controlled by the Information Division. On May 23, 1940, the Information Division established the "Committee for the Control of Paper for Newspapers and Magazines," and obtained control over the distribution of paper from the [Cabinet] Planning Board which was in charge of planning the mobilization of material resources. The "Newspaper Enterprise Decree" and the "Publishing Enterprise Decree" based on the "State General Mobilization Law" were issued after the outbreak of the war with the United States, but from the fall of 1938 the Information Division directed the "independent" consolidation of small newspapers throughout the country through the Police Bureau of the Home Ministry. By the end of 1940 a "one newspaper per prefecture" system had been established in some prefectures.

In July 1940, when the second Konoe Fumimaro cabinet was formed and proclaimed the movement for a New Order, the cabinet launched a policy of fusing all the information organizations of the various ministries and agencies into a single Information Bureau. In No. 210 of the *Weekly Report*, the cabinet made the following announcement, under the title of "A New Order for Propaganda."

> At the cabinet meeting this past August 13, the government decided as follows to expand the framework of the Cabinet Information Division: "We intend to reorganize the Cabinet Information Division so as to consolidate within it the work of the Information Division of the Foreign Affairs Ministry, the Information Division of the Army Ministry, the Naval Military Dissemination Division of the Navy Ministry, and the Reference Section of the Home Ministry, thereby facilitating and unifying information and instructional propaganda." . . . This action was the first step towards a new order in government administration.[10]

In this manner, the cabinet created a "uniform central propaganda system" consisting of five departments—planning and research (first department), direction and management of newspapers, publishing, broadcasting (second department), propaganda for foreign consumption (third department), censorship (fourth department) and cultural propaganda (fifth department)—with seventeen sections and 550 staff members.

Thought War as a Concept

Several previous studies have focused on "thought war" as the key concept governing the activities of the Cabinet Information Division and the Information Bureau. However, these studies fail to distinguish between materials for mass persuasion and those related to the planning of mass propaganda.[11] In this essay, I will be dealing with the internal discussions among information officers and information councillors at the core of national policy rather than the technical arguments of technocrats in charge of propaganda and announcements for the masses.[12] Attempts to investigate this esoteric sector, as it were, that is constituted by "the envisioned thought war," are indispensable to an analysis of the Japanese discursive space since the end of the war. It is not so much a question of what was achieved but rather what was meant to be achieved, that turns out to be the important issue for the total war system of a defeated nation and its postwar legacy.

The document that originated the Thought-War Symposium is *National Defense and Thought War*, included in the National Emergency Propaganda Materials (Secret). Section 4 of this document, "Thought-War Measures We Should Take," lists five "points that need improvement." These were, first, to establish "a system for national edification through both government and private groups," and the start of "scientific research on propaganda." Second, to provide "a scientific system and a theory of propaganda for Japanism [Nipponshugi]" that will be credible to non-Japanese. Third, to "improve the people's education" so that they will not be misled by negative rumors, and correct the tendency to "worship the West." Fourth, "through appropriate institutions and management of the political economy," to achieve the major premise of the thought war which is "stability in the lives of the people." And fifth, to complete the organization of warning systems and enlighten the nation regarding foreign plots.[13] In other words, the Thought War Symposia were created as sites for debate and research into the science of propaganda and the Japanese spirit, modernizing the political, economic, and educational systems, and strengthening the powers of surveillance.

In this connection, it is necessary to examine briefly the relation to the Nazi Ministry of Propaganda which has usually served as the object of comparison in studies of the Cabinet Information Division and the Information Bureau. Of course, it was widely recognized that in World War I Germany had "won in fighting battles but lost in propaganda." But it is important to note that the Thought-War Symposium did not include concrete reports on the Nazi Ministry of Propaganda. Cabinet Information Division Chief Yokomizo Mitsuteru mentioned the Third Reich in his basic report on "Modern Propaganda States" at the first meeting, but he concluded that propaganda war was just one technical aspect of thought war.[14] It is true that Yokomizo and representatives of the Army repeatedly pointed to the "modernity" of the Third Reich, but other speakers at the Symposium openly criticized the Nazi regime for suppressing media autonomy. Nazi propaganda was appreciated for its "modernity" and "planning," but criticized for being a "revolutionary state" which was "authoritarian" in nature.[15] In light of this, it would appear that analysis of the thought war should not be carried out via a framework of comparative "fascism," but rather in relation to the impact of World War I's "total war system," of which the Nazi propaganda itself was a product.

The Thought-War Symposia

A placard displaying a calligraphic rendition of "harmony is to be valued," the four-character opening to Shōtoku Taishi's "Seventeen-Article Constitution" (circa A.D. 645), decorated the wall of the conference room of the Cabinet Information Committee as it officially became part of the bureaucracy in 1936. The placard was written by then Prime Minister Hirota Kōki at the request of Yokomizo Mitsuteru, the Secretary of the Committee at the time, and later the chief of the Cabinet Information Division.[16] This fact is symbolic for an analysis of the discourse of the "Thought-War Symposia" which were sponsored by the Cabinet Information Division and held at the Prime Minister's residence for three years from 1938. The statements of high ranking bureaucrats and officers in charge of propaganda from the army, navy, Foreign Ministry and Home Ministry, along with the media representatives from newspapers, publishers, and so on, were mutually opposed and filled with contradictions. One could say that the inconsistency here exceeded even that among the views of the Japanese intellectuals who gathered at the "Overcoming Modernity" conference two years later. However, unlike that conference, which was premised on the eventuality of publication in the magazine *Bungakkai*, the Thought-War Symposia were based on the assumption that, as was indeed the case, the transcripts of lectures would be classified "top secret" or "secret." It was in such a closed discursive space that the propaganda policies of the total war system were conceived.

The 100 or so people gathered as "propaganda leaders" (150 attended for the third series) to listen to the lectures included "appropriate high level officials from regional and central bureaucracies, treated equally" and lieutenant colonels from the army and commanders from the navy.[17] The attendees received copies of a translated collection of European and American research on propaganda, entitled *Propaganda Research Materials*,[18] as well as materials related to each lecture. The series was held for one week each year, during the middle of February. Each series began on Monday morning with an opening ceremony, worship in the direction of the Imperial Palace, visits to Meiji Shrine and Yasukuni Shrine, and a lecture by Chief Yokomizo in the afternoon. From the second day there were lectures in the morning and study groups or field trips (to broadcast stations, newspapers, wire services, the thought war exhibition hall, etc.) in the afternoon. The closing ceremony was on Saturday afternoon. Concurrent with the lecture series, an exhibit for the general population, called "The Fight Without Weapons: An Exhibit on Thought War Throughout the World," was held at the Takashimaya Department Store in Nihonbashi. The exhibition featured aggressive and gaudy displays on foreign propaganda with titles like, "Sparks over the radio waves" and "Television and the future of propaganda."[19] But a different discursive space emerged inside the Prime Minister's residence. At the lecture series, Yokomizo noted that the definition of thought war that he gave in the Catalog for the Thought-War Exhibit—"thought war is a weaponless fight to bind the enemy to our will"—was but one aspect. "This definition forcefully expresses the aggressive, offensive aspects of thought war. It does not show the passive, defensive aspects. But I believe that the intellectual defense of the nation one often hears about places heavy emphasis on this latter kind of struggle."[20] In other words, "defensive, domestic thought war" was emphasized from the start, in contrast to the "aggressive, foreign thought war" for the consumption of the masses.

The lecturers and their topics for each year were as follows (their positions at the time of the symposium, during the war and after the war, are in parentheses).

1. The first Thought-War Symposium took place between Prime Minister Konoe's January 6, 1938 announcement of his government's refusal to deal with the Chinese Nationalists (the "*aite ni sezu*" proclamation) and the February 24 proposal of "The National Total Mobilization Law" in the Diet. This was the most comprehensive series, at which twenty-two lecturers from among the committee members, information officers, councillors, scholars, and so on, of the various ministries and agencies gave talks. They were as follows:

"The State and Propaganda," Yokomizo Mitsuteru (Chief of the Information Division; after the war, Consultant to the Judicial System and Research Department of the Minister's Secretariat at the Ministry of Justice).

"The Japanese Spirit and Thought War," Fujisawa Chikao (Part-time commissioner at the Information Division and Professor at the Greater Asia Culture Institute, Daitō Bunka Gakuin).

"The Current Situation in the International Thought War," Andō Yoshirō (Chief of Third Section of the Research and Planning Department of the Foreign Ministry; after the war, House of Representatives Diet member and President of Takushoku University).

"The China Incident and the International Situation," Yano Seiki (Information Division Committee Member and Chief of the Third Section of the Information Division of the Foreign Ministry; after the war, Council to the Foreign Ministry).

"War Leadership and Thought War," Takashima Tatsuhiko (Information Official at the Information Division and Lieutenant Colonel in the Infantry).

"War and Propaganda," Shimizu Moriaki (Information Official in the Information Division and Gunnery Lieutenant Colonel in the army; Information Department chief in the Army Ministry).

"An Outline of Japanese War Theory," Tada Tokuchi (Information Official at the Information Division, General Staff Headquarters; Army Infantry Colonel).

"America and England and the China Incident," Ogawa Kanji (Fifth Section Chief of the Naval General Staff, Captain in the Navy).

"The Anti-Japanese Thought War in China," Amamiya Tatsumi (Information Officer at the Information Department, Colonel in the Infantry).

"The Current Situation in Espionage and Counter-intelligence," Shirohama Hiroshi, (Kantō Army, Captain in the Military Police).

"On Freemasonry," Inuzuka Koreshige (Naval General Staff, Captain in the Navy).

"Thought War and the Police," Tomita Kenji (Information Division Committee Member, Chief of the Police Bureau of the Home Ministry; after the war, Diet Member, House of Representatives).

"On the Popular Front," Shimizu Shigeo (Information Division Committee Member, Public Safety Section Chief in the Home Ministry; after the war, Executive Director of the New Political Economy Research Association).

"The Current State of Thought Crimes," Hirano Toshi (Fifth Section Chief of the Bureau of Criminal Affairs in the Ministry of Justice; after the war, Trustee of Tōyō University).

"Overcoming Marxism," Hirata Susumu (Director of the Tokyo Protection and Supervision Center).

"The Problems of Student Thought," Ahara Kenzō (Information Division Committee Member, Chief of the Planning Section at the Edification Bureau of the Education Ministry; after the war, Chairman of the Japanese National Social Education Alliance).

"Thought War and Newspaper Studies," Ono Hideo (Part-time Commission at the Information Division, Manager of the Tokyo Imperial University Newspaper Research Room; after the war, Director of the Institute of Journalism at Tokyo University).

"Thought War and the Newspapers," Ogata Taketora (Council to the Information Division; after the war, Deputy Prime Minister in the Fourth Yoshida Cabinet, President of the Liberal Party.

"Thought War, Film and Theater," Kobayashi Ichizō (Council to the Information Division; after the war, President of the National Reconstruction Board in the Shidehara Cabinet).

"Thought War and the Publishing Industry," Masuda Giichi (Council to the Information Division, Chairman of the Japan Publishing Culture Association).

"Thought War and the Wire Services," Iwanaga Yukichi (President of the Dōmei News Agency).

"The Function of Radio in the Thought War," Tamura Kenjirō (Information Division Committee Member, Chief of the Telecommunications Bureau in the Communications Ministry)

2. The second Thought-War Symposium opened on February 20, 1939, in the wake of the resignation of the Konoe Cabinet and the organization of the Hiranuma Cabinet:

"The Reality and Theory of Thought War," Yokomizo Mitsuteru (Chief of the Information Division).

"The Current Situation in International Thought War," Inoue Kōjirō (Chief of the Eur-Asian Section of the Foreign Ministry).

"The Essence of the National Polity and Our Divine Spirit," Kakei Katsuhiko (Doctor of Law and Professor Emeritus at Tokyo Imperial University).

"The Present and Future of National Total Mobilization," Uemura Kōgorō (chief of the Industry Department at the Cabinet Planning Board; after the war, President of the Nippon Broadcasting Company, Chairman of Keidanren).

"The China Incident and Propaganda," Shimizu Moriaki (Information Official at the Information Division and Gunnery Lieutenant Colonel in the army).

"Conditions in the Soviet Union and Defense Against Communism," Kawamata Taketo (Section Chief at General Staff Headquarters, Army Infantry Lieutenant Colonel).

"The Basis of the Construction of a New China," Hidaka Shinrokurō (Information Division Committee Member, Chief of the Economics Department of the Greater Asian Board; after the war, Deputy Chairman of the Japanese United Nations Association).

"On the Problems of Naval Defense Thought," Sekine Gunpei (Rear Admiral in the Navy).

3. The third Thought-War Symposium opened on February 23, 1940, after the collapse of the Japan-United States Trade Agreement and the outbreak of war in Europe, and on the eve of the establishment of the Wang Ching-wei government in Nanking:

"An Outline of Thought War," Yokomizo Mitsuteru (Chief of the Information Division).

"The Japanese Spirit and the Thought War," Yasuoka Masahiro (Scholar of the Wang Yang-ming school; after the war, Involved in the Establishment of the New Japan Conference).

"Thought War Along With Military War," Matsumura Shūitsu (Information Division Committee Member, Army Gunnery Lieutenant Colonel; after the war, Diet Member, House of Representatives).

"Thought War Along With the Diplomatic War," Suma Yakichirō (Chief of the Information Department in the Foreign Ministry; after the war, Diet Member, House of Representatives, Director of the Association for the Advancement of Private Schools).

"Oceanic Thought and the Thought War," Kanazawa Masao (Chairman of the Naval Military Dissemination Division of the Navy Ministry, Rear Admiral in the Navy).

"Thought War and Propaganda," Koyama Eizō (Researcher at the Population Problem Research Center; after the war, Director of the National Public Opinion Research Center).

"Thought War, Newspapers and Wire Services," Furuno Inosuke (Council to the Information Division, President of the Dōmei News Agency; after the war, Kyōdō News Services Board Member).

"The Present and Future of the Regenerated New Chinese Government," Suzuki Teiichi (Information Division Committee Member, Chief of the Political Department of the Greater Asian Board; after the war, Class-A War Criminal).

"The Thought War in Manchuria," Okoshi Kenji (Kantō Army Headquarters, Army Infantry Major).

"America's Activities vis a vis Japan and America's Navy," Matsuda Chiaki (Section Chief of Naval General Staff, Admiral in the Navy).

"Domestic Thought War Activities and Counter-intelligence," Honma Akira (Information Division Committee Member, Chief of the Police Bureau of the Home Ministry).

"Thought War and the Public Finance Economy," Kaya Okinori (Director General of the North China Development Corporation; Minister of Justice in the Ikeda Cabinet; after the war, Class-A war criminal).

"Thought War and the Literary Arts," Kikuchi Kan (Council to the Information Division, President of Bungei Shunjū Company).

THE DISCURSIVE SPACE OF THOUGHT WAR

We can broadly divide the speakers at the symposia into the four categories of military men, bureaucrats, academicians and members of the mass media. Furthermore, we can divide the military men between army and navy, the bureaucrats between the Foreign Ministry and the Home Ministry, the academicians between theorists of the Japanese spirit and communications scholars, and the members of the mass media between the different private media (newspapers, publishing and film) and state media (NHK, Dōmei News Agency). Speakers from the Foreign Ministry, the navy and the state media consistently reported on the current situation, offering hardly any concrete proposals. A fairly broad range of claims are made in the reports, but there is general agreement on calling for the autonomy of informational activities and a conception of propaganda that emphasizes its efficiency as "technology." In the sections below, I will elucidate the "modern" aspect of the Thought War by taking up the typical arguments made by each group. In other words, I will examine the technology theory of the army, the claims made by the bureaucrats of the Home Ministry on the need for supervisory powers, the need for independence and active subjectivity (*shutaisei*) as seen by the private media and communications scholars, and the theory of the "Japanese Spirit," as presented by the Japan essentialists, in order to legitimize the above demands.

The Total War "Technology" Theory of the Military

In the completeness of their distributed materials, organization of argument, and degree of assimilation of the Army's research on total war, the lectures by Army officers, such as Takashima, Shimizu and Tada, who had been seconded from the Army Ministry and General Staff Headquarters and made information committee members and information officers in the Cabinet Information Division, set a high standard for the rest by providing a system theory of total war. After the war, Yokomizo referred to them as "divinely inspired" in the "style of Minoda Kyōki"[21] but we cannot swallow that whole. They believed in the need for autonomous support by the people, but were not simply relying on "spirit." Instead, they saw propaganda as analogous to military technology or troop formation.

Takashima, who had studied at universities in Berlin and Kiel during Hitler's rise, praised the Nazi leader's propaganda activities as "the classic example of well-planned preparation and independent leadership" and as "something truly admirable." Looking toward the completion of a self-sufficient state, he argued for "spiritual methods for carrying out the economic war in times of both peace and hostility." Moreover, Takashima's idea of "the necessity of profound sociological and anthropological studies as a basis" for "reaching the subtle emotions of the people of the opposing nation" is extremely technological. In addition, he argued that "competition in aviation technology, war preparation, physical and mental power, and state productive power all directly or indirectly amounted to forms of military power in times of peace." From a perspective of "total warfare as an organic union," which admitted of no distinction between military war and thought war, Takashima claims that "entering an undesired military conflict is proof of having already been defeated in total war."[22]

Shimizu was the man who proposed the Army pamphlet entitled, "The Essence of National Defense and an Appeal for its Strengthening" (1934), by which Japanese society at large came to know of the word "thought war." Thanks to his talent for languages, Shimizu had digested a great number of European and American propaganda studies, and his arguments were even more rational than Takashima's. "In essence, propaganda cannot be forced. Rather, it should enlighten by naturally permeating the environment, in the background of knowledge, while we enjoy ourselves. . . . Unfortunately, our nation's enlightenment is too abstract, conceptual and moralistic, and as a result remains merely a formal movement." From this perspective he went so far as to give examples of effective state-of-emergency propaganda that employed entertainment. Shimizu's "Items of Note in Propaganda" is scientific, and this attitude extends to his call for lectures on propaganda in universities and for the extension of surveillance to all aspects of daily life. In order to actualize a unified State propaganda, "we can use the network of schools, clubs, restaurants and bars, doctors, barbers and the entertainment trade network. We should also give consideration to development of a system of observers, and to surveillance from the standpoint of the propaganda needs of bureaucrats."[23]

At first glance, Tada's argument appears fanatical compared to those of Takashima and Shimizu. He attacked Kawai Eijirō's liberalism, Minobe Tatsukichi's organ theory of the emperor, and the critique of war made by Mutō Teiichi (a member of the editorial board of the *Asahi Shinbun*). He also gave consideration to mythic language in the *Kojiki* and *Nihon Shoki*. One might call his arguments the prototype of the discourse that was mass-produced after the outbreak of war with the United States. However, Tada employs the following concepts to situate the Japanese spirit in total war. He makes a distinction between the "state total-mobilization view of war" (*kokka sōdōinteki sensōkan*) that was typical of World War I, and the "state total-warfare view" (*kokka sōryokusenteki sensōkan*) that was current at the time of the lectures.

The former refers to the concentration, integration and activation of all state powers for military war. The latter, on the other hand, sees military war as a final unavoidable measure. At the same time, the latter view recognizes the priority of independent struggles in the realms of politics (domestic and foreign relations), economics, thought, religion, the arts, education, scholarship, and all other fields of culture. And the struggles across all these fields are developed in a unified and reductive—or to be more accurate, organic and holistic—manner in the operations of a single war."

He urged that attention be paid in the "state total-warfare view" to how "the myriad social phenomena—thought, economics, politics, military power, as well as all cultural enterprises such as religion and education—are interconnected and possess an organic and indivisible unity." Under this kind of system, "a situation which is neither peace nor war is likely to continue for some years to come." Thus, we can observe that Tada, who proclaimed the spirit of the *Kojiki*, arrives at an extremely modern system theory.[24] Tada's "state total-warfare view" was taken up at the second symposium by Yokomizo, the head of the Information Division, and became a common point of reference throughout the rest of the lecture series. This system concept appears as a realistic, technological, and everyday life-oriented demand. With erasure of the distinction between wartime and peacetime as a major premise, he directs attention away from specific events toward the everyday. Within the framework of such a quotidien, total-warfare system, it is possible to appeal to the importance of "entertainment" and to make claims for "freedom."

Then, how does Tada define "thought war"? "For the people of the enemy nation, it should lead to confusion regarding the right or wrong, good or evil, of the war from the standpoint of justice and humanity and, further, it should raise unsuppressable doubts and concerns regarding their country's prosperity, their own interests, and the welfare of humanity as a whole. . . . In the end, out of an irrepressible longing for peace it should generate ideals, feelings and desires receptive even to revolution, and bring such a process about."[25] This definition of "thought war" is surprisingly close to the Occupation censorship policy that Etō Jun criticized. If so, how much difference is there between the military's theory of total warfare which demanded "efficiency" as well as the "Japanese spirit," and postwar social theory, which pursued the same "efficiency" while proclaiming "democracy"? Shimizu called for media education and scientific propaganda studies from an understanding of thought war as technologized politics. In this way, military thought had incorporated a demand for the effective organization and rationalization of everyday life.

The Home Ministry's Theory of Surveillance Power

The issue of surveillance power in support of a total-war system was expressed in typical form, especially by Home Ministry and Ministry of Justice bureaucrats, and also by the military police who handled counter-espionage and thought problems. What is notable in the presentation by Tomita Kenji, chief of the Police Bureau of the Home Ministry, is the context of the so-called "overcoming modernity" line. "From the Meiji Restoration on we have been immersed in Western liberalism and democracy. The development of Japanese culture and the progress of material civilization today owe much to the influence of this thought. I believe there are many points for which we should be very grateful. . . . But it is also a fact that the impasses Japan faces in every area are also the result of those very influences." Therefore, he appealed for a "renovation" (*kakushin*) while in regard to the movements oriented to change, he notes, "'but in a larger perspective the arrests and enforcement are rather of secondary importance today. More than arrests what is necessary, if there is such a movement or information of some sort, is to be aware in advance of this discontent and dissatisfaction, or this movement for renovation, and to activate it politically. Politics would thus advance step by step, and improve along the way. I wonder if this is not where efforts should be made." Tomita was groping for an image of a power which could advance a renovation within Japan.[26]

For his part, Hirata Susumu, director of the Tokyo Protection and Observation Center, praised the outstanding function of the "Thought-Crime Protection and Observation Law" as "a truly Japanese law founded on the uniquely Japanese spirit of love." Hirata advocated allowing those who refused to renounce leftist beliefs to live freely under protection, unlike in Germany where such people were held indefinitely in concentration camps, or in China where the Nationalists had "self-reflection camps." Hirata went on to make an analogy between this "protection" and the "pacification" work carried on at the war front. For support, he quoted a letter from the former Communist Party leader Nabeyama Sadachika: "China must be Japanized from the bottom up. Reformed thought criminals should be mobilized for the great crusade of Japanizing China, so that we can repay our debt to the Imperial land."[27] In the background to this argument, we can see the intended formation of a disciplined subject, conceived according to the principle that "each and every citizen is a warrior in the thought war." The Thought Crime Protection and Observation Law aimed at "benevolent guidance in thought" through "cultivation of the Japanese spirit;" it sought to arouse non-reformed thought criminals to "a strong awakening so that they might be useful in the construction of a new Japan."[28] In addition to this argument, a theory of "counter-espionage" was offered which demanded a subjectively ascetic attitude toward information. This theory did not view the people merely as "receivers" but required them to take positive action in relation to information. From the perspective of the surveillance power that was formed in this manner, the fact that the "irrational 'propaganda' system that did not require an elaborate organization played the role, right down to the moment of defeat, of a somewhat surprising 'construction of conformity'" cannot be disposed of merely by characterizing it as "a problem that is deeply related to the spiritual structure of the traditional Emperor-system ideology that permeated our society from top to bottom."[29] In other words, it is more a problem of modernity itself than of the "traditional Emperor system." When our perspective is dominated by the "traditionality" of the Emperor system, we are prevented from realizing the renovationist nature of a power system that actively forms subjective consent. The mobilization of practical subjectivity is predicated on coercion brought about through the gaze of "protective supervision." The thought war, which projected upon the entire society the surveillance power already operating within the military, addressed the home front through counter-espionage and the thought problem in terms of a system of mutual surveillance. With reference to continuity with postwar history, it is possible to say that the Thought-War Symposia conceived of a panopticon in the form of an "information Emperor-system."

The Media Representatives' Theory of "Autonomy"

The media representatives can be divided into three categories: those from the control-oriented state media (NHK, the Dōmei News Agency), the communications scholars, and those from the private media (newspapers, film and publishing) that claimed autonomy. These divisions notwithstanding, they all shared the media's especially "efficient" tendencies. In the report on the function of radio made by the Chief of the Telecommunications Bureau of the Ministry of Communications, Tamura Kenjirō, the logic of "efficiency" was also reflected in the problem of entertainment in the thought war. Tamura argued,

> We often hear opinions that in times of emergency or war we should cut back on dramatic broadcasts and increase the number of lectures. But one might also make the point that this ignores the entertainment function of radio. Radio and the movies have immense propaganda power today because the people find them interesting.[30]

We can get the same kind of logic from Kobayashi Ichizō, President of Tōhō Film Productions. Kobayashi emphasized the special "effect" of entertainment and opposed the strengthening of control over film and theater, calling instead for "competition" among producers. He criticized the control of film content that limits the autonomy of producers, but the value of efficiency permeates the logic of his call for the aggressive introduction of controls over film distribution and management.[31]

Ogata Taketora, a lead writer for the Asahi Shimbun, gave a lecture that represents the newspaperman's attitude toward thought war. He asserts "reportorial freedom," but it is a freedom that is supported by efficiency-orientation and a logic of ends, so that there is no particular incongruity between this and the "technologism" of the military men. In fact, it is inescapably premised on a mobilization of independence and subjective involvement. "The most important condition for the development of modern newspapers is the freedom to report. Even if absolute freedom is not possible, it is the principle of freedom that counts." He calls for the active participation of newspapers in the wartime system on this basis. "There is no particular need to wait for enforcement from the government. The newspapers are taking the initiative in an extremely public-spirited manner. Thought war must be carried out in this form until the war is over, and even after it ends."

Naturally, this "freedom" does not apply outside the country. "The Japanese government's stand towards this incident [the war with China] is to completely uproot anti-Japanese thought in China. The most effective way to realize that goal is to reform Chinese textbooks and, at the same time, to form the same Public Relations Association in China as in Manchuria for the newspapers there. At least within the areas we occupy, we should thoroughly undertake the kind of newspaper policies Germany and Italy have adopted."[32]

If we change the "anti-Japanese thought in China" in this statement to "Japanese militarism," we have precisely the Allied Occupation's policy on the control of speech. In that sense, Ogata's freedom is the freedom of "a closed discursive space."

Ono Hideo, director of the Newspaper Research Center in the Literature Department of Tokyo Imperial University, claimed that communications studies would be able to contribute to the thought war as a "scholarly discipline" formed in response to the demand for propaganda sciences. "Contemporary control of newspapers should not take the form of passive pressure, in the manner of newspaper policy in feudal times. It should correct their distorted substance and use them to unify the spirit of the people. The essential function of this positive policy has been clearly manifested in research in the field of communications studies." That positive policy involved giving newspapers a sense of mission, and emphasizing their existence as media with "leadership and a psychologically unifying function" in social education and national unification. Ono criticized the power of prefectural governors to ban the sale of newspapers, as provided in the State General Mobilization Law Proposal, as irrational, like "censorship in autocratic times." Rather, he argued that newspapers should have the freedom to select content within the parameters of "the promotion of the welfare of the people." If the newspapers are given freedom and made to control themselves and respect their mission, "the newspapers will, of their own accord, move the masses spontaneously, since (the power of newspapers) isn't a power applied from the outside, like authority or a threat, but is a sense of power established within a universal interest." This is precisely how media power is formulated as a system to encourage the subjective mobilization of the masses. In the end, Ono criticizes the way newspapers have been continuously rendered powerless, complaining that "the government's newspaper policy has no scholarly basis." "The drain of power from newspapers is a drain of power from the spirit of the people, and will therefore detract from the National Spiritual Mobilization."[33]

Koyama Eizō gave a more practical presentation than Ono's, based on the same argument regarding the media's role in mobilizing subjectivity. As the only specialist doing academic studies of propaganda in this period, Koyama defined propaganda as "the decisive factor in the motivation of free will." This "free will," which was free in form but bound in substance, extended to include the "freedom" of Ono and Koyama themselves. Therefore, they could criticize the dictatorially-toned propaganda of Japan. On the one hand, Koyama placed emphasis on results, so that he saw "cultural propaganda" aimed at the U.S. as counterproductive, "like pouring oil on a fire." "For the cost of distributing pamphlets we can purchase more cannon rounds and quickly subdue the enemy." Further, he correctly evaluated the superficiality of the "Chinese Black Propaganda"—which was brought up so often at the symposium—as "merely dressing up reality as conveniently as possible." Koyama's instrumental rationalism, which led him to demand that "means be such as to bring about the desired end in the best and most efficient manner possible," was quite compatible with the "technological" thought of the military men. In conclusion, Koyama stated the following:

> Propaganda is not merely something handed down from above. It must also come from the people themselves, through local public organizations such as Youth Groups, Women's Groups, Local Assemblies, schools and so forth. This kind of propaganda, coming from communal social institutions, is the most effective. Moreover, through these organizations, it is possible to issue warnings and resolve at the local level the kind of situations that may arise among the masses.[34]

This kind of call for the organization of surveillance powers and subjective mobilization may appropriately be taken to express the goal of the Thought-War Symposium. The placement of Yasuoka Masahiro's "Japanese Spirit and Thought War" before the theory of logical propaganda technology in the edited version of the "Thought-War Symposium" was probably intentional. Technology, on the one hand, and the fetishized Japanese spirit in the rhetoric of propaganda, on the other, were not mutually opposed; but when subjectivity and autonomy were incorporated within a war system, they both became necessary together.

The "Spirit" Theory of the Japanists ("Nipponshugisha")

A Japanist was invited to each of the three symposia: Fujisawa Chikao to the first, Kakei Katsuhiko to the second and Yasuoka Masahiro to the third. Kakei was renowned for forcing his students to perform the Shinto hand-clapping ritual before his lectures at Tokyo Imperial University. Each Japanist lectured on the first day of a series, right after the Chief of the Information Division, suggesting that "discussion of the Japanese spirit" was largely ceremonial. Yasuoka, who called thought war a "low-class, militaristic way of thinking," argued that "the more one tries to carry out a thought war in a precise and technological manner, the more need one has for a philosophy or faith that fundamentally establishes our own self-identity."[35] Or, conversely, we could say that by beginning with discourse on the Japanese spirit, the military men and media-related theorists purchased the freedom to develop "a theory of propaganda technology."

Fujisawa claimed that "The true Japanese spirit is unique in the world as the concrete ethno-racial, spiritual manifestation of the truth of the universe." He even went so far as to claim that "the Nazis have imitated the Japanese national polity." However, inasmuch as this discourse on the Japanese spirit adhered to the illusion of "not externally subjugating the world but rather educating the countries of the world from within," arguments based on it could not be effective. As a result, in relation to "the liberalists who claimed the U.S. and Great Britain as their homelands" and the "Communists who claimed the Soviet Union as their homeland," the thought war descended to the vulgar level of rooting out dangerous thought in the manner of the traditional "thought problem."[36] As Suzuki Teiichi, later President of the Cabinet Planning Bureau, frankly expressed it, based on his experience since his days in the Newspaper Group of the Army Ministry, "The Chinese people have absolutely no basis for accepting the Japanese spirit or the spirit of the imperial way."[37] In effect, the actual mission of the thought war would end up being the formation of "a closed discursive space" centered on "the Japanese spirit." However, on the other hand, as Ahara Kenzō, Chief of the Planning Department of the Edification Bureau, Ministry of Education, commented on the attempt to focus on the Japanese spirit, the fact that the proponents of Japanism lacked a theoretical framework that could satisfy intellectual students was a serious problem.[38] Under such conditions, the rhetorical use of the Japanese spirit was revealed as fetishistic and fanatical in the same degree as the demands of the Thought-War Symposium were technological and rational.

Subsequent "Thought War"

Yokomizo Mitsuteru saw the Thought-War Symposium as "the kernel of the Total Warfare Research Center that followed."[39] One year before the outbreak of war with the United States, the "first desktop war games" were held at the Cabinet-sponsored Total War Research Center. The exercises ended in the conclusion that "if war should begin, Japan would inevitably lose" on each of the levels of military, diplomatic, intellectual and economic warfare.[40] In that sense, it would appear that the exercises inherited the rational thought of the "Thought-War Symposium."

However, during the US-Japan war, the Information Bureau was driven by the tide of the war so that the rationalist aspect was pushed into the background. As a result, the activities of the "Greater Japan Patriotic Opinion Association" which aimed at the "the establishment of the Japanese world view and the creation of thought-war volunteer writers' corps" became more prominent. But the Association, which began by fanatically suppressing speech, ended up as a fascist-style, antigovernment interest group.[41] Of course, this is quite a different phenomenon from the "Thought-War Symposium." One might go so far as to say that the thought war abandoned the rationalism conceived by the Information Division, and—in order to maintain the people's will to fight an "invisible war" in a Japan that had reached impasses on the military, economic and diplomatic fronts—was transformed into melodrama.

CONCLUSION: CONTINUITY WITH THE POSTWAR SYSTEM

In the end, the thought war developed as a leap of logic in a period in which Japan, as "a country that did not possess" a technological, rationalist "total warfare system," attempted to bring one into being by force. In any case, the conception of a thought war for "planning" the mobilization of subjectivity and autonomy as resources opened a space for the systematic consolidation of national unity. For example, even if during the war there were "feelings among the people of hatred for fanatical discourse and the news reports of the Imperial Headquarters, and desire for some kind of new discourse and information,"[42] the people still subjectively participated in the war even while feeling that dissatisfaction. The surveillance power conceived via the Thought-War Symposia was the kind of power that allowed space for the release of dissatisfaction with the system on the part of those who had already submitted to it.

In any case, the media and information system that had been organized and unified in response to the thought war survived to be incorporated almost intact into the Occupation system. Ariyama Teruo, who has analyzed the perception of Japanese newspapers in the American State Department policy proposal "PWC-288 CAC-237 Japan, Occupation; Media of Public Information and Expression," has said the following:

> The distribution of newspapers resulting from the consolidation of news organizations during the war was seen as "most likely making censorship and other forms of supervision much easier" for the Occupation Army. It goes without saying that the Newspaper Consolidation Policy had been used under the militaristic system to make the control of newspaper discourse more effective and to use newspapers as institutions for the mobilization of the people's consciousness. So in the large cities such as Tokyo and Osaka, the number of newspapers was kept small while in the provinces, a policy of one newspaper per prefecture was enforced. That system was convenient for the Allied Occupation Army which shared a concern for the control of information and media of expression. Naturally, reform of the newspaper consolidation system was not forthcoming.[43]

If we can say that "the information control system under Japanese militarism was applicable to the management of information under the Occupation," then this could be even more appropriately said of the later period of high economic growth.

In addition, if we follow not only the conceptions and the system, but also the individual paths of the lecturers at the Thought War Symposium, we can clearly read a pattern of "continuity," not "rupture." Apart from the military men and those who subsequently died, many of the speakers played important roles in postwar mass communications, education and politics. For example, Koyama Eizō went from a prewar history of being an investigatory official for the Planning Bureau, Chief of the First Department of the Volk (*minzoku*) Research Center in the Education Ministry, and Councillor to the Information Bureau, to being appointed the first director of the National Public Opinion Research Center in order to perform a public opinion investigation at the request of Commander Dyke, Chief of the Public Information and Education Bureau at GHQ.[44] Ono Hideo, who had encouraged the consolidation of newspapers likewise became a member of the Newspaper and Publishing Paper Allocation Committee and the first director of Tokyo University's Institute of Journalism, newly reestablished at the request of GHQ.[45] Newspaper studies and opinion polls were seen as necessary by the Occupation, just as was the Emperor system. Furthermore, it was Ogata Taketora who made efforts to establish the Cabinet Research Center as a postwar state information organization.[46]

Information Division Chief Yokomizo Mitsuteru was employed as the director of the Labor Culture Research Center at Japan Textile Industries, Ltd., during the period in which he was purged from public office. After being depurged, his public career included being a consultant to the Judicial System Research Department of the Minister's Secretariat in the Ministry of Justice, President of the National Publishing Association, Inc., and consultant to the National Public Records Archive. He left a line of publications, extending from his prewar work, *Keisatsu shūyōroku* (A Record of Police Training 1935) to *Gyōseidō no kenkyū* (Studies in Government Administration; 1978). As "Items of Government Administration," in the latter, Yokomizo lists "rigid discipline, administrative simplicity, cordiality and courteousness, loyalty and hard work, increasing efficiency, fairness and neutrality, consciousness of responsibility, and protection of secrets." In the final chapter he states, "The end of the war brought about a complete change in values. A time of vacillation appeared. The Imperial Japanese Constitution, said to be an immortal classic, was easily revised, and the new Constitution of Japan was born. . . . But I believe that even though the Constitution and administrative law may change in such ways, the way of administration never changes."[47]

Translated by Alan Christie

Notes

[1] Awaya Kentarō, "Taiheiyō sensōki no nihon no senden seisaku," in *Rekishigaku kenkyū*, no. 495 (1981): 17.

[2] Etō Jun, *Tozasareta gensetsu kūkan—senryōgun no ken'etsu to sengo nihon*, Tokyo: Bungei Shunjū, 1989, p. 130.

[3] Ibid., p. 118.

[4] Yamanouchi Yasushi, "Senjiki no isan to sono ryōgisei," in *Iwanami kōza: shakai kagaku no hōhō (3)—nihon shakai kagaku no shisō*, Tokyo: Iwanami Shoten, 1993, p. 157.

[5] Etō, op. cit., p. 13.

[6] Recent essays which argue for a theory of continuity include Ariyama Teruo, "Dōmei tsūshinsha kaisan—senryōki mejia shikenkyū," in Arima Manabu and Mitani Hiro, ed., *Kindai nihon no seiji kōzō*, Tokyo: Yoshikawa Kōbunkan, 1993, p. 358.

[7] Uchikawa Yoshimi, *Masu mejiahō seisaku shikenkyū*, Tokyo: Yūhikaku, 1989, p. 193.

[8] For a collection of materials see, Naikaku Chōsashitsu, ed., *Senzen no jōhō kikō yōran—jōhō iinkai kara jōhōkyoku made*, 1964. For essays on the system

see, Uchikawa Yoshimi, "Sōwa zenki masu mejia tōsei no hō to kikō" in Ibid., and Kōuchi Saburō, "Naikaku jōhōkyoku no keifu" in *Bungaku*, May, 1961.

[9] Takagi Noritsune, "Tennōsei shihai taiseika no genron no jiyū' in *Kōza: Gendai nihon no masu komunikeishon*, vol. 2, Aoki Shoten, 1972, pp. 86-111.

[10] Naikaku Jōhōbu, "Jōhō senden no shintaisei" in *Shūhō*, no. 210 (August 23, 1940), p. 34.

[11] Shibuya Shigemitsu, "'Shisōsen' no ronri to sōsasei" in *Taishū sōsa no keifu*, Tokyo: Keisō Shobō, 1991. Also, Akasawa Shirō, "Senden to goraku" in *Kindai nihon no shisō dōin to shūkyō tōsei*, Tokyo: Azekura Shobō, 1985. Taking up various arguments related to "thought war" during the Pacific war, Shibuya treats the "thought war" intended "for the masses" as a matter of storytelling designed for purposes of manipulation. He analyzes "the significance of the proclamation of an unreal thought 'war' during the engagement of an actual war" as serving to legitimize the beginning of the Greater East Asian War, to raise consciousness of the enemy, to unify emperor system ideology and to displace the dissatisfactions of the people.

[12] Kōuchi Saburō, "'Senden' kara 'fukyō' e no tenkan—senji senden ron josetsu" in *Kikan janarizumu-ron shikenkyū*, no. 4, 1976. Kōuchi deals with mass-oriented ideological works (such as Mizuno Masatsugu, *Shisō kessenki*) and the Information Technology Research Association, which explained propaganda technology (see the official organ *Hōdō gijutsu kenkyū*) as mutually supportive poles in order to analyze the genealogy of war propaganda. In particular, Kōuchi analyzes the emotional aspect of Mizuno's mass-oriented works, which looked down on thought war "technology" and "technique," and the technological aspect of the Information Technology Research Association whose activities were developed during the wartime and which became active in postwar advertising. This analysis works toward an understanding of the postwar "course of revival."

[13] Jōhō Iinkai, *Kokubō to shisōsen*, in Jikyoku senden shiryō dated August 15, 1937, not for distribution; pp. 18-21.

[14] Yokomizu Mitsuteru, "Kokka to jōhōsenden" in Naikaku jōhōbu, ed., *Shisōsen kōshūkai kōgi sokki*, no. 1 (secret), 1938, pp. 9-10.

[15] See for example, Ogata Taketora, "Shisōsen to shinbun," pp. 35-42, Kobayashi Ichizō, "Shisōsen to eiga oyobi engeki," pp. 54-58 in Naikaku Jōhōbu, ed., *Shisōsen kōshūkai kōgi sokki* (hereafter, *1938 Transcripts*) no. 4 (secret), Feb. 1938.

[16] Yokomizo Mitsuteru, *Shōwa-shi henrin*, Tokyo: Keizai ōraisha, 1974, p. 240.

[17] Yokomizo Mitsuteru, "Shisōsen kōshūkai," in *Senzen no shusho kantei*, Tokyo: Keizai ōraisha, 1984, pp. 97-104.

[18] Tsukanezawa Toshihiro and Satō Takumi, "Naikaku jōhōbu to 'jōhō senden kenkyū shiryō'" in Tsukanezawa Toshihiro and Satō Takumi, ed., *Naikaku jōhōbu/jōhō senden kenkyū shiryō*, v. 8, Tokyo: Kashiwa Shobō, 1994, pp. 394-404.

[19] Tsukanezawa Toshihiro, "*Shisōsen tenrankai kiroku zuran kaisetsu*," ibid., pp. 382-387.

[20] Yokomizo Mitsuteru, "Shisōsen no riron to jissai," in *(Hi) Dainikai shisōsen kōshūkai kōgi sokki* (hereafter 1939 Transcripts), Feb. 1939, p. 2.

[21] Naiseishi kenkyūkai, ed., *Yokomizo Mitsuterushi danwa daiyonkai sokkiroku*, Oct. 29, 1973, p. 35.

[22] Takashima Tatsuhiko, "Sensō shidō to shisōsen," *1938 Transcripts*, no. 2 (Top Secret), pp. 15, 30, 34, 40.

[23] Shimizu Moriaki, "Senden to sensō," *1938 Transcripts*, no. 2 (Top Secret), pp. 64, 101-102.

[24] Tada Tokuchi, "Nihon sensōron no gaiyō," in *1938 Transcripts*, no. 2 (Top Secret), pp. 163-64, 174.

[25] Ibid., p. 207.

[26] Tomita Kenji, "Shisōsen to Keisatsu," *1938 Transcripts*, no. 3 (Top Secret), pp. 128-29, 133-34.

[27] Hirata Susumu, "Marukushizumu no Kokufuku" *1938 Transcripts*, no. 3 (Top Secret), pp. 228, 235.

[28] For example, see Matsuyama Kazutada, *Shisōhan hogo kansatsuhō to ha*, Kyoto hogo kansatsujo, 1939, pp. 8-9.

[29] Uchikawa, op. cit., p. 205.

[30] Tamura Kenjirō, "Shisōsen ni okeru rajio no kinō," *1938 Transcripts*, no. 4 (Secret), p. 147.

[31] Kobayashi Ichizō, "Shisōsen to eiga oyobi engeki," *1938 Transcripts*, no. 4 (Secret), pp. 55-63.

[32] Ogata Taketora, "Shisōsen to shinbun," *1938 Transcripts*, no. 4 (Secret), pp. 26, 42-43, 41.

[33] Ono Hideo, "Shisōsen to shinbungaku," *1938 Transcripts*, no. 4 (Secret), pp. 12, 16, 24.

[34] Koyama Eizō, "Shisōsen to Senden," in *Shisōzen kōza*, no. 4, May, 15, 1940, pp. 21, 3, 25, 11, 45.

[35] Yasuoka Masahiro, "Nihon seishin to shisōsen," ibid., no. 3, pp. 16, 1.

[36] Fujisawa Chikao, "Nihon seishin to shisōsen," *1938 Transcripts*, no. 1 (Secret), pp. 30, 43, 61.

[37] Suzuki Teiichi, "Kōsei shinshina seiken no genzai oyobi shōrai," *Shisōsen kōza*, op. cit., no. 6 (Top Secret), p. 19.

[38] Ahara Kenzo, "Gakusei shisō mondai," *1938 Transcripts*, no. 3 (Top Secret), pp. 250-51.

[39] Yokomizo Mitsuteru, *Shōwa-shi henrin*, op. cit., p. 253.

[40] Ishikawa Junkichi, *Kokka sōdōin-shi/ge*, 1984, pp. 1237-1241.

[41] Akazawa Shirō, "Dainippon genron hōkōkukai—hyōronkai to shisōsen," in Akazawa Shirō, Kitakawa Kenzō, ed., *Bunka to fashizumu*, Nihon keizai shinbunsha, 1993, p. 210.

[42] Ariyama Teruo, "Amerika no senryo genron seisaku no keisei katei—senryōki mejia kenkyū josetsu," *Nenpō kindai nihon kenkyū*, no. 12 (1990), p. 296.

[43] Ibid., pp. 306-7.

[44] Koyama Eizō, *Yoron/shōgyō chōsa no hōhō*, Tokyo: Yūhikaku, 1956, p. 1.

[45] Tokyo Daigaku Hyakunen-shi Henshū Iinkai, ed., *Tokyo daigaku hyakunenshi: bukyoku-shi, yon*, 1987, p. 14.

[46] Kurita Naoki, "Koiso naikakuki ni okeru Ogata Taketora no genron seisaku," in *Nenpō kindai nihon kenkyū*, no. 12 (1990), p. 292.

[47] Yokomizo Mitsuteru, *Gyōseido no kenkyū*, Tokyo: Daiichi Hōki Shuppan, 1978, p. 467.

Glossary

1955 system

The political party system that resulted from the merger in 1955 of the Liberal and Japan Democratic parties into the Liberal Democratic party, and of the Socialist and Democratic-Socialist parties into the Japan Social Democratic party.

Arisawa Hiromi

(1896-) Economist, prof. of Tokyo University; formulated the priority production system in the early postwar period.

Cabinet Research Center

Established in 1935 as one of several committees and agencies that eventually provided the foundation for Prime Minister Konoe Fumimaro's New Order movement; merged with the Natural Resource Bureau in 1937 to form the Planning Board.

Cabinet Information Division

(Naikaku Jōhō Kyoku) Government agency established 1940 to handle propaganda and censorship.

China Incident

(Shina jihen) Also known as the Marco Polo Bridge incident, which marked the beginning of the Sino-Japanese War of 1937-1945.

Civil Information and Education Bureau

Office in charge of censorship under GHQ of the American Occupation.

Colonel Dyke	Colonel Kermit R. Dyke, director of the Civil Information and Education Bureau (CIE) in the Allied Occupation of Japan; replaced in May 1946.
Control Faction	(Tōsei-ha) Pejorative term for a loose grouping of Army officers who opposed the Imperial Way faction and favored further mechanization of the armed forces.
Dai-Nippon Sangyō Hōkokukai	(Greater Japan Industrial Patriotic Association) See Sangyō Hōkokukai.
debate on subjectivity	A debate among Japanese intellectuals, 1946-1949, over the meaning and normative force of the term *shutaisei*, meaning autonomy, identity, or subjective engagement.
Densan Wage	A wage structure, first demanded by the electric power union (Densan) in 1946, which became the model for demands by other unions all over Japan; it consisted fundamentally in a "livelihood guarantee" based wholly on need, and calculated according to age and family size.
Dodge Line	March 1949 program of austerity measures suggested by, and named after, Detroit banker Joseph M. Dodge.
Dōmei News Agency	(Dōmei Tsūshinsha) Established in 1936; government vehicle for propaganda that was replaced by Kyōdō News Service in 1945.
East Asian Community	(Tōa kyōdōtai) Ideal of a non-exploitative East Asian order to be led by Japan; conceived by philosopher Miki Kiyoshi in the late-1930s and developed among members of the Shōwa Kenkyūkai. See Shōwa Kenkyūkai.

Economic Stabilization Board	(Keizai Antei Honbu) Established in August 1946 to overcome the early-postwar economic crisis.
Employee Hiring Control Ordinance	(Jugyōin Yatoire Seigenrei) April 1939; prohibited workers in 93 occupations in the heavy and chemical industries from changing jobs without permission.
Etō Jun	(1933-) Literary critic and conservative spokesman; real name, Egashira Atsuo.
Fujita Shōzō	(1927-) political scientist and intellectual historian; professor at Hōsei University.
Fukutake Tadashi	(1917-) rural sociologist, professor of Tokyo University.
gonin–gumi	five-family groups established in the Tokugawa period (1600-1868) for mutual surveillance and aid; lost official status after the Meiji Restoration of 1868.
Gotō Ryūnosuke	(1898-) Politician; founder of the Shōwa Kenkyūkai; close associate of Prime Minister Konoe Fumimaro.
Gotō Fumio	(1884-1980) Home Ministry official, and leader of the so-called New Bureaucrats (shin kanryō), who were sympathetic to military rule.
Great Kantō Earthquake	Tokyo earthquake of 1923; measuring 7.3 on the Richter scale, it came at mid-day, causing widespread fires and massive destruction; killed around 100,000 people.
Greater Japan Industrial Patriotic Assoc.	See Sanpō
Greater Japan Women's Association	(Dainihon Fujinkai) Formed in 1942 through merger of the Greater Japan Women's Association for National Defense (Dainihon Kokubō Fujinkai) and the

Patriotic Women's Association (Aikoku Fujinkai); a component of the Imperial Rule Assistance Association.

Harmonization Society — (Kyōchōkai) Established Dec. 1919 with support of government and business to promote "harmony" in industrial relations; disbanded in June 1946.

Hokkaidō — northernmost of Japan's four main islands

Honshū — largest of Japan's four main islands

House of Councillors — (Sangiin) upper chamber of the National Diet under the 1947 Constitution.

House of Representatives — (Shūgiin) lower chamber of National Diet.

Housewives Federation — (Shufuren, or Shufu Rengōkai) Founded by Oku Mumeo in 1948; consumer organization that reached around a million members in 460 locals by the 1970s.

Imperial Rule Assistance Association — (Taisei Yokusankai) Established in October 1940 under government sponsorship; popular organization intended to be the focal point of Prime Minister Konoe's New Order; abolished June 1945.

Imperial Fleet faction — Group of conservative naval admirals led by Katō Kanji of the Naval General Staff.

Imperial Rescript on Education — Promulgated in the the name of the emperor on Oct. 30, 1890; provided principles of ethics and education for the Japanese nation; lost effect under the Allied Occupation in 1945.

Imperial Way faction — (Kōdō-ha) Army officer faction in the 1930s that stressed spiritual training and direct action.

Industrial Patriotic Association — see Sanpō

industrial unions — (sangyō kumiai) Japan's first agricultural cooperatives; established 1900, disbanded 1943.

Iwai Akira	(1922-) Secretary-General of Sōhyō, 1955-1970, the period in which the Spring Offensive began. See *shuntō*.
Japan Romantic Faction	Nationalistic literary group formed around the journal *Nihon Rōman-ha*, inaugurated in 1935; influenced by German romanticism.
Kamiyama Shigeo	(1905-) Japan Communist Party leader.
Kawai Eijirō	(1891-1944) Scholar of social policy and political philosophy; influenced by Thomas Hill Green.
Kawashima Takeyoshi	(1909-) Legal scholar, author, University of Tokyo law professor.
Kazahaya Yasoji	(1899-) Law professor; labor and social policy expert associated with productive forces theory (*seisanryoku riron*).
Kenseikai	(Constitutional Association) Political party, founded in October 1916; merged with the Seiyū Hontō to form the Rikken Minseitō in 1927.
Kojiki	mythohistorical account of the origins of Japan, completed in A.D. 712
Konoe Fumimaro	(1891-1945) Prime minister 1937-39 and 1940-41; scion of the aristocratic Fujiwara family; committed suicide in 1945.
Kōza-ha	"Lectures faction" of Japanese Marxists which adhered to the line of the Japan Communist party; in the debate on Japanese capitalism with the Rōnō-ha, it stressed the need for a two-stage revolution beginning with the bourgeois-democratic stage.
Kubo Sakae	(1901-1958) Playwright, producer, novelist. Joined the Tsukiji Little Theater in 1926; active in the prewar proletarian theater movement.

Kyōdō News Service

(Kyōdō Tsūshin) Postwar successor to Dōmei News Agency; established in 1945. Japan's largest cooperative news agency.

Kyoto School

Intellectuals, most often philosophers, who studied at Kyoto University in the 1920s and 1930s and were inspired by Japan's preeminent modern philosopher, Nishida Kitarō (1870-1945).

Labor-Farmer faction

See Rōnō-ha.

Lectures faction

See Kōza-ha.

Liberal-Democratic Party

(Jiyū Minshutō) Established 1955 by merging the Liberal and Japan Democratic parties; ruling party from 1955 until 1989.

Manchurian Incident

A September 1931 explosion on the South Manchurian railway, set by the Japanese Kwantung Army; used as a pretext for occupation and consolidation of Manchuria under Japanese control.

Maruyama Masao

(1914-1996) Intellectual historian and political scientist; professor in the Faculty of Law, Tokyo University; major theorist of Japanese modernization and postwar democracy.

Materialism Study Group

(Yuibutsuron Kenkyūkai) Marxist association, produced the journal *Yuibutsuron kenkyū*; active 1932-38.

Matsushita Keiichi

(1929-) political scientist, professor at Hōsei University.

Meiji Shrine

(Meiji Jingū) Tokyo shrine dedicated to the Meiji Emperor; completed in 1920.

Miki Kiyoshi

(1897-1945) Philosopher who analyzed the philosophical basis of Marxism and the problem of technology; arrested in

1930, and again in 1945; died in prison on the eve of surrender.

Military Service Law (Heieki hō) Passed by the Diet in April 1927; established universal conscription; replaced the conscription ordinance of 1873.

Minobe Tatsukichi (1873-1948) Tokyo University legal scholar, originator of the "organ theory of the emperor;" hounded by rightists in 1935, forced to relinquish his seat in the House of Peers and withdraw from public life.

Minoda Kyōki (1894-1946) Rightist scholar in the 1930s who led attacks against prominent liberal scholars such as Minobe Tatsukichi.

Minseitō (Rikken Minseitō) Political party, 1927-1940; along with the Seiyūkai, one of the two major parties of the prewar period; dissolved into the Imperial Rule Assistance Association in August 1940.

Mito School School of thought and reformist practice based on Confucian-Shintō syncretism; especially prominent in the late-Tokugawa period, when it championed imperial loyalism and expulsionism.

Mukyōkai Japanese Christian movement that rejects ecclesiastical organization and authority; organizes around local Bible study groups.

Munitions Corporations Law (Gunju Kaisha Hō) 1943; designated key firms as munitions corporations and subjected them to government control.

Nakano Seigō (1886-1943) Journalist, Minseitō politician; attracted to Hitler and Mussolini; jailed in 1943 for plotting the overthrow of Prime Minister Tōjō Hideki.

Nakasone Yasuhiro

(1918-) Prime Minister 1982-87; first elected to the House of Representatives in 1947.

National General Mobilization Law

(Kokka Sōdōin Hō) Formally decreed on April 1, 1938; provided overall legal authority for the mobilization of civil society and the economy; rescinded in Dec. 1945.

national spiritual mobilization

(*kokumin seishin sōdōin*) A campaign initiated in fall 1937 by the Konoe cabinet in order to rally popular awareness of and support for the Sino-Japanese War.

neighborhood associations (*chōnaikai*)

local organizations for communication, surveillance and mutual aid, which came into existence around 1920; made mandatory in 1940 for wartime social control; abolished by the Occupation in 1947, but have remained unofficially since then.

New Women's Association

(Shin Fujin Kyōkai) National organization that campaigned for women's right to participate in politics, 1920-22.

New Order in East Asia

(TōA Shin Chitsujo) Supposedly new form of association among China, Manchukuo and Japan, under Japanese dominance; proposed by Prime Minister Konoe Fumimaro in November 1938.

NHK

(Nippon Hōsō Kyōkai; Japan Broadcasting Corporation) Japan's national public broadcasting system.

Nihon shoki

Oldest official history of Japan, completed in A.D. 720.

Nishio Suehiro

(1891-1981) Labor leader and politician; founding member of the Democratic Socialist Party, January 1960.

oil shock

Precipitous rise in oil prices that accompanied the Middle East war of 1973.

"overcoming the modern" (*kindai no chōkoku*) The title and main topic of a famous round-table discussion among Kyoto School philosophers and Romantic writers, published in the literary journal *Bungakukai* in Sept. and Oct., 1942.

Peace Constitution Constitution of Japan since 1946; called the "Peace Constitution" because of Article Nine, the "Renunciation of War."

Perry, Matthew C. (1794-1858) American naval officer who commanded a mission to open relations with Japan in the early 1850s, resulting in the Treaty of Kanagawa of March, 1854.

Planning Board (Kikakuin) Established in October 1937 by Prime Minister Konoe Fumimaro to formulate economic plans for wartime; 10 of its members were arrested in spring 1941 for having goals similar to those of the Japan Communist Party.

Police Duties Bill 1958 legislation intended to broaden police powers; intensively opposed, and ultimately blocked, by progressive political forces.

Renovationist bureaucrats (*kakushin kanryō*) Government administrators who were close to the military and supported statist policies in the late-1930s and after; dominated the Planning Board

Respect for the Aged Day (Keirō no hi) National holiday, September 15.

Rōnō-ha "Labor-Farmer faction" of Japanese Marxists; stressed the bourgeois nature of Japanese capitalism in its prewar debate with the Kōza-ha.

Rōyama Masamichi (1895-) political scientist, professor of Tokyo Imperial University; resigned

	1939; president of Ochanomizu Women's University from 1954.
Sanpō	(Sangyō Hōkokukai; Industrial Patriotic Association) Government-controlled "labor front" founded on the model of the Nazi *Arbeitsfront*; became the Dainihon Sangyō Hōkokukai (Greater Japan Industrial Patriotic Association) in 1939; apportioned labor among essential industries.
Sanpō Renmei	(Sangyō Hōkoku Renmei; Industrial Patriotic Federation). Established July 1938; predecessor of the Sangyō Hōkokukai. See Sanpō.
Seinendan	Youth groups formed in the wake of the Russo-Japanese War to encourage patriotism; united in 1925 into a national youth association called, from 1934, the Greater Japan Youth Association (Dainihon Seinendan).
Seiyūkai	(Rikken Seiyūkai) Political party, 1900-1940; founded as a pro-government party by the Meiji oligarch, Itō Hirobumi; dissolved into the Imperial Rule Assistance Association in July 1940.
Shimomura Toratarō	(1902-) Kyōto School philosopher (see Kyōto School)
Shōtoku Taishi	(574-622 A.D.) Prince Shōtoku. Statesman and Regent for Empress Suiko.
Shōwa Kenkyūkai	Study group, founded by Gotō Ryūnosuke in 1933, which advised Prime Minister Konoe and influenced his New Order; disbanded in Nov. 1940.
shuntō	(Spring labor offensive) Begun in 1955; led by Sōhyō each April, with the objective of gaining a general wage raise in key

325

	industries which then set a standard for other unions.
Sino-Japanese War of 1937	War between Japan and China, 1937-45; initiated by the so-called Marco Polo Bridge incident on July 7, 1937.
Sōdōmei	(Nihon Rōdō Sōdōmei; Japan Federation of Labor) Established in 1921, and reorganized in 1946; affiliated with the right wing of the labor movement; dissolved into Zennihon Rōdō Sōdōmei (Dōmei) in 1964.
Sōhyō	(Nihon Rōdō Kumiai Sōhyōgikai; General Council of Trade Unions in Japan). Formed 1950; dissolved in 1989. Affiliated with the Socialist party.
Special Higher Police	(Tokubetsu Kōtō Keisatsu, or Tokkō) Formed in the Home Ministry in 1911 to monitor and prevent the spread of subversive thought.
Taisei Yokusankai	See Imperial Rule Assistance Association (IRAA).
Takamure Itsue	(1894-1964) Historian and feminist; pioneer writer of Japanese women's history.
Takano Minoru	(1901-1974) Leftwing Secretary-General of Sōhyō, 1950-55; replaced by the more moderate Iwai Akira.
Takashima Zenya	(1904-1990) Economist; specialist in economic sociology.
Taketani Mitsuo	(1911-) physicist, philospher of science; participant in the postwar debate on subjectivity.
Takigawa Incident	The ultimately successful attempt on the part of Rightist elements to force the resignation from Kyoto University of the liberal law professor, Takigawa Yukitoki;

vigorously protested by students and others.

Tsukiji Little Theater

Tokyo theater established in 1924 as a center of the Shingeki (modern theater) movement.

Uchimura Kanzō

(1861-1930) Christian scholar; inspired the "Nonchurch" movement in Japanese Christianity; accused of lése majesty in 1891 when, as a teacher at First Higher School, he failed to show sufficient respect for the Imperial Rescript on Education.

Umemoto Katsumi

(1912-1974) Marxist philosopher; major participant in the postwar debate on subjectivity (*shutaisei*).

Women's Association for National Defense

(Dainihon Kokubō Fujinkai) National women's association founded in 1932 under the sponsorship of the Army to prepare for national mobilization.

Yamada Moritarō

(1897-1980) Marxist economist; Kōza-ha leader. See Kōza-ha.

Yamamoto Yasue

(1906-) modern dramatic actress who, in 1966, established the Yamamoto Yasue no Kai, a group devoted to folklore and traditional theater.

Yasukuni Shrine

(Yasukuni Jinja) Tokyo shrine for the spirits of war dead; established 1869, renamed in 1879.

zaibatsu

Industrial and financial combines that developed between the Meiji period (1868-1912) and World War II; usually family-dominated.

CORNELL EAST ASIA SERIES

FORTHCOMING

Lives in Motion: Composing Circles of Self and Community in Japan,
    edited by Susan Long
*Ben no Naishi Nikki: A Poetic Record of Female Courtiers' Sacred Duties
    at the Kamakura-Period Court,* by S. Yumiko Hulvey
*Early One Spring: A Learning Guide to Accompany the Film Video
    February,* by Pilwun Wang and Sarah Wang

To order, please contact the Cornell East Asia Series, East Asia Program,
Cornell University, 140 Uris Hall, Ithaca, NY 14853-7601, USA; phone
(607) 255-6222, fax (607) 255-1388, internet: ceas@cornell.edu,
http://www.einaudi.cornell.edu/eastasia/EastAsiaSeries.html.

12-98/.5 M pb/.2M hc